Losing an Empire, Finding a Role

British Foreign Policy Since 1945

2nd edition

David Sanders
David Patrick Houghton

macmillan
education

palgrave

First edition 1990
Second edition 2017

Published by PALGRAVE

Palgrave in the UK is an imprint of Macmillan Publishers Limited, registered in England, company number 785998, of 4 Crinan Street, London, N1 9XW.

Palgrave is a global imprint of the above companies and is represented throughout the world.

Palgrave® and Macmillan® are registered trademarks in the United States, the United Kingdom, Europe and other countries.

ISBN 978–1–137–35715–1 hardback
ISBN 978–1–137–35714–4 paperback

This book is printed on paper suitable for recycling and made from fully managed and sustained forest sources. Logging, pulping and manufacturing processes are expected to conform to the environmental regulations of the country of origin.

A catalogue record for this book is available from the British Library.

A catalog record for this book is available from the Library of Congress.

Printed and bound by CPI Group (UK) Ltd, Croydon, CR0 4YY

Contents

List of Figures

List of Tables

Preface

It is a little over 25 years since the first edition of *Losing an Empire* first appeared on the bookshelves. Given some of the momentous choices that have been made about Britain's role in the world in recent years, it now seems an appropriate time for an update to appear. The book has proven reasonably resilient over the last couple of decades. The first edition is still used by some teachers to introduce the topic of British foreign policy in the classroom – though over the years it has become necessary to supplement the text with more up-to-date materials. This presented us with a challenge. It was clear enough what kind of empirical history needed to be added. But what would need to be done in a theoretical sense to bring it up to date? How would its core arguments fare, some 25 years after it first appeared?

Needless to say, we think the broad approach holds up well, and that the original argument – that economic interests and realist balances of power have been integral to the shape of British foreign policy – remains valid. In the first edition, David Sanders used Waltzian or Neo-Realist theory to reach a more or less liberal end: that membership of Europe was actually in the national interest of the United Kingdom. This remains a core proposition in what follows. But just as realist theory has changed and adapted, so have we. The debate about EU membership which raged in 2016 in the run-up to the referendum illustrated the importance of national identity, domestic politics and psychological perceptions of reality, not simply objective interests (however defined). This problem was what led a generation of Realist scholars to become what are usually called 'Neo-Classical Realists', and hence it produced a change in realism itself.

A reader familiar with the first edition will see that the argument has been updated along these lines. Although the analysis is not intended as a full 'test' of any theory, developments in IR theory are fully attended to in what follows. Twenty-five years ago, constructivism – for instance – was but a glint in the eye of Alexander Wendt, Nicolas Onuf and others. Could that approach be useful to us and our students? What about the Bureaucratic Politics approach, which was mentioned prominently in the original? And how might the psychological theories of someone like Robert Jervis be added to the mix? How, above all, could Neo-Classical Realism add to our understanding of events?

There are essentially two ways of writing a second edition. One is to add new empirical and theoretical material in a way that remains faithful to the original work. Another is to write what is fundamentally a new book, retaining a popular title but substantially changing the contents. We wanted to do the former, producing a second edition rather than a new book. We wanted to retain something that teachers and researchers liked, while acknowledging that IR and foreign policy theory have both changed significantly over the last two decades. In particular, we wanted to retain the Churchillian 'three circles' idea as the central organising device.

We hope we have been successful. We realise that in adding complexity, we sacrifice some parsimony that featured in the first edition. British foreign policy might appear a bit more 'muddy' than it was, after reading this book. But arguably, this is a complex topic, and we have sought to do it justice. The Introduction and much of Chapter 1 are substantially new, bringing the story up to date both theoretically and empirically. Chapters 3 to 6 are substantially new in some parts, although the basic shape of each chapter is retained throughout. The three circles come out strongly in this section, with a chapter (as before) devoted to the early post-World War II period and to each circle. Chapter 7, on post-war economic policy, is substantially updated, while Chapter 8, on Britain's defence policies, is substantially new. Chapter 9 is revised to bring the theoretical story into the 21st century, while Chapter 10 – speculating about the future of UK foreign policy – is entirely new.

Many people have contributed, directly or indirectly, to the writing of this edition. In particular, we want to thank Steven Kennedy at Palgrave Macmillan for his long-running efforts and determination to see this project through to the end. Steven was the original Editor of the book, and he prodded David Sanders at various conferences to come up with a new edition. We are glad that he did. We also particularly thank his replacement at Palgrave, Stephen Wenham, and his assistant Tuur Driesser. Most of all, of course, we thank our families for their patience and fortitude while this book was reworked and updated.

Professor David Sanders, Essex University
Professor David Houghton, US Navy War College
December 2016

Introduction

Three Themes: Churchill's 'Three Circles'; Realism; and Continuity and Change

The notion that Britain has foreign policy interests in 'three circles' was first encapsulated by Winston Churchill in a speech at a Conservative Party meeting in Llandudno, Wales, in October 1948. The speech had a rather small and select audience, perhaps insufficient to the scale of what the Opposition Leader had to say that day – even though only a small part of his speech explicitly mentioned circles. The problem Churchill addressed was a thorny one. But it was absolutely central to the thinking of those who were contemplating Britain's future in 1948, and it has remained so since. How could Britain retain a seat at the top table in an era of relative economic decline, in which the international system was becoming increasingly hardened into two great 'poles' focused on the United States and the Soviet Union? How could the country punch above its weight, as Douglas Hurd would later put it, given that Britain was massively in debt to the United States and had almost been broken by the economic, political and psychological demands of the war? The Cold War had not yet really begun and there was still something called 'the British Empire'. Churchill, moreover, was unaffected by the sense of long-term absolute and relative decline that is so commonplace in Britain nowadays, and the country was not yet seen as the 'mere' middle-range power it is today. Nevertheless, the issue he addressed was a timeless one, and it has been retained and 'updated' by politicians of both main political parties over the years.[1]

Churchill visualised Britain at the centre of three great, overlapping circles: the Atlantic circle (encapsulating the 'special relationship' with the United States and later NATO, which Churchill actually referred to in the speech as the circle of 'the English-speaking peoples'); the European circle (later centred on Britain in the European Union, although Churchill never envisioned us being an actual member of this federal 'United States of Europe'); and the Commonwealth circle (what remained of the old Empire and Britain's former possessions, still a particular concern for a Conservative in the 1940s). Central to this framework or metaphor was the notion of British *exceptionalism*: Britain was not just any old country. It was unique in and of itself, in the sense that it provided a vital

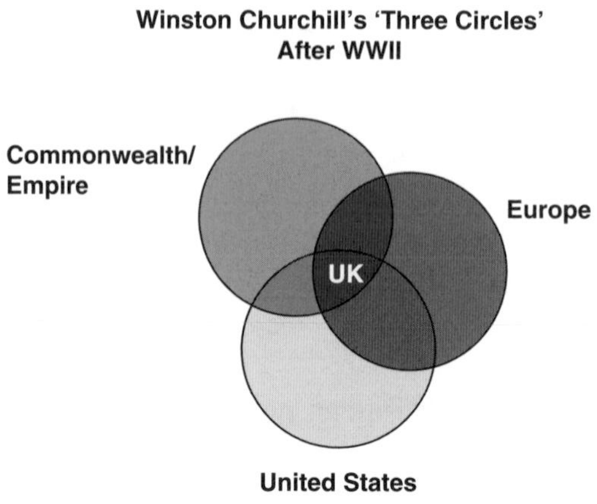

Figure I.1   **Winston Churchill's three circles after World War II**

connecting point between Europe and America, between the Old World and the New. Churchill himself brought out this sense of uniqueness by noting that Britain was 'the only country which has a great part to play in each one [of the three circles]'.

Nearly 70 years later, the three circles leitmotif continues to animate strategic thinking about Britain's role in the world, both among scholars and actual policymakers (see Figure 1.1). The idea of circles was embedded in Dean Acheson's 1962 critique, in which he infuriated the British policy-making classes by suggesting that the country was undergoing an identity crisis caused by its unwillingness to choose between spheres of influence. 'Great Britain has lost an empire and has not yet found a role', the former US Secretary of State suggested during a speech at West Point in 1962.

Although it was not immediately apparent to the British that they *needed* to choose, this does show the influence of the metaphor on American thinkers during the Cold War. The impact has, of course, been greatest in the UK itself. The notions of Britain as a transatlantic 'bridge' (James Callaghan and Tony Blair), a 'global hub' (Gordon Brown and David Miliband) or the centre of a 'networked world' (David Cameron and William Hague) all owe a considerable debt to the original three circles notion; indeed, in many ways they are merely a restatement or 'reshaping' of it.[2]

Like Callaghan before him, Tony Blair argued as British Prime Minister that the UK could act as a 'bridge' between Europe and the United States. Only Britain could talk to both in quite the same way, and only Britain could effectively bring them together. It was almost as if the UK were located somewhere at a mid-point across the Atlantic, and not just over twenty miles from continental Europe from its nearest point,[3] but the message was clear enough. As Blair put it in a November 1997 speech:

> Strong in Europe and strong with the US [*sic*]. There is no choice between the two. Stronger with one means stronger with the other. Our aim should be to deepen our relationship with the US at all levels. We are the bridge between the US and Europe. Let us use it. When Britain and America work together on the international scene, there is little we can't achieve.

As Blair saw it, Britain was a 'pivotal power' and there was no need to choose between circles, contrary to the position that Acheson had staked out years before. Blair saw a Britain that was 'adept at marshalling its unique combination of international relationships in making the vital difference to whatever crisis might present itself; crises – whether with a humanitarian, security or economic dimension – that invariably came to be viewed, like Britain's interests, through a transatlantic lens'.[4]

David Miliband sought to distance himself from the 'bridge' notion as Foreign Secretary under Gordon Brown in March 2008:

> I'm not sure the image of the UK as a bridge was ever right. It epitomised our ambivalent relationship with Europe, suggesting Europe was a bilateral relationship rather than an institution of which we are party. But with the rise of India, China and other emerging powers, the notion is even more inappropriate. I prefer to describe our role in the world as a global hub.[5]

This was presumably a reference to the fact that Churchill had never seen Britain as actually 'belonging' to the European circle itself. But for all his efforts to carve out a new niche in foreign policy – all governments seek to portray themselves as somehow 'different' to their predecessors – the basic idea was the same. Although power had moved since the 1940s from West to East, Britain was nevertheless still an exceptionalist 'hub' at the centre of things.

David Cameron and his former Foreign Secretary, on the other hand, saw Britain as the vital 'connector' within an increasingly 'networked world'. The 2010 and 2015 National Security Strategy (NSS) documents – about which we will have much more to say in Chapters 8 and 10 – are positively Churchillian in tone in some places. As Harvey has noted, the document observes that 'geographically Britain is an island, but economically and politically it is a vital link in the global network'. The notion that Britain remains the vital 'centre' of things was just as visible in the 2010–15 Coalition government as it was in the previous one.

In this book – in the second edition, much as in the first – we use the three circles as an analytical device to make sense of the ways in which Britain has attempted to project power and influence in an era of reduced circumstances. The notion is useful both because it is used by students of British foreign policy and because, as we shall argue, it remains the underlying metaphor that governs the thinking of policy-makers in Britain.[6] The foreign policies of governments from Atlee to Cameron have been animated, in one way or another, by the image of Britain still at the centre of things, acting as a vital pivot, bridge or hub in a world of external threats. To be sure, things have changed a bit since 1948. As William Wallace put it,

> [As] the Commonwealth connection shifted from apparent asset to apparent burden in the course of the 1970s, when the problems of Rhodesia/Zimbabwe loomed over British governments and the caucus of African governments within the Commonwealth replaced deference to Britain with demands on Britain, the preferred image shifted from three circles to two stepping-off points, the United States and western Europe, with Britain acting as the 'bridge' between them.[7]

As we shall see, Chapter 4 bears out this shift, arguing that by the 1970s the Atlantic and European circles had come to be seen as most critical of the three. It also probes the reasons behind this change.

A second theme of this book, as we shall see throughout the text, is the British emphasis on Realism or *realpolitik* as the 'default' approach to foreign policy. Under conditions of decline and austerity – but also during the heady days of Empire – the ingrained tradition of British foreign policy has always been an approach towards the rest of the world which emphasises the primacy of the national interest and the need to maintain regional and global balances of power. To be sure, perceptions of that interest have changed over time – most notably, Britain once took a 'wide view' of the world, in which the security of the Empire and its possessions across the globe were held to be synonymous with the security of the homeland, a position that was no longer economically or politically viable after the 1960s – but the emphasis on power and interest remained constant. This second theme, we suggest, reinforces the first. To the extent that British foreign policy is still about the projection of power and influence – and we would maintain that it mainly is – the three circles device retains its core utility, since the latter is essentially a way of thinking about how Britain retains a major role in the world and remains a 'player' in the game.

Although we shall emphasise Realism as a *descriptive* account of the images that UK policymakers often have in their heads, we will not necessarily assume that this *ought* to be the case; it is up to readers themselves to make up their minds about this, having first read the book. As we shall see in the following sections, this is not to say that other things (other, that is, than the naked projection of power) are unimportant in understanding contemporary UK foreign policy as well. During the last two decades in particular, British foreign policy has also emphasised Idealism, or the projection of values and ideals. 'What we believe' and 'what we stand for' are increasingly recurrent motifs in British foreign policy today, and the next chapter will stress the theoretical and practical 'war' between the rival visions of Realism and Idealism.

A third theme of the book is continuity and change. There are some aspects of British foreign policy that are relatively fixed and do not change with a change of government or political party. These are what Christopher Hill has called the 'givens' of UK foreign policy, constraints which are fixed over the short to medium term and which have left an especially visible mark.[8] But there are also major elements of change as well; one sees a quite discernable change of approach between Margaret Thatcher and John Major, for instance, and between Major and Tony Blair. This variability in approach is nothing new. It relates in part to the battle between Realism and Idealism, as we shall see in Chapter 1, since the 'power versus values' debate dates back at least to the rivalry between Benjamin Disraeli and William Gladstone. It also relates to a difference of opinion as to which of the three circles ought to be given priority over the others, especially to rivalries between the Europeanist and Atlanticist camps. Understanding British foreign policy today, we shall argue, requires an appreciation both of the things that are relatively fixed and of the things that change across individual leaders and administrations. In what follows, we shall stress this complexity, while attempting to give students a sense of the sources or 'drivers' behind these factors.

As emphasised in the First Edition, the authors remain convinced that 1956 continues to represent the most decisive 'turning point' in British foreign policy in the post-war era, not least because its profound psychological effect drove home a point that should have been clear in 1945. There have of course been a number of potentially significant points at which (or after which) Britain's place in the world and/or foreign policy approach might be said to have changed: (1) the end of World War II in 1945; (2) the Suez affair in 1956; (3) the withdrawal from 'east of Suez' after 1968; (4) the end of the Cold War around 1990 or 1991; (5) the 11 September 2001 attacks in the United States; (6) the 7 July 2005 bus and Tube bombings in Britain; and (7) the 2016 'Brexit' vote to leave the EU.[9] While the impact of all of these events will be noted in what follows, the role played by the Suez crisis was arguably the most critical, because it slowly dawned upon decision-makers in London after that crisis that

Britain could no longer pursue an 'independent' foreign policy without at least the tacit support of Washington DC. This said, as we shall see in later chapters, the end of the Cold War and 11 September 2001 also had profound effects that led to important policy changes.

Another significant commonality with the First Edition is our underlying conviction that *economic constraints* have had particularly large conditioning effects on the shape of British foreign policy. The move closer to Europe, for instance, reflected underlying movements in British trade as well as the gradual recognition that Britain should play a larger role in Europe because that is where its interests lie. Britain's waning economic resources have also played an increasing role in its foreign and defence policies, something which observers like F. S Northedge and Corelli Barnett recognised many years ago,[10] but which has also been evidenced more recently by the 2010 and 2015 defence reviews. It should also be stressed, however, that psychological factors, and not just structural forces, also have a significant effect on foreign policy. Nation-states may fail to recognise structural forces or there may be a 'time lag' in responding to them. In Britain's case, the pull of the past continues to war in the minds of policymakers with the recognition of structural realities. Britain's 'real' trading interests may lie with Europe, but the loyalties and identity of the country have made the process a slow and tortuous one. And as we will see in Chapter 5 in particular, the future of European integration continues to have a very divisive effect upon British politics today.

Continuity and Change in British Foreign Policy after 1945

There are certain constants which hold British foreign policy in place, and many of these are closely interrelated. These forces may be seen as providing the UK with opportunities on certain occasions, but most of them are more typically viewed as structural constraints that any British government must accept and consequently they lend a measure of stability. Like all constraints, they provide a certain amount of flexibility and are open to differing interpretations. Nevertheless, we shall attempt here to list those things that have generally been accepted by incoming administrations as factors they must live with, or else have proved to be so in the end.

One rather obvious 'given' is quite simply the loss of Empire and the related reality of long-term absolute and relative economic decline. As we shall see later in the book, for many years the makers of British foreign policy clung to the wider view mentioned earlier, namely that the Empire was synonymous with Britain's own position in the world and its own security. By 1968, that decline had proceeded so far that it necessitated a withdrawal of British forces east of Suez, and the need for that withdrawal has been wholly or partially accepted by British governments ever since. The partial exceptions were the Thatcher and Blair governments, both of which attempted to pursue the old wider view to some extent. Thatcher even attempted to reverse the course of decline itself, while Blair often acted as if the constraint was simply not there. But as we shall see in later chapters, both hit against very formidable economic constraints in the end and both were constrained, whether they saw the constraint as real or not.

A second constant, as we have seen already, is the British sense of exceptionalism. This can be viewed as part of the hangover of Empire. Both psychologically and politically, it is difficult to retreat inwards – adopting a policy of isolationism rather than internationalism – once a country has already played a global role for 200 years. The feeling that Britain is not just another country and can never be 'another Switzerland' – defending its homeland, but otherwise staying out of global affairs – has survived the loss of Empire. There is still an expectation that Britain should be involved in *some* way during any international crisis, although those expectations are far greater in the American case (and consequently harder to resist).[11]

A third given is that Britain's geopolitical position as an island nation helps to shape its strategic position, as well as its economy and its psychology.[12] In recent years, the British have perhaps underestimated the role that geography plays in shaping foreign policy.[13] On the one hand, the UK is dependent on global trade, since a small but populous island arguably cannot produce all the goods and services that its citizens need and demand. This dependence on overseas trade, moreover, gives the UK global interests and encourages that 'wider view' we mentioned already. On the other hand, Britain's island status makes it vulnerable to attack from outside, and UK strategy has therefore traditionally placed a premium on naval power; that power has been used for home defence, while also giving the UK the capacity to open up trading routes overseas. Some have tried to explain German militarism over the last few centuries and the relatively early onset of democracy in Britain, for instance – as well as the 'special relationship' with the United States – by noting that Germany is far less secure in its borders than the UK and that the latter had an Atlanticist orientation. Just as the United States was insulated in its infancy from outside security challenges by the gulf of the Atlantic Ocean, Britain is physically separated from mainland Europe by the North Sea and the English Channel. It is so close to mainland Europe, however, that it remains vulnerable, at least in a purely geostrategic sense.

Psychologically, the island status has had effects too. The British feel distant from Europe even though they are separated from the continent only by *La Manche* or the English Channel in the south and by the North Sea in the East. One cartoonist of the 1990s who disagreed with Tony Blair's bridging approach to Europe portrayed a tiny Blair sitting in the lap of a huge Helmut Kohl (the German Chancellor at the time). More significantly, the June 2016 British referendum on EU membership – won by the 'Leave' or 'Brexit' group – illustrated the mental schism which has grown up (or always existed) between the citizens of Britain and those of Europe, as well as divisions within the Conservative Party on this issue. At the same time, the British are not quite American either, and most Prime Ministers have shied away from appearing to be 'the 51st state' or 'America's poodle', a term used most notably of Margaret Thatcher by Denis Healey (again, Blair was an exception, on one occasion wearing cowboy boots and a ten-gallon hat during a visit to President George W. Bush's Texas ranch).

A fourth constant in recent years has been Britain's status as an increasingly multicultural society with a (somewhat tortured) history of immigration. As we will see in later chapters, the most enduring significance of the Commonwealth circle today is that the Empire has effectively 'come home'. The circle has in effect turned in upon itself. Immigration from the European circle (especially from Eastern Europe) has also made Britain far less homogeneous and more multicultural than at any time in the last thousand years.

Lastly, a final given – albeit one that often operates more as an opportunity than a constraint – is the kind of governmental system Britain has in foreign policy. The UK has a parliamentary system of democracy, but within that the executive tends to be highly dominant. There is no tradition of the House of Commons being consulted before major UK military interventions, and foreign policy powers are not shared as they are (technically at least) in the American system of government. Of course, Prime Ministers may submit a core issue to Parliament if they are unsure what to do and/or need the political 'cover' provided. David Cameron did this voluntarily in 2014, for instance, when the issue of intervention in Syria came up, and he surprisingly lost the vote 285–272.[14] He subsequently decided not to commit UK armed forces to that conflict. But there is no constitutional requirement to abide by such votes in the UK, and Prime Ministers need not be bound by the deliberations of Parliament in general. If the issue is controversial enough and parliamentary support is fragile – as it was in the case of the Coalition government which ran the UK from 2010 to 2015 – Prime Ministers may choose to be bound by Parliament on a controversial issue, but this is more a matter of political judgement than constitutional law or tradition. In 1982, for instance, Margaret Thatcher did not consult with Parliament before committing a task force to re-capture the Falklands; nor did Anthony Eden before the intervention at Suez in 1956; nor did the Major government in the 1991 Persian Gulf War, or the Blair government before its intervention in Kosovo in 1999. While a requirement to consult Parliament might (in future years) become one of those norms or conventions that govern constitutional behaviour, votes on Iraq and reversed votes on Syria remain slim reeds upon which to predict this, not least because the Cameron government was originally hampered by one of the smallest electoral majorities in the House of Commons that any Prime Minister had ever had to work with.[15]

Although we have portrayed the changes in UK foreign policy from Blair to Theresa May as more a matter of nuance than substantive change, it would be wrong to conclude that UK foreign policy never changes in its emphasis. Indeed, British governments have varied along the first two themes or dimensions with which we began this book. One regularly observed change in recent years has been the addition of British ideals into the mix. During the last three governments, policymakers have stressed the projection of *values* as well as the projection of *power*. Consider, for instance, the change of approach which occurred between John Major and Tony Blair. Major was a Realist, who hesitated to put out a 'conflagration' at the very heart of Europe in the former Yugoslavia – indeed, Major doubted whether Britain had the capacity to do much about troubles beyond its shores – replaced by a Prime Minister who was very much his opposite. Blair believed that Britain's true responsibility in the world was as much about spreading British values around the globe as it was to protect British power at home.

As well as changes in theoretical approach, we have also witnessed changes in the way that different governments see themselves interacting with the rest of the world. This is especially true of changes of emphasis within the three circles. While the pro-European Edward Heath saw Britain's future as being very much within the European circle, there was a huge change in the way that his successor as Leader of the Conservative Party, Margaret Thatcher, viewed Europe. While she did not contemplate outright withdrawal from the European Union, she was certainly one of the original 'Eurosceptics'. More recently, David Cameron was much closer to Thatcher than Heath, seemingly preferring an Atlanticist approach to foreign policy over a European one.

Britain's Place in the World

We can see elements of fundamental change when we look at how governments after 1945 viewed Britain's place in the world, as well as the steady accumulation of economic constraints we discussed in the previous section. For over two decades after 1945, successive British governments pursued a foreign policy strategy that sought to preserve their power and influence in all three of Churchill's circles. It was assumed – at least until 1968 – that Britain was still a Great Power with global interests and responsibilities, and that it should accordingly seek to maintain a world role in both the military and the economic spheres. However, Britain's continuing efforts to project this world role were confounded over the years by a series of changes in Britain's external environment. It had already been apparent in 1945 that the two emerging 'superpowers' – the United States and the Soviet Union – would henceforth be the dominant actors on the world stage. What had not been anticipated quite so clearly was the extent to which this changing alignment of forces would be supplemented by the growth of nationalism in the third world, a development that was destined seriously to weaken Britain's imperial grip. To make matters worse, the relative decline of the British economy, which had begun even before 1914, continued apace. In 1950 Britain's GDP per capita ranked the seventh highest in the world. By 1970 its position had slumped to eighteenth, by 1981 to twenty-first and by 2011 to thirty-third. In these changing circumstances, the British government's efforts to sustain its three-circle foreign policy strategy became increasingly overextended. Given the economic resources at their disposal, Britain's foreign policy makers found that they were simply trying to do too much. They were seeking to sustain a role in world affairs which reflected past rather than present capabilities. Sooner or later, Britain would have to bring both its aspirations and its commitments into line with its relatively reduced circumstances.

The resultant process of imperial withdrawal began technically with the decolonisations in India and Palestine in 1947–48. However, it was not until the late 1950s – when Macmillan's 'wind of change' brought a second and more far-reaching wave of decolonisation – that the retreat from Empire really gathered momentum. By 1968, most of Britain's colonial territories had been granted formal independence, and in 1971–72, as though to emphasise the fact that Britain had indeed abandoned its world role, British military forces were finally withdrawn from east of Suez.

The retreat from Empire, however, had two important corollaries. The first was that the declining importance of the Empire was counterbalanced by a concomitant increase in Britain's involvement in Western Europe. Even before the decolonisations in Africa and the Caribbean, it had been increasingly evident that the focus of Britain's external trade was already shifting away from the Empire and towards Europe. This, in turn, provided a powerful material motive for successive governments to emphasise the European dimension of their foreign policy. The second corollary of imperial retreat was that Britain's declining ability to project a world military role rendered it less able to assist American efforts to protect the general global interests of the West. Notwithstanding the continuing importance of Anglo-American collaboration inside NATO, the drastic reduction in the British government's ability after 1971 to conduct third-world operations served seriously to weaken London's ties with Washington. In short, the retreat from Empire in the 1960s was accompanied simultaneously by an upgrading of Britain's links with Europe and by a relative downgrading of its relations with the United States.

Yet, despite imperial withdrawal and the 'Europeanisation' of Britain's external policy, the extent and range of the British government's foreign relations remained immense. Indeed, one of the few things that could be said with certainty about Britain's foreign policy in the post-war period was that, like the weather, there was an awful lot of it about. During the late 1990s and the first years of the 21st century, British military interventions were undertaken in Afghanistan, Kosovo, Libya, Iraq and Sierra Leone, to cite but the best-known examples. The British government continued to participate in a diverse array of international bodies, ranging from single-purpose associations such as the World Trade Organization (WTO) and the Universal Postal Union to highly complex 'supranational' institutions such as the United Nations and European Union. London also maintained diplomatic contact with almost every other nation-state, with a plethora of embassies, consulates and High Commissions attempting to nurture innumerable sets of bilateral relations.

The Plan of this Book

A genuinely comprehensive analysis of Britain's post-war foreign policy would undoubtedly need to describe and to explain the changing course of Britain's bilateral relations with each and every one of the countries with which it has had dealings – a gargantuan enterprise given the extensive and highly variegated nature of London's post-war diplomacy. Fortunately, the present study has a more limited focus. Rather than providing an all-encompassing account of Britain's post-war foreign relations, this book attempts to outline the most important developments in British foreign policy which have occurred since 1945 and to review and assess the main explanations that have been offered for them. Of course, such an approach immediately gives rise to the question of what constitutes an 'important' development. We have been guided in this matter partly by what existing academic studies consider important and partly by the priority accorded to different issues by the policy makers themselves, as evidenced by their actions, by their public pronouncements and (where available) by the official public record. If this makes for a somewhat malleable notion of 'importance', so be it.

The descriptive part of the analysis presented here attempts to provide a straightforward outline of what Britain's major foreign policies have been during the period since World War II. The explanatory part is conducted in terms of both the policy calculations of the key decision-makers and the deeper structural factors that shaped those calculations. In the context of Macmillan's 'wind of change' decolonisations, for example, this involves not only a discussion of the government's calculations about the need for a rapid withdrawal of imperial control, but also an examination of the more general 'structural' preconditions (most notably the growth of indigenous nationalism inside the colonies) that caused London to reconsider its overall imperial strategy in the first place. This book accordingly constitutes a modest attempt to examine the effects of both structure and agency on Britain's post-war foreign policies. Neither is assumed to be more important than the other, but both are clearly necessary if a convincing account of the major developments of the post-war era is to be provided.[16]

British foreign policy did not suddenly 'emerge' in 1945, and it is of course rooted in much deeper historical traditions. Chapter 1 examines what those traditions are, outlining the historical background to developments after the end of World War II. From the 17th century until the early part of the 20th, British leaders essentially pursued a balance-of-power strategy in which Britain refrained from becoming a player in Europe itself ('Splendid Isolation'), but would intervene on the side of the weaker power or coalition in order to avoid the emergence of any single dominating force. This chapter looks in particular at the policy practices and ideas of Lord Palmerston, Benjamin Disraeli and William Gladstone, contrasting the Realism of the first two with the Idealism of the latter. In the 18th century, Britain focused mainly on buttressing the system which had emerged from the Congress of Vienna in 1814–15, but the moralistic and intensely religious William Gladstone – four times British Prime Minister between 1874 and 1894 – was the first to attempt an Idealist 'experiment' in Britain's approach towards the rest of the world. In the 20th century, Idealism then resurfaced with a half-hearted attempt to substitute cooperative diplomacy for aggressive *realpolitik*. This strongly reinforced Realist notions in the minds of Britain's foreign policy makers – a Realism that was further underpinned by six years of war. The lessons they drew from World War II played a significant part in the overextended defence strategy that successive governments pursued after 1945 in their efforts to resist communist expansionism, as the conceptual model that had been devised for dealing with Hitler and Mussolini was transferred wholesale to the activities of the Soviet Union. As generational replacement within Westminster and Whitehall occurred and memories of the 1930s diminished, Idealism then began to make a comeback in the early 1980s with the crusading approach of Margaret Thatcher and in the late 1990s in the guise of the 'Ethical Foreign Policy', associated in particular with Prime Minister Tony Blair and his Foreign Secretary, Robin Cook. The latter project in particular met with only mixed success, however, and Realism remains what we shall call the 'default' position among British foreign policy strategists.

Chapters 2 to 6 are organised around the major post-war developments in each of Churchill's three circles. Chapter 2 examines Britain's relationship with Europe and the superpowers during the early years of the Cold War. It describes how, against the backdrop of the growing Soviet threat to European security, the Attlee government went to considerable lengths to persuade the Americans to make a long-run military commitment to Western Europe's defence. The government's efforts – assisted in part by Stalin's short-sightedness – were rewarded with the creation of NATO in 1949. However, the indirect costs of American participation were to weigh heavily on the British exchequer in the years ahead. In return for Washington's assistance in Europe, Britain was expected not only to make a large contribution to NATO's continental land forces, but also to provide military support for Truman's global policy of 'containing' communist expansionism. It was this latter commitment that led to British involvement in the Korean war in the early 1950s and further exacerbated the problem of military overextension that had afflicted Britain's foreign policy strategy since 1945. As Chapter 2 also shows, however, while London was quite prepared to embroil itself in the defence of Western Europe, it was also determined to stand aloof from French moves to create a Western European economic community. In the early 1950s, Britain was still far too enmeshed in its 'three circle' strategy to entertain the idea that some part of its national sovereignty should be ceded to the incipiently supranational institutions of what was to become the European Union.

Chapter 3 assesses Britain's Empire circle policy between 1945 and the Suez crisis of 1956. It examines the relatively early withdrawals from India and Palestine and then describes Britain's post-1948 strategy of imperial retrenchment in the Far East, Africa and the Caribbean. It concludes that this final phase of full-blooded imperialism was carried out with remarkable skill, a series of well-timed constitutional concessions being employed to 'buy off' indigenous demands for full political participation. Suez, however, represented a symbolic watershed. The disastrous

British intervention not only damaged Anglo-American relations but also provoked a thoroughgoing reappraisal of Britain's three circle strategy. After Suez, traditional European imperialism was confronted with the realisation that indigenous third-world pressures for self-determination could not be resisted forever, perhaps not even for very long. After Suez, the question of a wholesale imperial retreat came close to the top of the British government's foreign policy agenda.

Chapter 4 discusses the 'wind of change', the circumstances that produced the second-wave decolonisations which by 1966 had deprived Britain of all but its smallest dependencies. It assesses the importance of the Wilson government's decision, in 1968, to withdraw British forces from East of Suez and discusses the extent to which the withdrawal succeeded in ameliorating the United Kingdom's problems of military overextension. Chapter 4 also analyses the fortuitous material shift in the pattern of Britain's overseas trade which (as noted above) was already beginning to occur before the post-Suez process of imperial retreat was fully under way.

Chapter 5 examines what was the clear counterpart to the retreat from Empire and the abandonment of Britain's world role: the British government's growing interest in Europe. Although Britain twice failed to join the thriving EU during the 1960s, the focus of its economic activities continued to shift markedly towards Europe throughout that decade. Indeed, with its accession to the now-renamed European Community (EC) in 1973, it seemed likely that Britain would subsequently follow a primarily European role in world politics, reflecting its increasingly European interests and its newfound international position as a middle-ranking European power. These expectations were confirmed during the 1970s but were at least partially confounded thereafter. Margaret Thatcher's 'Gaullist' unwillingness to cede any further sovereignty to EU institutions during the 1980s severely restricted the development of a European common foreign policy and also the development of the Union itself. Long after Thatcher's departure, moreover, the British Conservative Party in particular remained highly ambivalent about Europe, distancing itself from its EU partners in terms of both financial policy and Europe's political relations with much of the outside world. Throughout his time in office – which ended in July 2016 just after the so-called 'Brexit' vote to leave the EU – British Prime Minister David Cameron faced a revolt within his own party from so-called 'Eurosceptics', many of whom of whom favoured complete withdrawal from the Union.[17] Indeed, the relatively close referendum vote to leave the Union held the previous month showed that large numbers of British citizens remained psychologically distant from Europe, and at the time of writing it remains unclear just what Britain's future relationship with Europe will be.

Chapter 6 reviews the main changes that have occurred in Britain's 'special relationship' with the United States in the period since Suez. It discusses the rapid repair in relations that occurred in 1957–58 following the recognition by policy makers in both London and Washington that the main beneficiary of the Anglo-American rift over Suez had probably been the Soviet Union. The chapter examines the decay in bilateral relations which set in during the mid-1960s, as the Wilson government first refused to provide material support for the American war in Vietnam and then reduced its own geostrategic usefulness to Washington by withdrawing from east of Suez. During the 1980s, however, Britain ceased to be just another European power. As an instinctive Atlanticist, Thatcher was as convinced as President Reagan that the West could and should use force against any government or movement, communist or otherwise, that seriously challenged the global interests of the West. This foreign policy 'reboot' survived the end of the Cold War and was not restricted to the Reagan/Thatcher years, moreover. Fuelled both by ideological similarities and common interests, the Clinton/Blair years also saw a rekindling of the special relationship, even though the objective level of material support for allied military ventures that Britain was able to provide was, in reality, very restricted.

Chapters 7 and 8 focus on two areas of British foreign policy – economics and defence – which, although they are analysed *en passant* in other parts of this book, raise a series of technical problems that require special attention. Chapter 7, for instance, distinguishes between the two main phases of Britain's post-war foreign economic policy: before 1968, when successive governments sought to preserve the twin financial legacies of the Empire, the reserve role of sterling and the Overseas Sterling Area; and after 1968, when Britain experimented with a variety of approaches to currency policy at the same time as it brought its trade and investment policies increasingly into line with the requirements of the EU.

Chapter 8 focuses on UK defence policy, with a particular emphasis on the ways that successive governments have tried (and, arguably, failed) to make Britain's dwindling economic resources match its often ambitious strategic commitments. Repeated defence reviews since 1952 have attempted to cut back those commitments to match the available resources, the 2015 *Strategic Defence and Security Review* (SDSR) being only the most recent effort in a long line. This chapter also looks at one especially important aspect of Britain's post-war defence policy: the independent nuclear deterrent. The discussion of the independent deterrent analyses its role within Britain's overall defence posture and its importance, at least in the eyes of successive governments, as a symbol of Britain's continuing status as a power 'of the first rank'.

Chapter 9 is concerned with theoretical matters. It reviews a number of different approaches to the analysis of foreign policy with a particular focus on the four perspectives outlined in the next section of this Introduction – Neoclassical Realism, Bureaucratic Politics, Constructivism and Cognitivism. It assesses the extent to which each approach has informed the substantive analysis presented in this book. The chapter places particular emphasis on Realism, however – the theoretical model that in our view has dominated the foreign policy thinking of successive British governments for at least the last century. As argued elsewhere in this book, this commitment to Realist principles has exerted a powerful influence on the development of Britain's post-war foreign policy. However, we also note the renewed influence of a new Idealism – both on the right and the left – in British foreign policy since the Thatcher and Blair years. While this has not supplanted the standard Realist approach towards the rest of the world, the increasingly moralistic tone of foreign policy in Britain and the influence of domestic politics represents a challenge to the usual focus on alliances, power and interests, and both Constructivism and Cognitivism may be better placed than Realism to account for this.

Chapter 10 looks at the future of British foreign policy. Using the 2015 National Security Strategy and SDSR as a take-off point, it examines what the future threats to Britain are likely to be in the light of the hard and soft power capabilities the UK is likely to possess, as well as looking at how safe or 'endangered' Britain really is. This chapter draws together the main substantive themes that are explored throughout the book and examines the ways in which the very notion of 'threat' itself has changed since the end of the Cold War. It also assesses the extent to which, in spite of imperial withdrawal, Britain's post-war foreign policy strategy has continued to suffer from overextension – a kind of imperial overstretch without an empire – and discusses the changing role that Britain will play within the international system in the 21st century. It is argued that, although Britain did find a role, of a sort, in the post-imperial, post-Cold War world, its overall foreign policy strategy remained fundamentally ambivalent. During the Thatcher and Blair years in particular, the British government sought to maintain a prominent position within both the European and Atlantic circles. At a time when Britain's primary material interests were increasingly located in Europe – and when Britain was most likely to influence world events if it acted in concert with its European partners – the British government might have been better advised to commit itself more fully to the European Union. Britain is also increasingly committed to membership of, and action within, the North Atlantic Treaty Organization. NATO has proved remarkably resilient given that its original *raison d'être* has gone, but it is likely to play a particularly central role within UK foreign and defence policy in the future.

A Necessary Prerequisite: The Relevance of Foreign Policy Theory

It might at first sight seem rather odd to introduce a discussion of foreign policy theory into what should be a relatively straightforward historical or descriptive account of Britain's post-war foreign policy. At the time the first edition of this book appeared, works on UK foreign policy also exhibited what was perhaps a peculiarly 'British' aversion to theory. Fortunately, this is no longer as true as it used to be, although most studies today tend to privilege Constructivism as an approach rather than other perspectives, focusing on the ideational sources of foreign policy rather than the material ones.[18]

So why is 'theory' important? British governments, it might be observed, have pursued a particular sequence of foreign policies since 1945, and that sequence of policies has presumably been followed for a given set of reasons. All that an analysis of British foreign policy behaviour has to do is to specify the appropriate sequence of policies and then to identify the reasons why these policies were adopted. Where, it might reasonably be asked, does 'theory' come into it? The answer to this important question is simple, yet potentially perplexing: analysts of foreign policy invariably employ, either consciously or unconsciously, some sort of theoretical perspective when they approach their subject matter. Crucially, the perspective that is adopted not only colours the analyst's characterisation of 'that which is to be explained' (the 'appropriate sequence of policies' referred to above) but also strongly influences the specific explanations (the 'reasons') that are offered for it. In view of this profound influence of theoretical perspective upon both description and explanation, it is evident why the present aside is so necessary.

The discipline of Foreign Policy Analysis, as it is generally known in the academic world, has gone through a number of distinct phases over the years, but the most dominant perspectives today in both Europe and the United States are probably Neoclassical Realism, Constructivism, Bureaucratic Politics and the Cognitive approach. In the context of British foreign policy, Neoclassical Realism focuses on the use of military capabilities to maximise British power and national interests in an anarchical world. Britain, much like any other state, is concerned with the maximisation of its own interests, but it is restrained in that effort by its own much-depleted military and economic power.[19] For Constructivists, on the other hand, states do not actually have timeless or unchanging interests, and one must focus on what makes Britain 'different' from other states if we want to explain its actions abroad.[20] It is the British sense of identity – our self-image as well as our images of others – which shapes what we think our interests are in the first place. Identities tell us who we are and how we ought to behave. Bureaucratic Politics examines the infighting and compromise-making which goes on between organisations as they fashion foreign policy, looking at ways in which perception of 'the national interest' is coloured by organisational interests. Finally, members of the Cognitive school focus on the beliefs, personalities and psychological mindsets of leaders.[21] If we want to understand why Britain acts as it does in relation to the rest of the world, we need to delve into the cognitive beliefs and past experiences of particular decision-makers, and not just general or socially shared conceptions about what Britain is or ought to be doing.

As a handy mental guide to these four approaches, we might think of Neoclassical Realism as an approach which emphasises the role of *interests* (the British national interest, constrained by its power), Constructivism as a perspective which stresses *identities* (our collective images about ourselves and other nations), Bureaucratic Politics as examining *institutions* (organisational roles and the interests of particular bureaucracies) and finally Cognitivism as an approach that focuses on idiosyncratic *ideas* (individual-level psychological perceptions and misperceptions about the world). These distinctions are worth delving into in rather more detail.

Neoclassical Realism

Neoclassical Realism derives from the older Neorealist perspective and from the even older classical realist tradition, and it attempts to explain behaviour at both the structural and state levels of analysis. In a structural sense, it accepts that the nature of the international system, and the degree of material power which a state has within it, sets the broad parameters of a government's foreign policy. Britain's ambitions, for instance, are constrained by its material capabilities, and since the decline of Empire foreign adventures or interventions have been difficult to sustain and hence rarely undertaken. On the other hand, states do not just respond to external demands; while they are constrained by the polarity of the system (or number of superpowers within it), they enjoy a certain freedom to manoeuvre in choosing how to respond. There thus exists only an imperfect correlation between structural imperatives and the manner in which states actually behave (that is, between the amount of power we have and the nature and content of our foreign policy). As we shall see later in the book, Britain has sometimes stretched its military resources almost to breaking point, as happened in Iraq and Afghanistan under the leadership of Tony Blair. In other words, it is up to the 'agent' or state to decide how it responds to constraints, and internal or domestic factors (such as the balance of power between state and society, a general commitment to the spread of democracy or a desire to divert attention away from the domestic economy) may prompt a state to behave in ways that could not have been predicted by examining its material power or role within the international system alone, strictly construed. Neoclassical realists focus on a variety of unit-level or domestic factors which cause foreign policy to only broadly reflect structural demands or objective material power.[22] Nevertheless, this perspective is broadly based upon on the Rational Actor model. This seeks to understand foreign policy behaviour as the goal-directed consequence of rational calculation by decision-makers: rational calculations that aim in some sense to maximise the national interest. Since states are rational actors, then if we want to understand why state X did Y we need only to retrace the logical steps and reasoning processes through which we got to Y.

Social Constructivism

Constructivism is often only poorly understood because it is relatively new, but its basic features are easy enough to relate in a straightforward way. This approach makes a key distinction between 'brute facts' (things which are objectively there, like the weather or the existence of the Atlantic Ocean) and 'social facts' (things which are 'constructed' and only exist because we say that they do). Much of international politics, like all of politics, is made up of the latter: norms, conventions and rules which only 'exist' because we subjectively agree that they do. In other words, from this perspective our objective material capabilities – again, something which Realists tend to dwell upon more than anything else – are much less important than how we subjectively view our own place in the world; who and what we *think* we are is what drives foreign policy behaviour. Put differently, this approach focuses on identities and self-images. When Argentina invaded the Falkland Islands/Malvinas in 1982, for instance, it was simply unacceptable to Britain to allow this action to stand; the British self-image as an upholder of conventions like 'fair play', 'democracy' and 'state sovereignty' meant that the seizure of the Islands by a foreign dictator – and the subjugation of its citizens to Argentine rule under an autocratic general who refused to play by the rules – simply could not be permitted. Or when Tony Blair committed nearly 50,000 British troops to the 2003 war in Iraq, he often cited Britain's identity in justifying his actions. What we call our 'national interests' may be entirely shaped by who we think we are and what we think our role in the world is (or ought to be). So if we want to understand why state X did Y, we need to account for the way in which that state has constructed its own self-image or identity.

Bureaucratic Politics

Bureaucratic Politics treats foreign policy as both 'outputs' and 'result-ants'.[23] It recognises that politicians are not entirely free to set governmental priorities, not least because they are constrained by what the bureaucracy can deliver. In one sense, foreign policy is often an output of what particular organisations *know how* to do. They do not constantly reinvent the wheel, which would be both costly and time-consuming. Instead, they develop plans and standard operational procedures (or SOPs for short) which can be pulled down from the shelf as needed. Faced with the political requirement to invade a particular country like Iraq or Afghanistan, for instance, bodies like the Ministry of Defence (MoD) will dust off the last military plan they had for that task, revising it as necessary but following their 'standard' ways or routines in doing so. On the other hand, foreign policies can simply be that which remains after all the organisations (for example, the Foreign and Commonwealth Office, the MoD and the Treasury) have bargained and compromised with one another. This is foreign or defence policy as the 'least common denominator'. Since the Prime Minister is technically only *primus inter pares* and power is to some extent shared in any administration, each player in the game of policymaking has some resources to bargain with. An individual's position in that game can be strongly influenced by the job s/he does in the administration, hence the well-worn aphorism 'where you stand depends on where you sit'. Inter-service rivalry in the UK is especially acute, moreover, and defence reviews in particular – which in the British case have almost always involved decisions about cuts in particular services – can reflect bargains and deal-making, as much as any rational attempt to sit down and deal with a problem. To explain why state X took action Y, we need to understand the interplay of bureaucratic forces that underpinned the policy debate and decision.

Cognitivism

The Cognitive approach shares the emphasis of Constructivism on the subjective aspects of international politics and foreign policy. But where Constructivism is primarily sociological in nature, Cognitivism is shaped by a more psychologically based approach. Another way of saying this is that where Constructivism focuses on collectively held beliefs and norms that influence large numbers of people within a state, Cognitivism emphasises the more idiosyncratic beliefs and perceptions that are peculiar to particular leaders and decision-makers. It focuses on the way that the existing mindsets of individual decision-makers colour their interpretation of reality. Like Neoclassical Realism, the cognitive approach draws upon a long-established tradition within the study of international relations and foreign policy decision-making dating back to at least the 1950s. But it also rejects the Rational Actor assumption, arguing that actual decision-makers – due in part to the cognitive limitations of human beings as information-processors – are in fact 'boundedly rational'; in other words, there are major limits to our rationality. Instead of engaging in a comprehensive information search and considering the costs and benefits of an exhaustive list of options – both of which we would need to do in order to make a fully rational decision – we often rely on cognitive short cuts such as historical analogies or simple beliefs. When Margaret Thatcher compared General Galtieri of Argentina to Adolf Hitler in 1982, for instance – as Anthony Eden had done in 1956 when confronting Nasser over the Suez Canal – she was evoking the familiar Munich analogy, which shaped a whole generation of post-war thinking in Britain and in the United States. More recently, in 2011 Prime Minister David Cameron joined his allies in a NATO bombing campaign designed to free Libya from its long-time dictator Muammar Ghaddafi and to prevent a predicted genocide. The PM often argued that the bombing of Libya was necessary to save Benghazi and avoid 'another Srebrenica' – a reference to an incident in 1995 when UN peacekeepers had stood aside while Bosnian Muslims were slaughtered by Serbs.[24] This approach emphasises the role of beliefs and personality in shaping policy responses, so that different decision-makers can be expected to react differently to the same situation. So in summary, if we want to understand why state X did Y, we need to reconstruct the cognitive perceptions of the key decision-making actors, as well as showing how the short cuts they used influenced the whole process which led to the decision reached.

The utility of theory is clearest when applied to a specific case. As an illustration, consider the June 2016 referendum held in the UK between 'Remain' supporters (arguing that Britain was better off inside the European Union) and advocates of leaving the EU altogether (the so-called 'Brexit' or 'Leave' camp). We will have more to say about this development in Chapter 5. But how would our four approaches account for this potentially momentous development?

Neoclassical Realists would emphasise the dictating role of interests. By most standards, the 'true' interests of Britain lay in remaining inside the EU. In 2016, most of Britain's trade lay with EU countries and withdrawal would mean at best a long period of renegotiation and at worst recession and prolonged unemployment, caused by an inability to access the Single Market, which would play directly against UK interests.

However, there was a great deal of dispute during the referendum debate about this, and it has to be admitted that realists have some difficulty operationalising the somewhat fuzzy concept of 'national interests'. It is possible to argue, of course, that the interests of the UK had changed since 1975, so that its 'real' interests lay outside the EU. This said, most neoclassical realists would emphasise the degree to which systemic interests are distorted by domestic politics. In particular, by deciding to give advocates of the Brexit camp their own referendum, Prime Minister David Cameron was engaging in the political gamble that he could keep the Leave faction of his own Conservative Party at bay. For neoclassical realists, it is this distorting effect – and a not-wholly-rational effect at that – which explains how a focus on the national interest can sometimes *not* be the thing which dictates foreign policy.

For *Constructivists*, on the other hand, it is not interests but identity which shapes British foreign policy. It could be argued that the Brexit group won because of the challenge to the identity of many of the British people, especially to the older (mostly white and Anglo-Saxon) population that is traditionally associated with images of the British Isles. The 'British identity' was increasingly in crisis as a result of waves of immigration that followed the disintegration of Empire, the migration of workers within the EU (particularly after enlargement in the early 2000s) and, more recently, an EU-wide immigration crisis caused in part by refugees fleeing the conflict in Syria. The Eurozone crisis after 2009 – in which countries like Greece and Ireland defaulted on their national debts – did not help matters. By this reckoning, supporters of Brexit wished to return to a kind of 'pre-globalisation' past that had been viable in earlier times and, it was believed by some, could be again. But for Remain voters, this past had either had never existed in reality or could no longer exist because of changes in the way that international movements of people and capital were changing the basis of identity itself.

The *Bureaucratic Politics* approach would emphasise the differing roles of opinion leaders involved in the debate and the degree to which their positions emanated from positions within the government. Admittedly, this perspective has difficulty accounting for large-scale social movements and shifts in public perceptions, since it is focused on bureaucratic roles within a government and not on mass opinion within the nation-state. However, it would certainly stress the positions of the UK's foreign policy elites, arguing that even large votes like referendums are actually shaped by rather small numbers of people. It is notable, for instance, that Nigel Farage (leader of the UK Independence Party, but not a Member of Parliament) was essentially free to pursue his own ideological agenda, while David Cameron was caught between competing factions of the Conservative Party and tried (unsuccessfully, as it turned out) to keep both factions within the same tent. Cameron attempted to represent all of Britain simultaneously, as was his job, but it is difficult to do so when a country is as divided as the UK was over EU membership.

For advocates of the *Psychological* approach, finally, we should look to the mindsets of opinion leaders like Cameron, Farage and Boris Johnson (a former London Mayor and leader of the Leave faction within the Conservative Party) in shaping the debate, and at their perceptions (or misperceptions) of what was going on. Again, this approach finds it difficult to account for large-scale social and political movements, but it nonetheless argues that key individuals do shape mass opinions. Opinion leaders are not robots, but are themselves influenced by emotions like national pride (e.g. 'this is what it means to be British') and by competing cognitive beliefs (e.g. 'Britain is better off inside the EU'). They are also influenced by their perceptions of what Britain's 'true' interests really are. *Both* advocates of the Remain and Leave positions seem to have believed that they were acting in the larger national interest, positions which seemed resistant to empirical evidence as pro- and anti-European voters discounted information which failed to support their own strongly held positions. Both factions appear to have thought that they were acting in the best interests of the British state, but what those interests consisted of was largely in the eye of the beholder.

Although no one perspective is favoured in the discussion which follows – the intention is to provide the reader with a clear sense of how advocates of each would account for the history of British foreign policy since 1945, as well as the key decisions within that history – we shall give particular emphasis to Neoclassical Realism in much of the narrative. The reader should note, moreover, that Realism is not just a purported description of what exists – as, say, Constructivism is – but it is also a prescription for how leaders *ought* to behave. Economists like to distinguish between *positive* propositions (what the world is like) and normative ones (how we ought to behave in that world). Realism is in fact both, since it tries both to describe/explain what goes on in international relations *and* to prescribe how leaders should conduct themselves as they go about the making of foreign policy. It is fair to conclude that, since the end of World War II, British thinking about international affairs has been dominated by two sets of ideas: those of Realism and, to a lesser extent, of Idealism.

The 'Tug of War' Between Realism and Idealism

Idealism is based on the assumption that *all* states ultimately share a common interest in avoiding war and in maximising mutually beneficial international economic exchange. Its prescription is that, as far as possible, states should use the vehicles of cooperative diplomacy and international law in order to ensure that international disputes are peacefully resolved. Indeed, in the Idealist view, conflicts between states generally result either from injustice, mistrust or misunderstanding: a judicious combination of law and diplomacy can in principle remedy all three. Notwithstanding the British government's flirtation with Idealism in the 1920s, however, Idealist principles have rarely informed Britain's foreign policy, the only (partial) exception being the effort by Foreign Secretary Robin Cook to implement an 'ethical foreign policy' during the government of Tony Blair during the late 1990s, and Blair's own periodic attempts to inject a moral thrust into British foreign policy during that period and the early years of the 21st century. For the most part, since the late 1930s it has been the rival tradition of Realism that has constituted the foundation of the British foreign policy establishment's 'world-view'.

Although the principles of Realism are discussed in detail in Chapter 9, the frequent references to *realpolitik* logic that are made in Chapters 1 to 8 necessitate a further brief statement of Realism here – this time as a normative or prescriptive model.[25] Rejecting the notion that there is, or ever can be, a global harmony of interests, Realism is founded on the assertion that, in the absence of a single world government, the nation-state can never be sure that it is safe from external attack; the world of international politics is said to be 'anarchical'.[26] Every state permanently risks being confronted by at least one potential aggressor which, if it is given the opportunity to do so, will seek to dominate and exploit any other state weaker than itself. In these circumstances, argues the Realist, the overriding objective of a given state's foreign policy must be the achievement and maintenance of its security. This need to ensure security in turn requires both a strong defensive posture and the construction of alliances with other states which share similar security fears. (Thus, for example, in the late 1940s the countries of North America and Western Europe, fearful of the threat posed to their security interests by Soviet communism, joined together to form the NATO alliance.) Ensuring security also requires that the state does all it can both to weaken the strategic position of its opponents and to ensure that friendly governments are installed (or maintained in power) in as many other countries as possible. *Realpolitik* logic, in essence, is cynical, self-regarding calculation based on the paramount need to preserve national security.

Where does all this discussion of theories and the world-views of policy-makers leave us? Which of the theories, if any, are relevant to the analysis conducted here and how, if at all, do they relate to the world-views of Britain's post-war foreign policy makers? In order to answer these questions, it needs to be recognised that this book adopts an essentially 'state-centric' approach to British foreign policy. In so doing, it assumes that, in spite of the growing proliferation of transnational structures and processes, nation-states remain the most important actors on the world stage; that foreign policy analysis should still concentrate primarily – though not exclusively – on a given state's dealings and relationship with other states. This is clearly not the only approach to foreign policy analysis that could be taken – indeed, some scholars might regard it as being unnecessarily limited in focus – but it probably represents the one that has been used most frequently by mainstream analysts of post-war British foreign policy.

Who Makes British Foreign Policy?

Of course, any attempt to understand the decision-makers' world-views immediately raises the question as to who Britain's foreign policy makers actually are (or were). The ensuing text – like many others – is replete with phrases such as 'the government decided...', 'London's aims were...', and 'The British response was...'. To whom, specifically, do these synonyms refer? Who is it that actually makes British foreign policy? Any answer to these questions must begin by acknowledging that the British foreign policy making process, like its domestic counterpart, is a highly complex one, involving a variety of political and bureaucratic elites.[28] Figure I.2 identifies some of the main institutional actors involved in this process and describes the broad pattern of interrelationship among them.

Figure I.2   The National Security Council system

Source: UK Parliament.[27]

Formally, it is the Cabinet that is the key decision centre in all important policy matters.[29] It is the Cabinet that defines both the general and the specific goals of Britain's external policy. It is the Cabinet that defines where Britain's primary national interests lie. And whenever there is a major policy choice to be made – whether it involves a decision to use military force or a decision to negotiate a new trade treaty – it is the Cabinet that decides upon the general course of action to be taken. In practice, of course, the Prime Minister has frequently turned to some sub-set of the Cabinet, to a coterie of especially trusted advisers upon whom he or she relies for advice. In formal terms, this body is nowadays supposed to be the National Security Council (NSC), which is a sub-committee of the Cabinet.

The use of a National Security Council to make foreign policy is a relatively recent innovation in British politics (it was set up only in 2010).[30] The term derives from the American system, to which the US Congress added a National Security Council in 1947. Fearful that the President would not fully consult with the bureaucratic expertise around him, the intent of the law was that presidents would henceforth be *compelled* to seek advice. Ironically, American presidents have found ways to get around the law. Lyndon Johnson was rather typical in this regard, in the sense that he preferred to make foreign policy in small decision-making groups, and in America the NSC structure has become too large and unwieldy.

In Britain, however, the use of an NSC was driven by the executive branch's desire to rationalise the way that foreign and defence policy is made and to give a more formal structure to the process itself (an attempt at 'joined-up' government). Every four years, the government is now required to produce a National Security Strategy (NSS), which lays out the objectives it seeks to attain,[31] as well as a *Strategic Defence and Security Review* (SDSR), which details the ways in which these commitments will be met using the necessary resources. These are supposed to be drawn up with outside advice, external to the government itself, as well as materials generated internally. The post of National Security Adviser (NSA) – a permanent civil servant in Britain, as opposed to a political appointment in the United States – is supposed to ensure that the whole process runs smoothly and is as free from political 'interference' as possible, and the NSA actually chairs meetings on some issues as shown in Figure I.2. The making of British foreign policy probably does not work entirely in this idealised fashion, of course (see the discussion in Chapter 8). Like US presidents, British Prime Ministers may prefer to make their own policies (Tony Blair, for instance, was said to be uncomfortable with formal processes, relying instead on a 'sofa-based' system of government). Both Whitehall and Parliament can exert varying degrees of influence over particular policy issues, as do political parties, pressure groups and the mass media. In a democracy, governmental elites are not entirely free to choose the policies they like, as pressure within the Conservative Party to hold the 2016 referendum on EU membership shows. And even when the Cabinet or National Security Council arrives at a major decision, it is unlikely to be united in the kind of advice it provides. Not every member of these bodies will have an equal say in determining policy choices, moreover. It is obviously the case that there is frequently dissent within government and that some ministers have more influence upon (some) foreign policy decisions than others (see the top of Figure I.2, for example). It would be extraordinary, for example, if the Foreign Secretary and Defence Secretary failed to contribute significantly to decisions taken in the diplomatic and security spheres; or if the Chancellor of the Exchequer was unable to exert a powerful influence over decisions relating to external financial policy. Some issues may call for the National Security Adviser to chair, while others may produce prime ministerial involvement. The COBRA sub-committee of the NSC (which stands for 'Cabinet Office Briefing Room A') deals with crises or emergencies, for instance, and is usually chaired by the Home Secretary or Prime Minister because such issues are widely held to carry the greatest importance.

This said, patterns of ministerial influence vary from administration to administration. Through the use of the diverse political resources at their disposal, Prime Ministers constrain the decision-making autonomy of their individual ministers to varying degrees and in different ways. As far as this study is concerned, this means that references to 'the British government' (or to some synonym) should be taken to refer to the NSC or to the Cabinet – although in any given context it should also be recognised that the Prime Minister and one or two other ministers may well have exerted a disproportionately large influence upon the decision reached.

Conclusion

This book offers an unashamedly narrative account of Britain's foreign policy during the post-war era. It is a narrative, however, that is both guided and informed by theory. In keeping with the Neoclassical Realist model, the major shifts in Britain's post-war foreign policy strategy are analysed in terms of the changing pattern of Britain's material and security interests, while accepting that UK decision-makers have often deviated from the 'demands' of the system and that the identity of the British state as well as the psychology of particular leaders mattered as well. Following the outlines of the Rational Actor model, the policymakers' decisions are analysed primarily in terms of the calculations that were made as to how Britain's national interests could best be maximised, but the frequent deviations from comprehensive rationality are also noted.

The analysis also reflects the extent to which the rationality of Britain's post-war foreign policy makers was consistently constrained by their own Realist world-views. Constructivism and Cognitivism are especially useful here in highlighting the influence of a British 'strategic culture' or identity which has dominated the thinking of foreign policy makers in the country for many years, but which does not necessarily reflect any objective reality. In essence, the foreign policy calculations of successive British governments were based on the assumption that in a threatening world the primary foreign policy goal of maintaining national security could only be achieved by the possession of an effective defence capability combined with the determination to use it. For much of the post-war period this assumption was, on balance, justified. There were also occasions, however, when the magnitude of the 'threat' was seriously overestimated and when the application of *realpolitik* logic was accordingly misplaced. On these occasions, as will become evident, Britain's post-war foreign policy record was something less than glorious.

Chapter 1

British Foreign Policy Traditions

A revolt was going on against central rule by a ruthless and distant government. The government was responding by putting down all protest with extreme violence. Helpless citizens were being slaughtered in droves – men, women and children – as the central authority sought to quell all challenges to its rule. Western observers looked on appalled, as accounts of the mass killing appeared in the Western media. In Britain, humanitarians called for military intervention to stop the slaughter. In contrast, pragmatists quietly noted that Britain had no major national interest in trying to intervene in what was principally 'a domestic affair'. Some suggested that reports of atrocities were being exaggerated, while others noted that it was not entirely clear who was committing these acts. Questions of moral culpability became confused, as media reports began to appear of reprehensible acts committed by the initial victims in acts of apparent retribution.

The above paragraph could easily stand as a description of the humanitarian crisis still going on in Syria at the time of writing, as the regime of Bashar al-Assad sought to put down challenges to the rule of his personal family dynasty. It would do equally well as an account of the genocide in the former Yugoslavia in the early 1990s, as Bosnian Muslims and Croats were slaughtered by Serbs led by the genocidal Slobodan Milošević. In fact, however, the description refers to the Bulgarian crisis of 1876. The Ottoman Empire, centred on Istanbul in what is now modern Turkey, faced a revolt from the Bulgarians. In the summer of 1876 they revolted against Turkish rule, and the Turks responded by killing somewhere between 10,000 and 25,000 Bulgarians, as horrified onlookers helplessly recorded the atrocities. In Britain, reports of the events in Bulgaria sparked a debate as to whether (and how) the government should respond. Was this a moral matter in which the British were obligated to intervene, or did their real interest lie in allowing matters to run their own course?

This now-largely-forgotten crisis reveals just how old this kind of debate really is in the history of British foreign policy. The Liberal Party's William Gladstone, by then in semi-retirement following his defeat at the election of 1874, revealed himself during the Bulgarian crisis to be a morally driven Idealist, whose Christian convictions led him to take a simple but forceful approach to foreign policy. 'Nothing that is morally wrong can be politically right', he once insisted. By contrast, British Tory Prime Minister Benjamin Disraeli revealed himself to be a hard-headed calculator of the national interest in the Realist mould. He effectively sided with the Turks during the crisis, or at least failed to do anything that would prevent the slaughter, since support for the Ottoman Empire was part of a long-established balance of power strategy to counteract the position of Russia. For Gladstone, however, the issue involved the straightforward application of ethical principle. He penned an impassioned plea for British intervention in the crisis, written in just four days, called *Bulgarian Horrors and the Question of the East*. In it, he wholeheartedly condemned Disraeli for his amoral approach to the crisis and called for Britain to take a strong ethical stand. To be sure, the intense personal rivalry between the two men played a role in all of this, and Gladstone undoubtedly saw the potential of using the crisis to put one over on his old political rival (the two men harboured an intense dislike of one another). But at its root, this was a clash between two competing approaches, one stressing the primacy of identity and ideas (Idealism), the other the centrality of interests (Realism).

Since this book is primarily a history of British foreign policy since 1945, we can only sketch an outline of the pre-World War II traditions here. A full account of British policy in the 1800s or before, for instance, is beyond the scope of this project, and readers are encouraged to consult more detailed works on this topic.[1] Nevertheless, a brief outline is appropriate here, not least because British foreign policy (like the British political system generally) has evolved in an organic fashion. It did not spring up suddenly in 1945, but is the product of habits and traditions which stretch back for centuries. We will focus in particular on the development of Realist balance of power strategy after 1814, and on the ways in which this strategy was reinforced in the first half of the 20th century – notwithstanding a brief flirtation with Idealism in the 1920s and early 1930s. In order to understand why Britain has for many years suffered from a kind of 'imperial hangover', we also need to briefly describe Britain's rise to Empire and subsequent decline.

The Rise and Fall of British Power

In the mid-17th century, when the emerging European states system was in its infancy, England was a relatively unimportant regional power with primarily European interests. Over the next 250 years, with the gradual extension of its imperial acquisitions, Great Britain was transformed into a major global power with significant economic and political interests widely dispersed throughout the world.[2] By the late 1800s – in an era synonymous with the rule of Queen Victoria – the British stood at the head of an Empire which spanned much of the globe. As Jeremy Paxman notes in his well-researched history of this period:

> As her reign progressed, the tide of red – the colour chosen by the imperial cartographers to mark out British possessions – lapped across the world so quickly that maps had to be recoloured and reference books rewritten. By 1897 the ambitions of Germany were a cloud on the horizon, but there had really been no power to challenge Britain's pre-eminent status since the defeat of Napoleon at the battle of Waterloo in 1815. The army was twice the size it had been when Victoria ascended to the throne, the navy four times larger.[3]

Old maps of the British Empire, with two-thirds or more of the inhabited land mass of Planet Earth coloured red, can still be found in encyclopedias and museums. Of course, these maps were often more than a bit silly, serving better as geopolitical statements or exercises in nationalistic chest-thumping than literal geographic guides. For one thing, Britain itself was often presented as much bigger than Texas in such maps and sometimes as equivalent in size to the whole of the United States! But they bear genuine testament to Britain's 19th-century imperial pre-eminence and the cultural attitudes which frequently attend the possession of great power.

The growing strength of British sea power and the country's early industrialisation were crucial to this pre-eminent position. Equally, the emergence of a balance of power in Europe and a hundred years of peace (more or less) between 1814 and 1914 provided a kind of shield behind which early industrialisation and Britain's rise to pre-eminence could take place. It is no coincidence that the 'retreat from [global] power' which characterised Britain's foreign policy after 1945 should have had its origins in the relative decline of Britain's industrial capacity and in the failure to sustain the prominent maritime position of the Royal Navy in the period after 1870, and also no coincidence that the country's fall from grace in the 20th century took place against the backdrop of two vitality-sapping world wars that Britain could ill afford economically and in the context of the breakdown of the balance of power system before World War I.

First of all, the rise of Britain as a political powerhouse in the 19th century was associated with its status as the 'cradle' of industrialisation.[4] Large-scale mechanisation, the invention of the steam engine and the exploitation, production and mass transportation of commodities vital to industrialisation (such as iron, coal, textiles, glass and steel) played significant roles in the early transition of Britain from an agrarian society to an urban-based industrialised one. While the term 'Industrial Revolution' is misleading in some ways – it was, after all, a gradual rather than overnight process, occurring incrementally somewhere between the late 1700s and the mid-1800s – it nevertheless had a revolutionary impact on British economic, political and social life, not least through the creation of a large urban and industrial working class which arrived to work in the factories and coal mines of cities like Manchester, Newcastle, Liverpool and Leeds. Later on, as its major rivals industrialised – in many cases, several decades afterwards – Britain began a long, inexorable process of decline, but its head start in the process initially conferred very significant advantages.

The Royal Navy's prominent position and Britain's related status as a major maritime power were equally crucial to its imperial expansion.[5] 'Rule Britannia, Britannia rules the waves!' went the words of a patriotic song and poem of the 1700s which is still sung or recited today. Naval power – Britain's stock of naval and commercial ships was already several times the size of its closest rival in the mid-1700s, before the Industrial Revolution had even begun[6] – conferred both economic and security advantages. As an island nation, it was obviously vital to protect Britain from overseas attack from continental European threats such as France, Germany and Russia. But the navy played an often underappreciated economic role as well. The engine of free trade could confer significant advantages on Britain only if external markets were accessible to British goods. Via its role in the creation of Empire, the Royal Navy opened up the markets of the world, providing a demand for the products which British factories were churning out at an unprecedented rate.[7] Marxist historians like Eric Hobsbawm have argued that British foreign policy was totally subordinated to economic needs during the imperial period.[8] Whether this is true or not is debatable and we will not attempt to resolve this issue here. However, it is clear that while Britain 'ruled the seas', free trade operated to the country's considerable benefit. As Andrew Gamble notes, 'Britain exploited its advantage as the first industrial nation to the full by throwing open its markets and attempting to persuade or force all other states to do the same. Agriculture was sacrificed for the greater gains that flowed from specializing in manufactures.'[9]

The Empire itself was both the engine of all this growth and its product, creating a kind of virtuous circle in which economic, maritime and imperial power fed one another. As a result it is difficult to disentangle the exact causal chain by which Britain's rise to power occurred but it is clear that these relationships were mutually reinforcing, as Paul Kennedy suggests.[10] And along with this came the ideological justification for imperialism, making it seem 'natural' and 'proper' that Britain should play the role it did. Rather like the US notion of 'Manifest Destiny' and 'American exceptionalism', British imperialism came to be seen not as a self-serving practice – though in many ways, of course, it was – but a benevolent one. Britain, being so much more advanced than anyone else, had a moral duty to export its superior ideas and practices to the rest of the world.

It is probably true to say that all nations, to varying degrees, regard themselves as 'special', as particularly blessed by what earlier generations than ours called God and Provenance. All great imperial powers, moreover, seem to develop a self-justifying philosophy for expansionism (the French notion of the *mission civilisatrice* and the British-American notion of the 'White Man's Burden' come to mind here). Cecil Rhodes supposedly said that to have been born British was to have 'won first prize in the lottery of life'. Of course, one might expect an English-born South African supporter of colonialism, born in the mid-1800s when British power was at its height, to take such a jaundiced view. After all, the country we today call Zimbabwe was originally named after him – 'Rhodesia' – during the period in which it was part of the British Empire.[11] Today the name of Rhodes is synonymous with the scholarship system which allows American students to spend a portion of their academic training at Oxford University (as a young and relatively poor man, Bill Clinton spent time at Oxford on a Rhodes scholarship, for instance). But there is also a dark side to the family name associated with this vast fund: it derived from a one-time near-monopoly of the production of raw diamonds in South Africa. The Rhodes name is today synonymous not just with educational munificence but with the excesses of British imperialism, and the fortune of the De Beers company derived from expropriating the wealth of South Africa to London.

The British Empire no longer exists of course, but its few remaining remnants – most notably the rocks of Gibraltar in southern Spain and the Falkland Islands off the eastern coast of Argentina – remind us of what once was there. We will defer the story of how and why this Empire disintegrated until later on in this chapter and others, but it is important to note that the explanations of why Britain declined economically are still hotly disputed. Some blame the expansion of the British state into the domestic economy that occurred from the 1940s onwards, while others attribute national decline to the operation of unfettered market forces – and there are a variety of other explanations as well.[12] But what is not in dispute is that other nations simply 'caught up'. Britain's mastery of the seas was eroded in the late 19th and early 20th centuries by the growth of the German navy, and France, Germany, Japan and the United States would soon industrialise as well, often using protectionist measures that bypassed Britain's continued advocacy of free trade. By 1945, a Pax

Americana had replaced the Pax Britannica, and by the 1970s declinist works (of both British and American varieties) had become a veritable cottage industry. In spite of Britain's fall from economic grace, however, a well-worn set of Realist political and strategic traditions and precepts about how British power could be maintained and protected from external threat has persisted over the centuries, as well as a (usually subordinate) Idealist tradition that first emerged at the very height of Empire.

The Realist and Idealist Traditions in the 19th Century

Throughout most of the 1800s and 1900s, Realism was the 'default' position of British foreign policy, ingrained in a peculiarly European power-politics view of the world in which maintaining the balance of power (not moral or humanitarian concerns) was the overriding goal of policymakers. The logic of the balance of power is straightforward, and provides a relatively simple policy rule for those who make foreign policy: *prevent the emergence of a single preponderant power* within the international system by siding with the least powerful against the most. Sir Eyre Crowe's much-quoted 'Memorandum on the Present State of British Relations with France and Germany' of January 1907, written when Crowe was Senior Clerk at the Foreign Office, represents a classic encapsulation of this approach.[13] Crowe advocated the traditional balance of power principles upon which Britain had based its European foreign policy since the early 18th century. For him, the protection of Britain's vital material and security interests lay in the continued pursuit of a general strategy which sought to prevent any other state (or group of states) from achieving the sort of preponderance of power capabilities which might indirectly enable that state either to weaken Britain's links with its Empire or to challenge its dominant commercial position in world trade.

Balance of power politics involves a great deal of dexterity – not to say moral and ideological flexibility – on the part of decision-makers, as demonstrated by Disraeli's willingness to support the Turks over Russia regardless of the internal behaviour in which the former engaged. Idealists are often repulsed by the practices it implies, since changing domestic behaviour in the Realist approach is very often set aside in favour of other objectives. The overriding goal of this foreign policy strategy is stability or equilibrium: by 'tilting' towards the weaker coalition of states, we ensure that a balance is maintained and that no single power can predominate.[14] As Crowe put it in his famous Memorandum, Britain was 'the natural enemy of any country threatening the independence of others', and it had become 'almost a historical truism to identify

England's secular policy with the maintenance of this balance by throwing her weight now in this scale and now in that, but ever on the side opposed to the political dictatorship of the strongest single state or group at a given time'.[15]

Lord Palmerston famously summed up the standard British position when he said that we have 'no permanent friends or adversaries, only permanent interests'. Under this view, foreign policy was to be approached as a cautious and unemotional chess game rather than an exercise in moral imperatives, and he was known for favouring balance of power reasoning over his own personal political preferences (he opposed slavery, for instance, but favoured the Confederacy during the American Civil War simply because he thought a 'Disunited States' would better serve British interests). As Foreign Secretary for much of the period between 1830 and 1851 and then Prime Minister for most of the period from 1855 to 1859, Palmerston exerted a powerful and lasting impact on the shape of British foreign policy for nearly three decades. The cornerstone of his approach was support for the Ottoman Empire as a check against the growth of Russia and to counter French power in Egypt (and in favouring the Turks over Bulgaria later on, Disraeli was really only following Palmerston's blueprint).

In the 19th century under both Disraeli and Robert Gascoyne-Cecil (the Marquis of Salisbury), Britain pursued a related policy of what came to be known as 'Splendid Isolation'.[16] British policymakers kept a deliberate distance between themselves and Europe. They would enter into no permanent or long-lasting relationships with European states – avoiding what Thomas Jefferson in an American context had referred to disparagingly as 'entangling alliances' – but would intervene at crucial points to keep the balance, siding with one state or the other to keep the peace and thus protect vital British interests. In the Americas, for instance, US shipping lanes were protected in part by the British Navy, since British policymakers were preoccupied by the threat posed by Napoleon's France. America was initially too weak to play a world role so its first concern had to be self-preservation, and the early popularity of isolationism in the United States may in part have been an example of 'making a virtue out of a necessity'. Realists claim that states which lack power very often retreat into the rhetoric of moralism and isolation. Whether this is true or not, the balance of power in Europe certainly led to a hundred years of peace and helped to insulate America from the outside, while Britain acted as 'keeper of the balance' and protected the US from encroachment by other powers for its own reasons.[17]

Although the formal policy of splendid isolation was abandoned in the late 1800s and early 1900s – and Britain of course entered two world wars in the first half of the 20th century – a strong measure of isolation from Europe remains a central motif of British foreign policy, even as the UK joined the European Union. After World War II, for instance, Winston Churchill called for a 'United States of Europe' in a famous speech given in Zurich in 1946. That speech has often been mistaken as an argument for British entry into a federal Europe, but Churchill was actually advocating a federal union of *continental* Europe from which Britain would stand somewhat aloof. The notion that Britain would surrender its national sovereignty to such a body was anathema to him, as it was later most notably for Margaret Thatcher. And of course that sense of aloofness persists today, especially (though not solely) within the Conservative Party of Theresa May and the UK Independence Party. British foreign policy makers remain highly ambivalent about a permanent European role.

This sense of apartness almost certainly has some roots in geography as well as ideas. Geopolitical thinkers probably place too much emphasis on maps as a basis for understanding international relations, but it remains true that geography does have an impact on national identity and security interests (as we noted in the Introduction). 'Britain is an island close to continental Europe, and thus in danger of invasion through most of its history, giving it a particular strategic concern over the span of the centuries with the politics of France and the Low Countries on the opposite shore of the English Channel and the North Sea', Robert Kaplan notes.[18] While Realists would tend to agree, both Constructivists and Cognitivists would point out that 'brute' facts like geography don't speak for themselves (see our discussion in the Introduction). The fact that Britain and the United States face each other across the Atlantic could just as easily have led to enmity as friendship, were it not for other (non-geographical) factors. And why, for instance, has Germany abandoned militarism since 1945? Changing ideational factors, such as the fact that Germany seeks a peaceful Europe today (its social identity) and the fact that Angela Merkel is no Adolf Hitler (a leadership-based explanation), have to be taken into account as well.

It is hardly surprising that the association of a balance of power strategy in the minds of British foreign policy decision-makers with the maintenance of so many years of peace should have had a long-term effect. Of course, there were some challenges to this over time. Gladstone's administration of 1880 to 1885, for instance, was based on the Idealist notion that morality could be the only guide in British foreign policy. According to one of his most stringent critics, the historian and former policymaker Henry Kissinger:

Gladstone, perhaps the dominant figure of British politics in the nineteenth century, viewed foreign policy in much the same way as

Americans did after Wilson. Judging foreign policy by moral instead of geopolitical criteria, he argued that the national aspirations of the Bulgarians were in fact legitimate, and that, as a fellow Christian nation, Great Britain owed support to Bulgaria against the Muslim Turks.... Asserting that morality was the only basis for a sound foreign policy, Gladstone insisted that Christian decency and respect for human rights ought to be the guiding lights of British foreign policy, not the balance of power and the national interest.[19]

Like Tony Blair's much later experiment with an ethical foreign policy, Gladstone's Christian convictions led him to the conclusion that the morality of the state was as inviolable as the morality of the individual; policies pursued overseas had to be based on values practised at home. As Muriel Chamberlain puts it, Gladstone 'enunciated what he regarded as the fundamental principles which should guide British foreign policy. Peace, of course, was basic but it should be peace based on justice, which respected the rights of smaller nations and acknowledged the rule of law in international affairs.'[20] He favoured a Concert of Europe, a permanent body which would (in principle) act collectively against mutual threats. He also campaigned against imperialism in 1880, favoured nationalist movements (including Home Rule for Ireland) and wanted to pare down Britain's international commitments to what he thought the country could afford (he saw the risks of 'overextension' early on, a constant theme running through the history of British foreign policy from that point on).

The Concert of Europe proved a non-starter for states like Germany, however, and Chancellor Otto von Bismarck professed not to understand the new British Prime Minister at all (this was a clash of personalities, as well as ideas). Home Rule was later defeated in Parliament in 1886, during Gladstone's third spell as Prime Minister. Having recently attacked Realism so forcefully in his Midlothian campaign of 1880, in government he was often seen as continuing many of the foreign policies associated with Disraeli in South Africa and Afghanistan. And in a move that many observers have described as pure imperialism, Gladstone invaded Egypt in 1882, turning his back on the cause of 'Egypt for the Egyptians'.[21] The reasons why he did this are still debated by historians. Although British Consul General Edward Malet defended the action as necessary to 'defend Christendom' in the area, the action may have been motivated more by the desire to protect British economic investments and by an attempt to appease others within his fractious Cabinet. Gladstone does not seem to have been motivated by concerns about the security of the Empire or worries over the possible closure of the Suez Canal. He did, however, have to confront significant elements within his party (including his powerful rival Joseph Chamberlain) who favoured a continuation of imperialism over a moral foreign policy.[22] As Roy Jenkins notes

> Gladstone was constantly compromising between imperialist pressures and his own instincts, which were a mixture of Little Englander caution and Concert of Europe idealism. Neither pointed to the expansion of territory or colonial wars, which were nonetheless a frequent feature of the life of that government. They were mostly backed into without enthusiasm.[23]

Nowhere was this truer than in the Sudan, where a reluctant Gladstone – egged on by the imperialist British press – sent General Charles Gordon to Khartoum, then failed to rescue him in time from Islamists rebelling against British rule.

This was admittedly a brief interregnum in a long-established Realist orthodoxy, and subsequent British governments would soon return to that orthodoxy. And yet as Kissinger makes clear, Gladstone's vision of British foreign policy pre-empted many of the issues and concerns which would arise in more powerful form after the conclusion of World War I, a set of liberal or Idealist notions which are often known today as 'Wilsonianism'. The Concert of Europe notion echoes Wilson's League of Nations – which would be created over 40 years later – and Gladstone's second term represents perhaps the only serious effort in British foreign policy to depart from Realist principles before the period between World Wars I and II.

Britain and World War I

The guiding principle of Britain's pre-1914 foreign policy strategy after Gladstone remained the balance of power approach identified in Eyre Crowe's 1907 'Memorandum'. Crowe was then a relatively junior official at the Foreign Office, but he would rise up within that organisation in later years to become Permanent Under-Secretary. We have noted already that in Crowe's view, and that of many who preceded him, the name of the game in foreign policy was avoiding the emergence of any single predominant power that might challenge British interests. The focus of such efforts before 1815 had been Bonaparte's France, and after that the Russia of the Tsars had for a time seemed more threatening. But in Crowe's view and that of other major policymakers of the time like Foreign Secretary Sir Edward Grey, the *most* serious threat to British interests by the 1870s and 1880s was now Germany.

In the period before 1914 Britain's efforts to sustain the balance of power and prevent the emergence of a power preponderance elsewhere were directed towards four main areas. In *Europe*, the French defeat at the hands of the Prussians in 1871 ensured that suspicions of resurgent Bonapartism were replaced by fears of German hegemonism.[24] As a result, after 1870 the need to prevent Germany from making further territorial gains at the expense of the disintegrating Austro-Hungarian Empire became the major objective of Britain's European policy.[25] The counterpart to this strategy of German containment, of course, was a more sympathetic posture towards the French – embodied in the Entente Cordiale of 1904 – since a strong and independent France would constitute a bulwark against a further German advance in the West.[26] Notwithstanding this improvement in Anglo-French relations, however, the British government continued to entertain serious suspicions about French, as well as German, intentions in the Low Countries, the independence of which Britain had jealously guarded throughout the 19th century in order to prevent their use as a springboard from which a seaborne invasion of Great Britain could be launched. In the event, of course, it was Germany rather than France which in 1914 was seen as the greatest threat to the stability of the established European order; and it was the threat that German militarism posed to the integrity of the Netherlands and Belgium which was one of the important triggers to British involvement in World War I.

In order to maintain control of the *Empire* from the mid-18th century onwards, the main thrust of Britain's foreign policy was in the military sphere. This is not to say that London neglected the political need to enter into informal coalitions with local elites inside the colonies and dominions. Rather, it is simply to indicate that the fundamental means by which the Empire was maintained was (1) by the development of a relatively small but highly professional and mobile army and (2) by the commitment to maintain a navy which was larger than the size of the next two navies added together.[27] On this basis, the imperial possessions in India, Australia, Canada, Malaya and Africa could be provisioned, fortified and reinforced as and when circumstances demanded. And as long as Britain could sustain the Empire, it also maintained control of the vast material resources contained therein, thus depriving any potential rival of the opportunity of strengthening its own resource-capability position.

In the *Mediterranean and the Middle East*, the primary objective of British policy was to protect the military and commercial transit route to India. Thus the island bases in the Mediterranean (Gibraltar, Malta and Cyprus), the installation of a pro-British government in Egypt and the fortified bunkering facility at Aden were all required in order to allow the Royal Navy to exercise its imperial Pax Britannica and to prevent any other nation from interfering with British shipping en route to India. A second important objective in Britain's Middle East policy was the containment of Russia. In the Far East the fear of Russian expansionism had led to British involvement in the Afghan wars of 1838–49 and 1878–81. As we saw at the beginning of this chapter, in the Middle East this led to a consistent Realist policy throughout the 19th century of British support for the Ottoman Empire, the 'sick man of Europe' whose northern provinces were regarded as fertile ground for Russian annexation.[28] Close economic involvement with Germany – plus suspicions that Britain and Russia might be in the process of concocting a deal to partition the Ottoman Empire – led the Turks to enter World War I on the German side. However, the setback to British strategy in the Middle East which the Turkish defection represented was at least partially reversed by the mandates for Iraq and Palestine that were awarded to Britain by the League of Nations in 1920. Relations with Turkey itself were repaired after 1926.[29]

Finally, in the *Caribbean* the principal aim of British policy was not only to guarantee the security of the colonial territories themselves, but also to provide bases from which the Royal Navy could protect the shipping lanes that carried Britain's substantial and increasing trade with both North and South America. While the United States, acting under the Monroe Doctrine, exercised a dominating political influence in Latin America, it was Britain which – at least until 1900 – was the dominant economic power in the region.[30] Nonetheless, so long as the United States was prepared to ensure that *all* European attempts to engineer political hegemony in Latin America would be strongly resisted, Britain was only too happy to be allowed to continue to trade there without formal political entanglement or obligation. Indeed, after 1900, London was even prepared to hand over the effective policing of the Caribbean and Latin American trade routes to the US Navy, a move that was to be extended after 1921 to include the north-western Pacific.[31]

Yet if British strategy in each of these four areas had seemed to be generally effective during the 19th century, it gradually became apparent after 1900 that the overall position was weakening. The most obvious and immediate signs of the incipient decline were in the very sectors from which Britain had derived its 19th-century pre-eminence: the efficiency of its manufacturing industry and its preponderant sea power.[32] By the early 1900s, while Britain's hold over the indigenous populations of its colonies (South Africa excepted) was as strong as ever, it no longer enjoyed the luxury of a navy which could better the combined resources of the two next-largest naval powers. Germany, Japan and the United States now each possessed sufficient naval capacity to permit an alliance of any two of them to outnumber the Royal Navy.[33] In any case, within their own regions each was already mounting a significant challenge to British dominance. The era of Pax Britannica was thus effectively at an end. The tacit naval understanding with the United States in the Caribbean was an implicit admission that Britain could not police the seas alone; that the very underpinning of her dominant 19th-century global role was beginning to weaken.

Against this background of (1) a relative decline in Britain's sea power, (2) the loss of Britain's lead in industrial production and (3) profound suspicions that the British Army was too small and too ill-equipped to participate effectively in a continental war,[34] Herbert Asquith's government found itself in August 1914 embarking on a war which was to lay waste to Europe and to squander the resources of the Empire for over four years. Henry Kissinger's argument in *A World Restored* – and much later in *Diplomacy* – is that balances of power are only stable when they are also based on some legitimating principle which binds the states together. Metternich realised that the Concert of Vienna system after 1814 had to be based on such a principled consensus, otherwise a discontented power would seek to disrupt the balance. Both works are also paeans to Austrian Foreign Minister Prince Clemens von Metternich and British Foreign Secretary Lord Castlereagh, arguing that balances of power are not self-sustaining, emerging out of some sort of 'hidden hand'. They can operate only when created and sustained by skilful statesmen who recognise how the world really works and how interests can be interwoven to create lasting stability and peace. Of the two men, Kissinger mostly admires Metternich for coming closest to his ideal of how policymakers should fashion foreign policy, while he castigates William Gladstone and American President Woodrow Wilson for departing from Realist principles. But regardless of the 'skills' of statesmen or lack thereof, it is clear that by the beginning of the 20th century the basis of the old Vienna-based consensus had broken down.[35]

A large number of explanations have been offered for the outbreak of World War I, and it would be quite impossible to review them here.[36] Nonetheless there were certainly two fundamental and immediate motives (which were also to operate in 1939) that drew Britain into the conflict: the need to defend an Empire that had been assembled, with varying degrees of commitment, over the previous century and a half; and the need to prevent Germany from controlling France and the Low Countries, the ports and resources of which could readily be used for an attack on Britain itself.[37] Whatever causal factors 'really' operated, however, it is clear that Britain's international position in 1914 was markedly weaker than it had been a generation earlier. Yet by 1918, owing in part to the contribution of the United States after 1917, Britain had emerged as one of the victorious powers, a Great Power quite prepared to extend its global role and international commitments. With hindsight it is possible to discern that, as early as 1920, Britain was already beginning to pursue the 'overextended' foreign policy strategy which was to become so characteristic of the period after 1945. In the interwar period, however, 'overextension' was considerably less important than the tension between Realism and Idealism, as the respective protagonists of those approaches strove for mastery in the determination of Britain's foreign policy.

Realism versus Idealism in the Interwar Years

If the old practices of *realpolitik* had led to the horrors of World War I, then the new Idealism of the League of Nations promised a fresh start in which the systematic operation of 'collective security' would replace the haphazard and unreliable workings of the balance of power as the primary means of deterring war. But the Idealist experiment of the 1920s failed disastrously as a vehicle for preserving peace, and the main consequence of the failure of Idealism after 1938 was a deep commitment among British foreign policy makers to the principles of Realism. Without doubt this commitment to Realism served Britain well from the late 1930s until 1945. As will be seen in later chapters, however, thereafter it introduced a number of understandable but avoidable distortions into British foreign policy which probably operated to the country's long-term detriment.

Any event as universally traumatic as World War I was bound to have profound long-term consequences for all of the nations involved. As far as Great Britain was concerned, the 1914–18 war had three major consequences, though each had deeper and earlier roots. The first of these concerned the promises, soon to be broken, that were made to a variety of groups in the Middle East and the British Empire with the intention of securing their continued support during the war.[38] Indian nationalists were promised that their demands for greater self-government would be received sympathetically once peace with Germany had been secured. In Palestine, the Balfour Declaration of 1917 appeared to hold the promise of the coveted Jewish national homeland. And Arabs throughout the Middle East received a number of guarantees that their interests would be protected in any post-war dismemberment of the Ottoman Empire. The implications of these promises are discussed in a later chapter and so they need not detain us here.

A second major consequence of World War I was the expansion of the Empire, a development made possible partly by the general desire to deprive Germany of its colonial possessions and partly by the defeat of Turkey, which (as noted earlier) had entered the war on the German side in November 1914.[39] However, while the defeat of Germany and of Turkey released a large number of territories for distribution among the winning coalition, few of the victorious powers had a direct interest in acquiring them. The United States, at the instigation of the Senate, was in the process of withdrawing rapidly into isolation and was certainly not interested in burdening itself with quasi-colonial entanglements in either Africa or the Middle East. The new Soviet government – even if it had been consulted by the former allies of the Russian Crown – was deeply opposed as a matter of ideological principle to anything which resembled colonialism.[40] Japan was interested only in developing its power base in the Far East, and neither Germany nor Turkey had possessed territory in that region.[41] And Italy, whose participation in the war had been equivocal if not downright half-hearted, was thought not to deserve any of the spoils of war in any case, notwithstanding the promises made in the 'secret treaties' of 1915.[42]

Of the six victorious 'Great Powers', only Britain and France were in a position to acquire new 'responsibilities' like these. In consequence, as part of the Versailles settlement, Britain took control of the former German colonies of Tanganyika and South West Africa (now Namibia). By 1921, under the formal auspices of the League of Nations, Turkey had been stripped of Palestine, Transjordan, Iraq and the sheikdoms of the Persian Gulf, all of which were then 'mandated' to Britain. As H. A. L. Fisher observed later, this was 'the crudity of conquest draped in the veil of morality'.[43] The crucial point, however, was that, while Britain's quasi-imperial possessions had expanded, that expansion was almost entirely the result of a peculiar set of fortuitous circumstances rather than the consequence of a genuine increase in Britain's power capability. As early as May 1920 serious doubts were being expressed as to London's ability to maintain its direct control over the newly acquired territories as well as those which Britain already possessed. The Chief of the General Staff observed: 'Our small army is far too scattered ... in no single theatre are we strong enough.'[44] The British government's response was to adopt a tactic that decolonising governments were to emulate in the 1950s and 1960s. Under the terms of their respective mandates, nominally 'independent' governments were established in Iraq in 1921 and in Transjordan during the course of 1921 and 1922. Egypt, an effective British fiefdom since 1881, was accorded a similar status in 1922. As a result the British government maintained a position of considerable political and economic influence throughout the Middle East. What could have been a source of strength, however, was in fact a continuing source of vulnerability: the position of the 'thinly spread' army lamented by the Chief of the General Staff in 1920 was not substantially improved at any time during the interwar period.[45]

Even if the informal Empire was continuing to expand, the decline of Britain's economic and naval power led increasingly to a kind of 'imperialism on the cheap'. Many years later, after the US administration of George W. Bush invaded Iraq in 2003, the story of how Iraq became a state under effective British control would be dusted off. It re-emerged from the history books as later generations sought to understand why the country seemed composed of such fractious elements, but the story is primarily interesting to us for what it says about the continued functioning of the British Empire under increasingly severe financial and military constraints. How was a tiny island nation of only about 42 million (in 1920), with no standing army, able to continue to exert control over distant lands like this? How in particular was it able to do so even after the signs of imperial decline had become all too obvious?

One answer has to do with the co-option of local elites, friendly tribal or national figureheads who would nominally be in charge of their own regions but would in reality be beholden to London. This was done in India, for instance, where the now famous Gurkhas – initially a force of mercenaries – were enlisted to fight wars that Britain's own small and overextended army could not. As Jeremy Paxman notes, 'the British had learned from earlier experiences of empire and created thrones in the Middle East, on which sat pliant anglophiles with British advisers, high commissioners and residents. These generally well upholstered and harmless figures sent their sons to English schools and had armies trained, equipped and often commanded by British officers. Expanses of desert and mountain across which tribes wandered with herds of sheep and goats were turned into states.'[46] The answer also has much to do with the classic colonial strategy of 'divide and rule' and the deliberate creation of artificial states by imperial powers. The counterpart of the external balance of power approach was often the deliberate fashioning of *internal* balances of power. Fractious ethnic groups could be thrown together in the hope that they would spend more time fighting one another than they would challenging rule by London, and colonies might thus become 'self-regulating' (or so it was hoped). This was to be the fate of modern Iraq, a fake state cobbled together out of Kurds, Sunnis and Shiites who had little or nothing in common. The country is of course still living with the consequences today.[47]

A major consequence of World War I was psychological: the determination both within the governing elite and among the public at large that this kind of general war must never occur again. The determination was hardly surprising. Not only had millions of men been killed, but millions had experienced at first hand the horror and lunacy of prolonged trench warfare. The war poetry of Wilfred Owen, Rupert Brooke and Siegfried Sassoon gave sensitive expression to the mental and physical cruelty of life on the Western front, even when all was quiet. The rather more explicit details of all manner of ghastly experiences were gradually circulated among the general public by word of mouth, in direct contradiction of the government's wartime propaganda.[48] George Orwell observed that 'every [soldier and] junior officer looked on the General Staff as mental defectives' for having contemplated fighting this kind of war in the first place.[49] Arnold Toynbee later suggested that the experiences of World War I had rendered the British people 'prematurely humanised'. It had imbued them with a determination never to fight another war. Unfortunately the tide of history had not yet provided the sort of objective international conditions in which those with such unequivocally pacifist inclinations could hope to prosper. Toynbee's description was not intended as a compliment. But it was extremely appropriate.

Yet even if it was wrong for the age, the determination that World War I must not be repeated had powerful policy implications. Its major immediate effect was the British government's *public* commitment to the creation of a new international order which would espouse the principle of 'pacific settlement'. The new international order was to be constructed through two mechanisms, the twin pillars of interwar 'Idealism'. First, an embryonic international Leviathan was to be created through the further development of *international law*; law which had grown considerably in scope and volume since the Hague Conventions of 1899 and 1907.[50] Second, new *formal channels for cooperative diplomacy* were to be established which, along with existing bilateral arrangements and understandings, might act as a substitute for confrontation and the threat and use of force. Of central importance in this regard were to be the institutions of the newly created League of Nations.[51]

Even from the outset, however, the commitment of the British government to the central principle of Idealism was constrained by the position of the United States. Despite the central role played by Woodrow Wilson in both the post-war settlement and the formulation of the principles of the League, the United States subsequently withdrew into isolation following the failure of the Senate to ratify the League Covenant in 1919.[52] A second constraint on the commitment of successive governments to the principle of pacific settlement was that the publicly stated Idealism of the British government was never fully reflected in its private decision calculus. In private, the framers and movers of British foreign policy maintained a healthy scepticism as to the real potentialities of 'pacific settlement'. If the Gladstonian experiment with a moral foreign policy was hampered by his own need to compromise with other elements within the Liberal Party, the continued commitment of the British foreign policy bureaucracy to Realism ensured that Idealism was never really taken seriously. As many have argued, bureaucracies change slowly and incrementally (if at all), and it can be especially difficult to get an organisation like the Foreign Office to stop doing something it has been doing for hundreds of years.[53] As we shall see in later chapters, this problem also beset efforts to institute an 'ethical' foreign policy under Tony Blair many years later.

But if the illusion of pacific settlement could be maintained during the 1920s because the supranational decisions of the League fortuitously coincided with the interests of the powerful, that illusion could not be sustained for long. After 1930, it became increasingly apparent that *realpolitik* was once more (as perhaps it had always been) the fundamental determining force in international affairs. The disputes in Manchuria after 1931 and in Abyssinia after 1934 were settled not by the pacific mechanisms of the League – which possessed no coercive capability of its own to enforce its decisions – but by unadorned power politics: by military force. In Manchuria, the universally condemned Japanese invasion of a Chinese province went unpunished simply because none of the other Great Powers supposed that its 'vital' security or material interests were at stake. The Italian annexation of Abyssinia in 1935 attracted only token opposition (an ineffectual trade embargo) largely for the same reason.[54]

As far as the British government was concerned, however, the mismatch between public pronouncement and private calculation was all set to continue. In *private*, the Foreign Office view, typified by the position of Sir Robert Vansittart,[55] was that British interests were simply not affected by developments in Abyssinia. London also calculated that serious British opposition to Mussolini could either push him into a tighter embrace with Hitler or – if it damaged the Italian dictator's internal position – merely serve to strengthen the hand of the Italian communists.[56] Since both of these eventualities were patently unwelcome, it was better for the British government to reserve its judgement and await events: the Abyssinians would be left to their fate. In *public*, a somewhat different posture was adopted. In deference to the demands of public opinion, Britain consistently contrived to give the impression that it was seriously committed to the use of the League as an instrument for actively opposing aggression, a deliberately cultivated public image that was especially characteristic of the Baldwin government which was re-elected in November 1935. Not surprisingly, therefore, the bilateral Hoare–Laval Plan of December 1935 (which intended to recognise the ceding of large tracts of Abyssinian territory to Italy) was regarded as a clear violation of this self-avowed commitment to League-sponsored efforts at conflict resolution. A tremendous outpouring of public opposition to the plan resulted, in the wake of which Sir Samuel Hoare was obliged to resign as Foreign Secretary.[57] His replacement, Sir Anthony Eden, made rather more appropriate public noises but he could do nothing to retrieve the situation. Accordingly, the Realist advice of the Foreign Office that British interests remained unaffected was accepted and Italy was left in de facto control of Abyssinia. En passant, 'the credibility of the League as a coercive instrument [had been] ... completely destroyed'.[58]

Britain and World War II

If *realpolitik* calculation was by 1935 gaining the ascendancy in the British government's approach to the League, such calculations were less in evidence in the one context that (in retrospect) mattered most: Britain's dealings with Hitler's Germany. As early as 1928, five years before the Nazi regime emerged, Sir Horace Rumbold, the British Ambassador to Berlin, had warned that 'the satisfaction of one German grievance ... [serves merely to encourage] ... new demands'.[59] This was a pattern that was to be consistently repeated once Hitler achieved power in 1933; yet it was not until 1939 that the British government grasped the nettle and decided to meet Hitler's aggressive stratagems with a suitably coercive response. In spite of Rumbold's warnings in 1933 that war with Germany could be expected within four or five years,[60] successive British Cabinets took the line that a peaceful solution to the German problem was not only desirable but also *possible*.[61] In the fashion of the 'prematurely humanised' British public, they readily seized upon any evidence that would corroborate this belief.[62] The unfortunate consequence of the continuing belief in the possibility of a peaceful, compromise solution was that the cooperative diplomatic strategy which it engendered was bound to fail for precisely the reasons that Rumbold had articulated in 1928. That failure, in turn, led to the gradual castigation of cooperative diplomacy as 'appeasement', a denigration from which it has still not fully recovered.

Hitler's first major move to revise Germany's international position came in March 1934 when he made budgetary provision for large increases in German defence spending.[63] A year later the German government formally repudiated the clauses of the Versailles Treaty which had limited German armament levels, and reintroduced conscription. The Baldwin government's response to this deliberate act of confrontation was again to back down and to continue with its policy of cooperative diplomacy; the Cabinet still hoped to negotiate with 'Herr Hitler', perhaps even to the extent of restoring some of Germany's colonies if she would rejoin the League (which Germany had left in October 1933).[64]

In May 1937 Neville Chamberlain succeeded Stanley Baldwin as Prime Minister and the policy of appeasement continued to be the central feature of Britain's European diplomacy.[65] The period of Chamberlain's premiership provided the clearest examples of the ability of the Cabinet to seize upon any evidence that would corroborate the belief that cooperative diplomacy was the best way of dealing with Hitler. In stark contrast to the advice of the Foreign Office, Chamberlain chose to accept the judgement of Britain's Ambassador to Berlin, Sir Neville Henderson.[66] Whereas Vansittart had been calling for a determined stand against German militarism since the mid-1930s, Henderson's fundamentally benign views on the character of both Hitler and the German state held sway, bolstered by a convenient (to Chamberlain) Chief of Staff's report which concluded that Britain had no strategic interests in Eastern Europe and was therefore not threatened by any designs on the area that Germany might entertain.[67] As a direct result of the converging advice offered by Henderson and the Chiefs of Staff, Chamberlain's government simply acquiesced when Hitler's forces effectively annexed Austria in March 1938, on the pretext of being invited in by the Austrian Nazi government to restore order.

Worse was to come. In September 1938 Chamberlain travelled to Germany to discuss the Czech question with Hitler. At their final meeting in Munich – in consultation with representatives of both France and Italy, but not of Czechoslovakia – Chamberlain conceded Germany's right to annex the Sudetenland. He returned to London, waving the piece of paper which contained Hitler's assurances that he was now satisfied with the territory that had been 'retrieved' and that Germany would consult fully with Britain in the event of any future problems arising. In March 1939, in accordance with Rumbold's analysis of eleven years before, Hitler ordered his forces into what was left of Czechoslovakia. Even Chamberlain was forced to admit: 'As soon as I had time to think I saw that it was impossible to deal with Hitler after he had thrown all his assurances to the winds.'[68] The invasion of Czechoslovakia marked the end of Chamberlain's efforts to persist with a strategy of cooperative diplomacy and appeasement. Idealism, which had been comatose since 1936, was now well and truly dead. On 31 March 1939, the British and French governments announced the Polish Guarantee. With the Soviet threat to Germany effectively neutralised – for the time being – by the Molotov–Ribbentrop non-aggression pact of August 1939, Hitler's forces invaded Poland on 1 September. By 3 September Britain and Germany were at war.

With hindsight, of course, it was easy to see where first Baldwin and then Chamberlain had gone wrong. Baldwin had given his Foreign Secretary a fairly free rein to determine policy towards Germany but it was not until 1937 that Eden himself had been weaned away from appeasement. Chamberlain had relied far too heavily on the incompetent advice of Henderson, even when it was in direct opposition to almost everything else that the Foreign Office was telling him. Crucially, however, both Prime Ministers had failed to follow the first principle of *realpolitik*: potential aggressors will invariably remain unmoved by generous attempts to understand past injustices, by reasoned arguments about mutual interests in avoiding war or by patient efforts aimed at securing an equitable compromise. On the contrary, what potential aggressors really understand are firm and unambiguous threats – all the more disturbing if they are politely stated – backed by military force. Rumbold and Vansittart had been proved correct and the general model upon which their analyses had been based would provide the broad guidelines for policy in the future: Realism would remain firmly embedded in the hearts and minds of the policymakers for over a generation.

According to both his 'close confidant', Sir Samuel Hoare, and his official biographer, Keith Feiling, Chamberlain seems to have been prepared to accept the incorporation of the Sudeten Germany into the Reich primarily because he believed it was *morally right*.[69] It was this belief in the moral rectitude of Czechoslovak partition, together with his gullibility in thinking that Hitler's demands for more territory would stop there, that above all else discredited Chamberlain. The tragedy was that his strategy of cooperative diplomacy was discredited along with him. In spite of the fact that there was a significant element of Realist calculation in appeasement (a remilitarised and well-equipped Germany in possession of both Austria and the Sudetenland would be better able to resist Stalin), it was not Realism that was blamed for the failure to halt Hitler's programme of expansion. On the contrary, the blame was placed very firmly by the new Realist orthodoxy at the door of cooperative diplomacy, of appeasement, of Idealism as a whole. However contentious or injudicious the conclusion might have been, it was firmly in place. Henceforward, Realism would rule, OK.

The Impact of World War II on British Power

Throughout World War II, as in all wars, Realism was the fundamental determining factor in all the important decisions made by the major powers. The decisions as to which powers were to be regarded as allies and which enemies, when to provide support for a friend and when to delay it, when to attack an opponent and when to await events were all determined by calculations designed to protect and promote the security interests of the nation-state. In a classic Realist manoeuvre, Britain formed an alliance with the Soviet Union under the balance of power logic that 'the enemy of my enemy is my friend', a strategy which would not survive in the post-war world once Adolf Hitler was gone. While it would not be appropriate here to analyse the details of the military campaigns which finally produced the Allied victory – detailed accounts exist elsewhere, of course[70] – it is nevertheless important to understand the major effects that the war had on Britain's post-war international position.

World War II further damaged Britain's position in the world. First, as a direct result of the war effort itself, *Britain's financial and industrial position was appalling*. By 1945, the country's gold and foreign currency reserves were virtually exhausted: almost all of the privately owned income-earning foreign assets acquired since 1918 had been mortgaged or sold; enormous debts – for supplies received – were owed to India, Canada and Australia; and at least some reparation would soon have to be made for Lend-Lease, the programme through which the United States 'lent' funds and military equipment to Britain during the war.[71] In addition, the domestic economy was strongly geared to wartime rather than peacetime production, while exports were running at little more than a third of pre-1939 levels.[72]

A second major consequence of the war was *the weakening of Britain's grip on the Empire*. In what was almost a replay of what had occurred between 1914 and 1918, the exigencies of the developing situation during World War II produced a new set of promises to various nationalist groups throughout the Empire. In the period after 1945, however, the new promises could not be so conveniently forgotten. On the contrary, as will be seen in Chapter 3, indigenous nationalism, particularly in India and Palestine, emerged from the war more confident, more determined and better organised than ever before. The increasingly insistent demands for change could not be so easily resisted as they had been in the interwar years and, as a result, by the end of the war, Britain's hold on the Empire 'circle' was already weakening in the face of political and economic pressures which were set to grow inexorably in the ensuing years.

In relation to another of Churchill's 'circles', a third consequence of the war was clearly in evidence: *the geostrategic situation in Europe had been totally transformed*. The defeat of Germany created a political and military vacuum in central Europe which by the time of the Potsdam Conference had largely been filled by the Soviet Union. Before 1939, France and Britain together had appeared to provide some sort of counterweight to the growing German threat. Soviet Russia was only a distant worry and in any case any attempt at Russian expansionism would first have to deal with Germany itself. After 1945, with the German challenge eliminated by partition, the new threat was posed by the Soviets who appeared to possess a continental military capability far greater than any collective defensive response which the British and French might be able to muster. In these circumstances, it was only the massive American military presence in Western Europe which was capable of balancing Soviet power in the East. As the leading capitalist power in the post-war world, the United States had a considerable long-term interest in insulating Western Europe from the incipient communism which Soviet military hegemony already seemed to imply. Britain and France, of course, saw continuing American involvement as the only way of preserving their own immediate security: their problem in the early post-war years was to persuade the Americans of the magnitude of the Soviet threat to US interests in Europe and accordingly to encourage Truman to reverse Roosevelt's declared policy of evacuating American troops from Europe within two years of Hitler's defeat.

Of immense significance in this regard was a fourth consequence of the war: *the emergence of the Atlantic 'special relationship' between Britain and the United States.* Founded on both a traditional cultural affinity and a convergence of security interests arising out of the common wartime threat posed by Germany and Japan, the 'special relationship' had many facets. It began in the first few months of the war with a series of discussions which led to detailed technical cooperation in nuclear energy research.[73] Meanwhile the visit to London of President Roosevelt's envoy, Harry Hopkins, in January 1941, made important progress in political confidence-building.[74] The subsequent introduction of Lend-Lease in March 1941 meant that the United States was providing economic support for the British war effort on a scale unprecedented for a neutral state. And the Arcadia Conference in December 1941 not only reinforced the burgeoning economic ties (through the establishment of the Combined Boards) but also provided the institutional apparatus (the combined Chiefs of Staff Committee) for the intimate military relationship that was to follow. In short, at every level in the scientific, economic and military fields, there was a great 'mixing-up' of personnel, opinions and ideas.[75]

As the war progressed, Anglo-American collaboration increased. This was especially true with regard to atomic cooperation, which not only produced the first critical breakthrough in nuclear weapons research but also led to the Quebec Agreement of August 1943 in which the British and American governments agreed that each would only use nuclear weapons against a third party if the other had first given its consent.[76] Yet even this high degree of cooperation was surpassed in the military sphere where the complementary capabilities of the British and American armed forces were effectively integrated in a unified, global military campaign. Of course, there were inconsistencies, contradictions, reversals and occasional disasters;[77] but these would have occurred if the armed forces of a single country had been involved. As military allies the British and the Americans achieved an extraordinary degree of mutual reliance and integrated campaigning, an intimacy which was to be of considerable significance in the difficult years before the establishment of NATO in 1949. By the time of the Potsdam Conference in July 1945, moreover, the views of both the Harry Truman and Clement Attlee governments had converged on the need to prevent further Soviet encroachment westwards and on the necessity of challenging the Soviet Union's right to exercise permanent hegemony over Eastern Europe.

Yet, in spite of all these points of agreement, the 'special relationship' in 1945 was still marked by important political differences. In the *Far East* there was a significant divergence of opinion over the extent and timing of any post-war concessions that might be made to nationalism in India, Burma and Malaya; the anti-colonialist Americans favouring more and sooner, the British preferring less and later.[78] In the *Middle East*, while the Americans were intensely suspicious that London intended to restore its pre-war position of political and economic dominance, the British government for its part feared that US policy was designed principally to strengthen the position of American oil companies at the direct expense of their British counterparts; in which belief London was confirmed in February 1945 when (in the face of Senate opposition) Roosevelt was obliged to withdraw the 1944 Anglo-American Petroleum Agreement.[79] In *Western Europe* there were disagreements (in December 1944) over the composition of the new governments to be installed in liberated Belgium, Italy and Greece; with the United States rejecting British calls for the return to power of anti-radical pro-monarchist factions which, rightly or wrongly, were regarded by the Americans as little more than Nazi collaborators.[80]

By the end of the war, then, the 'special relationship' was distinctly ambivalent. In the *military* and *technical* spheres, the degree of bilateral cooperation achieved had been remarkable. In *economic* matters the United States had rendered an invaluable service to Britain by the provision of Lend-Lease, though its sudden termination had come as a serious blow. In terms of the broader global *political* issues there were a number of significant differences which counterbalanced the common interest that Britain and the United States shared in opposing communism and in promoting capitalist liberal democracy. Not surprisingly, as we will see in later chapters, the subsequent course of the special relationship was to prove critical in the overall development of British foreign policy.

A fifth consequence of the war which merits brief attention here was *the reinforcement of the policymakers' Realist world-views*. If the late 1930s had promised the future pre-eminence of *realpolitik* calculation, the experiences of the war years assured it. It had been only by the exercise of Churchillian Realism that Britain had survived and then triumphed. The callous ceding of the Burma Road to the Japanese in July 1940, for example, which had seriously damaged the war effort of allied China, was a simple reflection of the fact that Britain could not at that time afford to be at war with both Germany and Japan. Similarly, the German invasion of Russia in June 1941, by transforming 'my enemy's collaborator' into 'my enemy's enemy', provided the classic 'power politics' motive for Britain's near-spontaneous alliance with the Soviet Union; although, once the common threat had disappeared, the alliance itself disintegrated. The crucial point was that Churchill had played a hard *realpolitik* game and had won. The problem was that so had Stalin. And Stalin was *still* playing that game in a situation in which he no longer appeared to be 'on our side'. In classic Realist fashion, post-war British foreign policy makers reasoned that, if *one* party plays 'power politics' in an anarchical system, then all other parties whose interests are in consequence threatened *are also* obliged to play the same Realist game. The central concern of Britain's post-war foreign policy was thus the achievement of security in the face of the Soviet communist threat. The direct implication was that, even though the war itself was over and the demands for demobilisation irresistible, Britain could not afford to dismantle its defences. Any British withdrawal anywhere – if the Americans could not immediately substitute their own troops for the British forces thus removed – would leave a vacuum which either the Soviets or their communist agents would be only too pleased to fill. In these circumstances, London appeared to have little choice but to attempt to maintain a military presence in all those parts of the globe that were deemed vulnerable to communist insurgence and/or expansionism. This, in effect, meant almost everywhere, and as a result Britain embarked on a global strategy which was bound to produce massive military overextension. With growing demands for more domestic consumption at home, this was the last thing that new Labour Prime Minister Clement Attlee or Foreign Secretary Ernest Bevin really wanted. However, as practitioners of *realpolitik* (and after the experiences of the previous decade how could they be anything else?), it was something they could not avoid. Very difficult times lay ahead.

Summary and Conclusions: The Roots of Overextension

In the period after 1918 successive British governments made a series of half-hearted attempts to follow a new, more 'Idealistic' style of diplomacy. If at all possible, the *legal and quasi-legal processes* of the League of Nations and its attendant institutions, with their provision for 'collective security', were to be used in order to resolve international conflicts. If this strategy failed, then the new commitment to *cooperative* diplomacy – in which the spirit of compromise reigned supreme – might still permit conflicts to be peacefully resolved. The problem, of course, was that, although most of the powers of the state system ostentatiously signed the General Treaty for the Renunciation of War in 1928, none of them had the slightest intention of actually renouncing war as 'an instrument of national policy'. Although the leaders of the Great Powers paid public lip service to widespread demands for pacific settlement, their deliberations in private were strongly coloured by Realist calculation about the 'vital interests' of their respective nation-states.

The irony was that, while this element of power politics calculation was sufficient to ensure the failure of both the League and the new cooperative diplomacy which it inspired, the commitment to Realism was itself so diluted by vestigial Idealist sentiment that effective strategies of coercive diplomacy were not followed either. For Britain in particular, this unfortunate cocktail of Realism and Idealism was of considerable importance. By the mid-1930s Hitler and Mussolini were pursuing policies of unashamed *realpolitik*. In contrast, the Baldwin and Chamberlain governments, perhaps the victims of fifteen years of their own propaganda, retained a residual commitment to cooperative (compromising, appeasing) diplomacy, long after the objective logic of the situation (and almost the entire Foreign Office) had suggested that a coercive response might have been more appropriate. Not surprisingly in these circumstances, the appeasement strategy of 1935–38 (notwithstanding the possibility that it provided a useful 'breathing space' during which time Britain was better able to prepare itself for war) failed to prevent war.

The failure both of the League and of Chamberlain's 'cooperative diplomacy' led after 1938 to a general rejection of Idealist principles. In their place came a return to the basic maxims of *realpolitik* (persuade and cajole if it is at all possible, but balance power and threaten serious consequences if it is not), a commitment which the war years – inevitably – served to reinforce. But the conclusion of World War II also produced a major dilemma for British foreign policy decision-makers. On the one hand, the Soviet Union was beginning to emerge as a potentially serious threat to British interests both inside and outside the European theatre; and that threat, somehow, had to be met. On the other hand, the weakening ties with the Empire and the parlous state of the economy, both engendered by the war, meant that the potential threat could only be countered (in the short term at least) at the cost of sacrifices which the British public were not prepared to make. The post-war solution to this dilemma was to exploit the ambivalent – but, it was hoped, still 'special' – wartime relationship with the United States, in an effort to persuade the Americans that their own best long-term security interests lay in defending Western Europe against Soviet expansionism. As we will see, however, even though the Americans did remain in Europe, Britain's overseas commitments remained seriously overextended: the price of American support was that the British government be seen to play *its* part in the defence of the free world. As a result, Britain was obliged to maintain both a sizeable military force on the continent of Europe and a significant military presence in a variety of theatres throughout the world. The forms which this overextension took, together with their consequences, are examined in subsequent chapters.

Chapter 2

From Potsdam to Cold War: Relations with Europe and the Superpowers, 1945–55

This chapter examines the development of Britain's foreign policy in Churchill's 'Atlantic' and 'European circles' in the decade after 1945. The simultaneous examination of these two areas of policy is by no means accidental. As will be seen, developments in both circles were intimately related, not least because successive British governments were convinced that a revitalised 'special relationship' with the United States was essential if Western Europe was to be effectively defended. Britain's main problem in this context, of course, was that the 'Big Three' allies had not emerged from the war united. As the previous chapter indicated, even before Potsdam British fears of the coming Soviet threat in Europe were already taking shape and, despite the closeness of Anglo-American relations in the technical and military spheres, there were certainly significant political strains in the 'special relationship' which gave cause for concern. As things turned out, relations with the Soviet Union were to deteriorate progressively over the next ten years and as a result Britain's military links with Western Europe were to be substantially strengthened. Relations with the United States were actually set to worsen before they improved after July 1946.

This chapter begins by describing Britain's main economic and military problems in 1945. The second section examines the events in Europe which transformed American perceptions about the need to withdraw from Europe and led the United States to restore the 'special relationship' to some semblance of what it had been during the war years. At the root of this transformation, of course – in true *realpolitik* fashion – was an increasing sense that the material and security interests of Britain and the United States were again converging, with the Soviets beginning to mount a serious challenge to the global interests of Western capitalism. In the third section of the chapter the main consequences of this renewed interest convergence are discussed: a renewed economic intimacy and increased military collaboration throughout the world. As will become clear, what was crucial in all these developments was the *realpolitik* view of the world taken by British and (slightly later) by American foreign policy makers. It was their mutual fear of Soviet communism that produced both the sense of interest convergence and the additional military commitments that they were subsequently to make both inside and outside Europe. These extra commitments, in turn, were to result in a significant *overextension* of Britain's military and financial capabilities by the mid-1950s.

Britain's International Position in 1945

The Economic Problems

Partly as a consequence of nearly six years of war, by the second half of 1945 the British economy was in serious trouble. In order to support the immediate needs of the war effort, the government had forcibly sold off almost all the foreign assets held in Britain by private individuals and companies, issuing interest-bearing bonds to the former owners by way of compensation. In the short run, this had provided the government with much-needed foreign exchange with which to purchase raw materials and munitions. In the immediate post-war period, however, not only were the interest payments to bondholders a considerable drain on the Exchequer, but the economy as a whole was deprived of the invisible export income which before the war had flowed into the country in the form of repatriated profits.[1]

This problem was compounded by the size of the debts (£3,567 million) owed to India and the Dominions as a result of materials supplied during the course of the war. Payment for these supplies had been deferred by building up the so-called 'sterling balances' in London. The interest that Britain had to pay on these balances to the countries of the Overseas Sterling Area (OSA) was yet another drain on the British economy's slender resources. Moreover, although the 'sterling balance' debts appeared to be partially offset by gold and foreign currency reserves in July 1945 of £610 million, these reserves were earmarked for the protection of the external value of sterling and accordingly could not be used for debt-reduction purposes.

A further problem deriving from the war years concerned the level of (mainly industrial) exports. In the first nine months of 1945 exports were running at some 42 per cent of the pre-war level at a time when the Treasury estimated that they needed to be at 175 per cent of the 1938 level for the balance of payments to be in equilibrium.[2] Part of the difficulty was that, under the conditions of Lend-Lease, British manufacturers had been prevented from exporting any equipment or materials of the type imported by US firms into Britain. The refusal of the Americans to relax this ruling, even for a transition period, as long as Lend-Lease continued meant that British entrepreneurs had no opportunity to attempt a *gradual* penetration of overseas markets. As a result, when Lend-Lease was abruptly ended in September 1945, British exporters were simply not equipped to produce the massive increase in export levels that was required in order to equalise the balance of payments. The only good news about the termination of Lend-Lease was that, although Britain had received over £31 *billion* worth of supplies since March 1941, the US government finally decided that only £650 *million* of it would have to be repaid.[3] However, even this remarkably generous concession constituted a request for monies which Britain at that time simply did not possess.

In addition to these war-related problems, of course, Britain's postwar economy was also suffering from long-term structural weaknesses which were made to appear all the more acute precisely because of the difficulties outlined above. In 1860, Britain had been involved in 25 per cent of the total world trade in goods and services; even before the war, in 1938, its share had dropped to 14 per cent. In the 1860s, 42 per cent of Britain's exports had gone to other industrial countries; by the late 1920s industrial markets had been 'lost' to such an extent that the corresponding figure in 1927 was 25 per cent.[4] At the root of these problems, of course, were the historically low levels of domestic industrial investment that Britain had constantly achieved in comparison with its industrial competitors. While it would not be appropriate here to enter the prolonged and contentious debate about the *origins* of this low-investment pattern,[5] it is worth noting that there has been something decidedly odd about Britain's historical tendency to export capital in vast quantities during times of peace, only to mortgage it all each time it finds itself engaged in a major war.

Whatever the causes of Britain's long-term industrial decline, however, the combination of long- and short-term problems mentioned above served to produce a severe balance of payments crisis which was to last throughout the 1940s. Making the external debt problem even worse, Britain's balance of payments deficit in 1945 was £704 million; in 1946 it was £386 million; in 1947, £652 million; in 1948, £496 million; and in 1949, £488 million.[6] It was against this background of wartime debt and accumulating post-war deficits that the Attlee Cabinet had to confront not only irresistible demands for the extension of the welfare state at home but also the problem of the ever-present and growing Soviet threat in Europe. If Bevin and the Foreign Office and the service ministries had not been imbued with the spirit of Realism they might have decided to ignore Stalin's machinations in Eastern Europe and to hope for the best.

Who knows what might have happened if they had? As it was, however, their Realist analysis told them that there clearly was cause for alarm and that remedial political and military action had to be taken. The problem was that, in the aftermath of victory, Britain was not only economically exhausted: it was also militarily overextended.

The Military Problems

Britain ended the war with over five million men under arms and – as in 1918 – tremendous domestic pressure for rapid demobilisation.[7] Military personnel were cut to three and a half million by December 1945 and to under one million by March 1948.[8] Before 1939, Britain in peacetime had not required a large army. It did not need to keep a military presence on the continent of Europe and the Empire could be effectively policed with a relatively small but professional mobile force. In this latter task, the British government was assisted in no small measure by a large (and loyal) locally raised Indian army; by the fact that throughout the Empire local nationalist groups were almost invariably conveniently divided among themselves; by the Colonial Office's expertise in manipulating indigenous elites; and by the fact that the strength of the Royal Navy insulated Britain's imperial possessions from effective third party challenge or infiltration. By mid-1945, everything had changed. In Europe, Britain was already making an important contribution to the occupying forces in Germany, Austria and Italy. In the Empire, and especially in the mandated territories acquired after 1920, local nationalist groups were rapidly acquiring both a greater sense of determination and a wider popularity among indigenous populations. They were also discovering new and more effective techniques of guerrilla warfare which were to render their future suppression much more difficult.

In consequence, although the size of the armed forces was being rapidly reduced in the face of domestic demands, and although the economy was already significantly enfeebled, Britain found itself in a position where its overseas military commitments were both enormous and growing. As Table 2.1 indicates, in 1945 Britain had a significant military presence in over 40 countries, for the purpose either of suppressing the local population or of deterring adventurism on the part of some potential external aggressor. In almost every theatre throughout the world, Britain was somehow involved: in the North Atlantic, the South Atlantic, the Caribbean, the Mediterranean, the Indian Ocean and the South China Sea; in Central Europe and Mediterranean Europe; in North Africa, the Middle East and the Persian Gulf; in West Africa, Southern Africa, East Africa and the Horn of Africa; in India, Burma, Hong Kong,

Table 2.1   Countries where British forces were stationed in 1945

Austria	Burma	Aden
Belgium	Hong Kong	Cyprus
Britain	India	Egypt/Suez
France	Indonesia	Jordan
Germany	Japan	Libya
Gibraltar	Malaysia/Singapore	Muscat and Oman
Greece		Palestine
Italy		Trucial States
Netherlands		
Bermuda	British Somalia	
British Guyana	Ethiopia	
British Honduras	Gambia	
Falkland Islands	Ghana	
Jamaica	Kenya	
	Mauritius	
	Nigeria	
	N. Rhodesia	
	S. Rhodesia	
	Sierra Leone	
	South Africa	
	Tanganyika	
	Uganda	

Sources: CMND 6743, *Statement Relating to Defence* (Feb. 1946); CMND 7327, *Statement Relating to Defence* (Feb. 1948); CMND 7337, *Navy Estimates 1948–49* (Feb. 1948; CMND 9075, *Statement on Defence 1954* (Feb. 1954); CMND 9072, *Memo of the Secretary of State for War relating to the Army Estimates for 1954–55* (Feb. 1954).

Japan, Malaya and Singapore and Indonesia. For the government, the reason for this massively overextended commitment was clear:

> The objectives of our [external] policy derive *directly from our obligations and commitments as a Great Power*. It remains the firm intention of HMG [His Majesty's Government] to maintain the forces which are needed to support its international policy, to ensure the security of the UK, to maintain its interests throughout the world, and to enable it to play its full part in the preservation of world peace. The forces which we maintain in place must be sufficient to provide an adequate nucleus for expansion in war, to meet the need for garrisons overseas … and to furnish our contribution to the UN Armed Forces. All these duties are the inescapable responsibilities of a great Power intent on preserving peace.[9]

For a Great Power recently victorious in war, the proud possessor of a great Empire and Commonwealth which had held together through the vicissitudes of war, such commitments seemed entirely reasonable. For a medium-sized European nation-state, exhausted by six years of war, its colonial links and its economic base dangerously weakened, the commitments in many respects seemed ludicrously overextended. But Bevin et al. were committed to a *realpolitik* view of the world. If Britain did *not* fulfil its obligations (and the Americans did not yet seem ready, even if the Attlee government had wanted it, to step into the breach that would have been thus created) then the ever-watchful Soviets – or their proxies – would without doubt seize the opportunity and further extend their own sphere of influence. In these circumstances, Attlee and Bevin had no choice: overextend or leave the stage free for Soviet expansionism. They chose to overextend.

Differences over the 'Soviet Threat'

A third aspect of Britain's international position in 1945 that merits brief attention concerns the divergence in British and American opinions about the seriousness of the Soviet threat. In Britain, Stalin's uncompromising attitude at Tehran and Yalta had certainly led Churchill to recognise Stalin as a fellow practitioner of *realpolitik*. And the subsequent Soviet-inspired coup in Romania in March 1945 and the continuing Soviet refusal throughout the summer of 1945 to allow genuinely free elections in Poland were an unmistakable indication of things to come. The ruthlessness which Stalin had demonstrated inside Russia in the 1930s clearly continued unabated in his present foreign policy. For Churchill, and latterly for Bevin, Stalin's 'real' intentions for Eastern Europe – and for anywhere else he could dominate – were all too plain: Soviet-style socialist regimes subservient to Moscow would be installed wherever possible.

Yet, in spite of this profound conviction as to Stalin's malevolent *realpolitik* intent, Bevin at Potsdam and after was for a brief period prepared to concede the *possibility* that the Council of Foreign Ministers and the UN Security Council might somehow usher in a new era of peace and cooperation. While Bevin was rapidly disabused of this optimistic belief, the Americans took somewhat longer. They had in any case always been more hopeful both about the potential of the United Nations for peaceful conflict resolution and about the Soviets' supposed desire to enter the post-war world in a spirit of partnership rather than confrontation. American analysis of the Soviet position was also coloured by lingering suspicions of Britain's intentions: in late 1945 US policymakers were still wary of the possibility either that there might be a post-war revival in

British imperialism or that in contrast the new Labour government might look to Moscow rather than Washington for political leadership and ideological inspiration. Although each eventuality was unlikely, neither was to be welcomed. In any event, by early 1947 the American position had changed dramatically and, by the end of the year, the incipient 'cold war', in which Britain and the United States were very much on the same side, was fully underway. How, then, did this transformation come about? What were the major causal factors responsible for it?

Decline and Recovery: The Transformation in Anglo-American Strategic Relations, 1945–48

The sudden termination of Lend-Lease in September 1945 was followed in December by the disbanding of the wartime Combined Boards for raw materials and for production and resources. The decline of the special relationship was further hastened, however, by the McMahon Act of August 1946, in which the United States effectively ended collaboration with Britain in atomic research and development. At a time when the possession of nuclear weapons, at least in Western eyes, was intimately bound up with the whole notion of 'Great Power' status, this was a serious blow both to Britain's nuclear ambitions and to its postwar role aspirations. Yet from this low point in the summer of 1946, Anglo-American relations rapidly recovered. In July 1946 the 'American loan' had already come to the rescue of the struggling British economy; in September 1946, Secretary of State Byrnes acknowledged that American forces would not be speedily evacuated from Europe; in March 1947 the 'Truman Doctrine' was proclaimed; and finally in June 1947 the Marshall Plan announced a programme of economic reconstruction that was to revitalise Western European capitalism and thereby strengthen its resistance to communist infiltration and encroachment.

Although each of these developments has been cited as a decisive 'turning point' in the course of post-war Great Power relations,[10] it seems likely that the drawing together of Britain and the United States, and the simultaneous growth of their common hostility towards the Soviet Union, resulted from the operation of rather more gradual processes. In particular, the improvement in Anglo-American relations, which was to prove so crucial in Britain's subsequent foreign policy, was the consequence of two underlying factors that were much more obviously 'gradual' in their respective effects: (1) Stalin's obstructive diplomacy in the Council of Foreign Ministers and at the Paris Peace Conference in 1945–46; and (2) his ruthless overt and covert 'consolidation' of Eastern Europe between 1945 and 1948.

Stalin's obstructiveness rapidly became apparent at the first meeting of the Council of Foreign Ministers held in London in September 1945. The main express purpose of the meeting was to establish a viable framework for the peace treaties with the defeated powers, a post-war settlement which, it was assumed, would bring the hostilities of World War II to a formal close. However, Molotov's insistence on the Soviet Union's right effectively to determine the political complexion of all post-settlement governments in Eastern Europe – a position that was clearly unacceptable to both Britain and the United States – ensured that the conference failed in all important respects. The foreign ministers of the 'Big Three' subsequently met again in Moscow in December 1945, but their first tentative steps towards agreement on the peace treaties were rapidly reversed by the Persian complaint to the UN Security Council in January 1946 that Soviet occupation forces had still not withdrawn from the Azerbaijan Province of Eastern Persia, where they were actively fomenting communist-inspired demands for concession. By April, Molotov had in fact relented on Azerbaijan and the Soviets agreed to evacuate their forces by May 1946.

However, this small (and uncostly) gesture of Soviet goodwill did little to improve the atmosphere at the second meeting of the Council of Foreign Ministers in Paris in April 1946. It had been hoped that in Paris real progress would be made on the future of Germany. Unfortunately, it rapidly became clear that, unless the Western Powers retained their de facto military control of Germany west of the Elbe, Moscow would use every means at its disposal to transform it into a Soviet-dominated client state. Meanwhile the Western Powers would be permitted no say whatever in the affairs of Soviet-occupied East Germany. It was more than a little ironic, therefore, that at the very time that the McMahon Act was driving a wedge between Britain and the United States in the *defence* field, Britain and American negotiators were finding a new common *political* purpose in opposing Soviet diplomatic intransigence in respect of the 'post-war settlement'. The immediate result was that the Paris meeting achieved nothing except a growing realisation among American policymakers that Churchill's 'iron curtain' – evoked in his speech at Fulton, Missouri, in March 1946 – was indeed 'descending across the continent of Europe' and that there was little in practice that they could actually do about it.

In July 1946, negotiators from all the Allied powers met in Paris in order to devise draft peace treaties for Bulgaria, Hungary, Romania, Italy and Finland. To the surprise of the Western Powers, the Soviet delegation accepted the principle that disagreements over the content and wording of the drafts could be resolved by majority voting: fairly rapid progress was accordingly made. Yet when the Council of Foreign Ministers met for the third time in New York in November 1946 in order to finalise the wording of the five draft treaties, Molotov rejected all of those parts of the drafts where a majority decision (in July) had overridden Soviet preferences. With the negotiations stalemated, the US delegation threatened to withdraw from the treaty-making process altogether. As a result, the Soviets relented and in December 1946 final agreement on the five treaties was reached. Notwithstanding this agreement, however, the diplomatic damage had been done. Thereafter negotiations aimed at achieving a formal peace treaty with Germany progressed no further. Indeed, in American eyes, the Soviets had shown themselves, at least since April 1946, to be largely untrustworthy negotiators who used the treaty-making process more as an opportunity for the dissemination of vitriolic propaganda than as a vehicle for achieving peaceful compromise. This was precisely what Churchill had been telling them in no uncertain terms since Yalta; and they were now starting to believe it: the ingredients for a revitalised 'special relationship' were beginning to come together.

The crucial factor underlying the transformation in Anglo-American relations between 1945 and 1948, however, was the cynical manner in which Stalin manipulated the governments of those countries that the Red Army had liberated before the German surrender and over which the Soviet Union now exercised potential – if not actual – military dominion. The first concrete intimation of Stalin's 'defensive expansionism' to come was the Soviet-inspired coup in Romania in March 1945, only one month after the 'spheres of influence agreement' at Yalta.[11] This was followed in July 1945 by the installation of a Soviet-backed government in Poland. The outcome of the Hungarian election in November 1945 (in which the Communist Party vote was small) suggested that the Soviets might not invariably seek to subvert the promise made at Yalta that they would hold free elections throughout liberated Europe, but any optimism about Soviet actions in this regard was short-lived. Over the next two years, Soviet-inspired intriguing undermined the stability of a series of East European governments that dared to delay the advent of 'People's Democracy'. Poland was the first to succumb in January 1947 when a new socialist-communist coalition government was elected in highly suspect circumstances. By the end of 1948, the Soviet-inspired communist elements within the coalition had achieved a clear ascendancy and a People's Democracy subservient to the will of Moscow was accordingly declared. Similar fates befell the Romanian government in March 1947, the Hungarian government in August 1947 and the Bulgarian government in December 1947. In Czechoslovakia, where competitive elections in May 1946 produced a communist-led coalition government that showed few signs of converting itself into a one-party regime, the transition to a People's Democracy was achieved in February 1948 by the simple mechanism of a *coup d'état*. The only countries in Eastern Europe that escaped Stalin's efforts to consolidate the Soviet Union's strategic 'buffer' zone were Yugoslavia and Albania, which had strong and independent communist parties of their own, and Austria, where British and American forces were still in occupation.

At one level, of course, all of these Soviet machinations were understandable, if not entirely 'acceptable', to both Washington and London. After all, at Yalta it had been acknowledged that the countries involved (Czechoslovakia excepted) were outside the Western sphere of influence: it had been recognised that Britain and the United States were powerless to resist determined intriguing aimed at installing regimes favourably disposed to the Soviet Union. Yet the machinations were so self-evidently the direct consequence of Stalinist *realpolitik* that they inevitably served to reinforce the reciprocal Realism that was already growing among policymakers in Britain and the United States. Even more worrying for Realists in London and Washington was the fear that Stalin's defensive expansionism would soon begin to extend beyond the confines of the existing Stettin–Trieste 'iron curtain'. In France and Italy, recent elections had returned relatively large numbers of communist deputies. In Greece, following an electoral victory for the right-wing Populist party in March 1946, civil war had broken out with communist-inspired insurgents reportedly receiving assistance from Albania, Yugoslavia and Bulgaria. And in Turkey the nationalist regime was attempting to withstand the double pressures exerted internally by communist insurgents and externally by Soviet demands for its navy to be allowed unrestricted passage through the Black Sea straits. Of course, all of this might not actually be an orchestrated campaign by Moscow, but the combination of threats to Western strategic interests certainly gave cause for alarm.

The final straw was Stalin's blockade of West Berlin, which began in May 1948. This was viewed in the West as a clear attempt to dislodge the Allied occupation force from Berlin where negotiation had failed: a preliminary step to extending Soviet influence in Germany more generally. The response of the Western Powers was correspondingly determined. A protracted RAF/USAF airlift ensured the survival of the British/French/American garrison in Berlin and a counter-blockade on Soviet-controlled Eastern Germany encouraged Stalin to look for a compromise solution. After various diplomatic manoeuvrings, both blockades were lifted in May 1949. Whatever Stalin's 'real' aims had been in initiating the Berlin blockade, however, its main effect – coming on top of everything else that the Soviets had done in Eastern Europe – was to bring his capitalist enemies closer together and to convince the Americans that their continued military presence in Europe was still required, even if it was now Russia rather than Germany which threatened both the liberal values and the economic stability of capitalist Western Europe. As Arnold Toynbee remarked, 'the Russians' feat of curing the Americans of isolationism staggers the imagination'.[12]

By the middle of 1948, therefore, Stalin had succeeded in reinforcing the perception among British and American policymakers that their security and material interests strongly converged. The communist encroachment in Europe provided the classic *realpolitik* raw material for a renewal of the Anglo-American 'special relationship'. The collective interests of the free, capitalist democracies were clearly threatened by a wily and mendacious aggressor playing a skilful Realist game apparently based on the 'salami' tactic of the piecemeal incorporation of adjacent territory into the Soviet 'Empire'. Inevitably, that aggressor had to be confronted by a united *realpolitik* response. A mere convergence of interest, however, was not on its own sufficient to sweep aside all of the political doubts and suspicions which had characterised Anglo-American relations in the immediate post-war years. In peacetime, when the urgency generated by fear of imminent attack is neither so pervasive nor so strong as it is in war, a convergence of vital interest has to be supplemented by a political meeting of minds in order to effect a genuine transformation in bilateral relations. The shared sense of Realism which dominated both the State Department and the Foreign Office was of course a useful start. But the crucial 'added ingredient' necessary for the full restoration of the 'special relationship' was British diplomacy.

At Potsdam Attlee and Bevin had rapidly dispelled American fears that the new Labour government, clearly 'socialist' in its domestic programmes, would look to Moscow rather than Washington for political support in resolving the post-war 'German problem'. In a number of diplomatic forums during the course of 1946 and 1947, Bevin consistently voiced his suspicions about Soviet aims and intentions and in so doing established his credentials as a worthy successor to Churchill, as a stout defender of liberal values squarely confronting the new totalitarian threat. Yet at the same time that Bevin could reasonably claim to be Churchill's heir in matters of European security, the Labour government's progressive stand on the Empire also enabled him to portray Britain as a power which fully recognised the moral importance of self-determination. And if American suspicions that this was mere public posturing still lingered, the decolonisation in India in August 1947 demonstrated that Britain was prepared to pursue colonial policies rather more in keeping with American conceptions of the way a *liberal* Great Power ought to behave. This was progress indeed. And even if this new-found spirit of British liberalism was far less important as a source of interest convergence than the threat posed by Soviet acquisitiveness in Eastern Europe, it nonetheless made Britain a far more acceptable partner for the United

States in its post-war role as primary defender of the interests of Western capitalism. This partnership, in turn, was to prove crucial in the development of British foreign policy over the next 20 years.

The Consequences of Anglo-American Interest Convergence, 1946–55

The fundamental consequence of the renewed sense of interest convergence shared by British and American foreign policy makers in the period after 1946 was the tacit acknowledgement that, if Western capitalism was under threat worldwide from totalitarian communism, then it was better to confront that threat together rather than separately. And if the United States was now set to take over the major role in the containment of communism by virtue of its superior military and economic capability, Britain and the Empire could still perform an enormously important subsidiary role by providing the United States with both moral and material support. Obviously there would still be policy differences over Europe, the Middle East and the Empire but these could not be allowed to divert the re-emerging partnership from its primary task of opposing the communist threat.

The Economic Consequences of Interest Convergence

In the economic sphere, Britain and the United States had already begun to make joint plans for the post-war international *monetary* system at the Bretton Woods Conference in 1944. The International Monetary Fund thereby established was designed to facilitate international trade payments and thus to encourage the growth of world trade. Under the new system, the two major 'reserve' currencies were to be the dollar and sterling: joint symbols of Anglo-American dominance in the post-war capitalist world. The benefits and costs that accrued from sterling's status as a reserve currency are examined in Chapter 7 and so they need not detain us here. The important point, however, was that, as Britain and the United States grew closer together in the political-military sphere, so their established economic collaboration took on a new significance: the junior partner in the new monetary system – Britain – was now also emerging as the junior partner in the coming political-military struggle to defend the 'free world' against the ubiquitous threat of world communism.

If Britain was to play an effective 'lieutenant's' role in the defence of Western capitalism, however, it had to do so from a sound economic base. And if the iron curtain was not to be extended Westward in Europe, where the greatest threat in 1946–47 was perceived to be, then the West European economies also needed to be considerably strengthened. The putative solution to this problem – the American Marshall Plan announced in June 1947 – in fact offered to provide *all* of Europe, both East and West, with the financial resources necessary for rapid economic reconstruction. However, Soviet suspicions that the extension of the Plan to Eastern Europe was merely a ploy to insinuate American capital (and therefore influence) into the Soviet sphere of hegemony led to the rejection of the offer throughout the Soviet bloc. As a result, when the distribution of Marshall Aid actually began in March 1948, it effectively became a vehicle for rebuilding the economies of *Western* Europe.

This had two obvious benefits: not only would the provision of a solid economic base head off deprivation-induced dissent at home, but it would also provide the resources necessary for a more formidable West European defence against external attack. As far as Britain was concerned, Marshall Aid provided the economic underpinning for the new North Atlantic politico-military partnership that was already emerging. For the Americans it was, in addition, a means of strengthening Western Europe's commitment to capitalism. In any event, the provision of Marshall Aid had a profound impact on the recipient economies, laying the foundation for the economic rejuvenation of Western Europe in the 1950s.

The Political-Military Consequences of Interest Convergence

The main consequences of the renewed convergence of British and American interests in the late 1940s, however, were in the politico-military sphere. Inside Europe, it led to a new military alliance which, although always subject to important strains and tensions, was to provide the foundation for British defence policy for the next 40 years. Outside Europe it produced defence collaboration in a variety of theatres aimed at protecting Western interests worldwide.

Anglo-American Co-operation Inside Europe, 1946–55

Several of the 'milestone' events which marked Britain's closer ties with the United States from mid-1946 onwards have already been mentioned. In July 1946, Congress ratified the Anglo-American Financial and Trade Agreement – the 'American Loan' of $3.75 billion which provided (on very reasonable terms)[13] a desperately needed boost to the flagging British economy. The loan not only indirectly enabled Britain to maintain throughout Europe and the Mediterranean military forces which otherwise might have had to be withdrawn, but also 'seal[ed] Anglo-American political solidarity' to such an extent that 'subsequently Stalin had to face a common Anglo-American front'.[14] In September 1946, Secretary of State Byrnes tacitly acknowledged that the Truman administration had reversed its previous commitment to Roosevelt's policy of withdrawing American troops from Europe as quickly as possible. Indeed, in a speech at Stuttgart, having stressed the United States' 'permanent and inescapable involvement' in global affairs, he asserted: 'I want no misunderstanding. We will not shirk our duty. We are not withdrawing. We are staying here. As long as there is an occupation army in Germany, American forces will be part of that occupying army.'[15]

The Truman Doctrine of March 1947 proclaimed the Administration's determination to provide assistance to any 'free peoples who are resisting attempted subjugation'.[16] Although never as all-embracing in practice as it sounded in principle, the doctrine constituted an important symbolic affirmation of America's global responsibilities in the defence of the 'free world'. The main practical effect of the doctrine, however, was that the United States took over the primary responsibility for supporting the beleaguered Greek and Turkish governments in their separate domestic struggles against subversion, a responsibility which in February the British government had announced it was shortly to abandon as a result of its overextended military commitments.[17]

Finally, the Marshall Plan, announced in a speech by the new Secretary of State at Harvard in June 1947, not only provided for the economic reconstruction of Western Europe but also marked the formal abandonment of American hopes that the Great Powers might act in concert in the post-war world. As early as April 1946, the UN Security Council had degenerated into little more than a propagandising talking-shop, and a similar fate had befallen the Allied Control Commission in occupied Germany. Marshall's Harvard speech was the first major public affirmation of the US commitment to 'one *free* world' rather than to the more general 'one world'.[18] The rhetorical switch was not accidental: after the Harvard speech, the *containment* of the Soviet communist threat became the main concern of Anglo-American strategic thinking.[19] The world was clearly dividing – if it had not divided already – into two antagonistic camps, each convinced of its own moral superiority and its opponent's aggressive intent. As far as the Truman and Attlee governments were concerned, for two years one cooperative diplomatic gesture after another had met with a Soviet rebuff. The time for sterile talking with Stalin was over; what was now needed was a liberal dose of *realpolitik*.

As the Marshall Aid funds began to flow in March 1948, however, its European recipients remained concerned that the main intention underlying Washington's generosity might actually be to 'get Europe on its feet and off our backs'.[20] These fears were compounded by the suspicion that the Brussels Treaty of March 1948, in which Britain, France and the Benelux countries, with American approval, had created the 'Western Union' and bound themselves together in a mutual assistance pact, would be viewed in Washington in the same detached way. Perhaps this demonstration of European determination on security matters would simply provide the Americans with the excuse they were looking for to withdraw from Europe. With Marshall Aid serving to strengthen Europe's economic base, US military assistance might no longer be considered necessary. Fortunately for London, there was an alternative (and rather more accurate) interpretation of American intentions. As Bevin correctly predicted, the Brussels Treaty was in fact seen in Washington as a clear indication that the Europeans were prepared to make an effort to help themselves.[21] Such fortitude, moreover, was deemed to deserve American support. Five days before the Brussels Treaty was signed, the Truman administration entered into preliminary negotiations with a view to establishing some sort of Atlantic Pact.[22] The Vandenberg resolution, passed overwhelmingly in the Senate in June 1948, confirmed American intentions. Although the wording of the resolution was imprecise, its import was undeniable: the United States would provide material support to any regional security organisation in the Western sphere of influence which sought to bolster collective resistance to the communist threat.

The process of increasing American involvement in European security culminated in the signing of the North Atlantic Treaty in April 1949: the Brussels Pact was extended to create NATO, which from January 1950 onwards became a mutual assistance pact with a permanent military command structure. The message to the Soviets was unequivocal. The United States was now tied formally and directly to the defence of Western Europe: any Soviet incursion in Western Europe would without doubt be met with the combined resistance of all the Western Powers, and in particular with the full force of the US Strategic Air Command.

Yet, in spite of this uncompromising external stance, London remained concerned throughout the early 1950s about the real extent of the American commitment to European security. The problem was that, throughout the negotiations that preceded the formation of NATO, there had been two conflicting strands of American strategic thinking – one associated with the State Department and one with the National Security Council (NSC) – about the role that the United States should play in NATO. Even after the Berlin crisis of 1948–49, the State Department view – associated particularly with George Kennan, the head of its Policy Planning Staff – was that the Soviets were already strategically overextended and that they were consequently extremely unlikely to attack Western Europe in the foreseeable future. For Kennan, the creation of a US-dominated North Atlantic alliance would inevitably provoke the remilitarisation of Europe, divided into Eastern and Western camps. This was undesirable for two reasons. First, it would divert resources away from the fundamental task of economic and political reconstruction which in the long term was the best defence against the real threat of Soviet-inspired subversion *inside* Western Europe. And second, remilitarisation would lock both the United States and the Soviet Union into a set of European entanglements from which they might not subsequently be able to extricate themselves even if they so desired. For Kennan, therefore, the primary responsibility for the defence of Western Europe should lie with the Western Europeans themselves, with Washington providing only limited assistance if absolutely necessary and for a limited time period.

The position of the National Security Council, however, was rather different (and rather more simplistic). The NSC had witnessed Stalin's ruthless consolidation of Eastern Europe between 1945 and 1948, his provocative posturing over Berlin, his covert support for communist subversion in the Mediterranean and in Western Europe and his overt backing of the communists in the Chinese Civil War; from all these actions, the NSC deduced an aggressive, expansionist Soviet *intent*. According to American intelligence reports, moreover, whereas the Red Army had 175 divisions at its disposal at the beginning of 1949, Western Europe had a combined total of 12: here was a massive superiority in *capability*.[23] For the hard-line realists in the NSC, intent plus capability meant only one thing. At the first sign of a weakening in the West's resolve, the Soviets would be likely to attack. Since little could be done about Stalin's intentions, in these circumstances it was absolutely essential that the capability imbalance in Europe be redressed; a situation that could only be remedied – in the medium term at least – by a significant and continuing *American* military presence in Western Europe.

The views of the NSC were embodied in a document (NSC-68) published in April 1950, which called for a 'massive projection of American military power abroad' in the fight against communist expansionism.[24] Yet even though NSC-68 became official administration policy on 25 April, the State Department's position was at that time still being accorded considerable weight in Washington. What swung the balance decisively in the NSC's favour was the outbreak of the Korean War in June 1950. (The war itself is discussed below.) Suspecting that the Korean episode might simply be a feint to divert the West's attention and resources away from the defence of Western Europe, the Truman administration became all the more determined to strengthen its commitment to NATO.

The difficulty for the administration, however, was that in the short term it needed to concentrate its limited resources on the war effort in

Korea. The position was further complicated by the fact that Truman also needed to persuade the British to make as large a contribution as they could to the Western force. This latter requirement gave Washington a powerful incentive (1) to play down the seriousness of the Soviet threat to Europe (how could Britain send troops to Korea if a Soviet attack in Europe was imminent?); and (2) to encourage the Europeans (and especially the British, who in 1950 were still producing 30 per cent of all West European industrial output) to increase their overall defence spending to more 'realistic' levels. Not surprisingly, this combination served to fuel British fears of a revival of incipient Kennanism: notwithstanding NSC-68 and Washington's formal membership of NATO it was possible that the Americans were once again contemplating trimming their European commitment.

The Attlee government's response in December 1950, as it had been in early 1948 when Bevin had instigated the Brussels Pact, was to demonstrate the seriousness of Britain's commitment to the defence of Europe and the free world. In addition to despatching the Commonwealth Brigade to Korea in July 1950 as a show of solidarity, on 19 December 1950 Bevin announced the government's plans for a massive rearmament programme.[25] If the expected cost was to be a doubling of defence spending over the next three years, the intended benefit would be a further strengthening of the American commitment to Europe.

Unfortunately, even while British and American troops were fighting side by side in Korea, the controversy about the extent of Washington's European commitment continued unabated as a result of disagreements over the *European Defence Community* (EDC). The French had produced the Pleven Plan for an EDC in October 1950 and its main attraction had been its proposal to create a West European army to which the newly independent Federal German Republic could subscribe:[26] NATO would obtain a sizeable increase in the number of divisions at its disposal without the (then) politically unacceptable reconstitution of the Germany Army. Britain's response to the plan, as it had been to its economic counterpart, the (May 1950) Schuman Plan for a European Coal and Steel Community (ECSC), was sympathetic but non-committal. Like Truman, Attlee and Bevin were in favour of the Europeans doing more to build up both their defences and their economic strength. In contrast to American preferences, however, the British were not willing to participate directly in either the EDC or the ECSC. Britain was prepared to accept some sort of associate membership of the EDC, but anything more would compromise both its sovereignty and its '*global* responsibilities'. As a result, when the EDC treaty was signed by the continental European powers in May 1952,[27] the Eisenhower administration and the new Churchill government merely signed an appended bilateral agreement stating that they would assist the signatory states if they fell victim to some future aggression, a commitment which they had already made in any case through their joint membership of NATO.

However, in the months after the signing of the EDC treaty, and before it had been ratified by the various national Parliaments, Secretary of State Dulles became increasingly concerned that Britain should assume a more prominent role in European defence. He warned Foreign Secretary Eden publicly that the US commitment to Europe would have to undergo an 'agonising reappraisal' if the EDC plan foundered, though he largely left open the question as to whether it would be the British or the Americans who would suffer the most 'agony' if this did indeed occur.

To the consternation of the British government, in August 1954 the French National Assembly failed to ratify the EDC treaty. The alacrity with which Eden toured the capital cities of Western Europe in September 1954 was a measure of the importance that Britain accorded to Dulles's threats. However, following a series of meetings in London and Paris in September and October of 1954, a satisfactory compromise solution among all the Western allies was reached. The plans for a European Defence Community were shelved but the now clearly rehabilitated Federal German Republic would be allowed to join NATO in 1955, the size of its military contribution to be determined by the newly constituted Western European Union. However, the crucial development in the last months of 1954 was that the Americans, having secured the principle of German rearmament within a political framework that was acceptable to the Europeans, were now genuinely committed to making a permanent and substantial military contribution to the defence of Western Europe: henceforward over 300,000 troops would be permanently stationed in Europe. With the constant fear of the continuing Soviet threat, this was precisely what British policy in both the European and Atlantic 'circles' had been aiming for since 1946. To be sure, there had been a convergence of British and American security interests in Europe, with their common interest in opposing the Westward expansion of the Soviet Empire, since the time of the American loan. But the course of true *realpolitik* interest convergence never runs smooth: it had taken almost a decade of manoeuvring on both sides of the Atlantic to achieve a mutually acceptable compromise on the practical form that the Western alliance should take.

Yet, even though a lasting compromise had now been achieved, there was still a sting in the tail. Just as Bevin had been obliged to strive for European agreement on the Brussels Pact in 1948 (and to initiate a costly rearmament programme in 1950–51) in order to convince Washington of Britain's commitment to European defence, so Eden had to pay a heavy price for America's renewed commitment to NATO in 1954–55.

Over 50,000 combat personnel – four divisions of the British Army of the Rhine and the 2nd Tactical Air Force – were to be assigned to the defence of continental Europe for the indefinite future. The open-ended commitment thus engendered was to contribute significantly to the military overextension that was to plague successive British governments for the next 25 years.

What has been repeatedly suggested in this section, then, is that the basis of Anglo-American collaboration in post-war Europe was the joint perception that both countries were confronted by a common Soviet threat: the long-run interests of both Britain and the United States would have been seriously damaged if Western Europe had succumbed to Soviet domination, leaving almost the entire Eurasian landmass under Stalin's control. It has also been suggested that the fundamental character of the NATO alliance was stabilised only after several years of tortuous negotiation. While the British believed an effective European defence was impossible without the participation of the United States, the Americans were not prepared to make a *permanent* commitment unless the Europeans would shoulder a larger share of the defence burden. The delay in resolving these differences was not the result of the policymakers failing to appreciate the urgency of the situation: achieving the right compromise in an extremely complicated situation simply took a long time.

Anglo-American Cooperation Outside Europe, 1946–55

Outside Europe, collaboration between Britain and the United States was based on the community of interest that the two countries shared in insulating pro-Western regimes throughout the third world from communist infiltration.[28] In the decade after 1946, this shared interest was of particular importance in the Middle East and in Korea.

The *Middle East* was of interest to Britain and the United States in the post-war period for three main reasons. First, as noted above, according to the 'bipolar' Realist model which Western policymakers were increasingly employing in their dealings with Stalin in Europe, any territories which 'defected' from the Western sphere of influence constituted an automatic gain for the 'other side'. There was therefore a continuing incentive to ensure that as few territories as possible were left 'unguarded', so as to avoid leaving a vacuum that the Soviets might fill.

A second reason underlying British and American interest in the Middle East derived from the strategic contingency plans that the Chiefs of Staff in Washington and London were obliged to make during the post-war period. Whatever assumptions were made about the likely extent of a Soviet advance in Europe – whether it was assumed that the Red Army could be held at the Elbe, the Rhine,[29] the English

Channel or the Atlantic – the network of British bases stretching across the Mediterranean and North Africa into Egypt, Sudan, Iraq and the Gulf took on considerable strategic significance. All of the bases were potential springboards for future counter-offensives in Southern Europe and those bases East of Cairo could in principle be employed as sanctuaries for long-range strategic bombers capable of launching air attacks (nuclear or otherwise) on Soviet cities. It was of course hoped that such contingency plans would never need to be put into effect, but at the same time conditions in Europe were sufficiently tense to underscore the enormous potential importance of these strategic assets.

A third reason for Anglo-American interest in the Middle East, inevitably, was oil. If it was important to prevent the Soviets from encroaching into any of the territory currently within the Western sphere of influence for fear of the additional resources which the Soviets might accordingly control, it was doubly important that a region rich in such a vital strategic resource as oil should not fall prey to Soviet machinations. Anglo-American collaboration in oil policy had in fact begun in the 1930s when Iran and Iraq had been tacitly acknowledged as the preserve of the British, and Bahrain and Saudi Arabia the preserve of the United States; Kuwait had enjoyed the privilege of being plundered by them both.[30] In the immediate post-war era there was no pressing need to alter these rather comfortable arrangements: the question of whether it was British or American companies that held the oil concessions was less important than the fact that the oil states were solidly entrenched in the Western sphere of influence.

All this said, the actual collaboration between London and Washington in terms of concrete policy was rather limited, notwithstanding Marshall's announcement in December 1947 that the two countries would henceforward be pursuing 'parallel policies' in the Middle East.[31] Although the Americans did provide considerable assistance in restoring the Shah of Iran to power in August 1953, which resulted in the British-owned Anglo-Iranian Oil Company (later British Petroleum or BP) receiving some compensation for the assets that had been nationalised in May 1951, this barely merited the description 'Anglo-American collaboration'.[32] Indeed, the most tangible aspect of Anglo-American co-operation that occurred in the Middle East in the decade after 1945 was the encouragement that the Americans gave to British efforts to maintain their network of bases throughout the region.[33] Defence planning in both countries from 1947 onwards was predicated on the assumption that, in the event of war with the Soviet Union, American forces would have free access to Britain's Middle East bases as and when they needed it. As things turned out, of course, the bases were never actually required: war in Europe never materialised and by the late 1950s rocket technology and doctrines of mutual assured destruction had substantially reduced the military potential of the bases anyway. However, their availability was an important ingredient in the increasing closeness of relations between London and Washington in the late 1940s: for the Americans, Britain's possession of the bases made it an ally worth having in the Middle East; for Britain, American support for at least a part of its global role was a welcome symbolic acknowledgement of Britain's continued status as a Great Power. The United States, of course, did not provide any specific financial assistance to Britain in order to support the upkeep of the bases. Nonetheless the American loan and then Marshall Aid did provide a general subsidy to the British economy which enabled the government to continue to service its overextended global military commitments without having to make hard choices (yet) about where those commitments should be reduced. As a result, in spite of the withdrawal from Palestine in May 1948 and the downgrading of the British presence in Egypt after the Arab nationalist coup in 1952 (both of which are discussed in Chapter 3), Britain maintained a significant military capability in the Middle East throughout the Cold War.

The main arena for Anglo-American collaboration outside Europe, however, was in Korea where Western involvement was predicated mainly on the *realpolitik* need to avoid 'losing' territory to the communist 'enemy'. The Korean peninsula itself had been dominated by the Japanese since its military victories over China (in 1896) and Russia (in 1904–5). The Japanese had then used the area as a base for further expansion into Manchuria and beyond in the 1930s and 1940s. After the Japanese defeat Korea had been subjected to de facto partition along the line of the 38th Parallel, the point where the advancing Soviet and American liberation forces had met (and briefly negotiated) in 1945. Predictably, in the years after 1945, there were significant local tensions between the communist North and the American-backed South, with each side seeking to achieve reunification on its own preferred terms. In January 1950, however, notwithstanding the State Department's avowed global strategy of containing communist expansionism, Truman and Secretary of State Acheson both made speeches indicating that South Korea, unlike Japan and the Philippines, was *not* included in what was described as the United States' 'defence perimeter'. It seems clear that it was this statement, together with assurances of support from Moscow, that provided the trigger to the North Korean invasion of the South in June 1950. The South Korean government immediately appealed for assistance to the UN Security Council where, with the Americans having second thoughts about the 'real' extent of their 'defence perimeter', their request met with a favourable response. By accident or design the Soviet delegation was at that time boycotting the Council[34] and as a result the American forces which supported the South Koreans from July 1950 onwards did so under the auspices of the United Nations. By January 1951, in support of the American effort, Britain had despatched a 10,000-strong Commonwealth Brigade – which constituted the largest non-American contingent in the UN force – together with a sizeable naval task force that was to be stationed in Korean waters.

But why was Britain involved in this relatively obscure part of the Far East when there were so many prior and pressing commitments elsewhere? The immediate justification at the time was that the action was necessary to uphold the UN Charter, though it now seems fairly clear that this claim was no more than moralistic window-dressing. A second explanation advanced (later) by a junior foreign minister in Attlee's government was that British support for the US action had been an 'instinctive reflex': not to have provided assistance to Britain's closest ally would have been, quite simply, unthinkable.[35] While there may be an element of truth in this explanation, it seems likely that British involvement was based on a rather more calculated assessment of the risks and benefits involved. Of particular importance in this context was the belief that, if Britain wanted continued American support in Europe in the future, then it would have to provide a clear demonstration now of its moral and material commitment to the 'defence of the free world'. As the Cabinet was told in November 1950,

> If we were to withdraw our support for US strategy in the Far East, the US government would be less willing to continue their policy of supporting the defence of Western Europe: and without their full assistance in Europe, we have little chance of withstanding a Russian aggression there.[36]

There was also a significant element of hard calculation in the government's assumption that, by joining the United States in its Korean campaign, Britain would be better able to restrain the Americans from taking a course of military action that might lead to an escalation of the conflict. Bevin and Attlee did not want to see either the Chinese or the Russians drawn into the war since it might then prove extremely difficult to prevent the conflict from spreading to Hong Kong or Malaya or even to Europe.

Perhaps the most important of all the factors underlying British involvement in Korea, however, was the fundamentally 'Realist' set of assumptions adopted by the leading members of the British Cabinet in their analysis of the developing situation. Although more recent historical research has tended to emphasise the local tensions between the two Koreas as the primary source of the conflict,[37] it was widely believed at the time that the Soviets were not only supplying the North Korean war effort, but had *instigated* it as well. In July 1950, Secretary of State Acheson informed Foreign Secretary Bevin in no uncertain terms that 'the aggression was *ordered* by the Kremlin and is being actively directed by key Sov[iet] personnel [emphasis added]'.[38] Whether or not the information was correct, it was in general believed.[39] Certainly Attlee and Dalton believed it, and inside the Cabinet their views carried considerable weight. The invasion of South Korea was seen as a Soviet-inspired act of aggression not dissimilar in its fundamentals to Hitler's expansionist strategies of the 1930s. It was 'America's Rhineland' and accordingly the failures of appeasement must not be repeated.[40] The least that Britain could do was to assist its ally in its attempt to resist aggression and thereby prevent further communist encroachment: if action was not taken in Korea now, then Indochina, Hong Kong and Malaya would soon be the next targets on the communists' list.[41] In these apparently threatening circumstances, and with the need to provide the Americans with a public show of support, it was perhaps not surprising that the Attlee government should find itself embroiled in a war in a far-off country with which Britain had no historical ties.

In October 1950, however, the position worsened considerably. A UN General Assembly resolution sympathetic to the reunification of Korea was used by General MacArthur, the Commander-in-Chief of the UN forces, as a pretext to invade North Korea.[42] The Chinese in turn used the incursion into North Korea as a pretext to launch their own intervention, in November 1950, against the UN force. They made rapid progress and by the end of the month were threatening to overrun South Korea itself. Amid rumours that the Americans were considering using nuclear weapons against the Chinese or the North Koreans, or both, Attlee hastened to Washington in early December with the express purpose of persuading Truman of the immense folly of such a course of action: it would not only be immoral but would also encourage an escalation of the conflict well beyond the confines of the Korean peninsula. It is possible, of course, that Truman had no intention of crossing the nuclear threshold, but in any event Attlee emerged from their discussions satisfied that the Americans would not use atomic weapons without first consulting Britain.[43]

Attlee's success in Washington did little to calm the Cabinet's fears of imminent war with the Soviet Union. Even though Bevin had been able to inform the Cabinet in September 1950 of his belief that 'the Soviet Union wishes to avoid provoking a major war', by December 1950 the Chiefs of Staff Committee was reporting to Cabinet that 'preparation for war should be based on the formula, "war probable in 1952; possible in 1951"'.[44] While these estimates, which were also typical of those being supplied to Britain by the United States,[45] were clearly a reflection of Soviet *capabilities* rather than an estimate of Soviet *intent*, they were nonetheless extremely alarming. They certainly served to reinforce the pervasive sense that Britain's vital interests were seriously threatened by the Soviet Union and in so doing made any chance of a thawing of the Cold War for the foreseeable future seem increasingly remote. It is not clear whether Stalin was deterred from extending the Korean conflict by the massive British and American rearmament programmes that began in 1951 or whether he had no serious intention of risking war in the first place. In any event, notwithstanding the dire warnings of the strategists, a major global war was avoided: the Soviets continued to supply the Korean war effort but never gave the slightest indication that they were prepared to become directly involved in the fighting themselves. In Korea itself, by March 1951, with MacArthur removed from his command, the military position had stabilised at the 38th Parallel, the original line of partition. Two years of military stalemate ensued and an armistice signed at Panmunjon finally brought a formal end to hostilities in July 1953.

As far as Britain was concerned, however, the legacy of Korea was to endure well after Panmunjon. The distorting effects on the domestic economy of the 1951–54 rearmament programme were considerable. And the deep suspicion of China and the Soviet Union – of communism generally – had been strongly reinforced. But perhaps the most important consequence of the Korean episode stemmed from the very obvious fact that the UN forces had successfully achieved their primary objective of containment. In the final analysis the 38th Parallel had been maintained. Whereas Britain and France had failed to act in Manchuria in 1931 and in the Rhineland in 1936, in Korea the United States and Britain had actively opposed aggression and, in the end, opposed it successfully. To be sure, the costs in terms of lives and materials had been considerable, but this did not vitiate the fact that the seductive appeal of appeasement had been successfully resisted and a cynical aggressor forced to withdraw. Indeed, London and Washington were so convinced of their own joint determination to continue to resist communist aggression in the Far East that they speedily assembled SEATO (in September 1954), a defensive alliance of capitalist powers in South-East Asia, the security of which would be jointly guaranteed by Britain and the United States. The crucial point, however, was that without doubt an important lesson had been learned: aggressive expansionism *could* be profitably resisted if appeasement was avoided and a determined political and military stand taken. Unfortunately, within three years, this entirely valid principle was to be horribly misapplied in Egypt. That way lay Suez.

Summary and Conclusions

Underlying all of Britain's dealings with the European and Atlantic 'circles' in the decade after 1945 was a continuing perception that Western interests were seriously threatened by an aggressive and potentially expansionist Soviet Union. As a direct response to this perceived threat Britain sought both to strengthen its political and military ties with Western Europe and to convince the United States that it should join the Europeans and underwrite their collective defence. By 1947, when the Cold War began in earnest, the Americans were fairly receptive to London's overtures. They could see that, if the Soviets were allowed to dominate Western Europe, the resources of the industrial economies therein would not only be denied to North American capitalism but would instead be at the disposal of Moscow's strategic planners. At the same time, however, the Americans also remained convinced that the Europeans themselves were sufficiently well equipped to mount their own response to the Soviet threat. A combination of Soviet diplomatic intransigence, Stalin's strategy of 'consolidation' in Eastern Europe and Bevin's diplomacy transformed the American position. By 1949, Washington was ready to join the Atlantic Pact and to make Strategic Air Command formally available as a deterrent to Soviet aggression in Western Europe. Yet even though American involvement in European security now had an air of permanency about it, Washington's long-term commitment to NATO was still extremely tenuous. In consequence the British government not only had to make the correct noises and gestures to assuage American reservations about unnecessary European entanglements, but it also had to take appropriate *action* as and when required to persuade Washington to maintain its European presence. Britain's involvement in the Korean war, its financially crippling rearmament programme between 1951 and 1954, and its decision to station 55,000 troops permanently in Germany in 1954 were all essential demonstrations of Britain's commitment to the defence of the West. Without them, the Americans might simply have left Western Europe to fend for itself. And, in the view of successive British governments, the Europeans, Britain included, would not have been equal to the task.

The extra commitments thus engendered, however, were additions to an already overstretched British defence capability. The problem for the government was that no compensating reductions could be made to existing commitments: the security of what was left of the Empire still had to be maintained; and the global aspects of the renewed 'special relationship' required the preservation of the bases in the Mediterranean and the Middle East. The result was that Britain's foreign policy strategy in the period after the war remained fundamentally overextended.

The overextension, moreover, was likely to continue for the foreseeable future. The main reason for this was that the foreign policy makers themselves remained convinced that Britain was still a Great Power of the first rank with global responsibilities. The Soviet threat had to be met and if the United States was not yet prepared to meet it alone – and no other country in the period after the war possessed the capability even to consider it – then Britain would have to shoulder a significant share of the burden. In these circumstances existing commitments could not be cut or new commitments refused unless there was either a significant reduction in the perceived magnitude of the Soviet threat or a radical revision in Britain's perception and definition of her role in world affairs. The problem was that, while Soviet antagonism towards the West remained unabated, Britain had not yet suffered the sort of external trauma (such as a defeat in war) usually associated with a fundamental role reappraisal. Throughout the late 1940s and early 1950s, therefore, the intense fear of the Soviet Union, the belief in Britain's Great Power status and the overextended strategy were all sustained, draining ever greater resources from the fragile British economy. Perhaps fortuitously, both a softening in the Soviet attitude and the requisite external trauma – Suez – were close at hand.

However, the concern with the Soviet threat and the consequent need to re-establish the 'special relationship' in the decade after 1945 had serious consequences for Britain's relations with Western Europe. Following the framework outlined in the Schuman Plan of 1950, European economic 'reconstruction' became increasingly based on the principle of economic integration. The European Coal and Steel Community was created in 1952 and by 1957 the 'functional cooperation' that it inspired had led to the creation of the European Economic Community. In the early 1950s, the Americans encouraged Britain to consider leading West European efforts at integration. The British, however, demurred: they were not yet ready to cede sovereignty to a supranational institution such as the ECSC and they feared that participation in Europe would damage relations with the Empire and Commonwealth. With hindsight, it was relatively easy to see that, with its diminished capabilities after 1945, Britain's best long-term interests lay primarily in the European 'circle'. As Nicholas Henderson observed: 'We had every Western European Government eating out of our hand in the immediate aftermath of the war. For several years our prestige and influence were paramount ... we could have stamped Europe as we wished.'[46] What was evident to later observers, however, was not so obvious to contemporary policymakers who had to make decisions amid genuinely felt fears of the ubiquitous Soviet threat. Britain flirted with Europe economically and politically, but concentrated most of its European efforts in the *military* sphere: in the Brussels Pact and NATO, where the European and Atlantic 'circles' overlapped. This of course was the very aspect of the European circle which not only incurred the most clear-cut cost but which also produced the least tangible gain. Though the security which NATO provided was obviously crucial to *survival* (the 'gain'), the *effort* which went into sustaining it (the 'cost') did nothing to reverse Britain's fundamental long-run problem: the decline of its economic base. In any event, the opportunity to lead Western Europe economically and politically had been missed. And when Britain was finally allowed to join the European club in the 1970s it was very much on the terms laid down by the existing members. In the meantime, however, there was still the Empire.

Chapter 3

The Road to Suez: British Imperialism, 1945–56

Throughout the 19th century, Britain's dominance as an imperial power extended well beyond those territories that were administered from the Colonial Office and the India Office. In addition to the *formal* Empire of the colonies and dominions, London also exercised considerable economic and political influence in China, Latin America and the Middle East. By 1914 Britain's position in China and Latin America had been undermined by commercial and naval competition from Germany, Japan and the United States. However, the consolidation of Britain's *informal* empire in the Middle East progressed steadily as the government took effective control of Egypt in the early 1880s and then acquired possession of the 'mandates' over Iraq and Palestine in 1920.

This chapter reviews the major developments in both the formal and the informal empire between the end of World War II and the Suez debacle of 1956. The story of the period, somewhat paradoxically, is simultaneously one both of 'withdrawal' and of 'retrenchment'. The first section examines the build-up of forces that led to the rapid withdrawal of British authority in India and Palestine in the late 1940s. It is argued that these withdrawals derived principally from indigenous pressures for autonomy that in the years immediately after 1945 grew irresistibly. The second section, in contrast, briefly describes Britain's strategy in Malaya, in the Caribbean and in Africa where the government's main concern after the war – partly as a result of what had happened in India – was a retrenchment aimed at preventing any further erosion of the British sphere of influence. It is argued that this retrenchment is best explained by classic *realpolitik* security calculations: the counterinsurgency operation in Malaya after 1948 was largely a response to the global Cold War tensions of the period; British policy in Africa and in the Caribbean reflected the belief of successive governments that Britain could ill afford to make further major concessions to nationalist movements which, if they proved successful, might conceivably look to Moscow rather than London or Washington for moral inspiration and material support. Finally, consideration is given to the Suez affair, in which an unsuccessful attempt at Imperial retrenchment was followed by an enforced and embarrassing withdrawal necessitated mainly by the external pressure exerted by the United States.

India and Palestine apart, Britain in the late 1940s and early 1950s still possessed sufficient military capability to resist nationalist pressure throughout the Empire and Britain was accordingly able to maintain much of the imperial status quo. After Suez, though not necessarily because of it, the balance between British capability and nationalist pressure was to be quickly reversed and, in consequence, as we will see in later chapters, substantial changes to the status quo were to be rapidly introduced.

Withdrawal: India and Palestine

India

Nationalist resistance to imperial domination had always been a force in India since the early days of British involvement. The Indian Mutiny of 1857, though triggered by religious rivalries and differences, was fundamentally a nationalist rebellion which expressed the resistance of the indigenous population to the legal and social changes that the Raj had introduced. The suppression of the Mutiny did not mean the end of Indian nationalism. Though not supported by the traditional Indian elites, anti-British nationalist sentiment continued to make gradual progress throughout the late 19th century inside both the Muslim and Hindu communities, punctuated by periodic civil disturbances which served to remind the British that eventually some sort of concession to nationalist demands for autonomy would have to be made. The first clear sign of compromise came with the Montagu Declaration of December 1917, in which Lloyd George's government announced its intention to introduce 'self-governing institutions with a view to the progressive realisation of responsible government in India'.[1]

The 'Montagu-Chelmsford reforms' embodied in the 1919 India Act which followed held out the promise of a future 'dyarchy' in which the British would retain responsibility for the internal and external security of India while the Indians themselves would progressively obtain control of all other areas of policy.[2] The promise failed to materialise, however, and in 1927 the Simon Commission was despatched to India to consult with the All-India Congress and other interested parties in order to assess the possibilities for future constitutional reform. The eventual result of Simon's investigations, after much heart searching and discord within the ruling Conservative Party,[3] was the 1935 India Act. Under the provisions of the Act, while the Indian provincial governments were to achieve fuller self-government, the dyarchy principle at federal level was to be retained: in federal matters the Viceroy would still maintain control of the key areas of internal and external security. The 1935 Act, however, like its counterpart in 1919, failed to have any real practical effect. Indian nationalists of varying religious and ideological persuasions soon came to recognise the Act for what it was: a continuation of the British policy of side-tracking demands for independence, a device for diverting nationalist pressure and sentiment away from the issue of fundamental reform. Indeed, if anything, the Act had the opposite effect of that which had been intended: instead of acting as a kind of safety-valve by siphoning off dissent, it merely served to convince nationalist leaders that the proposed concessions were a sign of British weakness. Moreover, such displays of weakness merely invited further demands.

The progress of Indian nationalism was interrupted, albeit briefly, by World War II. Some nationalists, inevitably, regarded the war as just the opportunity they had been waiting for: the anti-colonial forces should strike against British rule while the imperialists' attention was focused on their own survival. Gentler counsels prevailed, however. Notwithstanding the occasional riot and Gandhi's civil disobedience campaign of 1940–41 there was relatively little serious open resistance to the Raj during the war years. This absence of outright nationalist opposition was partly a reflection of the recognition that the Japanese – poised to attack India from their bases in Burma – were even more undesirable as potential colonial masters than the awful British. It was also partly a consequence of the widespread confidence that internal pressures for change would be so great once the war was over that the British would in any case be obliged to introduce fundamental constitutional reform. Indeed, nationalist leaders were so confident of major concessions to come that they rejected the Cripps plan of March 1942, which would have instituted post-war reforms that went well beyond anything envisaged in the Acts of either 1919 or 1935.

In any event, after 1945, it rapidly became clear that the rule of the Raj was drawing to a close. The British were obviously incapable of resolving either of the two major (and interrelated) problems that confronted the Indian subcontinent: the growing civil unrest which produced intercommunal violence of increasing ferocity, and the refusal of the Moslem League to accept the Hindu-dominated All-India Congress Party's plans for a united post-imperial India.[4] A significant turning-point was the Great Calcutta Killing of August 1946, in which a Moslem massacre of Hindus produced a Hindu retaliation of unprecedented proportions.[5] Amid the repeated and escalating counter-retaliations which followed, the three-million British and Indian troops of the Raj were simply unable to maintain anything approaching law and order. Aware of the danger that the resultant anarchy might provide fertile ground for ideological zealots even more unattractive than the Moslem and Hindu fanatics who were actively fomenting the present intercommunal strife, the Attlee government decided to adopt a high-risk strategy. In February 1947 – before any agreement between the rival Islamic and Hindu factions in the nationalist struggle had been reached – it was announced that June 1948 had been set as the date for Indian independence. The effect of the announcement was salutary. Having observed the scale of the slaughter on both sides of the religious divide which had occurred since August 1946, the Congress leaders realised that their attempts to pacify the secessionist demands of the Moslem League would in all probability be no more successful than those of the British. As a result, Congress elected to compromise and to accept the principle of partition. Yet it was not until June 1947, when Mountbatten announced that the date for independence would be brought forward to August 1947, that agreement was reached on the precise form that partition would take. On 15 August India and a geographically divided Pakistan became independent nation-states, their newfound independence being accompanied by mass migrations of Moslems to Pakistan and Hindus to India. Over 500,000 people were killed in the continuing intercommunal strife which the migration provoked and as a result the British were roundly condemned for adding to the slaughter by their precipitate withdrawal. However, given Britain's proven inability to maintain civil order after August 1946, it seems probable that further delay would only have made matters worse.[6] To its credit, the British government had granted independence to two states which were subsequently to achieve a degree of domestic stability. The added bonus as far as Britain was concerned was that both India and Pakistan (and Ceylon, which achieved its own independence in February 1948) decided to remain with the Commonwealth, thus maintaining many of the economic and diplomatic ties which were of potential benefit both to the former colonies and to the ex-imperial power.

Crucially, the Attlee government had firmly eschewed the interwar strategy of seeking to delay – or even to avoid – decolonisation by promising constitutional reforms which in the event failed to materialise. It had recognised that the Raj could not be preserved in the face of continued and growing nationalist-inspired civil disorder. In these circumstances it had been far better to cut and run, leaving a relatively well-disposed Congress in control, than to attempt to maintain British hegemony and to risk fuelling further dissent: this might conceivably have produced an anarchic power vacuum and thereby have provided an opening for Britain's Cold War enemies. Given how awful things could have been, Indian decolonisation had been a remarkable success.

Palestine

Throughout the Middle East, as in India, there had long been indigenous pressures for greater local autonomy. Indeed, as the dominant European power in the region since the late 19th century, Britain had not been averse to encouraging nationalist sentiment in certain contexts, particularly if temporary support in the prosecution of some greater struggle could be bought by vague promises of future independence. This was precisely what had happened during World War I when London had succeeded in making mutually contradictory promises to the rival Arab and Jewish communities in Palestine. In order to encourage an Arab revolt against their then Turkish masters, the McMahon letter of June 1916 had promised that Britain would 'recognise and support the independence of the Arabs'; in order to appease Jewish opinion both at home and in Palestine, the Balfour Declaration of November 1917 had announced the British government's commitment to the principle of a national homeland for the Jewish settlers who had been arriving in Palestine since the 1880s. If Britain had had no formal responsibilities in the Middle East after World War I, these promises could have been quietly forgotten, or someone else blamed for their non-implementation. However, the acquisition of the Palestine Mandate in 1920 meant that the British government was obliged to confront the competing demands of both Arab and Jew. In fact, throughout the interwar years, notwithstanding a series of Arab riots in 1936, Britain still possessed sufficient military capability to contain the more aggressive elements within both communities.

Britain's hold on Palestine was seriously weakened, however, by developments during World War II. The Nazi holocaust in Europe not only swelled the numbers of Jewish immigrants into Palestine but also simultaneously stiffened the Zionist resolve that in future the Jewish people must be masters of their own destiny.[7] At the same time the growth in Palestinian Arab nationalist consciousness – itself partly the result of the accelerated influx of Jewish settlers after 1930 – increased Arab demands for complete autonomy from British rule. In the immediate post-war period these different demands found expression in escalating intercommunal violence and in increasingly ferocious attacks on the beleaguered British garrison forces. In these circumstances, the Attlee government was confronted with an unenviable choice. On the one hand, withdrawal was not an attractive option. Not only was Palestine important in its own right if Britain was to retain its dominant position in the Middle East, but the base facilities which Palestine provided could also be offered to Washington's strategic planners as part of the price for the continuation of an American military presence in Europe. In these circumstances, a complete British withdrawal from Palestine – since the bases would presumably then be unavailable to both London and Washington – might prejudice Bevin's entire Atlantic/European strategy. On the other hand, if withdrawal was undesirable for reasons of strategic *realpolitik,* the internal security situation had deteriorated so badly by the beginning of 1946 that there was also no point in trying to sustain the status quo. The 'natural' solution which presented itself in this difficult situation was to instigate some form of *partition* – if Arabs and Jews could not live together in the same state, then the problem could be resolved by creating two separate states – in the hope that close relations with at least a part of the divided territory might be restored at a later date. Unfortunately, in 1945 and 1946, the fear that partition in Palestine would reinforce demands for partition in India (where London's policy was still predicated on the paramount importance of post-colonial unity) meant that even this sort of compromise solution had to be rejected.[8]

What freed the British government from its state of near-impotent immobility was the growing conviction during the course of 1947 that, with Palestine ungovernable, the British military bases there were in any case an unusable resource. Moreover, once the decision to abandon India to partition had been taken in June 1947, there was clearly no longer any need to deny the possibility of partition in Palestine merely to prevent the contagion spreading to the Raj. With a specially constituted UN Commission backing the principle of partition, Britain announced in December 1947 that it would withdraw the mandate on 15 May 1948: Palestine east of the River Jordan – the mandated territory of Transjordan – would achieve independence as the Hashemite Kingdom of Jordan; the fate of Palestine west of the river would be determined by negotiation between the rival indigenous and settler communities. The British tactic of announcing a date for withdrawal had produced a negotiated compromise (albeit a bloody one) in India: why not reproduce the experience in the Middle East?

Unfortunately what had worked – just about – for India was not appropriate for Palestine. Between December 1947 and May 1948 no serious negotiation between the Arab and Jewish communities took place. On the contrary, intercommunal violence increased as militias on both sides of the religious divide prepared for armed confrontation once British troops had departed. Outrages were undoubtedly committed by both sides but, following the Deir Yassin massacre in April 1948, there was a mass exodus of Palestinian Arabs from the territory that David Ben Gurion proclaimed as Israel when the British did indeed withdraw in mid-May. The surrounding Arab states immediately initiated the first Arab–Israeli war, seeking to destroy the infant Zionist state at birth. Their efforts proved unsuccessful, however. Israel tenaciously held on to (what were at that stage) its preferred borders and the Palestinian Arabs merely retained the so-called 'West bank' territory, which was formally incorporated into Jordan in May 1948, being subsequently seized by Israel in 1967. Not surprisingly, the Arabs felt that their interests had been betrayed by Britain: through their rapid withdrawal the British had tacitly offered their approval to the emergent Zionist state at the direct expense of the indigenous Palestinian Arabs. This had certainly not been London's intention but that was the way things were viewed in Cairo, Damascus and Amman: Anglo-Arab relations were set to be discordant for several years to come.

What, then, can be deduced from the withdrawals in India and in Palestine? How can they best be explained? What implications did they have for Britain's subsequent external policy? Consider, first, the main alternative *explanations* for the withdrawals. In the context of India and Palestine, there was very little justification for arguing – as British politicians were inclined to do when discussing the 'second-wave' decolonisations in the late 1950s – that independence had been granted because the colonial peoples, after years of British tutelage, were now 'ready' for self-determination. Such a thesis was immediately disproved by the horrible massacres that were occurring on all sides in both territories. There was also no real basis for arguing that beneath the indigenous challenge to imperial rule in India and Palestine lurked the insidious machinations of some Soviet-inspired communist conspiracy. The fact that neither Moscow's diplomacy nor Marxist ideology made any significant progress in either India or Israel (where the *Kibbutzim* movement certainly had socialist aspirations) in the years after the British withdrawal suggested that such 'external subterfuge' arguments were largely irrelevant.

As has been repeatedly intimated, it seems much more likely that the root cause of the British withdrawals of the late 1940s was the increasing strength of indigenous nationalism in India and Palestine and the concomitant inability of the British-sponsored security forces to maintain internal order. Without doubt, the British government would have preferred to maintain a presence in both countries if it had been at all possible: in Palestine, because long-range aircraft based there could reach targets in the Soviet Union, and in India, because of the lingering suspicion that Lord Curzon's gloomy prediction might actually prove correct – that without India Britain would 'drop away as a third rate Power. The rest would become the tollgates and barbicans of an Empire that has vanished.'[9] In both India and Palestine, however, the meagre British forces were unable to cope with either the generalised mass rejection of British rule or the blind fratricidal hatred of rival religious groups. The combination of both proved irresistible. Even the *timing* of the withdrawals was conditioned largely by the pattern of events inside the colonial territories: in each case, to have delayed further would have been pointless. Withdrawal was a recognition of the new facts of colonial life: it simply brought the *de jure* position into line with *de facto* conditions on the ground.

The major *implications* of the two withdrawals were also relatively clear-cut. Their most immediate and unambiguous consequence was the decline in Anglo-Arab relations that resulted from the manner of the British withdrawal from Palestine. The rapidity of the evacuation and the failure to achieve a prior negotiated settlement were widely perceived in the Arab world as evidence both of London's pro-Zionist sympathies and its determination to do nothing to protect the interests of the indigenous Arab inhabitants of what had become Israel. Far more important than Arab resentment, however, was the additional impetus to *further* withdrawal which the two decolonisations had provided. Further withdrawal was in principle now more likely, for two reasons. First, Indian decolonisation had again raised the possibility that the loss of India would significantly impair the strategic coherence of the Empire. The British bases both in the Middle East and in Singapore, for example, had been acquired primarily as vehicles for protecting the routes to India and the removal of India from the system of imperial defence undoubtedly diminished their immediate strategic relevance: why not execute further withdrawals, therefore, and ease the financial crisis at home? A second reason for supposing that further withdrawal would be more likely in the future was that developments in India and Palestine had clearly increased the danger of an imitative increase in nationalist consciousness elsewhere in the Empire. Unchecked, the contamination would undoubtedly spread and could only serve to increase the pressures for greater local indigenous autonomy in the future. However, in spite of these increased pressures for further withdrawal, successive governments – ever convinced of Britain's Great Power status – stood firm. The deepening Cold War of the late 1940s made it imperative that Britain should follow the *realpolitik* principle of ensuring that potentially useful strategic sites remain within the Western sphere of influence. In consequence, the process of withdrawal was suspended and a new policy of retrenchment adopted. For the next decade or so nationalist demands of independence would in general be contained wherever possible: only when the indigenous pressure proved irresistible would real concessions to local democracy actually be made.

Retrenchment: Malaya, the Caribbean and Africa

From mid-1948 onwards the British government was determined both to prevent a repetition of the violence that had occurred in India and Palestine and especially to avoid making further major concessions to demands for self-determination. This desire to retain as much as possible of the old imperial sphere of influence was in turn a response to 'natural' *realpolitik*-motivated fears that were increasingly exacerbated after 1947 by the Soviet/communist Cold War threat. Throughout the remainder of the Empire, the result was a policy of careful but consistent retrenchment: while local nationalists might be granted some concessions by way of greater participation in local decision-making, the ultimate power of decision on major issues would still lie with either the British government or its representatives.

Malaya

The Malayan peninsula and adjacent islands had been under British domination since the early 19th century. Before the Japanese occupation in 1942 Malaya had been more a 'geographical expression' than a political entity: a collection of Crown colonies (Sarawak, North Borneo and Singapore) and internally autonomous British protectorates (notably Brunei). After the Japanese surrender in September 1945, the Attlee government became increasingly concerned to consolidate the position of Malaya within the Western sphere of influence by achieving some sort of political union among the various Malay states. Unfortunately its plan for a Malay Union outlined in 1947 was rejected by most indigenous Malay groups on the grounds that it gave too much (that is, a proportionate share of) power to the large ethnic Chinese minority. The announcement in February 1948 of a modified plan for a Malay Federation – which restricted Chinese participation in the political process – merely served as the trigger to a communist-inspired insurgency among ethnic Chinese Malays that necessitated the declaration in June 1948 of a state of emergency which was to last until 1958.

Arguably Malaya was the first genuinely 'hot front' of the Cold War, if only because the insurgency posed such an obvious threat to Western (and particularly British) interests in the Far East: Malaya not only provided one-third of the world's rubber and one-half of its tin, but it also provided the Overseas Sterling Area (OSA) with over a third of its dollar earnings, without which the OSA would very probably have collapsed.[10] What made the situation even more alarming was the victory of Mao's communists in the Chinese Civil War in October 1949. Thereafter the communist insurgents in Malaya had an obvious community of interest and outlook with the regime in Beijing. The need for Britain to resist the insurgency was reinforced even further by the outbreak of the Korean War in June 1950. Indeed, with the entry of the Chinese into that conflict the following November, the whole situation in the Far East looked as though it might erupt into the sort of generalised capitalist versus communist conflagration which – whatever its consequences for Korea itself – would almost certainly overwhelm the relatively meagre British forces in Singapore and Hong Kong and threaten the whole of Asia with a communist takeover.

Notwithstanding the covert material support which the Beijing regime provided to the Malayan revolutionaries, however, the British-backed counterinsurgency campaign eventually proved successful. The estimated number of active terrorists, which in 1951 had been over 8,000, was reduced by January 1956 to 3,000.[11] Indeed the security situation was so improved by the end of 1956 that Malaya was granted independence in August 1957 and in the following year anti-terrorist operations were ceased altogether. Two principal factors had underpinned Britain's success. The first was the pursuit of a patient military strategy closely tailored to the contingent needs of the situation. While the Royal Navy had made it increasingly difficult for the insurgents' backers to provision their island-based guerrillas with supplies, the Army, in conjunction with local security forces, had succeeded in isolating the revolutionaries from their potential support base by developing a system of 'protected' settlements which the guerrillas were increasingly unable to penetrate. Turning Mao's dictum on its head, the counterinsurgency campaign had effectively prevented the revolutionary fish from swimming in the sea of the people. Sound military strategy on its own would never have been sufficient to contain the insurgency, however. The second – and critical – factor was the widespread support which the majority non-Chinese Malay population gave to the British-sponsored anti-terrorist campaign. Although the majority population wished to be free of British interference, it certainly did not want either to be ruled by ethnic Chinese communists or to see Malaya fragmented into rival communist and non-communist mini-states. In these circumstances, it was hardly surprising that the British government should have received the support of the majority community and that, partly as a result of that support, the British-led military campaign should have proved successful.

The favourable outcome of the Malayan campaign nevertheless had two disturbing implications for Britain's subsequent foreign policy. First, the achievements in Malaya seemed to provide additional confirmation that the British government's overall foreign policy strategy of maintaining Britain's position of influence in all three of Churchill's 'circles' – of maintaining the 'world role' – was being successfully prosecuted. The strategy had been devised, of course, on the assumption that, while close links with Western Europe and North America were necessary for Britain's immediate defence, it was also essential to nurture the forces of anti-communism in the Empire if the long-term economic and political interests of the West were to be protected. The tactical success in Malaya served to dispel the suspicions – which had been increasingly voiced after the rearmament programme of 1951 – that the three-circle strategy itself might be damagingly overextended: in doing so, it indirectly contributed to the continued pursuit of the strategy at a time when it was becoming increasingly apparent that Britain no longer possessed the economic capability to sustain it.

A second and even more troublesome implication of the Malayan campaign was its reinforcement of the belief that the communist threat to Western strategic interests in the third world could be productively resisted by military means. If Korea had shown that *external attack* could be successfully opposed by a determined strategy of Western confrontation, Malaya demonstrated that the same principle applied with regard to communist-inspired *internal subversion*. As a result, in the period before Suez, the Malayan campaign – like Korea before it – served to strengthen the commitment of Britain's key foreign policy makers to Realism. Since Western interests throughout the world were increasingly open to challenge by the agents of communism, appeasement should at all costs be avoided. A decisive and determined stand must be taken against any attempt to subvert the international status quo. Suez beckoned.

The Caribbean and Africa

In the immediate wake of the withdrawals from India and Palestine, indigenous demands for change in Africa and the Caribbean were neither sufficiently focused nor so intense as to oblige the British government seriously to contemplate similar acts of decolonisation elsewhere. To be sure, during the course of 1948 there were riots in both the West Indies and West Africa which, though partly the result of purely local grievances, were also a potentially ominous manifestation of the sort of imitative 'contagion' effect that the imperialists feared.[12] The disturbances were not particularly well organised, however, and in the event were quickly and relatively easily suppressed. The longer-term task that confronted the Foreign and Colonial Offices was how to prevent the situation in the remaining parts of the Empire from degenerating into the sort of ungovernable chaos which had characterised India and Palestine in the run-up to independence.

The specific tactics that London subsequently pursued in Africa and in the Caribbean obviously varied from country to country. Nonetheless, in a wide range of contexts, the same basic principles seem to have been followed: (1) retain British authority for as long as possible and in as many policy areas as possible; and (2) keep internal dissent to a minimum by increasing indigenous participation in the local legislature and – if absolutely necessary – in the local executive. As in the Indian case, the motivation underlying these principles could be interpreted in two rather different ways. On the one hand, Britain could be portrayed as a benign liberal power that was gradually preparing its subject populations for self-rule: colonial peoples needed a gradual introduction to the ways of responsible government and administration; independence would come only when indigenous populations were ready for it. On the other hand, Britain could also be characterised as a self-interested Realist power which in the face of growing indigenous nationalism sought to postpone independence by making constitutional concessions which would divert dissent into politically acceptable, institutionalised channels: relatively minor concessions made at the appropriate time would enable Britain to retain control of the major levers of power. Inevitably, it is extremely difficult to establish which of these characterisations is correct. Indeed, there is probably an element of truth in both of them. Nonetheless, the fact that Britain did so little in real terms to prepare its black subject populations for power – apart from the self-educative benefits of imprisonment which it bestowed on most of their more prominent leaders – suggests that the *realpolitik* characterisation was perhaps the more accurate of the two.

It is clearly not possible here to provide a detailed description of the constitutional developments that occurred in each of Britain's colonial territories in the immediate post-war period. A brief summary of the main changes that were introduced is worthwhile, however, since it shows that the policy of retrenchment – pursued after the loss of India and Palestine as a means of stemming the tide of imperial decline – was already exhibiting signs of erosion well before Suez. Of course, in some of the colonies, limited constitutional reforms had been instigated even before 1948. *Nigeria,* for example, had already been favoured with a modest increase in African representation in its national legislative council in 1946, and similar reforms were introduced in *Sierra Leone* in 1948, though in both cases the councils remained firmly under the domination of British-sponsored nominees. In the Caribbean, a similar adjustment had been effected in *British Guiana* in 1943 and new constitutions based on adult suffrage (yet which still left ultimate power in the hands of the Governors) had been introduced in *Jamaica* in 1944 and in *Trinidad* in 1946. In terms of real black participation in government, of course, all of these reforms had been largely cosmetic. Moreover, as noted above, after the withdrawal from Palestine successive governments had become even less well-disposed to the notion of radical colonial change. However, events on the ground were soon to force a series of breaches in this strategy of imperial retrenchment, although, by the introduction of various transitional arrangements, London doggedly sought to delay the full transfer of power for as long as possible.

Despite the best endeavours of successive governments, between 1948 and 1956 *Sudan* followed the model that had been established in India in the period after 1918. Although nominally an Anglo-Egyptian condominium, Sudan had been effectively controlled from Whitehall since 1899. In June 1948, however, Sudanese representation on the legislative and executive councils was increased, and in 1952 – partly as a result of Egyptian pressure aimed at securing Sudanese-Egyptian union – the powers of the councils were expanded and those of the British-appointed Governor commensurately curtailed. In August 1955, an army mutiny was followed by widespread insurrection and in the midst of the chaos (in January 1956) Ismail al-Azhiri's National Unionist Party issued a *de facto* declaration of independence which Britain was both powerless to resist and (since Nasser's designs on Sudan would thus be thwarted) willing to accept. A not-dissimilar developmental path was simultaneously being followed in *Ghana* (Gold Coast). The reforms of 1946 – which had produced a black majority in the legislative council – did nothing to prevent serious rioting from occurring throughout the colony in February and March 1948. Britain's eventual response was to hold elections in 1951 and 1954 which produced clear victories for Kwame Nkrumah's nationalist Convention People's Party. In the face of further nationalist pressure the powers of the governor were radically circumscribed during the course of 1955 as a prelude to the granting of full independence in March 1957.

In East and Central Africa, partly as a result of the existence of small but influential white settler communities, nationalist progress in the decade after 1945 was slower. In *Uganda*, where African participation in the legislative council had first been permitted in 1945, appointed colonial officials continued to dominate both the legislative and executive councils well into the 1950s. In *Tanganyika*, it was not until 1948 that four African and three Indian representatives were allowed to participate in the 24-member legislative council, though the revised 1955 constitution did accord equality of representation to the (variably sized) African, Indian and European communities. In *Kenya*, where the white settler community was more firmly entrenched and more determined to sustain its racial dominance, progress was only achieved after four years (1952–56) of Mau-Mau guerrilla insurgency; constitutional reforms introduced in 1956 mirrored the changes introduced a year earlier in Tanganyika by instituting equality of representation among the three main racial groups. Throughout East Africa, however, serious reforms favouring the interests and aspirations of the indigenous majority would have to await Macmillan's 'wind of change' in the early 1960s.

A similar delay would also prove to be in evidence in central-southern Africa where the protectorates of *Northern Rhodesia* and *Nyasaland* and the self-governing colony of *Southern Rhodesia* were joined together in August 1953 under the auspices of the British-sponsored Central African Federation. The Federation was widely seen as a vehicle for sustaining white rule and throughout its ten-year existence was subject to sporadic but increasingly violent opposition from black nationalist groups. The challenge to the existing order was insufficient, however, to require much in the way of a concessional response and it was not until 1964 that Northern Rhodesia (as Zambia) and Nyasaland (as Malawi) achieved independence under conditions of majority rule.[13]

What conclusions are suggested by these various developments in Africa and the Caribbean? What is clear is that, after India and Palestine, the fear of contagion led successive British governments to conclude that further demands for self-determination should be resisted. Not only was it unseemly for a Great Power to be seen rapidly to divest itself of long-cherished imperial possessions, but there was also the question of who else might benefit from British withdrawal: the exigencies of the Cold War dictated that Britain, as the second-ranked Western power, could not retreat from its imperial responsibilities only to allow Moscow to make easy progress in the territories thus vacated. Indeed, for the next eight years or so it seemed that the historical pattern established in India and Palestine would be repeated throughout the remainder of the Empire and possibly even over the same time-frame: indigenous nationalists would demand greater autonomy but London – using whatever means were at its disposal – would delay self-determination for as long as possible. In the hope of diverting dissent and, therefore, of delaying fundamental change, concessions would be made only when the strength of indigenous pressure was irresistible. By 1956, Sudan, no longer governable from London, had actually been granted independence, and significant (though not necessarily democratic) moves towards local self-determination had been made in Ghana, in Kenya, Uganda and Tanganyika, in the Rhodesias and Nyasaland, and in the West Indies. For the time being, however, the post-1948 policy of imperial retrenchment appeared to be working. The Empire was still largely intact and the separate decisions of India, Pakistan and Ceylon (though not Burma or Palestine) to remain within the Commonwealth boded reasonably well for the maintenance of British influence in the future. However, indigenous pressures for change were already gaining in strength and momentum throughout the Empire. And they were about to be given an important psychological boost.

Retrenchment and Withdrawal: Suez

Writing in the late 1950s, Martin Wight observed that, although Suez ranked with Ireland and the United States as one of Britain's greatest imperial failures, the episode itself had been 'of small historical effect'.[14] With hindsight, Suez does seem to have been much more of a 'turning-point' than Wight implied.[15] To be sure, Britain's position of relative power was in decline well before Suez, just as indigenous pressures for change in the Empire were already growing apace. However, the crucial significance of the Suez affair was that it provided an important external psychological shock – analogous, perhaps, to defeat in war – that enabled British foreign policy makers to undertake a fundamental reappraisal of Britain's role in the world and the changing nature of its imperial system.[16] Although some of the consequences of the reappraisal were not felt immediately, Suez was an important watershed in Britain's post-war history: the perhaps necessary prelude to the large-scale withdrawal from the Empire and the shift towards Europe which occurred after 1960.

Britain's close political and military involvement in Egypt itself had begun in 1881. What had started as a classic piece of gunboat diplomacy – a debt-collecting mission – ended with London in effective control of a semi-autonomous Egyptian government which, though notionally a part of the Ottoman Empire, in effect became a British strategic base from which the routes to India could be protected. After 1881, Egypt, and especially the Canal Zone, was very much a part of Britain's 'informal empire' and in 1914, when the Turks sided with Germany, Asquith declared it a protectorate. In 1922 Egypt was granted independence, though Britain retained both formal control of the Canal Zone and a considerable amount of informal influence over the Egyptian government. Under the terms of the Anglo-Egyptian Treaty of 1936, although Egyptian autonomy was strengthened, the British government maintained the right to garrison the canal. Together with the condominium status of the Sudan, this continued military presence represented a continuing affront to the Egyptian government's desire to exercise sovereignty over what it perceived to be all of its rightful territory.

In the years immediately after 1945, Egypt, under its conservative monarchy, was not particularly troublesome to Britain, in spite of its attack on Israel in 1948 in the cause of pro-Palestinian solidarity. The Neguib-Nasser coup of July 1952, however, drastically changed the character of the Egyptian regime, providing it with a new commitment both to land reform and to Pan-Arab nationalism.[17] Long suspected as the power behind Neguib's throne, Nasser assumed full control of the Egyptian state in December 1954. Although highly critical of Britain's historical role in Egypt, Nasser in fact showed a preparedness to negotiate which suggested that some new sort of Anglo-Egyptian accommodation could be reached. The Agreement on the Canal Zone of July 1954, however, seemed to involve the British government doing most of the accommodating. Indeed, according to one account, London's agreement to withdraw its troops from the zone within 20 months was enough of a concession to merit it being described as the 'equivalent of the [1947] transfer of power in India';[18] though as a supposedly independent sovereign nation Egypt had every right to expect that such a concession would be made.

It has been suggested that, if the 1954 Anglo-Egyptian agreement had remained the basis for subsequent Anglo-Egyptian relations, then the Suez fiasco might never have happened.[19] Unfortunately events proved otherwise. Throughout 1955 and early 1956, the Egyptian government entered into separate negotiations with Britain, the United States and the Soviet Union with a view to securing finance for a series of development projects. In early June 1956, the Suez garrison completed its withdrawal from the Canal Zone and a few days later Nasser was elected President of Egypt. Given the new President's penchant for socialist rhetoric and his continuation of the ousted Neguib's policies of land reform, Nasser's continued discussions with the Soviet Union increased concern in London and Washington that he might be about to move Egypt into the Soviet sphere of influence. In the hope of weakening the Egyptian leader's domestic position, on 19 July the Eisenhower administration withdrew its offer to provide finance for the Aswan Dam project. A week later Nasser nationalised the Anglo-French Suez Canal Company. Although on the Canal question the Egyptian government was acting well within its rights under international law, Prime Minister Eden was outraged. He regarded the nationalisation as a clear violation of the spirit of the 1954 Agreement and in response established the Egypt Committee – a six-man inner cabinet – which engaged in three months of intense analysis of the implications of Nasser's actions.

Anglo-Egyptian relations remained tense throughout the summer of 1956, despite several attempts at negotiation involving both the UN Security Council and an 18-Power Canal Users Conference in London in September. The real obstacle to an improvement in Anglo-Egyptian relations was that, while Nasser had adopted an immovable stance on the Canal, the Egypt Committee's main concern from the beginning was not to seek a further compromise but to conjure a set of circumstances in which Britain could take effective military action against the Egyptian government.

In spite of strenuous denials at the time, it is clear that Britain colluded with France and Israel in order to create politically acceptable conditions in which – it was hoped – the two European powers could intervene against Nasser.[20] The arrangements were finalised at a series of meetings in Sevres between 22 and 24 October. Israel would provoke a 'border conflict' with Egypt; Britain and France would intervene on the pretext of 'separating the combatants'; the Egyptians would be obliged to withdraw from the Canal Zone; and, it was hoped, Nasser would be toppled from power and someone more amenable installed in his place. The Israeli attack began on 29 October; the next day an Anglo-French ultimatum demanding the withdrawal of Israeli and Egyptian forces from the vicinity of the Canal was rejected by both sides; on 31 October British aircraft bombed Egyptian airfields; and on 5 November British troops were parachuted into the Canal Zone itself.

Unfortunately for the British government, world opinion was not at all taken in by Eden's stated pretext for military action. The Americans in particular were astonished both at the apparent collusion and at the crass attempt to revive 'gunboat diplomacy'. They were strongly critical both of the *means* (force instead of law) which Britain had used in its attempt to weaken Nasser and of the *timing* of the invasion, which not only came in the politically sensitive run-up to the presidential election but also let the Soviets off the propaganda hook over their intervention in Hungary on 24 October.[21] Apart from using the normal channels of diplomatic persuasion, the Eisenhower administration also took concrete action to thwart Eden's plans. The Sixth Fleet, stationed in the eastern Mediterranean, was ordered to use all peaceful means to obstruct Anglo-French operations.[22] Far more significant, however, was the dramatic run on sterling which occurred during the first week of November. Reputedly orchestrated from Washington, this financial crisis was made all the more serious by the US Treasury's insistence that the International Monetary Fund (IMF) would not be permitted to bail Britain out. London's near-instantaneous response on 6 November was to call a halt to its military action (the French rapidly followed suit). In the face of continuing American threats to let the pound sink even further if Britain did not withdraw altogether, British forces were completely evacuated from Suez by mid-December.[23] In a matter of days – which from a purely military viewpoint had been quite successful – Britain had experienced a symbolic political reversal which had demonstrated prominently to the world what even Eden had already suspected: that Britain could no longer compete with the two superpowers in the race for global influence.[24] Relations with the United States had been damaged, but they would soon be repaired. The blow to Britain's prestige, however, would prove rather more permanent in its effects.

But why had it happened? Why over Suez had Britain embarked on a strategy that seemed bound to incur both near-universal condemnation and the extreme displeasure of Britain's closest ally, the United States? Why, against the advice of almost the entire Foreign Office,[25] did the Egypt Committee choose to take military action to resolve Britain's dispute with Nasser? Given the many analyses of the Suez episode that have been offered since 1956, it is hardly surprising that a wide range of explanatory factors have been cited as having been partly responsible for the Egypt Committee's decision to intervene militarily. Three factors seem to have been especially important, however. The first of these was the legacy of the Egypt policy that successive governments had pursued between 1881 and 1952. Throughout the period Britain had contrived to preserve its economic and political hegemony through a combination of threats and carefully judged elite manipulation. This in turn had enabled London to maintain a military presence in the strategically vital Canal Zone. For Britain, the 1954 Anglo-Egyptian Agreement had constituted an acceptance of the fact that British dominance over Egypt could no longer be sustained. However, Nasser's nationalisation of the Canal within days of the evacuation of the British garrison looked suspiciously like an attempt to replace British dominance with British subordination; an unequivocal abuse of London's liberal gesture of 1954. For Eden, such a situation was intolerable. It demanded a retrenchment – a reversion to the pre-1952 *status quo ante* – that would remove Nasser from power and enable a more malleable government to be installed. This was what the Suez invasion was supposed to provide: a means of restoring Britain's traditional position of dominance in Egypt. The disastrous political outcome of the intervention merely meant that such hopes were irretrievably lost.

A second major factor underlying Britain's military intervention was (yet again) the fear of 'contagion'. In view of the nationalisation of the Anglo-Iranian Oil Company in 1951, the danger was that the nationalisation of the Canal might encourage the development of a pattern; in which case British-owned assets throughout the Middle East, and possibly further afield, would be increasingly at risk. In these circumstances a determined show of force was perhaps necessary *'pour décourager les autres'*, to warn other third-world nations that similar acts of nationalisation would meet with severe sanction. Of course, as things turned out – as will be seen below – the *failure* of the British strategy counter-productively served to reinforce the aggrandising tendencies various radical regimes were soon to display: for the next decade and more, Arab radicals were to hold up Nasser's achievements against British imperialism as a model which could be used for liberation throughout the Arab world.

The third, and by far the most important, factor underlying the Egypt Committee's decisions, however, was the influence of Realism; especially the Realist world-view of Sir Anthony Eden. As with many of his contemporaries, Eden's political beliefs had been profoundly influenced by the events of the 1930s. In Eden's case, the impact was particularly strong, if only because of his direct association with 'cooperative diplomacy' (as a junior minister at the Foreign Office) between 1935 and 1937 and his subsequent public rejection of 'appeasement' (by resignation) in February 1938. For Eden all the major international conflicts that occurred in the years after 1938 – German and Japanese expansionism, Stalin's ruthless 'consolidation' in Eastern Europe, the Communist aggression in Korea – served to reinforce his belief in the importance of *realpolitik* calculation and, especially, to demonstrate the need to confront aggressive dictators with force rather than mere diplomacy.

From the outset of the Suez crisis in July 1956, Eden clearly identified Nasser as being very much in the mould of the great dictators of the 1930s. This perception, given Eden's dominant position in the Cabinet, seems in turn to have coloured all the deliberations of the Egypt Committee. Britain had made important concessions to Egypt in July 1954 and now Nasser was seeking to make further political and economic gains directly at Britain's expense by the use of the *fait accompli*. For Eden the parallels with Munich were all too obvious: Chamberlain's 'paper agreement' with Hitler had done nothing to prevent German troops marching into Poland one year later; the 1954 agreement had failed to prevent Nasser nationalising the Canal. Where would it all lead? Would Sudan be next? Or Libya? As Eden commented in his memoirs,

> To take the easy way, to put off decisions, to fail even to record a protest when international undertakings are broken on which the ink is scarcely dry, can lead only one way. It is all so much more difficult to do later on ... the insidious appeal of appeasement leads to deadly reckoning.[26]

Given Eden's determination to resist 'appeasement', the Egypt Committee's major calculation became not whether to intervene against Nasser but when. The Soviet intervention in Hungary which began on 24 October may have had some small effect on the timing of the Anglo-French-Israeli action, but far more significant were the practical logistical problems of organising the military campaign and the political problems of agreeing a joint strategy with France and Israel. In any event, when the intervention did come it met with enormous political resistance both from Britain's enemies and from its friends. Crucially, even the Americans – in spite of all the difficulties they had experienced by rejecting the temptation to adopt a strategy of appeasement in South Korea – remained unconvinced that Nasser's Canal policy constituted part of some greater plan aimed at securing Egyptian hegemony in either North Africa or the Middle East.

Eden's main failing throughout the Suez affair had been his application of the wrong historical model to Nasser's behaviour. Although he was right to see the nationalisation of the Canal as a challenge to Britain's immediate economic interests, in the period after 1956 there was in fact never any question of restrictions being introduced on the free movement of commercial shipping through the Canal. Eden's fundamental error, however, lay in assuming that the way to treat Nasser was the way (he now believed) Hitler *should* have been dealt with over German rearmament in 1935, over the remilitarisation of the Rhineland in 1936 and over the annexation of the Sudetenland in 1938: by determined resistance and, if necessary, by force.

Unfortunately, as historians have frequently noted, the comparison between the expansionism of Hitler's Germany and the nationalist aspirations of Nasser's Egypt was not well founded. After 1936 Hitler clearly had his sights set on the territory of *other* countries, whereas, over Suez, Nasser was simply trying to regain full sovereignty over a piece of *Egyptian* territory which, under foreign control, had represented a continuing affront to Egyptian national pride. Similarly, whereas Hitler wilfully and openly violated international legal commitments in pursuit of his grand strategy, in nationalising the canal Nasser was acting well within his rights under international law. The historical comparison which Eden perhaps should have made was not between Nasser and Hitler or Mussolini but between Nasser and Kemal Attaturk, the Turkish dictator of the interwar period. Indeed, the parallels between Anglo-Turkish relations during the period 1923–36 and Anglo-Egyptian relations in the early to mid-1950s – though never apparently considered – were striking.

First, both Nasser and Attaturk were dictators who nonetheless enjoyed mass popular support in their respective attempts to carry out a radical domestic policy programme. Second, both were nationalist leaders whose respective countries had just achieved some semblance of 'real' independence: Attaturk's Turkey after the 1920–23 War of Independence; and Nasser's Egypt after the 1952 Neguib coup and the 1954 Anglo-Egyptian agreement. Third, the countries which they led were both being vigorously courted by the Soviets. In Attaturk's case this was partly because the Soviet leadership in the 1920s saw Turkey as a fellow victim of Western imperialism and partly because of the strategic importance to the Russians of having an ally which could in principle control the straits between the Black Sea (wherein lay the Soviet's only warm-water ports) and the Mediterranean. In the Egyptian case, Nasser was viewed as an agent of 'progressive' change in the Middle East whose success could only serve to weaken the West's political and economic stranglehold over that region. Fourth, when each leader had achieved power his country had enjoyed very poor relations with Britain: in Attaturk's case this was because the 'War of Independence' had been fought primarily against what was seen as a British-sponsored attempt to dismember the Turkish national homeland; and in Nasser's case, the 1952 coup had ousted Britain's preferred candidate for the Egyptian leadership, King Farouk. Finally, with regard to the major source of contention in each set of bilateral relations, neither nationalist leader was seeking to annex any foreign territory. On the contrary, both were simply seeking to (re)gain national control of what was perceived as an important national asset: Attaturk wished to return the Straits – which had been internationalised in 1923 under the Treaty of Lausanne – to Turkish sovereign control, Nasser to take charge of a strategic asset which had for too long been a symbol of foreign domination in Egypt.

Notwithstanding this series of remarkable similarities, the British government apparently paid no heed to the fact that a strategy of patient and unaggressive diplomacy towards Attaturk had been extremely successful in transforming Anglo-Turkish relations from a position of extreme antagonism in 1926 to one of firm cordiality by 1932.[27] Eden, of course, plainly believed that quite enough 'patient diplomacy' towards Nasser had already been practised between 1952 and 1954 and that the time was now right for decisive *action*. Yet Nasser was asking for no more in 1956 than Attaturk had requested, and duly received, when in 1936 under the terms of the Montreux Convention Britain had accepted Turkey's right to remilitarise the Straits. The Egypt Committee seemed unable seriously to consider the possibility that a continued strategy of non-violent cooperation towards Egypt – even in the face of the loss of ownership of the Canal – could have maximised Britain's long-term interests. Rather than regarding the nationalisation as a hammer-blow to British interests in the Middle East, London could have chosen to accept it as an inevitable concession to what after 1954 was in effect a newly independent state striving to achieve a sense of national identity. The continued ownership of the Canal by British citizens was not sufficiently important to merit the British government's seriously damaging its relations with the entire Arab world by resorting to force. Indeed the logic of self-interest – as well as the need for a Great Power to be seen to adhere to international legal norms – suggested the reverse: that Britain's wisest strategy was patient diplomacy aimed both at maximising the compensation payable for the forfeiture of the Canal and at preserving Britain's good relations with the Arab states; and that a policy of persuasion and accommodation was far more likely to promote Britain's long-term goals in the Middle East of securing oil supplies, retaining strategic bases and maintaining pro-Western regimes wherever possible. The Foreign Office was well aware of the depth of feeling in the Arab world generally about the importance of Egyptian control of the canal; and it advised Cabinet accordingly. Eden, however, chose to ignore that advice. Within the confines of his particular version of Realism, Nasser was seen as an expropriator who must be opposed, if necessary by force, rather than appeased. The potential lessons offered by Britain's interwar Turkey policy were in consequence ignored and disaster ensued.

Summary and Conclusions

Britain's 'Empire circle' policy in the years immediately after 1945 was a combination of withdrawal and retrenchment. In India and in Palestine – where as late as 1946 it had been hoped that some sort of British presence could be maintained – Britain was obliged to effect rapid withdrawals: a simple response to the fact that in each country London was no longer in *de facto* control. By way of contrast, in the Far East, in Africa and in the Caribbean, a broadly successful policy of *retrenchment,* designed to maintain British dominance, was facilitated by the relative weakness of indigenous nationalism. In Egypt, a brief attempt in 1956 to reverse a policy of withdrawal that had been grudgingly accepted two years earlier met with such determined resistance from the United States that an immediate and ignominious withdrawal was unavoidable.

The decolonisation in India in 1947 was the culmination of a long sequence of events in which Britain had periodically introduced limited constitutional reform with the intention of softening dissent and thus enabling British dominion to be maintained for as long as possible. By 1947, however, the diversionary potential of the British strategy had been exhausted. In these circumstances the British withdrawal merely represented a *realpolitik*-inspired recognition that in conditions of near anarchy a quick transition to independence – rather than further delay – would be more likely to leave behind regimes relatively well disposed towards British interests. In Palestine, the post-war situation was not dissimilar, though obviously the time-scale of British involvement had been much shorter and the building of indigenous pressures for change more rapid.

The critical factor underlying Britain's loss of control in Palestine and her resultant withdrawal was Hitler's anti-Semitic extermination campaign in Europe. The holocaust not only swelled Jewish immigration into Palestine but also increased Zionist determination to achieve a Jewish national homeland at a time when guilt and compassion had rendered London's will to resist those Zionist pressures correspondingly weak. All things considered, however, the British withdrawals from India and from Palestine were accomplished with only minimal damage being done to British interests: India and Pakistan joined the Commonwealth; Jordan and Israel remained in the Western sphere of influence. In the conditions of the time these two outcomes were probably the best anyone could have hoped for.

After 1948, Britain's imperial strategy became broadly one of retrenchment, though it was a retrenchment sufficiently flexible to permit further withdrawals when circumstances were clearly beyond London's control. In fact, in Malaya, where the desire to avoid imperial withdrawal was overlain with a determination to prevent further communist gains in the Far East, no major concessions were necessary, at least in the period before Suez. This was largely because the communist threat had been successfully resisted – thanks partly to an outstanding military campaign and partly to the ethnic composition of the Malayan population (which undermined the popular appeal of the ethnic Chinese communist insurgents). In Africa and the Caribbean the danger of communist subversion was considerably smaller than in the Far East. Nonetheless the continuing need to protect British political and commercial interests and the corresponding need to keep the remaining colonial territories firmly within the British sphere of influence meant that the Colonial Office had to carry out the chosen strategy of imperial retrenchment with caution and sensitivity. It did so with considerable success. As in India between the wars, nationalist demands for full self-determination were, for the time being, held at bay by a variety of constitutional concessions which allowed for some (and often increasing) indigenous participation in the decision-making process, but which simultaneously ensured that the British government remained the source of final authority. This was not to say, however, that nationalist pressures could everywhere be contained. Where indigenous demands for autonomy were especially strong and/or the problems of ungovernability particularly intense, then Britain was still prepared to bow to the inevitable and withdraw: hence the agreement to evacuate Suez by 1956 and the abandonment of the Sudan at the end of 1955.

Yet it was in relation to Egypt that the whole post-1948 imperial strategy began to founder. In 1954 Britain had accepted that the new Egyptian government had the right to full sovereignty over the Canal Zone and had set out a timetable for British withdrawal. However, the subsequent nationalisation of the Canal Company itself was regarded as such a provocation that Britain opted for a return to the strategy of retrenchment: of attempting to restore Britain to the position of influence which it had enjoyed in the period before 1952. Unfortunately, the specific form of collusion that was adopted by the Egypt Committee displayed neither the subtlety nor the understanding of local conditions which had characterised Britain's policy of retrenchment in Malaya and Africa. Indeed the politically unacceptable nature of the intervention in Egypt led to the rapid abandonment of the attempted retrenchment; a complete and permanent withdrawal quickly followed.

What is clear from the foregoing discussion, however, is that the Realist world-views of Britain's foreign policy makers were extremely important in generating this variegated pattern of retrenchment and withdrawal. It was certainly Realism – in both the everyday and the technical senses of the term – that led Britain to evacuate India and

Palestine: a simple recognition of the fact that, when the imperial power is no longer able to govern its dependencies, then its own interests are best served by achieving an accommodation – on the most favourable terms possible – with those who look as though they can. It was certainly Realism, given the apparently growing communist threat to Western security interests in the Far East, which underlay Britain's determination to eradicate the Marxist insurgency in Malaya. It was certainly Realism that led to the strategy of retrenchment in Africa and the Caribbean: while there was no serious *security* threat to Western interests in these areas in the late 1940s and early 1950s, the twin necessities of maintaining safe overseas markets and protecting the sterling area's dollar earnings meant that material-interest *realpolitik* calculation continued to dominate British government policy. And it was certainly Realism – forged out of the experiences of World War II, the Cold War and Korea – that encouraged Eden to misapply the principle that aggressors should be actively resisted rather than passively appeased, with such unfortunate consequences at Suez.

The real paradox of imperial policy in the decade after 1945 was that a string of *tactical* successes could have added up to something approaching *strategic* failure. As has been repeatedly observed, the decolonisation in India and the withdrawal from Palestine were completed with minimal damage to British interests; the guerrilla insurgencies in Malaya and Kenya were successfully resisted; nationalist pressures in Africa and the Caribbean were successfully contained. Yet Britain's military capabilities, given its Cold War commitments in Europe, the North Atlantic and Korea, were seriously over-stretched. The competing resource demands of rival spending programmes at home and the chronic balance of payments difficulties that the British economy was encountering merely made things worse. In this curious situation of faltering strategy and tactical success it was more than a little ironic that the one notable tactical failure of the 1945–56 period, Suez, should have been largely responsible for the broad strategic reappraisal which subsequently took place. Without the trauma of Suez, Britain might have attempted to sustain its overextended 'three circle' strategy well after 1956, continuing to improvise brilliantly in increasingly difficult circumstances. Without Suez, the subsequent self-conscious analysis of Britain's diminished role in the world of the superpowers might not have been so intense or the indigenous demands for change in the colonies so insistent.

The road to Suez had been tortuous and by no means inexorable. If the Conservative Party had decided to skip a generation and pass over Anthony Eden when the question of Churchill's successor arose in April 1955, it is possible that Suez might never have happened at all. In the event it was perhaps just as well that it did. Without the stimulus of humiliation, Britain might have stumbled on in its strategy of overextension, determined to hang on to its remaining imperial possessions until they were forcibly prised from its grasp. It was far better to recognise the strength of the 'wind of change' that was blowing through the Empire; to come to terms with reality quickly; and to act accordingly.

Chapter 4

The Wind of Change: The Empire Circle after 1956

In the years after 1956, Britain progressively withdrew from the Empire 'circle'. Although the pace of withdrawal varied – at times accelerating and on occasion even going into temporary reverse – it nonetheless proceeded inexorably. At the root of this process, of course, was the relative decline in Britain's international economic position which had begun well before World War I. However, while Britain's relative economic decline might have been a necessary condition for the downgrading of the Empire, it was never a sufficient condition for such an eventuality. Crucially, in the period after 1956, economic weakness was complemented by two other processes that encouraged withdrawal: the increased intensity of *indigenous nationalist pressures for real local autonomy* and the seemingly *autonomous shifts that were taking place in the pattern of Britain's overseas trade.* In the decade or so after Suez, the juxtaposition of these three factors produced tremendous pressures for a strategic shift in Britain's external policy. Fortunately successive governments after 1957 were sufficiently well schooled in the principles of *realpolitik* to recognise not only that the economic significance of the Empire had diminished but also that Britain's traditional military position within it could no longer be sustained.

This chapter begins with a review of the major effects which Suez had on Britain's international position. Although the affair itself does not seem to have provoked a thorough-going formal reconsideration of Britain's world role,[1] it undoubtedly gave added impetus to deep-seated changes that were already occurring within the Empire; changes which were quite beyond the British government's ability to control. The second section of the chapter provides a brief account of the 'second wave' decolonisations that occurred throughout Africa and the Caribbean in the decade after 1956: as with India and Palestine, the critical factor in this process was the pressure of indigenous nationalism. The third section examines the withdrawal from East of Suez after 1968, a manoeuvre of enormous symbolic significance which was undertaken largely in order to reduce the size of the overseas defence budget. The final section reviews British policy towards the Empire circle in the period since 1968 and attempts to assess how far Britain – despite its formal imperial withdrawal – can still be regarded as an imperialist power.

The Effects of Suez

Notwithstanding the domestic political furore which accompanied the Suez crisis in the fall of 1956, the affair itself did not in the short term appear to have a major effect on the British government's empire circle strategy. In one sense this was odd. It might have been expected that Britain's most serious diplomatic humiliation in modern times would have occasioned a major review of Britain's international position in what was now clearly the age of the two superpowers. Yet no such review took place. Indeed, in the immediate aftermath of Suez the main political fallout was limited to the discreet removal from Cabinet of those politicians who had so consistently chosen to ignore Foreign Office advice. As a result, Britain's overextended, three circle strategy – including its commitment to an imperial world role – continued largely undiminished, at least for the time being.

The wider ramifications of Suez were considerable, however. In Britain's informal Empire in the Middle East, the government's standing plummeted. The Iraqi government suggested publicly that Britain should be expelled from the Baghdad Defence Pact; Jordan abrogated the 1953 Anglo-Jordanian defence treaty; Syria and Saudi Arabia broke off diplomatic relations with London; and at a summit meeting in Beirut, the Arab heads of state considered the possibility of combined economic sanctions against Britain.[2] Inside the Commonwealth the response was little better. Although Australia, New Zealand and South Africa were non-committal, Canada publicly announced its regret that Britain had failed to engage in consultation with its allies; Ceylon conveyed its vigorous disapproval of British policy; and Pakistan and India expressed their outright condemnation of Britain's actions.[3]

These immediate responses were of less significance, however, than the longer-term implications of the Suez affair. While it is clearly not possible to describe all of the consequences which Suez had for Britain's international position, three of the more important ones – which were of direct relevance to the subsequent pattern of imperial withdrawal – require brief review here. The first of these was the damage which Suez inflicted upon Britain's prestige abroad and in particular upon its ability to pose as a champion of international morality. From the mid-19th century onwards British military involvement in both Europe and the third world had always been more or less plausibly justified in terms of some moral principle or other. Wherever the British government had been obliged to resort to force it had done so either to uphold international law or to defend some weak state threatened by external aggression, internal subversion or both. Even if in the mid-20th century the maintenance of colonial control could no longer be justified as part of 'the white man's burden', Britain could still claim that it had an obligation to discharge its responsibilities of 'trusteeship' towards its colonial dependencies in order to provide appropriate conditions in which self-government could eventually be introduced. The problem with the Suez intervention was that none of these moral justifications applied. Nasser was operating within his rights under international law; he was clearly not acting aggressively against some weak third party; and Britain could in no sense claim a 'trusteeship' over internal developments in Egypt. In these circumstances the British intervention was widely interpreted by the international community as evidence of London's general preparedness to resort to power politics if it failed to get its way by persuasion. After Suez, foreign diplomats and nationalist leaders pressing for independence were even less likely to believe that British diplomacy was instinctively more civilised and more benign than that exercised by either the United States or the Soviet Union (both of which made significant advances in the Middle East in the decade after 1956). An important reserve of goodwill had been lost and without it subsequent demands for self-determination were to prove much harder to resist.

A second long-term consequence of Suez concerned the Commonwealth. The more ardent imperialists at home had always hoped that the Commonwealth would help Britain to maintain its post-war world role by acting as a kind of surrogate Empire.[4] In the mid-1950s there had been several good reasons for supposing that the strategy might be successful: the cultural ties which bound the Commonwealth together were still strong; trade interdependence was still high, bolstered by the monetary underpinning of the sterling area; and the participation of the Commonwealth Brigade in the recent Korean War suggested that Commonwealth governments were agreed that cooperation among the liberal democracies was still important in resisting the global threat of communist expansionism.[5] However, Suez meant that, although the Commonwealth survived as a formal institution, it lost what coherence it had possessed as an economic and diplomatic bloc. Of particular importance in this context was the reaction of India. Prime Minister Nehru was so incensed at Britain's aggressive manoeuvring that he initiated a series of diplomatic moves which were to result in 1962 in the creation of the Non-Aligned Movement. Crucially, Nehru gained the strong support of Kwame Nkrumah, Prime Minister of the newly independent state of Ghana and the leading African nationalist of the period. While the Non-Aligned Movement itself never achieved the diplomatic coherence that its creators had hoped for, the support which the 'new' (black) Commonwealth members accorded it in turn meant that London was unable to use the Commonwealth as a device for sustaining British influence in the rest of the third world. On the contrary, during the 1960s the Commonwealth increasingly provided little more than a forum in which ex-colonial states could express their disapproval of the British government's domestic and foreign policies and at the same time seek to secure special concessions from Britain's overseas aid budget.

A third major consequence of Suez was that Britain had demonstrated a new vulnerability in its dealings with less powerful states. Even with its superior military capability – which was in any case already diminished in comparison with that of the two superpowers – it could not prevail over a weak opponent. Here was a lesson for would-be nationalists both in the 'informal Empire' and in the remainder of Britain's colonial possessions: with the right political strategy 'perfidious Albion' could be successfully resisted. In the Middle East Nasser's example was soon to provide the inspiration for a series of attempts to subvert the Western-dominated status quo. In the immediate aftermath of Suez, oil pipelines throughout the Gulf region were sabotaged; Bahrain and Kuwait were subject to a wave of strikes and serious rioting; and there was an upsurge of anti-government guerrilla activity in Yemen.[6] In July 1958, the pro-British Iraqi monarchy was ousted in a *coup d'état* following a radicalisation of the Syrian government which had taken place during the course of 1957. Notwithstanding the changed climate in the Middle East, however, the most profound effects of Britain's new vulnerability were felt in the increasingly insistent demands for decolonisation in Africa, the Caribbean and the Far East. To be sure, Suez itself had not *created* these demands for change, but it certainly gave them a significant boost. It is these developments which are now examined.

The 'Second Wave' Decolonisations: Africa and the Caribbean after 1956

As noted in Chapter 3, some concessions to African nationalism had already been made well before Suez. Sudan, for example, had effectively been granted full independence in January 1956. The plans for decolonisation in Gold Coast (Ghana) had been formalised several months before Nasser nationalised the Canal. Yet, in spite of these concessions, it was still London's broad intention in mid-1956 to continue its policy of 'trusteeship' over its remaining colonial territories into the indefinite future. However, partly as a result of the new 'vulnerability' that Suez revealed, in the period after 1956 there was a fairly rapid change both in Britain's overall imperial strategy *and* in the conditions on the ground inside the colonies. In terms of the overall strategy there was an increasing recognition both in Cabinet and in the Foreign and Colonial Offices that Britain no longer possessed the military and economic capability to sustain its imperial role in the third world. Crucially, by the early 1960s it was also recognised that a fairly rapid withdrawal would be less painful for all concerned than a lengthy campaign to retain control of possessions that would eventually be lost anyway: to move quickly would permit a transition to a cordial interdependence between ex-colonisers and ex-colonised; to delay would be to risk an escalation in violence and the possible development of irreconcilable antagonisms.[7]

The immediate reason for this transformation in the collective perceptions of the British foreign policy establishment was the changing balance of grassroots political forces inside the colonies themselves. Quite simply, indigenous nationalist sentiment in the late 1950s and early 1960s was rapidly becoming more articulate, more widespread and more determined. Throughout Africa and the Caribbean, political discourse was experiencing a radicalisation. Anti-imperialist propaganda received much wider currency than ever before and the membership of nationalist organisations accelerated significantly. A new generation of black intellectuals – Fanon in North Africa, C. L. R. James in the West Indies, Nyerere in Tanganyika and Nkrumah in Ghana – found its ideas gaining increasingly wide acceptance, especially among the politically active sections of the colonial populations. A black political consciousness was emerging that was all too aware of the nature and extent of the oppression and exploitation that colonialism engendered. The new generation of nationalist leaders was much less ready to accept a slow retreat from Empire and far more prepared to countenance the use of active and, if necessary, violent resistance to imperial domination.[8]

The result of this strengthening of indigenous nationalism was a series of acts of decolonisation which by 1966 had left Britain with the merest residue of an Empire, consisting of territories considered too small to be viable as independent nations. Between 1957 and 1966 Britain granted formal autonomy to some 22 major colonial territories. Independence was not granted unconditionally, however. If the Realist world-views of the policymakers had forced the recognition that imperial control could no longer be sustained in the face of rising indigenous demands for independence, then Realism also required that, wherever possible, the newly sovereign regimes should be well disposed to Western – and especially to British – interests. The British government had gone to great lengths in Malaya, resolutely suppressing a guerrilla insurgency in the decade after 1948, both to ensure the survival of a friendly government after independence and to guarantee the installation of a Westminster-style political apparatus through which subsequent political conflicts could be resolved. Following classic *realpolitik* principles, the Colonial Office made great efforts to ensure that this pattern of well-disposed governments, underpinned by liberal-democratic constitutions, was continued throughout the subsequent decolonisation process in Africa and the Caribbean. If the Westminster model was in fact inappropriate to societies riven by ethnic and linguistic divisions – where the need to achieve a sense of national unity and identity was more important than the possession of a competitive party system – then this was unfortunate but unavoidable. The British government believed in the virtues of liberal democracy and the least that it could do was to bestow liberal-democratic institutions upon its newly liberated colonial peoples. The fact that liberal democracy was so short-lived in so many of the ex-colonies is a sad testament to the failure of successive governments fully to comprehend the depth of the economic and political problems that Britain bequeathed to the colonies which it had ruled so benignly, yet exploited so thoroughly.

Explaining the Rise in Indigenous Nationalism

But if the pressure of indigenous nationalism was the critical factor which induced decolonisation, what had been responsible for the upsurge in nationalist sentiment in the first place? Had the retreat from Empire been unavoidable? Or could something have been done either to divert or to suppress the rising tide of nationalist demands? As has been repeatedly intimated, a key factor in Britain's inability to resist the increase in nationalist pressure was Britain's long-run relative economic decline. If Britain had retained the industrial and financial pre-eminence which it enjoyed before 1914, then it might have remained impervious to nationalist demands. Certainly a thriving economy might have provided the British government with the physical wherewithal to suppress a widespread outbreak of colonial dissent. However, while economic decline was almost undoubtedly a precondition of imperial withdrawal, it certainly does not explain the *timing* of the second-wave decolonisations. Neither does it explain the upsurge in nationalist demands for self-determination which actually provoked the decision to decolonise.

At least three general explanations for this upsurge in nationalist activity can be identified. One explanation, frequently advanced in the popular press of the time, attributes the upsurge to *the machinations of the Soviet Union* and its agents at home and abroad: the Soviets were alleged to have trained nationalist leaders, supplied them with arms, assisted with the dissemination of anti-British propaganda, or some combination of the three.[9] While it seems unlikely that Soviet agents were entirely uninvolved in the various nationalist struggles around the world in the

1950s and 1960s, there is no evidence to suggest that their participation was in any sense decisive in the groundswell of indigenous support for rapid decolonisation. While the covert nature of anti-status quo operations obviously militates against the discovery of any direct evidence of Soviet intrigue, it is worth noting that in the years after independence none of Britain's ex-colonies moved into the Soviet sphere of influence. Apart from Somalia – which briefly strengthened its commercial and military ties with the Soviets, between 1971 and 1977 – none signed a Friendship Treaty with the Soviet Union and none was induced to enter the Soviets' economic club, Comecon, as Vietnam did in 1979 after the withdrawal of US forces. Such a record of subsequent Soviet exclusion provides indirect support for the claim that Soviet involvement in the process of decolonisation itself was never significant: otherwise, it seems likely that the Soviets would have sought to realise their 'investment' as quickly as possible by supplanting Britain as the 'sponsoring' external power.

A second explanation for the increase in nationalist resistance to imperialism in the late 1950s and early 1960s concerns the mutually reinforcing *contagion effects of British and French (and to a lesser extent Belgian) decolonisations*. The argument runs along the following lines.

1. The crucial feature of the post-war world was the shift in the global locus of power away from Western Europe and towards the United States and the Soviet Union. With the loss of their hegemonic position, it was only a matter of time before the great Western European empires collapsed. Indeed, Britain initiated the process by conceding independence in India and Burma.
2. Notwithstanding *Britain's* subsequent attempts at imperial retrenchment, the success of these 'first wave' decolonisations acted as both *a stimulus and a model* to nationalists in Indochina. Accordingly *France* was obliged to withdraw from Laos, Cambodia and Vietnam in the mid-1950s.
3. The success of South-East Asian nationalism in turn encouraged nationalist liberation movements in French North Africa, provoking the crisis in Algeria in the late 1950s.
4. Inspired by the Algerian model, Ghanaian nationalists demanded their own independence, which they were granted in 1957.
5. Once one of the major *British* West African states had achieved autonomy, the demands for independence from *French* West Africa became irresistible, and accordingly the French decolonised their West African possessions in 1960 (at the same time as the Belgians were obliged to withdraw from the Congo).

6. This 'wind of change' was clearly far too strong for a liberal power like Britain to resist. Unable either to offer any plausible public justification as to why it should retain control of its colonies or to provide the military capability which might render such a public justification unnecessary, the British government bowed to the inevitable. Following the French example, in 1961 it effectively foreclosed on the Empire by initiating a sequence of major decolonisations throughout Africa and the Caribbean which was to last until 1966.

While the 'contagion' explanation has a ring of intuitive plausibility to it, it is extraordinarily difficult either to determine what the precise transmission mechanisms of such 'contagion' effects actually were or to demonstrate that such effects did indeed operate. More importantly, the contagion explanation does not really address the fundamental question as to why the colonial populations were *susceptible* to 'contagion' in the first place. The post-war shift in the global balance of power might explain why Soviet and American imperialisms replaced Western European imperialism in the period after 1945. It might explain the loosening grip of the Western European powers on their respective colonial possessions. It does not explain why indigenous nationalism should almost universally have become such a potent force for change in the 1950s and 1960s.

It is in this context that a third explanation – what might be termed the 'social mobilisation' explanation – assumes relevance.[10] This explanation centres on the long-term economic and political effects which imperialism itself had on the colonial territories of the European power. It suggests that, *by developing the colonies, the imperial powers created the very conditions which encouraged the colonised peoples to challenge imperial rule.*[11] The process began with the improvements in long-range transportation which accompanied the second industrial revolution of the late 19th century and which accelerated the incorporation of the newly acquired third-world colonies into the emerging global economy. This insertion of the African and Caribbean economies into the international division of labour produced important changes within those economies. People began to move away from subsistence agriculture in the rural areas to paid employment in the cities and small towns. In the early part of the 20th century the extent and importance of this migration was limited. In the period after 1945, however, as the world economy entered a 30-year period of increasing prosperity, there was a dramatic increase both in the productive capacity of the colonial territories and, crucially, in the numbers of people moving to the urban centres. It is difficult to overestimate the profound consequences which rapid urbanisation can have for an undeveloped society and economy, especially when it is combined, as it was throughout the Empire in the post-war years, with an expansion of the available channels of political communication. Of particular importance is the fact that the entire social and political milieu of the newly urbanised migrant is totally transformed. Old loyalties, allegiances and social networks are broken. The migrant is exposed to new ideas and to the influence of new organisations – on the streets, in the workplace, even in the home.[12]

In conditions of rapid urbanisation – of *social* mobilisation – the potential for *political* mobilisation of the frequently impoverished urban migrant under the banner of any *new* ideology is inevitably greater than the equivalent potential encountered under the static conditions of rural subsistence.[13] In the 1950s the rate of social mobilisation in Africa and the Caribbean was at historically unprecedented levels; and the new ideology with the most obvious mass appeal was anti-colonial nationalism. In these circumstances it was perhaps not surprising that indigenous nationalism should have experienced such an upsurge in the late 1950s and early 1960s and that it should have had such profound consequences for European imperialism.

Yet the pressures of social mobilisation and contagion did not produce decolonisations everywhere in Africa. For several years three of the major Western European colonies apparently remained immune to indigenous nationalism: the white settler regimes in Mozambique, Angola and Southern Rhodesia. The critical factor in their survival was their geographical proximity to the apartheid regime in South Africa: with the firm political and economic support of Pretoria they were able to fight temporary holding operations in order to delay the transition to majority rule.[14] It was Rhodesia – the only British colony of the three – which held out the longest. Confronted with the imminent introduction of universal suffrage, Ian Smith's government had made a Unilateral Declaration of Independence in November 1965. From the outset, the illegal Smith regime posed severe difficulties for the British government. To have handed over the problem to the United Nations (as some critics advised) would have involved an abdication of British responsibility and sovereignty that was unacceptable to a country which still aspired to Great Power status. To have attempted to remove Smith from power by military force (and there was no guarantee that such a strategy could be effected successfully) would have seriously overstretched Britain's military capability and split both Parliament and Cabinet at a time when the Labour government had a Commons majority of only four. In the event, successive governments, in collaboration with the United Nations, chose to apply economic sanctions against Rhodesia and to await developments.

Throughout the 1970s, as indigenous demands for majority rule grew progressively stronger, the Smith regime's efforts to resist the combined guerrilla onslaught of Robert Mugabe's ZANU and Joshua Nkomo's

ZAPU became increasingly ineffective. By the late 1970s the security position of the settler regime had been so weakened that Smith was ready to negotiate. In January 1980, after a series of diplomatic false starts, the British-sponsored Lancaster House Conference reached agreement on a new, compromise constitution that was acceptable both to ZANU and ZAPU and to the ruling Rhodesian Front Party. Although Britain had never been in a position to exert a determining influence upon the military situation in Rhodesia itself, British Foreign Secretary Lord Carrington's diplomatic efforts were undoubtedly important in persuading Smith that a rapid transition to majority rule was inevitable and that the interests of the settler community would be best served by accepting the limited constitutional concessions to the white minority that Mugabe and Nkomo were still prepared to make. Crucially, at Lancaster House, Britain had fulfilled its formal legal obligations as the decolonising power: with the independence of Zimbabwe, in April 1980, the second-wave phase of decolonisation was complete.

Why, then, did the second-wave decolonisations occur? In one sense, the answer is fairly clear. The decision of the Macmillan government to opt for a broad strategy of imperial withdrawal was based on classic *realpolitik* calculation. In the face of escalating indigenous demands for independence abroad and a relatively weakened economic base at home, decolonisation was a simple matter of trimming Britain's overseas involvement to match its declining overseas capability. Such an answer, however, immediately gives rise to another question: what factors were responsible for producing the conditions that underlay this *realpolitik* decision? As we have seen, the 'external subterfuge' argument – in the absence of any compelling evidence to support it – cannot be seriously entertained. A similar conclusion can be drawn with regard to the frequently articulated contemporary claim that independence could now be granted because, thanks to Britain's previous 'educative' endeavours, the colonial peoples were now 'ready' for full self-rule: such a contention is strongly contradicted by the dismal record of militarism and instability which characterised much of British Africa after independence.

But if these factors were not particularly important, certain things did matter. Britain's relative economic decline and its post-war eclipse as a leading world power were undoubtedly significant as background preconditions. However, the two major conditioning factors underlying the Realist decision to curtail Britain's imperial responsibilities were (1) the acceleration in social mobilisation which accompanied economic development inside the colonies; and (2) the imitative contagion effects which seem to have linked different nationalist movements in various parts of the third world. The economic development of the colonies created the structural conditions in which indigenous nationalism could flourish; the achievement of independence in one colonial territory served as both an inspiration and a model for nationalists elsewhere. The process was inexorable and the imperialists had neither the will nor the capability to resist it.

The Withdrawal from 'East of Suez'

In spite of its commitment to the process of decolonisation, Britain in the mid-1960s still retained much of the global network of bases that it had assembled in order to protect the Empire. Sizeable military forces were still maintained in the Far East (in Singapore and Hong Kong), in the Middle East (in Aden and the Persian Gulf), in Southern Africa (at the Simonstown base in South Africa) and in the Mediterranean (in Malta and especially in Libya, which had become increasingly important since the 'loss' of Egypt in the 1950s). There were three major reasons why successive governments attempted to sustain this partial Pax Britannica. First, Britain still had unambiguous treaty obligations which required it to assist in the external defence of its allies. Under the SEATO 'Manila Pact' of 1954, Britain was obliged to defend Malaysia, the Philippines and Thailand; under the CENTO 'Baghdad Pact' of 1955, it had a responsibility towards Pakistan and Turkey;[15] and under a series of separate bilateral treaty arrangements it was also committed to defend Malta, Libya, the South Arabian Federation, Bahrain, Qatar, Muscat and Oman, the Trucial States and Kuwait.[16] Clearly, if Britain was to discharge its responsibilities in all these contexts effectively, it had to maintain military forces locally which would not only act as a deterrent to any potential aggressor but which could also be rapidly deployed should the deterrent fail.

In addition to these formal legal commitments, a second reason why Britain remained apparently wedded to its global military role was the potential military-strategic value of British bases. To be sure, the strategic rationale of those bases had been questioned both after the loss of India in the late 1940s and after the loss of Suez itself in 1956. Nonetheless, even if Britain, having now abandoned all of its major colonies, no longer needed to protect exclusively British interests in the third world, it could still provide a useful supplement to American efforts to defend the general interests of the West: interests which in an era of decolonisation the Soviet Union was doing its very best to subvert. In these circumstances, the continued deployment of British forces in areas where London had traditionally exercised an imperial influence represented a very convenient way of insulating the global status quo from communist-inspired challenge. Thus, in terms of strategic contingency planning, the bases in Singapore and Hong Kong could still be used for the 'forward defence' of Australia and New Zealand and for the protection of Malaysia; the British presence in the Persian Gulf was still required to ensure that the West retained a firm grip on Middle Eastern oil supplies; and Aden and Simonstown were necessary for the protection of the increasingly important oil tanker traffic which used the Indian Ocean and the Cape. A continued British presence was obviously no guarantee that Western interests in these regions would be safeguarded, but equally obviously it would reduce the chances that Soviet intrigue would prove successful in the future.

A third factor underlying British involvement East of Suez in the early 1960s was the 'bureaucratic inertia' of the foreign policy making process itself, and the general tendency of Britain's foreign policy makers to avoid hard choices and to delay making a major decision until events foreclosed on all the options. This tendency has certainly been evident in Britain's foreign policy making throughout the post-war period and, according to Wallace, was undoubtedly involved in the matter of the British military presence East of Suez in the early 1960s.[17] On this account, a major reason why Britain retained its far-flung network of bases in the face of both decolonisation and the loss of Suez itself was simply that British forces had been stationed East of Suez for over a century. While a conscious strategic decision was necessary to end this involvement, the highly bureaucratised nature of the decision-making process itself militated against such a radical policy departure unless circumstances made it unavoidable,[18] which until 1966 they did not.

The Decision to Withdraw

When Harold Wilson's Labour government achieved office in October 1964, it did so committed to retaining a British military presence East of Suez. Indeed, in the face of Parliamentary Labour Party (PLP) criticism, Wilson was still defending the need to maintain Britain's global role as late as June 1966.[19] There were several good reasons for doing so. In the Middle East, following the shock administered to the American defence establishment by the Cuban missile crisis of 1962, Britain's naval presence in the Gulf now had the blessing of the United States.[20] In the Far East, Britain's support for Malaysia in its border dispute with Indonesia after September 1963 had been invaluable in preserving Malaysian territorial integrity: without it, there was no telling how the situation might have escalated. In addition, in the face of the rapidly growing communist threat to Indochina, the Americans were now prepared to accept the need for an indefinite continuation of Britain's military role in the Far East. It appeared that Britain, having lost an Empire, might conceivably have confounded Dean Acheson and found a role acting as the United States' second lieutenant, defending Western strategic interests where the Americans – for whatever historical or contingent reasons – feared to tread.

But if this was the way things appeared in 1965, the situation was not to last beyond the publication of British Secretary of State for Defence Denis Healey's Defence Review in February 1966.[21] Although the Review stated that the Labour government intended to retain its naval presence in Singapore and Malaysia, it also placed great emphasis on the 'overstretch' of Britain's defence capabilities. By insisting that this 'overstretch' was to be eliminated at the same time as the defence budget was to be cut from 7 per cent to 6 per cent of Britain's gross domestic product, the Defence Review effectively anticipated the end of Britain's presence East of Suez. Against a background of overall defence cuts, it was only possible both to maintain Britain's commitment to NATO (now clearly designated as the first priority) and to avoid 'overstretch' by reducing Britain's global commitments. The Review also asserted the government's clear intention to withdraw from Aden in November 1967, when South Arabia was scheduled for independence. In February 1967, the process of withdrawal was further bolstered when the annual Defence White Paper asserted that British forces would withdraw from Simonstown in a matter of months and that only Britain's 'core responsibilities' would be maintained in the Gulf. Finally, in July 1967, it was announced that Britain would withdraw all of its forces from East of Suez by the early 1970s. This was confirmed formally in the 1968 Defence Review, which expressed the government's intention to evacuate British forces from Singapore, Malaysia and the Gulf by the end of 1971.[22] In anticipation of the fact that these withdrawals would effectively prevent Britain from discharging its existing treaty responsibilities, Britain would also cease to 'declare' ground forces to SEATO from March 1969 onwards, convene a special five-power conference to arrange for the future defence of Malaysia and Singapore by delegating greater responsibility to Canberra, and make bilateral arrangements with each of the Gulf States in order to ensure their continued security.[23] The new – and much diminished – world role that Britain might play in the future was neatly symbolised by the tiny contingent of unarmed British 'bobbies' that was despatched to the Caribbean dependency of Anguilla in the summer of 1967: in combination with some skilful diplomacy, the contingent's benign presence brought a potentially dangerous constitutional crisis to a swift and peaceful end.

Explaining the Withdrawal from East of Suez

But why had it all been necessary? Why had the British government found it expedient to bring to an end a traditional commitment that was intimately bound up with the perception – both at home and abroad – of Britain as a world power? Why had London wilfully turned its back on the 'second lieutenant' support role, apparently well suited to Britain's post-colonial status, which dovetailed so neatly with the American view that the Western powers could operate a mutually beneficial division of labour in the defence of Western interests in the third world?

Several factors seem to have been important. At the decision-making level, by far the most important consideration in all the deliberations over East of Suez policy was cost. By 1965, although Britain still had an abundance of post-imperial responsibilities, it no longer possessed the financial capability to discharge them. In terms of GDP per capita Britain had declined from seventh position in the world 'league table' in 1950 to twelfth position in 1965, having been 'overtaken' by France, West Germany and Denmark. With the exception of the United States, it was spending a higher proportion of its GDP on defence than any of its major industrial competitors.[24] And given the Wilson government's determination to increase state spending on both industrial investment and social welfare provision, the Treasury not surprisingly insisted on commensurate cuts in defence expenditure.[25] In 1965 Britain had over 55,000 military personnel stationed East of Suez, at a cost of £317 million per year or 15 per cent of the total defence budget of £2,120 million.[26] Notwithstanding the support which the British military presence East of Suez provided for a number of friendly regimes, it was not easy to see how this considerable drain on defence funds actually contributed to British security. The two major bases East of Suez – Aden and Singapore – had originally been acquired in order to defend, respectively, the western and eastern approaches to India. With the 'loss' of India – and it was certainly lost after 1956, if not in 1947 – both bases had lost their principal strategic *raison d'être*. It might well have been worth paying 15 per cent of the annual defence budget in order to defend the Jewel in the Crown; it was certainly not worth paying simply to maintain isolated pockets of British influence in the third world – or to curry favour with the Americans – when serious financial crises threatened at home.

These cost concerns were exacerbated, moreover, by the suspicion that the same wind of change that had produced the second-wave decolonisations was also responsible for increasing the extent to which Britain's commitments East of Suez were being activated. The pacification of the old empire had always been a relatively easy task: rarely, except during the years of the two world wars, had it been necessary to wage campaigns in more than one territory at any given time. However, the early 1960s had witnessed a violent confrontation between Malaysia and Indonesia, serious internal subversion in Bahrain and in Kuwait, and a prolonged armed insurrection in the South Arabian Federation; all of which required a determined and sustained military response from the British government. If this pattern was representative of things to come, reducing Britain's overseas commitments might well be preferable to increasing the resources available for fighting the necessary military campaigns effectively. In these circumstances, given that it was the Atlantic Alliance which was at the core of British security concerns, the commitment to maintain forces East of Suez was an obvious target for defence cuts: as with decolonisation, it was a matter of trimming involvement to match capability.

But if cost was the major reason underlying the *policy decision* to withdraw from East of Suez, there was another important *structural* factor which also operated to encourage the retreat from empire. This concerned the changing pattern of Britain's international trade, and in particular the changing pattern of its export markets. The essence of the change was that while the second-wave decolonisations were actually taking place – and immediately prior to the withdrawal from East of Suez – Britain's vitally important export trade was experiencing a dramatic shift away from the Empire circle and towards Western Europe and the United States. To be sure, as Table 4.1 shows, exports to the Overseas Sterling Area (OSA) countries of the Empire and Commonwealth increased between 1955 and 1965. However, while exports to the OSA increased by £403 million, total exports to Western Europe and North America – from a lower base – increased by the much larger figure of £1,390 million. As Table 4.2 indicates, between 1955 and 1965 the share positions of the two groupings were almost exactly reversed: the OSA share of total exports *fell* from half to a third while the Europe/United States share *rose* from a third to half over the same period.

Now, of course, it is extremely difficult to establish that these shifting trade patterns were in any sense a 'cause' of imperial withdrawal. It

Table 4.1   British exports to selected areas, 1955–65 (£ million)

	1955	1965	Change 1955–65	
African and Caribbean	57	235	+ 178	total change
Old Commonwealth	731	866	+135	in OSA
India/Pakistan/Ceylon	188	183	-5	exports
Malaysia/Singapore/ Hong Kong	99	159	+60	+403
Gulf States	0	35	+35	
Western Europe+USA	993	2,383	+1,390	

Source: Annual Abstract of Statistics (HMSO, various years).

Table 4.2   Percentage of British exports destined for selected areas, 1955–84

	1955	1965	1975	1984
Exports to W. Europe + USA as % total exports	34.2	50.5	56.3	70.5
Exports to OSA as % total exports	49.2	34.8	22.3	13.2

Source: Annual Abstract of Statistics (HMSO, various years).

is entirely possible, for example, that the relaxation of imperial control associated with the second-wave decolonisations had the effect of 'losing' British export markets to foreign competition. However, even if the relative decline in imperial trade can be thus explained away as a consequence of decolonisation, it is less clear why imperial withdrawal should have so radically stimulated Britain's export trade with Europe and North America. It was not the decision to decolonise which accelerated Britain's export trade with Europe and the United States. Rather, it was the changing consumption patterns in those advanced economies which autonomously increased the demand for British goods and services. The reason for this was simple. The economies with the fastest-growing market potential in the 1950s and 1960s were those of the rich industrialised world. As a result, British exporters increasingly found it easier to sell their goods and services in Europe and the United States rather than in the generally poorer economies of the Empire and Commonwealth. Crucially, the focus of Britain's *economic* activity was shifting away from the Empire and towards Europe: as a result of the aggregate effect of innumerable individual business decisions in Europe and the United States, trade with the Empire circle was becoming progressively less important to the British economy. In these circumstances, it was only a matter of time before the British government's *political* commitments followed the same path: if Britain's material-economic interests were shifting autonomously towards Europe, then in classic *realpolitik* fashion its military-strategic commitment was sure to follow. Viewed in this light, the political downgrading of the Empire circle associated with both the second-wave decolonisations and the withdrawal from East of Suez was simply the policy response to deep-seated economic forces which were already operating inside the rich Western economies and which were drawing the locus of Britain's trading activity away from its imperial roots.

In addition to Britain's long-term economic decline, then, the two major factors that led to the withdrawal from East of Suez were also primarily economic: (1) the need to cut the size of the overseas defence budget; and (2) the changing pattern of Britain's export trade. But if these underlying preconditions made an eventual withdrawal from East of Suez inevitable, the *timing* of the decision to withdraw was also shaped by a number of shorter-term – mainly *political* – factors. First, while Britain was supporting Malaysia in its border dispute with Indonesia between 1963 and 1966, a strategic withdrawal from East of Suez was unthinkable; however, once the local participants had settled their differences, as they did in August 1966, the constraint was clearly removed. A second short-term factor was the endemic sterling crisis which plagued the Wilson government between 1966 and 1968 and which created enormous pressure for cuts in public spending. Given Britain's declining international economic position and the recent discarding of its imperial possessions, defence expenditure was an obvious target for cuts. Decolonisation had enormously diminished Britain's world role: why not now take the process to its logical conclusion by terminating a military commitment which had originally arisen primarily as a means of protecting an Empire that had now disappeared? The final short-term factor was the fact that a Labour government was now in power. Although the Conservatives had presided over much of the process of decolonisation, a Conservative government would also have been sorely tempted to retain a presence East of Suez both to preserve the appearance of a continued British 'world role' and to appease the influential Tory right wing. A Labour government was far less likely to experience internal party dissent as a result of a decision to end a military commitment which had outlived its political and economic usefulness. It was consequently far better placed to carry through a policy that squarely faced up to economic realities by offering a symbolic affirmation of the fact that Britain no longer had pretensions to an imperial role.

Political Entanglements in the Empire Circle after 1968

Not long after the decision to withdraw from East of Suez had been publicly confirmed, a serious blow was dealt to British interests in the Mediterranean. The Libyan monarchy, which since 1956 had increasingly been regarded as Britain's major ally in the Near East,[27] was ousted in a coup which brought to power Colonel Muammar Ghaddafi, champion of Arab nationalism and ardent anti-imperialist. British interests were almost certain to be damaged by the change in regime, as indeed they were in January 1972 when Libya dissolved its alliance with Britain, and again, in September 1973, when all foreign-owned companies were nationalised.[28] However, the Heath government responded with commendable circumspection. There was no question of a repetition of the sort of crass intervention which had produced such calamitous results at Suez. With some justification, Britain was unwilling to confront the international opprobrium which would undoubtedly have greeted any attempt to intervene in the internal affairs of a sovereign nation-state: as a result, the opportunity to engage in yet another piece of modern-day gunboat diplomacy was firmly rejected.

A similarly responsible reaction greeted Idi Amin's coup against Milton Obote's government in Uganda in January 1971. Although it was rumoured at the time that Amin's actions had the blessing of the Foreign and Commonwealth Office (FCO)[29] because of Obote's recent shift to more radical domestic and foreign policies, there is no evidence whatsoever that the British government had any part in either the planning or the execution of the coup. On the contrary, Britain certainly did not benefit from it. It seems far more likely that London's policy from the outset was designed to avoid any British involvement in the internal conflicts of an ex-colony. This was certainly the position that had been adopted with regard to the coups in Nigeria and Ghana in 1966 and with regard to the Nigerian Civil War of 1967–70. It was a policy which was also to be adhered to as further coups afflicted West Africa after 1970.[30] As with Libya, in all these cases the British government's awareness of its own physical inability to impose a military solution – as well as the strongly antipathetic international reaction which intervention would have invoked – counselled a policy of caution. It was better to do nothing and risk a gradual loss of influence and investments than to embark on a vainglorious campaign to restore pro-British regimes which could only survive with continued – and substantial – military support. This was classic *realpolitik* calculation on the part of the British government, but in the straitened economic circumstances of the time it implied post-imperial *non*-involvement rather than further efforts at colonial subjugation.

Throughout 1971, as the date for the final withdrawal from East of Suez approached (and as promised in the 1968 Defence Review), the Heath government negotiated a series of defensive and quasi-defensive treaties with the countries from which British forces were to be removed. Between August and December 1971, a series of Friendship Treaties were signed with the Gulf States which variously provided for the future stationing of British forces in the Gulf in certain circumstances.[31] However, the newly unobtrusive nature of Britain's post-imperial involvement in the third world was best expressed in the agreements which Britain signed separately with Singapore and Malaysia in December 1971. Intended as a direct substitute for Britain's hitherto intimate involvement in the defence of the region, the texts of these agreements revealed clearly that it was the governments of Malaysia and Singapore which would dictate the terms and conditions of any future British involvement in their defence. The United Kingdom-Malaysia Exchange of Notes, for example, asserted that the *Malaysian government* '*may* after mutual consultation *permit a UK force to be stationed or present in Malaysia* upon agreed terms' [emphasis added].[32] It was also made clear that all future rights and facilities accorded to British forces would have to be agreed with the Malaysian government.[33] As far as the British government was concerned, these residual commitments were in no sense a surreptitious vehicle for the maintenance of indirect imperial domination. On the contrary, they were simply assurances that London felt obliged to make in order to avoid leaving friendly governments cruelly exposed should their security be threatened by some nearby regional conflict (such as the war in Indochina, which was then raging).

But if a relatively benign view can be taken of the arrangements that Britain made for the protection of its allies after its withdrawal from East of Suez, rather more cynicism is in order with regard to the Diego Garcia Agreement which Britain reached with the United States in October 1972. The British evacuation of both Singapore and Aden had not only signalled Britain's unpreparedness to provide strong material support for the United States in its global efforts to defend the strategic interests of the West. It had also left the Indian Ocean exposed to Soviet infiltration. With the radicalisation of the People's Republic of South Yemen after 1968, Soviet warships had begun, by the early 1970s, to use the port facilities which the British had vacated in Aden. In addition, Siad Barré's coup in Somalia in 1969 had led to a Soviet-Somali Friendship Treaty which in turn had given the Soviet navy access to the deep-water facilities at Mogadishu. The combined effect of these changes was a significant increase in Soviet naval activity in the Indian Ocean, a development which was construed, rightly or wrongly, by strategic planners in London and Washington as a threat to Western shipping. The British response was swift. Having already granted limited port facilities to the United States Navy on the strategically placed Indian Ocean island of Diego Garcia in 1966,[34] London decided that, if the Royal Navy was no longer able to police the Indian Ocean, Britain should at least provide the Americans with the means to do the job properly. As a result of the 1972 Agreement (which was reinforced by a subsequent Exchange of Notes in February 1976)[35] the United States was given a virtual *carte blanche* to fortify and enhance the facilities of the Diego Garcia base as it wished. This may not have been overt neo-imperialism on the part of the British government, but it was certainly yet another example of *realpolitik* calculation intended to maximise the strategic interests of the West rather than the interests of a subject population over which Britain still exercised sovereignty.

Meanwhile, in Southern Africa, the Rhodesian crisis slowly rumbled on throughout the 1970s. As the decolonising power that had so far failed to decolonise properly, Britain had residual responsibilities towards Rhodesia which it exercised after 1965 by supporting the diplomatic isolation of the Smith government and by orchestrating an international campaign of economic sanctions against the rebel regime. Given the fairly sophisticated sanctions-breaking operation which, with South African assistance, was subsequently put into effect, it is unclear how far British policy was actually responsible for the downfall of the Smith regime. None the less, as noted earlier, as the armed struggle of the black nationalist movement reached its climax in the late 1970s, London returned much more directly to the fray by organising the Lancaster House Conference, which, in January 1980, established a framework for a peaceful transition to formal independence and majority rule. In strictly legal terms, Britain's actions in 1980 were those of an imperial power. Realistically, however, the government possessed no practical capability to influence events on the ground: Lord Carrington's skilful diplomacy merely provided a suitable environment in which black and white Zimbabwean leaders could agree to resolve some of their more significant differences. This was certainly not imperialism in any malign sense: it was simply Britain undertaking a minor role on the world stage which, by virtue of its imperial past, it was uniquely qualified to perform.

With Zimbabwe independent, it seemed as though virtually all of Britain's overt imperial responsibilities had been discharged. In future – with luck – Britain's imperial role would be limited either to the sort of occasional minor policing operation that had been undertaken so successfully in Anguilla or to providing training assistance for the armed forces of ex-colonies which specifically requested British advice.[36] However, such calculations reckoned without the Falklands affair of 1982.[37] Britain had occupied the Falkland Islands since 1828. Throughout the ensuing period, successive Argentine governments had claimed sovereignty over the islands but had taken no overt military action to reclaim them, a result principally of Britain's obvious determination to retain control over what had always been regarded as an important strategic base. The 1981 Defence White Paper, however, had announced significant cuts in the size of Britain's surface fleet.[38] One consequence of these cuts was the withdrawal in November 1981 of the only remaining Royal Navy frigate to have been permanently stationed in Port Stanley.

This action was clearly viewed in Buenos Aires as an indication of Britain's weakening commitment to maintaining a presence in the South Atlantic. With negotiations over the possession of the islands deadlocked, General Galtieri's government decided to wrest control of them by a *fait accompli*. In a case of mutual misperception, the British did not expect Argentina to act as it did.[39] Equally, the Argentine invasion of March–April 1982 had not, however, anticipated the reaction of the Thatcher Cabinet, which immediately began preparations for the repossession of the islands. Three factors were crucial to Thatcher's position. First, after 150 years of continuous occupation, Britain had a strong claim to ownership of the islands under international law. Second, as an attack on a British colony, the invasion was a direct challenge to British sovereignty, which could not go unpunished. And third, the vast majority of the islands' 1,800 inhabitants fervently wished to remain under the British Crown.[40] As a result of an outstanding military campaign, by October 1982 British forces had regained control of the islands and British sovereignty had been restored. At the considerable expense of the British taxpayer, a substantial garrison and naval contingent were permanently stationed in and around the islands thereafter. This continuing military presence not only acted as a deterrent to further Argentine aggression but also represented an unequivocal public affirmation of Britain's intention to carry out its remaining imperial responsibilities to the full even if the scope of its Empire had been radically compressed since decolonisation.

Yet, in spite of the scale and the determination of the British response to the Argentine intervention, the Falklands episode was nothing more than a temporary reversal of the long process of imperial retreat. It provided a welcome 'shot in the arm' at a time when Britain needed it most, but it did not fundamentally change the existing balance of power. After 1982, the possibility of any British withdrawal from the Falkland Islands was remote, and in 2015 there were about 1,000 UK troops stationed there, compared with about 3,000 islanders, a 1:3 ratio. But it was equally unlikely that the British government would seriously consider embarking on a similar venture of (post-)imperial self-assertion elsewhere in the world. Quite apart from the fact that there were now so few colonial dependencies left, there were two main reasons why this should have been so. The first was cost. By 2010–11 the cost of maintaining the base was about £75 million per year, a figure that was set to rise as a result of British Defence Secretary Michael Fallon's announcement in March 2015 that the existing force would be expanded.[41] During the Cold War an *additional* commitment of a similar magnitude would have seriously prejudiced the defence of Western Europe, and was quite simply unaffordable in any case. Second, the decision to send the task force to repossess the Falklands was based in part on a Realist assessment of international circumstances that were themselves unlikely to be repeated in the foreseeable future. Although much of the third world was opposed to the British government's policy, the United States (after four weeks of attempted mediation between London and Buenos Aires) and the European Community countries provided firm backing for Thatcher's stance. The then-Soviet Union, for its part, could not be seen to provide material assistance to one of the most odious right-wing military governments in Latin America. Thus, deprived of potential support from

powerful allies, Argentina was from the outset a relatively weak opponent whose military campaign could be effectively stifled through the
intelligent use of the Royal Navy's superior sea power. Crucially, given
that such a fortuitous combination of strategic and diplomatic circumstances was unlikely to recur, the resurgent imperialism which characterised Britain's Falklands War was clearly an ephemeral historical
aberration. Rather than presaging a renewed attempt to restore Britain
to its world role, the Falklands campaign merely represented the last gasp
of imperialism in retreat.

That the heyday of perfidious Albion was long gone was confirmed
in Britain's negotiations with the People's Republic of China over the
future of Hong Kong between 1983 and 1985. Although the size of the
Hong Kong garrison had been reduced at the time of the withdrawal
from East of Suez, a continued presence had been maintained there after
1971. This was partly to accord with the wishes of the indigenous population and partly because to have withdrawn in the immediate aftermath
of the Cultural Revolution might have been construed in Beijing as an
invitation to intervene. With the gradual softening of China's position
towards the West during the 1970s, the prospects for a negotiated settlement over the future of the colony increased. Yet in the early 1980s
there was still reason to suppose that such a settlement would prove
elusive. Britain had consistently been unprepared to concede sovereignty
to Argentina over the Falklands question: why should it behave any
differently towards China over Hong Kong? The two situations, after
all, were in many respects similar. In both cases, the territory had been
acquired by military force over 100 years before; the adjacent power
had a longstanding – though contentious – legal claim to possession
of the territory; and the indigenous population, apparently, wished to
remain under the Crown in order to avoid being dominated by a much
larger neighbour. Yet where Britain had refused as a matter of principle
to make concessions to Argentina, by December 1984 it had formally
agreed to a complete withdrawal from Hong Kong by 1997, after which
date – with certain safeguards – the territory reverted to the People's
Republic.[42]

The reason for these very different approaches to two similar problems was in fact very simple: *realpolitik*. Whereas Britain could have
reasonably expected to resist any Argentine threat to the Falklands, it
would have been powerless to resist had Communist China – itself no
stranger to Realism – chosen to take Hong Kong by force. In the wake
of the Falklands War, the agreement on Hong Kong represented a rapid
reversion to the long-term pattern of gradual imperial withdrawal that
had first found expression in the decolonisation of India. As always,
even if diplomacy had been important in determining the timing and the
conditions of withdrawal, at the root of the withdrawal itself were the

ubiquitous forces of Realist calculation: with Britain's military capability in progressive relative decline, a major diplomatic concession on Hong Kong had always been inevitable.

To summarise, then, Britain's political actions in the Empire circle after 1968 – with the notable exception of the Falklands War – were those of an imperial power in continuous retreat. To be sure, as the process of withdrawal proceeded, prudence demanded that help be given to old friends. But it was help generally given on terms determined by the recipients; and when British assistance was firmly rejected, as in Libya after 1969, the rejection was accepted in London with good grace. As in the Macmillan years, frantic efforts to subvert the forces that were pressing for further imperial withdrawals were studiously avoided. But if responsibility, admittedly inspired by Realism, reigned almost supreme in the political sphere, what of Britain's *economic* activities in the Empire circle?

PostImperialism: The Economic Record after 1968

It has become almost an axiom of Marxist political economy that formal decolonisation made no difference to the economic exploitation of the third world. In spite of the relaxation of formal political control that occurred in the 1960s, the forces of international capital, using the rich 'Northern' capitalist states as their instrument, continued to extract a large 'economic surplus' from the impoverished 'South'.[43] According to this view, in the economic sphere the British government did not need to take any specific action after 1968 in order to continue to be 'imperialistic'. Simply by participating in the existing international division of labour – by maintaining the exploitation of the 'South' – the British government laid itself open to the charge of 'imperialism without colonies'.

What specific evidence is there that Britain continued to extract an 'economic surplus' either from the third world in general or, more particularly, from the territories that were formerly under its direct colonial control? Given the large volume of writing on the relationship between Northern affluence and Southern poverty, it is somewhat surprising to discover that there is in fact little hard evidence to show that Britain – or for that matter any other rich country – does indeed 'exploit' the third world. While British companies certainly extract profits from their operations in the South, for example, it is also the case that they can only do so once they have brought desperately needed investment funds to the 'host' economy. Moreover, contrary to what is often claimed by critics of Western neo-imperialism, the notion that the level of repatriated profit exceeds the extra income which is generated by the investment activities of foreign corporations still awaits firm empirical corroboration.[44] The fact that most third-world governments, notwithstanding their awareness of the potentially exploitative behaviour of multinational corporations, continue to welcome foreign capital suggests that they at least must believe that the domestic benefits of foreign investment outweigh the costs incurred as a result of profit repatriation.[45]

A similar problem of lack of evidence is encountered in relation to *trade*. Critical observers of North–South relations feel instinctively that the North benefits disproportionately from its trade with the South; that the terms of trade favour the former at the expense of the latter. However, while it is possible to show that the third world's overall terms of trade did become less favourable during the 1980s,[46] it is extremely difficult to demonstrate that the North extracts a measurable economic surplus simply by trading with the South. The core of the problem is that, if Southern countries derived no benefit from exporting their products to the North, they would presumably cease trading altogether: the fact that they do not implies that trade must be to some degree mutually beneficial. The question as to whether the North benefits 'more' than the South – to an 'exploitative' degree – in these circumstances essentially involves a normative judgement that is not susceptible to empirical corroboration.

This failure to demonstrate that trade of itself involves the extraction of an economic surplus does not mean, however, that those trade statistics which are available are entirely irrelevant to the question of Britain's possible post-colonial 'imperialism'. On the contrary, even if it is assumed that any North–South trade does involve the extraction of an economic surplus from the South, the available evidence suggests that since decolonisation Britain has, in relative terms, extracted substantially less of an economic surplus than it did previously. In the mid-1950s all of the countries in the Empire circle sent a significant proportion of their exports (average: 28.5 per cent) *to* Britain and received a significant proportion of their imports *from* Britain (average: 35.2 per cent). By the mid-1980s the position had altered considerably with corresponding figures of 6.9 per cent and 9.4 per cent respectively. This diminution in British economic dominance was clearly not an *intended* consequence of the government's post-colonial foreign policy. (Successive governments would obviously have preferred British companies to have retained those markets which, after decolonisation, were increasingly opened to foreign competition.) Nonetheless, the failure to maintain market share has meant that protagonists of the benevolence of Britain's post-imperial role can reasonably claim that decolonisation was followed by a reduction in British economic domination within the Empire circle. Even if trade with the third world necessarily implies the extraction of an economic surplus from it (and there are good reasons, identified above, for doubting whether it does) Britain was a much less serious offender in the 1980s than it had been in the 1950s. Ironically, Britain's relative decline as a world trading power – the result of its own inefficiency – meant that charges of a continuing neo-imperial role after decolonisation were increasingly ill-founded.

Where does this leave us? Was Britain's more benign political approach to the Empire circle after 1968 matched by a concomitant reduction in the extent of its economic imperialism? Unless the orthodox Leninist line is taken – that all advanced capitalist states are *by definition* imperialist – the answer must be equivocal. In terms of its failure to press for a 'fairer' deal for the South – for a New International Economic Order – Britain could be adjudged to be passively imperialist: its inactivity helped to maintain an international economic system which appears to sustain the economic underdevelopment of the South. Yet in terms of the crucial indicator of neo-imperialism – the extraction of an economic surplus from the 'periphery' – the evidence is both sparse and indecisive. On the one hand, there is no systematic evidence whatsoever that the economic surplus which accrues to Britain as a result of repatriated profit exceeds the economic surplus which accrues to the third world as a result of British investment. On the other hand, the available information on trade flows suggests that since decolonisation Britain's economic dominion over the Empire circle has significantly diminished. This weakening dominion is likely to continue in the future; the plausibility of claims that Britain remains a neo-imperialist power is likely to decline with it.

Summary and Conclusions

The story of the Empire circle after 1956 was fundamentally one of withdrawal. As the Empire simultaneously became both less manageable and less crucial to the preservation of Britain's vital interests, so London relaxed its imperial grip and progressively abandoned the 'world role' which Britain had played for almost two centuries. The major step in the process of imperial retreat was obviously the second-wave decolonisations that took place between 1956 and 1966. The withdrawal from East of Suez in 1971 represented the British government's symbolic affirmation that the retreat was to be both comprehensive and irreversible.

Yet in spite of the seemingly inexorable nature of the forces which provoked this 'retreat from power', successive governments from the late 1950s onwards had good reason to hesitate. Their main fear was that British withdrawal, in addition to bruising innumerable egos in both Cabinet and Whitehall, would leave a power vacuum in the third world which the Soviet Union, either directly or indirectly, would be only too happy to fill. In the colonial territories themselves the dilemma was resolved (if only temporarily, given later developments) by installing friendly governments and liberal democratic constitutions before independence and by making ad hoc defence arrangements with the newly independent nations on request. In the strategically important Indian Ocean – vacated by the Royal Navy after the withdrawal from East of Suez – the solution was to provide the United States with facilities at Diego Garcia that would enable it to replace Britain as the guardian of Western strategic interests in the region. Despite the occasional set-back, the strategy was in general fairly successful: Soviet influence in Britain's ex-colonies remained limited and the American naval presence in the Indian Ocean effectively counterbalanced any threat which the Soviet navy might pose to Western shipping.

But why had the withdrawal itself been necessary? The *decisions* over both decolonisation and the withdrawal from Suez were undoubtedly based on classic *realpolitik* cost–benefit calculation. On the one hand, Britain increasingly lacked the military capability to contain the growing demands for independence inside the colonies. On the other hand, the focus of Britain's material economic interests was shifting away from the Empire and towards Europe. If the potential communist threat resulting from a British military and political withdrawal could be effectively neutralised – which, as we have seen, was possible in principle – then the obvious solution was to reduce Britain's overseas commitment to a level commensurate with its remaining capabilities: better to do less effectively than to attempt more and fail ignominiously.

However, to assert that the decision to opt for a strategy of imperial withdrawal was based on Realist criteria does not explain why the particular circumstances arose that made such a decision necessary. It has been argued in this chapter that, in addition to Britain's long-term relative economic decline, two principal 'structural' forces were responsible for the 'emptying out' of the Empire circle.[47] The first of these was the increase in indigenous nationalism which arose from the economic development of the colonies. The acceleration in world economic growth that occurred in the post-war years created economic and social conditions throughout the colonial world in which nationalism could thrive. Rapid urbanisation and the move away from subsistence agriculture combined to produce a major social upheaval which rendered almost all of Britain's colonial peoples much more susceptible to the appeal of anti-imperialist ideologies. As a result, nationalist movements throughout the Empire – with their views clearly articulated by a new post-war generation of third-world intellectuals – found increasing support. It was this indigenous nationalist pressure which constituted Macmillan's 'wind of change': a force for imperial retreat that could not be sensibly resisted.

The second major 'structural' factor underlying the withdrawal from the Empire circle was the apparently autonomous change in the pattern of Britain's external trade which occurred from the mid-1950s onwards. Between 1955 and 1965 – *before* the end of the Sterling Area and *before*

Britain's entry into Europe – the Empire circle declined significantly as a destination for British exports. This was almost certainly not a result of any policy decisions taken by the British government. It was simply a reflection of the fact that European and North American consumers expanded their demand for the sort of goods and services that British business was increasingly willing and able to supply. The main consequence of this secular change was that Britain's economic ties with the Empire circle became progressively less important for the health of the domestic economy: here was a powerful economic force which could only serve to reinforce the existing political pressures for an imperial withdrawal.

After the withdrawal from 'East of Suez' in 1971, the retreat from Empire continued. In the political sphere, this principally involved the granting of independence to most of the remaining smaller colonies and resisting the residual temptation to intervene in those parts of the third world where indigenous regime changes threatened to damage British commercial or strategic interests. It also meant playing a diplomatic role in the formal decolonisation of Zimbabwe in 1980 and in the 1984 agreement to return Hong Kong to the People's Republic of China by the end of the century. The only major departure from this long-term trend was the Falklands crisis of 1982, which led to a powerful reassertion of Britain's commitment to the defence of the islands. However, in spite of the fact that this particular commitment seemed destined to continue for the foreseeable future, the Falklands episode was likely to remain an isolated exception to the general rule: that Britain had indeed retreated from its world role and that it no longer possessed the capability to sustain it.

Even in the economic sphere, British imperialism continued to retreat. From the mid-1950s onwards, largely as a result of increased competition from other industrialised countries, Britain found its share of Empire circle markets in serious decline. Indeed, by the mid-1980s, Britain's economic dominance in the third world had declined to such an extent that accusations of a specifically British neo-imperialism seemed misdirected. The only sense in which Britain might have been deemed to participate in the continuing imperialistic exploitation of the third world was as one of the large group of rich Northern powers which exercised a generalised dominion over the world economy; but even in these circumstances there was no compelling evidence to demonstrate that Britain actually extracted a disproportionate economic surplus from its dealings with the South.

Chapter 5

The Uncertain Search for a New Role: The European Circle after 1956

As noted in earlier chapters, throughout the post-war period successive British governments found it increasingly difficult, in the face of Britain's long-term relative economic decline, to sustain the strategy of maintaining British influence in all three of Churchill's 'circles'. In Chapter 4 it was suggested that, from the mid-1950s onwards, partly as a result of indigenous nationalism and partly because of the diminishing importance of Britain's imperial trade, Britain's involvement in the Empire circle was gradually reduced. As will be seen in Chapter 6, by the 1960s, with the process of decolonisation well under way, Britain was also becoming less important to the United States as a strategic ally in the global struggle against 'communist expansionism'. The obvious corollary to this reduction of influence in both the 'Empire' and 'Atlantic' circles was for the focus of Britain's foreign policy to shift towards Europe. It was increasingly recognised in the years after Suez that it was here that Britain's primary economic and political interests were located; that if Britain wished to retain a significant voice in world affairs, then it would have to do so in concert with its allies in Western Europe. The strategic shift towards Europe was not accomplished without great difficulty, however. Significant problems were encountered in the 1960s as Britain attempted to institutionalise its European connections. And even after Britain finally 'joined Europe' in 1973, its residual commitments and responsibilities in both the Empire and Atlantic circles frequently served to reinforce the widely held impression that the British were fundamentally 'reluctant Europeans', only partially committed to the ideals of European cooperation that the original six members of the European Union (EU) had so strongly – and productively – embraced.[1]

More recently, this reluctance has taken the form of overt 'Euroscepticism' among some important segments of the British polity, which eventually resulted in the June 2016 vote to leave the EU.[2] This was the first time since the 1975 referendum that ordinary voters had been asked whether they wanted to remain in the European Union. Although it was rarely presented as such, voters were essentially being given a choice about how Britain could best maintain its three circles of influence: through the primarily EU-focused route that it had increasingly followed since 1973; or through a route that stressed the UK's independence and autonomy in determining how it should manage its affairs with Europe, the US, and the rest of the world. Would the EU remain an indispensable and increasingly important part of people's lives or would Britain again try to go it alone? Somewhat contrary to expectations – the polls had been uncertain, but many had suggested that the Remain camp would win – the Brexit argument narrowly won the day, with 52 per cent supporting withdrawal against 48 per cent to stay in the EU.[3]

The British government was thrown into almost immediate crisis. Prime Minister David Cameron, who had argued strongly for the Remain camp, decided to resign the day after the vote, and the Conservative Party scrambled to find another leader (he was replaced in July 2016 by the former Home Secretary Theresa May). Cameron had been pressured by advocates of Leave within his own party to hold the vote in the first place – he had had been following a manifesto commitment to hold a referendum on Britain's EU membership before the end of 2017 – and had recklessly gambled that he could somehow win the referendum which resulted. The pound dropped precipitately and the stock market tumbled, as the British economy and polity were confronted by a period of great uncertainty that seemed likely to last until at least 2018.[4]

This chapter begins with a brief review of Britain's increasing involvement in the European circle in the period up to 1972. It examines Britain's failure to participate in the early efforts at European economic cooperation in the 1950s and then describes both its abortive attempts to join the (then) European Economic Community (EEC) in the 1960s and its successful accession in 1973.[5] The second section seeks to identify the principal causal factors that lay behind the strategic shift towards Europe. At the decision-making level, the crucial factor was the apparent benefit which it was believed EU membership would bestow upon the British economy; at the structural level, the major causal influence was the autonomous shift in the pattern of Britain's external trade – away from the Empire and towards Europe – that was observed in Chapter 4.

Finally, Britain's evolving relations with Europe in the period since 1973 are examined. In the late 1990s and 2000s in particular, Britain shed at least a part of its 'reluctant European' image and – with reservations – joined with other EU members in their efforts to achieve some degree of foreign policy coordination within limited policy areas. The period since Tony Blair and Gordon Brown served as Prime Ministers has seen a reassertion of that reluctance, however, and the austerity measures of the early 21st century made a common European foreign and defence policy an increasingly remote possibility. The Eurozone crisis after 2009 – in which several EU states defaulted on their national debts – and the Greek financial crisis of 2015, as well as the determination of some members of the British Conservative Party and UK Independence Party (UKIP) to leave the EU, again threw Britain's membership into question. This culminated in the June 2016 referendum vote to rescind British membership, and at the time of writing, it was unclear what form Britain's future relationship with the EU would take.[6] Over the longer run, however, the movement from purely economic cooperation to something more akin to a deeper *political* union, particularly after the signing of the Maastricht Treaty in 1993, intensified strains between Britain and what has always been seen by some as a 'foreign' government on the continent of Europe.

Increasing Involvement in the European Circle, 1956–72

As observed in Chapter 2, in 1945 Britain's position as the dominant power in Western Europe provided it with the capability to play a determining role in the political and economic evolution of the entire region. Yet, in spite of American efforts to persuade London to take a leading role in establishing a new European cooperative political order, the Attlee government demurred. Although Ernest Bevin was actively involved in the formation of the Council of Europe in May 1948,[7] the Council itself never became anything more than a 'talking shop' in which European foreign ministers (in the 'Committee of Ministers') and Parliamentarians (in the Council's 'Assembly') could exchange views on matters of current concern. Jealously guarding the principle of national sovereignty, the British and Scandinavian delegations insisted from the outset that the Committee of Ministers should play the primary role in the Council's activities. This in turn prevented the Assembly from developing any sort of authority, thereby dashing the hopes of contemporary European 'federalists' who had hoped that the Council as a whole – but especially the Assembly – might provide the basis for an embryonic European federation analogous to the model developed in the late 18th century in the United States.[8]

The response of European internationalists to the limitations of the Council of Europe was to develop the idea of *functionalist integration*. Federalist internationalism had foundered because of the refusal of national governments to cede any part of their sovereignty to the would-be federal body. The central principle of functionalism was that the process of economic and political integration in Western Europe could be started without the need for an open-ended commitment on the part of national governments to transfer decision-making power to some supranational institution. On the contrary, the integrative process could be started by achieving functional cooperation in a limited number of narrowly defined areas of economic activity. Once the benefits of such functional cooperation became evident, there would be pressure to extend it elsewhere: functional collaboration in one sector would 'spill over' into others.[9] In short, greater political and economic integration – which was impossible to achieve in the short run because of the continuing commitment of national governments to the preservation of their own sovereignty – would be achieved by 'stealth' over a period of time.

The French-sponsored Schuman Plan of 1950 was very much a reflection of this new functionalist logic and in January 1952 it resulted in the creation of the European Coal and Steel Community (ECSC). Under the terms of the enabling legislation, the constituent members of the Community delegated a large measure of decision-making power to the 'High Authority'. This meant that the High Authority was from the outset a genuinely supranational body which did not require the unanimous consent of member governments for its actions: it was thus able to develop a common policy for the coal and steel industries of the member countries on the basis of *majority* decisions. However, the British coal and steel industries remained outside the High Authority's purview. Fearful of the damage that membership of the ECSC might inflict on Britain's Empire circle trade, London was still unprepared to accept any diminution of its sovereignty even in so specific a policy area: British involvement was accordingly limited to an agreement in December 1954 which regularised Anglo-ECSC relations.[10]

Even without British participation, however, the ECSC flourished. Indeed, it was such a success that at a summit meeting in Messina in June 1955 the member governments decided to act upon the 'spill-over' principle and extend their collaboration by forming the European Economic Community (EEC) and the European Atomic Community (EURATOM). The Treaty of Rome of March 1957 duly established that these two additional 'functionalist' institutions would be created in January 1958. The three main aims of the EEC were (1) the elimination of intra-community trade barriers; (2) free mobility for capital and for labour; and (3) a common external tariff. As with the ECSC, however, the British government expressed no desire to join the new venture. In the mid-1950s, first of all, Britain had yet to experience the autonomous shift in the balance of its external trade – away from the Empire circle and towards Europe – which was to become so evident over the next decade.[11] Second, it was widely feared that a common external tariff would seriously damage what was left of 'imperial preference', the special trade relations with the Empire and Commonwealth which had been established at the Ottawa Conference in 1932.[12] The result of London's prevarication was clear, however: Britain again 'missed out' in Europe, as it had in 1952, at a time when the EEC was still young enough for the UK to have decisively influenced its rules and structure. Britain turned instead to the creation of the European Free Trade Association (established in 1960 with the three Scandinavian countries, Austria, Portugal and Switzerland) – though this was largely a diversion that London was content to pursue temporarily until the time was right for a close British relationship with the Six.

The Abortive Attempts to Join the EEC, 1961–62 and 1967–68

In the 1960s, certain changes were taking place – both in Britain's bilateral relations with the major European powers and inside the European communities – which were to lead to two British attempts to join the EEC. Throughout the late 1950s and early 1960s, British collaboration with Western Europe increased in a wide range of policy arenas. More significant, however, was the return to power of General de Gaulle in France in December 1958. De Gaulle was committed to the principle of national sovereignty and deliberately tried to put a brake on the integrative, supranational momentum of the EEC. He wanted it to remain an association of independent sovereign states which would collaborate pragmatically for the sole purpose of their mutual economic benefit,[13] a view that squared well with the British government's long-held view of European cooperation.

In October 1961, Prime Minister Macmillan entered into a series of negotiations aimed at securing Britain's entry into the new 'Gaullist' EEC. De Gaulle for his part welcomed Britain's approaches, hopeful of building a genuinely European *security* community – independent of the United States – as well as an economic one more suited to his liking. Negotiations continued for over a year, with apparent success. However, in December 1962, the 'special relationship' – the 'House that Jack and Mac built'[14] – interposed itself. For largely technical reasons, the Americans cancelled the Skybolt nuclear-tipped missile system which Britain had contracted to buy in order to strengthen its deterrent capability in Europe. De Gaulle apparently regarded the cancellation as a great opportunity both to develop Anglo-French military – and especially nuclear – collaboration and for Britain to reduce its military links with the United States.[15] Macmillan was ready to draw closer to Europe in economic terms but he remained unconvinced that such involvement should in any way prejudice London's close military and political relationship with Washington. Within a week of the Skybolt cancellation, Macmillan met President Kennedy at Nassau, where, by way of replacement, he negotiated the purchase (on extremely favourable terms) of the submarine-launched Polaris missile system.[16] On 14 January 1963, however, the French government announced its intention to veto the British application. By convincing de Gaulle that the United Kingdom still retained strong political and military ambitions inside the Atlantic 'circle' – that Britain was still in effect a near-dependency of the United States – the special relationship, as manifested at Nassau, had succeeded in preventing Britain moving more fully into the European 'circle'.

The incoming Labour government in 1964 was not in favour of British membership of the EEC. The Labour left had always regarded the Community as a 'capitalists' club' which should be studiously avoided if socialism was to make any progress either in Western Europe in general or in Britain in particular. In July 1966, however, George Brown, the party's deputy leader and an ardent Europeanist, became Foreign Secretary. Under his influence, first the Prime Minister and subsequently the Cabinet and the Parliamentary Labour Party were gradually persuaded of the merits of UK membership.[17] As a result, in May 1967, Britain initiated its second attempt to enter the newly designated 'European Communities'. Negotiations over the terms of UK entry proceeded for almost a year before being halted in February 1968 by the 'Soames Affair'. In a private dinner conversation with the British Ambassador to Paris (Sir Christopher Soames), General de Gaulle had indicated that the French would favour British entry provided that it meant (1) less European reliance on the United States, (2) a change in the character of the EEC, making it principally a free trade area with special provisions for agricultural prices, and (3) a more powerful decision-making role for the largest member countries.[18] This conversation was then leaked, however, causing a diplomatic furore. Anglo-French relations plummeted to their lowest point since January 1963, while the remaining Community members were highly suspicious of British motives. With the Council of Ministers deadlocked on the question of British entry, the Wilson government decided to withdraw the application.

Entry, 1972–73

De Gaulle's resignation from the French presidency in April 1969 and his replacement with Georges Pompidou proved to be a turning point. The latter was far more inclined towards a supranationalist view of the Community itself and helped convince other leaders of the merits of a British application. The election victory of the Conservative Edward Heath – a longstanding advocate of British entry into the Community – in June 1970 provided the final trigger. Formal diplomatic negotiations began in May 1971 and in January 1972 a series of treaties were signed confirming Britain's accession to the Communities as from 1 January 1973.[19] For good or ill, Britain's long journey into the European circle had been given formal, institutional expression, but in later years it would always play an ambiguous 'in or out' role, uncertain as to whether this would at last provide an answer to Acheson's digging question about Britain's role in the world, or whether the 'special relationship' would prevail over all else.

At the same time, important changes were also occurring in British policy towards the communist countries of Eastern Europe. To be sure, underlying these changes was the continuing conviction that the Soviet Union and its Warsaw Pact allies[20] constituted the major threat to the security of the West. And, as a key member of NATO, Britain was obviously obliged to maintain its strong deterrent military posture towards the Soviet bloc. But successive British governments did engage in 'partial cooperation' with the Warsaw Pact countries in relatively non-contentious policy areas well removed from security matters, and this cooperation would of course intensify in the years after the Cold War ended.[21] In the early 1970s the Heath government, for instance, extended the principle of partial cooperation to embrace the rest of the Warsaw Pact. In April 1971 a long-run trade agreement was reached with Poland,[22] and similar accords were achieved with Hungary, Czechoslovakia and Romania during the course of 1972.[23] While none of these agreements signalled a major breakthrough in Britain's relations with Eastern Europe, they were nonetheless indicative both of the more Eurocentric focus of UK foreign policy in the 1960s and 1970s and a determination to build diplomatic bridges wherever possible. In spite of the added East–West tensions which were generated as a direct result of the Soviet invasion of Czechoslovakia in August 1968, Britain continued to operate the kind of 'dual-track' strategy towards opponents that Churchill had counselled in 1953.[24] This was also in accordance with the classic *realpolitik* maxim that statesmen should 'speak softly and carry a big stick'.[25]

Explaining the Shift towards Europe

Any major foreign policy development is obviously the consequence of a large number of causal factors, but there were probably four critical ones which were of overriding significance in Britain's strategic shift towards Europe after 1956. At the decision-making level the three most important considerations were (1) the apparent economic benefits of Community membership, (2) American approval of closer British ties with Europe, and (3) the declining political significance of the Empire-cum-Commonwealth. At the structural level, the principal influence was the shift in the focus of Britain's overseas trade.

The Economic Benefits of Closer Ties with Europe

The economic benefits of ECSC membership were already becoming evident by the time the Six signed the Treaty of Rome in 1957. All of

Table 5.1   Percentage growth in industrial production in selected countries, 1950–56

Federal Republic of Germany	100
Italy	63
France	49
Belgium	36
Britain	21

Source: Mancur Olson, *The Rise and Decline of Nations: Economic Growth, Stagflation and Social Rigidities* (Cambridge, MA: Harvard University Press, 1982) p. 17.

Europe – Britain included – was benefiting from the worldwide post-war economic boom which Marshall Aid and the expansion of the US economy had done so much to create. Unfortunately, Britain's economic performance lagged significantly behind that of its European competitors. As Table 5.1 shows, even by 1956 it was clear that, in comparison with other major Western European economies, Britain's record on industrial growth was unimpressive. The continental European countries, with their economies shattered by the war, had begun their industrial expansion from a lower production base, which in turn meant that they could achieve relatively large *percentage* increases in production rather more easily. It was also widely suspected that an overvalued pound, inefficient British manufacturers protected from foreign competition, and unnecessarily powerful trade unions were also, in their separate ways, contributing to Britain's poor economic performance. A final possibility, moreover, was that the ECSC, with its supranational orientation, its factor mobility and its common external tariff, was genuinely achieving better collective results for its members than any of them could have secured individually. Indeed, as noted earlier, it certainly appeared after Messina in 1955 that the Six themselves were sufficiently convinced of the benefits of functional cooperation for them to elect to expand the functional domain of the entire community.

As the debate about the relative merits of Britain's fuller participation in Europe gathered momentum in the early 1960s, the available evidence on different national growth rates certainly suggested that Europe was performing rather more effectively than Britain. As the first column of Table 5.2 indicates, throughout the 1950s the average annual growth rate within the ECSC/EEC countries was 4 per cent compared with a figure of 2.3 per cent for Britain. There was, of course, some reason to suppose that functional cooperation among the Six was *not* the critical factor in the genesis of these differential growth rates: Belgium, for example, was inside the Community and yet had a lower growth rate than the United

Table 5.2   Average annual growth of GDP in selected countries, 1950–80 (%)

	1950–60	1960–70	1970–80
Belgium	2.0	4.1	3.2
France	3.5	4.6	3.0
FRG	6.6	3.5	2.4
Italy	4.9	4.6	2.1
Netherlands	3.3	4.1	2.3
(Av. ECSC/EEC)	(4.08)	(4.2)	(2.6)
Denmark	2.5	3.9	2.2
Ireland	1.8	3.8	2.3
Britain	2.3	2.3	2.0
Austria	5.7	3.9	3.8

*Excluding Luxembourg.

Source: Mancur Olson, *The Rise and Decline of Nations: Economic Growth, Stagflation and Social Rigidities* (Cambridge, MA: Harvard University Press, 1982) p. 6.

Kingdom; Austria was outside and yet had a growth rate almost as high as West Germany. The main comparison that *was* made, however, was between Britain and the three other countries which since the late 19th century had been regarded as the most important powers in continental Western Europe: France, Italy and West Germany. Here the contrast was clear-cut: an average annual growth rate of 2.3 per cent for Britain, compared with 5 per cent for the other 'Big Three'. The inference that was drawn accordingly was that, if Britain had been a member of the ECSC/EEC from the outset, its economic growth might have been considerably greater. Compounded over the years – and, more importantly, projected into the future – these differences in growth performance were alarming. Certainly by the early 1960s the Macmillan government was convinced that, if the British economy was not to be further disadvantaged in the future, Britain would have to become a full member of the Community. This perception even extended to 'public opinion': in December 1962, immediately prior to the French veto, two-thirds of the respondents to a Gallup survey who expressed a preference declared themselves to be in favour of British entry.[26]

Britain's overall economic performance continued to stagnate throughout the 1960s. As column 2 of Table 5.2 shows, between 1960 and 1970 even the lowly Belgian economy outperformed its British counterpart. Indeed, while British growth remained stuck at 2.3 per cent per annum, the average EC rate rose to 4.2 per cent. In these circumstances the tempting prospect of easier access to an expanding market of over 250 million consumers was quite enough to persuade both Conservative and Labour leaders that somehow or other Britain must join the European Club. The tragedy was that, shortly after Britain finally did accede to the Community in 1973, Community growth rates – for a variety of exogenous reasons discussed below – fell sharply (see column 3, Table 5.2). The result of this fall was that for the 1970s as a whole there was a levelling-down of Community growth rates rather than the levelling-up of British rates which had been anticipated. With hindsight, it seems sensible to conclude that it was *not* Britain's exclusion from the ECSC and EEC which led to its comparative low post-war growth rates: the causes of Britain's economic failure lay much deeper than its non-membership of a successful economic club.[27] However, this is not to suggest that the *promise* of economic improvement was anything other than a crucially important element in the decision calculus of successive governments in their respective attempts to join the EEC.

The Importance of American Support

A second continuing factor underlying Britain's greater involvement with Western Europe was the consistent support lent to the idea by successive American administrations. As observed in Chapter 2, immediately after World War II Truman and his Secretary of State Dean Acheson encouraged Ernest Bevin to take a leading role in stimulating political and economic cooperation in Western Europe: a strong united Europe, which was inconceivable in 1945 without British participation, would be a solid bulwark against Soviet expansionism. As also noted in Chapter 2, however, what the Americans failed to appreciate in 1945 was that Britain could not simultaneously lead the process of (Western) European unification *and* maintain its strong imperial links. Nonetheless, the fact that through to the late 1950s successive governments chose to emphasise London's ties with the Empire circle rather than with Europe did not prevent US leaders, ever suspicious of a resurgence in British imperialism, expressing their continued desire to see Britain pursuing a primarily European role in world affairs. Increasingly after 1949, Britain's economic integration with the rest of Western Europe was, for the Americans, the natural corollary to Britain's military role in the European wing of NATO.

But why should the British government have been concerned to receive United States approval for any of its actions? For one thing, Britain's national security relied heavily on a strong American commitment to NATO and in particular to the continued presence of a large United States conventional force in Western Europe. No British government after 1949 would have been prepared to entertain a projected foreign policy strategy which might weaken that commitment, even with the Cold War a thing of the past; the 2015 budget announced by Chancellor George Osborne, for instance, re-affirmed that Britain would continue to spend the NATO-required 2 per cent of its national budget on defence. A second sense in which the United Kingdom was concerned to appease American sensibilities was in the context of the British independent nuclear deterrent. The continuing belief within the Cabinet that Britain's status as a Great Power required the maintenance of an effective and up-to-date nuclear capability was confronted from the late 1950s onwards with the unpleasant fact that Britain could no longer afford to build one itself. This in turn meant that London was increasingly obliged to rely on the Americans for the necessary technology. Yet, if the Nassau agreement of December 1962 was a symbol of this dependence, the fact that no other nation received such preferential treatment was an affirmation of the special place which Britain still occupied in United States global strategy. To have deliberately flouted Washington's longstanding preference for a closer British association with Western Europe after the withdrawal from 'East of Suez' would undoubtedly have been to undermine Britain's privileged position as the sole overseas recipient of American nuclear technology.

Britain's formal passage into Europe was both hesitant and protracted, but if it had attempted to join Europe in the face of American *resistance*, that passage would have been even more difficult. It would also have put at risk both the unity of NATO and the survival of the independent deterrent, neither of which Britain was prepared to countenance. Britain certainly did not join the European Community simply to please the Americans, but Washington's approval of London's repeated applications was a welcome facilitating condition, essential to the success of British efforts to give formal institutional expression to the United Kingdom's increasing involvement in the European circle.

The Declining Significance of the Commonwealth

A third major factor underlying Britain's shift towards Europe after 1956 was the further decline of the Commonwealth as an instrument for maintaining British influence inside the old Empire circle. Originally, it had been hoped that the Commonwealth would act as a sort of surrogate Empire, fostering the preservation and spread of Anglo-Saxon democratic principles across the black–white racial divide. With luck, it might even provide the nucleus of a global network of alliances among democratic states capable of resisting any challenge which the communist states might collectively pose. As noted in Chapter 4, however, such hopes were soon dashed. The Suez affair seriously tarnished Britain's image in the eyes of both the recently liberated and the soon to be liberated colonies. Combined with the new third-world consciousness of oppression that was already developing in the mid-1950s, the general disillusion with Western neo-imperialism that had been exacerbated by Suez led to the emergence of a new international political bloc which sought to establish a 'middle way' between the rival imperialisms of East and West. Moreover, the fact that two of the Commonwealth's most prominent third-world leaders – Nkrumah and Nehru – were among the prime movers of this Non-Aligned Movement was a clear signal to London that the new Commonwealth nations felt very little diplomatic allegiance to the old 'mother country'; a conclusion which was soon to be reinforced by the tendency of those nations to fail to support the Western Powers in critical votes in the UN General Assembly.[28]

The internal coherence of the Commonwealth was further weakened by a series of crises during the 1960s, which affected Britain's already limited ability to exercise political influence over the association's new members. Indeed, it was doubly unfortunate from Britain's point of view that this further erosion of its *political* influence should have coincided with the decline of the Overseas Sterling Area (OSA), an international monetary arrangement which since the 1940s had operated to the mutual advantage of Britain and the majority of the 'Empire circle' countries.[29] With the final abandonment of the OSA in 1968, Britain lost not only a valuable source of international liquidity but also a potential *economic* lever that could have been used to exert pressure on individual Commonwealth nations had the need arisen. In a situation where Britain found it increasingly difficult to exert either political or economic pressure on individual Commonwealth members, the Commonwealth itself rapidly began to look less like the surrogate Empire of the post-war imperialists' imaginings and more like the loose association of (somewhat like-minded) sovereign states which the founding Statute of Westminster had formally envisaged in 1931. By the mid-1960s the British government's calculations, based, as ever, on sound *realpolitik* principles, suggested a very simple conclusion. If Britain's ties with the Commonwealth – with the residue of Empire – were no longer benefiting the United Kingdom either politically or economically, then there was absolutely no point in allowing those ties to hamper Britain's relations with Europe, as they had done since the early 1950s when London had first rejected the Schuman Plan. In these circumstances, Britain might just as well accept that its principal material interests now lay in the European rather than the Empire 'circle'.

The Increasingly European Focus of Britain's Trade

The fourth – and probably the most important – factor which underpinned Britain's strategic shift towards the European circle after 1956 was the changing pattern of Britain's overseas trade. As we discussed in Chapter 4, the focus of Britain's trade shifted dramatically away from the Empire circle and towards Europe from the late 1950s onwards. The fact that the change was already occurring well before Britain's entry into the EEC in 1973 is shown very clearly in Table 5.3, which reports the percentages of British exports to and imports from the EEC countries for selected (but representative) years between 1935 and 1983. In the prewar period, about 20 per cent of Britain's trade was with the eight countries that were destined later to become members of the EEC. As a result of the industrial devastation engendered by the war this figure fell slightly after 1945. However, by 1954 the prewar share had been restored, a position which remained more or less stable until 1960. Yet by 1971, *before* Britain's membership application had been successful, the EEC share in Britain's trade had risen to almost 30 per cent. This trend continued after 1971, so that by 1979 the EEC share had risen to well over 40 per cent.

This 'Europeanisation' of Britain's external trade was not confined solely to the *EEC* countries, however. Britain's trade with the *whole* of Western Europe increased considerably after 1955: Sweden, Switzerland, Austria, Greece, Portugal and Spain also became much more significant as United Kingdom trading partners in the period after 1955. Allowing for inflation and the overall increase in trade which occurred between 1955 and 1984, the increasingly European focus Britain's trade pattern

Table 5.3   Percentage of British exports to and imports from the EEC*

	British exports to EEC as % of all British exports	British imports from EEC as % of all British imports
1935–38	21.7	18.6
1948	16.7	13.1
1954	21.5	18.4
1960	20.9	20.2
1971	29.3	29.9
1979	41.8	43.1
1983	43.8	45.6

*All figures include the Six + Ireland + Denmark

Source: *Annual Abstract of Statistics* (HMSO, various years).

was striking. France and Germany, for example, were four times more important as destinations for British exports in the mid-1980s than they had been in the mid-1950s; Western Europe as a whole became twice as important as a destination over the same period.[30] In short, Britain's major trading interests were becoming ever more concentrated in Western Europe. Here was a powerful material reason why, during the 1960s and 1970s, the leaders of all three major political parties should have begun to stress Britain's role as a primarily European power: this was, increasingly, where Britain's main material interests lay.

Britain's Relations with Europe after 1972

Once Britain (along with Denmark and the Irish Republic) had actually joined the European Communities in January 1973, the main foreign policy question that arose was how far membership would affect the government's general European circle strategy. The broad answer was 'not very much': although changes did occur in certain policy areas, they were invariably both slow and incremental (much as the later end of the Cold War would mean only gradual changes in approach). British policy towards Eastern Europe, for example, exhibited remarkable continuity: the strategy of partial cooperation – of gradually building bridges in non-contentious policy areas – continued steadily with yet more trade and scientific cooperation agreements being negotiated with the countries of the Warsaw Pact. However, the main focus of London's European circle activities after 1972 was in the West. Here, too, Britain's overall foreign policy posture was largely unaffected by its membership of the EC. As the first part of this section indicates, Britain's relations with the other Community members – though always good in comparison with non-member states – were consistently marred by the continued British preference for an organisation in which sovereignty, especially in foreign affairs, ultimately remained with the *national* governments. As the second part shows, this continued preference was a major reason why the EC and then EU had failed to develop a coherent common European foreign and defence policy even by 2016.

Britain's Foreign Policy towards Other Community Members

The fictitious Whitehall mandarin of the early 1980s, Sir Humphrey Appleby, frequently referred to Britain's new European partners as 'our European enemies'.[31] The sentiment underlying the description – though not the characterisation itself – was probably an accurate portrayal of the continuing belief in both Cabinet and Whitehall that the fundamental task of government in the field of foreign relations was the protection of

Britain's national interests. Wide-ranging and protracted international cooperation of the sort engendered by the EC was all very well, and always welcome, but it could never be permitted to interfere with the vital national interests of the United Kingdom. It could also be safely assumed, moreover, that several other EC member governments viewed the organisation in a similar light.

Notwithstanding this important reservation, however, Britain's relations with other EC members were from the outset remarkably good. There were obviously periodic diplomatic disagreements, but these were never so important as to impair the fundamental convergence of material interest which had motivated the British government to apply for EC membership in the first place, and which continued to inform relations with the Community thereafter. After all, the United Kingdom's new European partners, though still 'enemies' in the sense that they were by definition not actually British, were far closer to Britain economically and politically than any other sovereign country or group of countries. They shared with Britain not only geographical proximity but also a common commitment to competitive party democracy, common membership of NATO and an increasingly interdependent trade network.[32] All of these shared interests had made for comparatively good relations before Britain's entry and, not surprisingly, they continued to do so afterwards.

In formal-legal terms, from the time of its accession to the EEC, Britain's behaviour towards the Community's institutions was exemplary. As anticipated at the time of entry, during the 1970s London accepted without question a new form of international legal obligation – the regulations and directives of the European Communities – which circumscribed the behaviour of member states in a variety of different contexts.[33] Similarly, the decisions of the supranational Commission, in areas where, by prior agreement, it was competent to make them, were generally accepted without challenge, as were the decisions of the European Court of Justice. In spite of this formal obeisance to the supranational practices and institutions of the Community, however, the British still gave the impression that they remained somewhat 'reluctant Europeans'. This reluctance was reflected in the two major issues which arose between Britain and its European partners in the years after 1972: the 'terms of Britain's entry' into the EC and the continuing problem of the Community budget.

Each of Britain's three attempts to join the Community in the 1960s and 1970s had encountered difficulties with regard both to the size of Britain's contribution to the EC annual budget and the implications which Community membership – and especially participation in the Common Agricultural Policy (CAP) – would have for British farmers and existing overseas foodstuff suppliers. As a subject for international bargaining, the size of the budget contribution was a fairly simple matter to resolve. Britain obviously wanted to contribute as little as possible to central Community coffers, but at the same time it would have to make a contribution that was acceptable to the existing members. This was clearly a position which was always capable of being resolved by simple haggling.

The agricultural problem was rather more intractable, however. In the early 1960s, Britain had still wanted its Commonwealth suppliers to retain their privileged access to British markets. At the same time, British farmers were extremely unhappy about the change in the system of farming subsidies which would be necessary if Britain were to accept the principles of the CAP. In the event, of course, the United Kingdom government's failure to secure membership before 1972 meant that difficult choices could be delayed. By the time Britain's successful negotiations were under way in 1971–72, however, London had already downgraded the Empire circle in its overall foreign policy strategy. In consequence, notwithstanding the special arrangements made for Commonwealth sugar and for New Zealand butter and lamb, the interests of Britain's Commonwealth suppliers could be largely disregarded. Meanwhile Britain's farmers were not sufficiently important as a domestic lobby for the United Kingdom to risk prejudicing its entire application solely on their account. The result was that, as part of the 1973 terms of entry, the Heath government not only accepted the imposition of a discriminatory tariff against *all* non-EEC imports to Britain, but also acquiesced in the indefinite preservation of the CAP.

However, having achieved membership of the Community on terms apparently agreeable to all sides, London soon began to recant. In 1975, in order to appease the left wing of the Labour Party, the recently elected Wilson government was obliged to hold a referendum on whether or not Britain should remain inside the Community. Lord knows what would have happened if the popular verdict had been in favour of withdrawal. Fortunately, the referendum produced a strong statement of approval for Britain's continued membership.[34] The die had been cast, however. For Britain's partners in Europe the fact that London could even consider subjecting Britain's continued membership of the Community to such a grave risk was clear evidence of its lack of commitment to European ideals. The error was compounded by the attendant efforts of both the Wilson and Callaghan governments to 'renegotiate the terms of entry' in 1974–75 and again in 1978–79. The results of their endeavours in terms of a 'better deal for Britain' were at best marginal, the disillusion with the recalcitrant British which their efforts occasioned considerable.

With Mrs Thatcher in power after June 1979, European suspicions of Britain's lack of commitment to the Community intensified. Even if it was now impossible to renegotiate the 'terms of entry' yet again, Britain was still unprepared to accept that the contribution which Britain was obliged to make to the EU budget was 'fair'. Accordingly, from 1980 onwards, the Thatcher government engaged in a form of 'megaphone haggling' which invariably resulted in an annual budget settlement that London at least clearly regarded as unsatisfactory. A breakthrough of sorts was eventually reached at Fontainebleau in June 1984, however, where the Community heads of government, meeting as the European Council, finally agreed on an algorithm for budgetary contributions which took account of the fact that income per capita in the United Kingdom was among the lowest in Western Europe.[35] Yet even after this achievement Britain did not retreat substantially from its 'reluctant European' image. Until its departure from the scene in 1990, the Thatcher government made strenuous efforts to effect a major revision in the CAP: the policy not only resulted in excessive over-production but also constituted both an enormous drain on the Community budget and a serious violation of the free-market principles in which the Thatcher Cabinet so firmly believed. Indeed, London was so determined to force the pace of reform that, in June 1987, Thatcher effectively vetoed the entire EC budget for the coming financial year – to the considerable consternation of the other EC heads of government.

British recalcitrance towards the Community, then, transcended the party political divide. From their different ideological standpoints, Labour and Tory governments in the period after 1972 were equally obstructive in their general approach towards Europe. But *why* should successive governments, notwithstanding the significant convergence of material interests that Britain shared with other EC member states, so consistently have advertised their own latent anti-Europeanism in their policy towards the Community? At least three possible explanatory factors can be identified. The first of these can be dismissed fairly rapidly. It might be expected that the obstructionism of successive British governments could have resulted from *the ideological opposition of other member governments*: the 1974–79 Labour government, so the argument runs, suffered from a predominantly right-wing European political environment, the Conservatives after 1979 from a predominantly socialist one. Unfortunately, this appealing hypothesis is simply not borne out by the facts: the European political balance in the 1970s if anything inclined towards the left; in the 1980s it certainly shifted to the right.[36]

A second factor that encouraged Britain's diffident posture towards the Community after 1972 was the fact that her relatively late entry meant that she joined a Community in which *the economic interests of the original Six were already well entrenched and in which French and German political influence predominated*.[37] In this sense, the continual wrangling over the 'terms of entry' and Britain's budget contribution simply reflected the government's attempts to effect changes in the EC's internal economic and political arrangements that would enable Britain to play a role in intra-Community affairs rather more commensurate with its status as a Great Power. By the mid-1980s, this particular objective had in fact to some extent been achieved, and as a result Britain was beginning to behave – and was being seen to behave – as a more 'normal' member of the Community. And although the UK government still clearly had important reservations about the current and projected supranational character of the Community, it was no longer quite the 'late-comer in search of self-aggrandisement' which it had appeared to be before the Fontainebleau settlement in 1984.[38]

A third factor underlying Britain's continued recalcitrance towards the EC concerned *the decision-making arrangements of the Community itself*. As detailed descriptions of these processes exist elsewhere, it is unnecessary to review them here.[39] It is sufficient to note that all major policy decisions of the Community required the assent both of the supposedly supranational Commission and of the nationally nominated Council of Ministers. The critical feature of this dual arrangement was that in all important matters the Council required unanimous agreement: this in turn meant that each member government possessed an effective power of veto over any new Community initiative with which it disagreed. Britain had entered the EC in the full knowledge that it could use its ministerial veto in order to prevent the Community as a whole from introducing changes in either institutions or practices which appeared contrary to British interests. (Indeed, if such a protective provision had not already been available, Britain would never have joined the Community in the first place.) Once Britain had secured membership, however, the United Kingdom was all too ready to use the threat of the veto not just as a means of preventing progressive supranational change within the EC, but also as a bargaining counter with which it might extract concessions from other member states in its attempts to produce a Community more to its liking. The decision-making apparatus of the Community, by making provision for legitimate nationalist reservations, simultaneously armed Britain – a state which felt increasingly during the 1970s that EC rules and regulations worked systematically to its disadvantage – with the diplomatic weaponry necessary to prosecute its own narrow, nationalist case. Many Europeans had feared that a British government steeped in centuries of *realpolitik*-based diplomatic practice would find the temptation to use such weapons irresistible, even among friends. London's behaviour after 1972 merely served to confirm their suspicions.

The French, of course, were not entirely disappointed with this turn of events. As noted earlier, under de Gaulle they had always preferred to see the EC develop as a highly cooperative association of sovereign states rather than as a genuinely integrative supranational community. Under

Giscard in the late 1970s and Mitterrand in the 1980s they were quite content to witness the rapid dissipation of the supranational momentum of the Community under the weight of British membership. Like the British, they were also anxious to admit yet more members to the EC. When Spain, Portugal and Greece joined the Community in the mid-1980s, the prospects of diluting the Community's supranationalism were enhanced even further. The Gaullist vision of the Community which had proved so embarrassing at the time of the Soames Affair in 1968 was now surreptitiously becoming a welcome reality. The remaining founder members of the Community were not quite so amused.

In 1973, then, Britain had joined a Community which had already achieved quite a high level of economic integration (in terms of a common external tariff and the free internal mobility of goods, capital and labour) and which was advancing along the road to supranational decision-making. Even before Britain's entry, however, both the process of economic integration and the moves towards supranationalism had already begun to peter out. Although this stagnation was certainly exacerbated by British intransigence, London was by no means primarily responsible for it. Indeed, the response of the Community's main protagonists was not to apportion blame but to search for new policy areas where Community-wide cooperation would yield such obvious benefits that the impetus towards supranationalism would be restored. What seemed to offer the most promise in this regard was the development of a greater political union and a common European foreign and defence policy. One of the original attractions of the Community had been the idea that its members might at some stage wield a collective influence in world affairs which was greater than the sum of their individual contributions: if this could indeed be achieved now, then the supranational momentum of the EC as a whole might be revived.

Change Afoot? The Maastricht Treaty 1993 and the Birth of the EU

Thatcher's government did not seriously question Britain's membership of Europe, but it did increasingly concern itself with 'clawing back' cash from Brussels. John Major, her successor, continued this policy with less visibility, but suffered the indignity of having to resign from the European Exchange Rate Mechanism in 1992 (which some say contributed to his defeat at the 1997 General Election). Ironically, perhaps, it was under the Realist-minded Major that the pace of European integration was to increase, and the British Prime Minister seemed to be pulled along in its wake. In 1993 the Maastricht Treaty was passed, creating the new 'European Union' and laying out the framework for the introduction of the single European currency, or 'euro' (formally introduced in January 2001). Maastricht was regarded by its supporters as the first stage on the road to a federal Europe, or at least a very significant one. The treaty also established 'European citizenship' and spelled the end for the old British passport emblazoned with three lions on the front. In its place came a somewhat smaller, burgundy passport which established that the bearer is first and foremost a citizen of the European Union. And before this change had come, the Schengen agreement of 1985 – and later the Schengen Convention of 1990 – ushered in what was in effect an 'open border' policy within the EU itself: the restricted movement of European peoples across borders was seen as a major inhibition to the creation of a genuinely open internal market, but now at last the major barriers to the exchange of people and services were coming down. That these changes happened under Conservative governments openly opposed to further political integration is perhaps highly significant. Although the UK opted out of the Schengen provision, in practice the UK Border Agency now operated a policy in which all EU citizens (while required to show their passports) were free to travel within the territory occupied by the member states.

Until 1997, Britain's highly ambiguous approach to Europe, as evidenced by its insistent and continuing demands for opt-outs, was apparent under both Labour and Conservative governments. With the election of Tony Blair in 1997, there was some expectation that Acheson's nagging criticism might finally be answered and that Britain might now assume the role of 'committed European'. In the 1970s, figures like Peter Shore on the left of the Labour Party had actively opposed EC/EU membership, but Blair's 'New Labour' project was almost universally pro-European, at least on the face of it. It envisioned a fundamentally different relationship with Europe than that which had existed under Thatcher and Major, and even harked back to the heady first days of Britain's membership under Heath.

As we saw in the Introduction, Blair saw Britain, in classic Churchillian fashion, as occupying a middle ground or critical linkage space between the United States and Europe. As a rhetorical position this was not altogether new, since his predecessor John Major and Foreign Secretary Douglas Hurd had said much the same thing (albeit rather more quietly and less enigmatically). But Tony Blair clearly had a more ambitious, Idealist vision for the country, and he saw no contradiction between 'doing what was right' and Britain's core interests.[40] Most importantly, he argued that if Britain was to be an effective bridge between the two circles, it needed to be fully *trusted* in Europe, and this would mean playing a much more whole-hearted role within it than hitherto (not the ambiguous one which had almost always been in evidence). In a November 1997 speech, for example, Blair pledged to 'end the isolation of the past twenty years and be a leading partner in Europe'.[41] Moreover, Britain had now supposedly found that elusive role in the world, at long last. As Blair put it in 1999, 'nearly forty years ago Dean Acheson's barb – that Britain had lost an Empire but not yet found a role – struck home … I believe that search can now end. We have a new role … not as a superpower but as a pivotal power, as a power that is at the crux of the alliances and international politics which shape the world and its future.'[42]

The UK would also have to be far more proactive on the issue of a common defence. One of the most concrete expressions of this new foreign policy approach was Blair's commitment to the enhancement of a Common Foreign and Security Policy (CFSP) for Europe.[43] This had actually been agreed to already some years before, but the existing programme had lacked teeth. Now the British Prime Minister determined that he would give it some. At St Malo in 1998, Blair and Chirac agreed to take concrete steps to create a common European defence.[44] 'The long standing taboo of associating the EU with defence policy was broken' at this meeting, according to Alastair Shepherd.[45] Although the CFSP had actually been created in 1993 – when it was initially known as the European Security and Defence Policy (ESDP) – it sought to fashion a single European position on foreign policy and security issues. The obvious hope was that the EU would become more 'state-like' thereby, expanding European cooperation and revitalising the body as a whole. Like its companion the Common Security and Defence Policy (CSDP), CFSP seeks to pool security resources collectively and make the EU a 'global player'. Both of these Common Policies emerged from the signing of the Treaty of Lisbon in 2007, entering into force in 2009.

In practice, however, the CSDP in particular has come under strong criticism. While the EU has engaged in a relatively large number of interventions under its auspices – by one estimate, it had engaged in 30 such operations by 2014[46] – these have all uniformly been what might be termed 'least common denominator' operations, relatively minor instances where all parties could agree that action was necessary. This is because the launching of any initiative requires *unanimity*; all 28 members have to agree that the security interest at stake is sufficiently significant to merit EU intervention.[47] Naturally enough, in such a large body the member states often do disagree with one another and tend to put their own national interests first. These interests and priorities differ. Just as importantly, they may also not be prepared to put in sufficient equipment and resources, not least because there is a 'you intervene, you pay for it' rule within the CSDP (a sort of European version of Colin Powell's dictum, 'you break it, you own it'). As Menon puts it, 'those member states willing to contribute forces for an EU mission also pick up the tab'.[48] The financial incentives, then, are weighted very much *against* intervention, a factor which can prove especially decisive in an age of austerity. Usually, EU operations have 'borrowed' equipment from the better-funded NATO. We will return to this topic in the final section, where we examine the history of a common foreign and defence policy for the EU.

But if Blair seemed more committed to Britain's involvement in the Union than any of his predecessors, he still kept a healthy distance in some respects. In a 2012 speech, long after he had left office, he repeated what he had said about the EU during the 1999 Kosovo crisis. Britain needed to be inside the EU fighting for its interests, not outside looking in. Speaking against those who favoured a UK withdrawal, Blair said that

> I believe such a policy would be politically debilitating, economically damaging and hugely destructive of Britain's true long-term interests. Our country faces a real and present danger by edging towards exit. The correct policy is to engage, to make it clear Britain intends to be a strong participant in the debates about Europe's future, to build alliances and to shape an outcome to those debates consistent with the right way forward not just for Britain but for Europe as a whole.

But even Blair postponed debates in Britain about joining the euro, and he disavowed any commitment to a European 'superstate'. Clearly, any reference to 'federalism' – which had become the new 'F word' – was still unacceptable in British politics, and 'stay in, but reform internally' was the new mantra.

Much to his credit, Blair at least recognised that structural forces were pushing Britain towards Europe, whether the country liked it or not. One of the central difficulties in applying Churchill's 'three circles' notion to policymaking, however – or at least a major problem with seeing one's country as a 'bridge' – is that the various elements do not necessarily pull in the same direction. Anthony Eden saw the three circles as 'not disparate, not incompatible, but complementary'.[49] But in the Iraq War in 2003 (which we will discuss in more depth in Chapter 6) they *were* incompatible. Blair had said in a 1997 speech in Paris that 'mine is the first generation able to contemplate the possibility that we may live our entire lives without going to war or sending our children to war'. Yet he would end up putting British troops in harm's way more often than any other British Prime Minister since Churchill, notably in Kosovo, Sierra Leone, Iraq and Afghanistan. He saw the war in Iraq as a moral issue. On the other hand, almost all other leaders within the EU (with the notable exception of Spain's Prime Minister Jose Maria Aznar, who soon lost his job over the war) could see no compelling interest for themselves or anyone else to be involved. Most visibly, French President Jacques Chirac and German Chancellor Gerhard Schröder were dead set against any European involvement in what they both saw as an unnecessary war of choice. But when it came down to a choice *between* the circles, Blair chose the transatlantic one. As we will see in Chapter 6, Britain sided with the United States, much to the chagrin of many in Europe.

While New Labour became more cohesively 'pro-European', the UK Conservative Party was moving in the opposite direction. Somewhat ironically, the Conservatives had become much more 'anti-European' by this stage than their former leader Edward Heath was, and those 'Heathites' who remained at the pinnacle of power – most notably Kenneth Clarke and, for a time, Michael Heseltine – always suffered from the fact that their policy positions on Europe were not favoured by a majority of the wider Conservative Party faithful. Clarke contested the leadership of his party no less than three times, for instance, but lost on all three occasions, arguably because of his European convictions.

In 2010, the Labour government was replaced by a coalition of the Conservatives and Liberal Democrats under David Cameron. Openly, Cameron favoured the same position of 'staying in but obtaining reform' that Blair had articulated. But his government often seemed buffeted both by opposition to a federal Europe from the 'Eurosceptic' right of his party and by a much smaller (an often older) group of Conservatives still sympathetic to Europe. The position was further complicated by the fact that his Liberal Democrat Coalition partners were strongly pro-EU. Cameron resolved both his party and his coalition difficulties by indicating that, if re-elected in the 2015 general election, his government would hold a referendum on whether or not Britain should remain inside the EU, similar to that held in 1975. Cameron was re-elected with a Conservative majority in May 2015. In line with commitments made in the Conservative manifesto, he indicated that he would begin immediate negotiations with the EU to revise the terms of Britain's membership and that he would put any resultant agreement to a referendum vote before the end of 2017.[50]

By 2015, immigration into the UK had become a particular rallying cry on the right, as critics of the European project found British hotel desks (for instance) staffed by Poles who had come from low-wage jobs in Eastern Europe.[51] This kind of 'internal' immigration was often conflated by its critics with immigration from *outside* the EU, and it came to a particular head in the 2015 Calais crisis, when seemingly hundreds (or even thousands) of African and Middle Eastern refugees attempted to enter Britain by hiding in lorries. Worries that immigrants were changing the identity and culture of Britain fuelled Euroscepticism and a wider sense that immigration must be halted altogether among what were rather derisively referred to as '*Daily Mail* readers.' Supposedly, huge swathes of immigrants were swarming into Britain, from both inside and outside the country, because of the welfare and unemployment benefits still to be had within the UK system.

In some ways, this recalled the still-simmering results of immigration to Britain as part of the old Empire circle. In 1968, Enoch Powell had destroyed any hope he might have had of continuing a Conservative front-bench career by expressing the view that 'rivers of blood' would flow in the streets as a result of immigration to Britain from the Commonwealth. In reality, most of the immigrants had arrived in Britain under a condition of 'overfull employment', in which there were too many workers chasing too few jobs, and the old Empire circle proved rather useful to British decision-makers in this sense.

Without a doubt, from the vantage point of 2016, immigration had risen sharply in recent years, but there was little evidence to suggest that the UK was bearing a disproportionate share of the resulting burden within the EU (if indeed, it is seen as a burden). Moreover, much of the impact of rising immigration was psychological in nature. About 13 per cent of the population in both Germany and the UK were immigrants, for instance. But research by the German Marshall Fund in 2013 found that the two populations viewed this simple fact very differently. As a report in *The Guardian* derived from that study notes, '64% of people in the UK see immigration as a problem compared to 29% who see it as an opportunity. In Germany those numbers flip almost perfectly, with just 32% seeing immigration as a problem compared to 62% viewing it as an opportunity.'[52]

We cannot get too heavily here into the debate about the economic importance of the EU to Britain – notwithstanding the various economic crises which the former has weathered – but the vast volume of trade which the country conducted with its European counterparts continued to be a powerful force behind 'staying in'. In 2016, the EU remained by far the UK's major trading partner; in fact, more than 50 per cent of the UK's trade in goods and services (about £400 billion in total) came from the Union. And yet matters were about to come to a head. David Cameron had committed Britain to holding a referendum on EU membership in his party's 2015 election manifesto. He had done so in order to appease those on the Right who 'wanted out', as a way of staying in political power in No. 10. But he then faced a stark choice – either to hold the referendum as promised, or to postpone this until some later date, much as his predecessors had dragged their feet on membership of the euro. For whatever reason, he chose to gamble. As noted earlier in the chapter, he lost this gamble, throwing 40 years of EU membership into question (and with that, Britain's future role in the world).

In mid-2016 it was clear that it would take at least two years to disentangle the country from its existing economic and political arrangements with the EU, now that Britain had chosen to pull out. It was also widely believed that any withdrawal from the EU was likely to slow economic growth and increase unemployment – which is why a whole range of states were clamouring to get into the EU rather than to stay out. Britain's decision to 'go it alone' or rely solely on its transatlantic relationship, meant that it would have to find a vast number of new buyers for what it sells. Just as favourable trade movements had eventually convinced decision-makers in Whitehall that Britain should move closer to Europe, so the continuation of those linkages became a formidable force against 'getting out'. However, that force did not prove quite as powerful as the political movement (popularly known as 'Brexit') ranged against EU membership.[53]

In terms of EU foreign policy, we may have settled into a situation where – as a *de facto* matter rather than anything to which anyone has agreed – NATO does 'hard power' and the EU (seemingly incapable of moving beyond its state-based focus in this arena, and apparently now minus the UK) does diplomacy and 'soft power'.[54] As we shall see in the next section, the 2011 Libyan intervention was conducted largely under the remit of NATO, and was therefore a source of particular disappointment for those who believed that the CDSP (and CFSP of which it is a part) had acquired any real teeth. Back in 1998 and after the St Malo meeting, the Clinton administration in particular voiced concern that an independent EU foreign and defence policy might well reduce the significance of NATO, over which America still exerts a high degree of influence. Then Secretary of State Madeleine Albright made a speech in which she expounded the famous 'three Ds': no *duplication* of what NATO already does, no '*decoupling*' of NATO from the US, and no *discrimination* against non-EU members (she had states like Turkey in mind here).[55] Albright need not have worried, though. NATO – enjoying something of a new lease of life after the end of the Cold War and acquiring a new *raison d'être* – has almost always done the 'heavy lifting' in the absence of a coordinated or cohesive European Union. In the final section, we examine the history of attempts to create a broader European defence, and we show that this issue of Union weakness in foreign and defence policy is far from new.

A Common European Foreign and Defence Policy?

Although a common European foreign policy had always been on the political agenda of the European federalists, the integrative activities of the Six during the 1950s and 1960s were almost entirely restricted to the economic and social spheres. The first real sign that a common European foreign policy might indeed be emerging was the introduction of the so-called 'Davignon Procedure' in 1970.[56] The resultant system of European Political Cooperation (EPC) aimed to extend the principle of harmonisation – previously confined to the economic and social policies of the Six – to include foreign policy as well. EPC provided a set of procedures whereby European foreign ministers (including those of the Six and of the EC's four intending members: Britain, Denmark, Norway and the Irish Republic) could engage in detailed consultation and negotiation prior to a major policy decision being taken. This was a considerable departure from the previous diplomatic practice, which even at its most cooperative had been restricted to the exchange of 'information' and 'assessments'.[57]

Within months of Britain's accession to the Community in 1973, European Political Cooperation appeared to bear its first (small) fruit. With the outbreak of the fourth Arab-Israeli war in October 1973 and the subsequent Arab threat to Western oil supplies, Europe found itself more or less united in its opposition to American policy in the Middle East. While the United States firmly maintained its position of 'Israel right or wrong', the Europeans – fearful that their oil supplies might dry up altogether if they antagonised the oil sheikhs still further – were rather more sympathetic (in public at least) towards the plight of the Palestinians. (The rift with the United States, although serious, was rapidly repaired at the NATO Heads of Government Conference in Ottawa in June 1974).[58] What seemed especially promising from the European point of view was that the European nations, in the face of stern American opposition, had established something approaching a common position on what was undoubtedly a highly complex and difficult issue. However, in case anyone should get carried away with enthusiasm, it was also recognised that the achievement of this common position had probably been due less to the procedures established under EPC and more to a clear convergence of material interest in an urgent and threatening situation. The protagonists of EPC nevertheless remained undaunted. In the years after 1973 the foreign ministers of the Nine continued to attempt to carve out a distinctively European position on the whole Middle East question. Their efforts culminated in the June 1980 Venice Declaration, which recognised that negotiations aimed at achieving a Middle East peace settlement must include the Palestine Liberation Organization (PLO). The declaration also initiated a long-running dialogue between Western Europe and the more moderate Arab states that was intended as Europe's contribution to the Middle East peace process. Unfortunately, European efforts in this regard, though commendably 'harmonised', had '[very little] influence on the affairs of the region' itself.[59]

In retrospect, however, it is clear that such optimism was misplaced. In many respects the Venice Declaration and the agreements on defence were merely 'islands of agreement amid a sea of matters'.[60] They were exceptions to a general pattern of *non*-agreement in matters external to the Community; isolated examples of the successful coordination of national foreign policies rather than the embryonic embodiment of an emergent Community foreign policy. The main reason for this dearth of genuinely European foreign policy was simple. It is extraordinarily difficult for any group of nation-states, no matter how ingenious the procedural arrangements which it has established, to achieve agreement on complex matters of external policy when individual members of that group continue jealously to guard their own national sovereignty and national interests. Notwithstanding the sentiments underlying both the Treaty of Rome and EPC, this was precisely the position inside the European Community throughout the 1970s and 1980s. Ceding sovereignty to NATO in the military sphere had been unavoidable and ceding sovereignty to the Commission in the internal economic sphere had been positively beneficial, but political relations with states outside the Community remained the prerogative of the national governments. It would only be possible to achieve a common foreign policy on those rare occasions when, for whatever external reasons, the different national governments found themselves in agreement.

The British government, moreover, was one of the prime offenders in this regard. During the *Lomé negotiations* on EC trade with the third world in the late 1970s, the British delegation frequently seemed to imply that, as a result of Britain's long experience with the Empire and Commonwealth, it was better placed than its European counterparts to understand the needs and aspirations of the impoverished peoples of the South – a posture which inevitably made it much more difficult for the EC negotiators as a whole to reach agreement with the ACP group. Similar problems arose in the mid-1980s with regard to the *Middle East* 'island of agreement'. Having accepted in 1980 the terms of the Venice Declaration, which recognised that the PLO had a crucial role to play in any attempted peace settlement, Mrs Thatcher's government unilaterally abandoned this position in October 1985 when it prevented a joint Jordanian-Palestinian negotiating team (which it had previously invited) from entering Britain. The express reason offered for the cancellation of the invitation was that, as PLO members who subscribed to the Palestine National Covenant, the Palestinian delegates did not accept Israel's right to exist within secure borders. This was a clear defection on Britain's part from the agreed European position which had insisted that, despite the hard-line stance adopted in the Covenant, no progress on a negotiated settlement could be achieved without the participation of the PLO. Here was an 'island of agreement' that was rapidly sinking back into the sea, and at the British government's behest.

The fact that British diffidence had tarnished the EC's would-be common foreign policy even in those few areas where it had achieved limited success was not lost on Britain's European partners. They were equally irritated by the United Kingdom's posturings in areas where *no* common European position had been reached. In the context of *Latin America*, for example, where several of the continental European countries had extensive investments as well as a significant share of lucrative markets, London's actions during the Falklands crisis were a distinct embarrassment. On the one hand, the need to protect Europe's economic interests in Latin America pointed to a quiet neutrality; on the other, Britain *was* a partner in Europe and there *was* intense diplomatic pressure from both London and Washington aimed at persuading all of the Community countries to express their public support for British policy. In the event, Britain's European partners came out solidly in favour of the United Kingdom's robust stance against Argentina.[61] The consequence, however, was the loss of a considerable amount of Latin American goodwill; a loss which was immediately translated into a commensurate European irritation with Britain. The British refusal even to negotiate with the civilian Alfonsin regime after 1984 merely served to reinforce that irritation.

By the late 1980s, then, Britain appeared to be adopting a rather different position from the rest of Europe on a series of policy issues which might otherwise have provided the nucleus for an emerging Community foreign policy. Indeed, there *was* no common European foreign policy during this period. At best, the consultative procedures of EPC ensured that the foreign policies of the Twelve were *coordinated*.[62] And the British government's determination to pursue a very public 'independent' line ensured that even this coordination was severely limited. What was especially disappointing for serious supporters of further European integration was the declaration by the Community in 1985 that henceforward members would (1) 'inform and consult' one another on foreign policy matters and (2) 'develop and define ... common principles and objectives'.[63] This was past failure masquerading as good intent: (1) had been official policy since the inception of EPC in 1970; and (2) was merely an example of the classic bureaucratic formula which recommends that the insoluble problems of today should be left for resolution (preferably by someone else) tomorrow.

But then came the activist government of Tony Blair, which saw itself as operating 'at the heart of Europe'. Blair wanted to use the EU as a force for good, and the hope which emerged at St Malo in 1998 was that it would finally begin to act cohesively to attain that goal. In practice, however, this bold idea was scuppered by at least two crises, both of which suggested that NATO was far more suited than the EU to confront the spectre of 'evil in the world': the Kosovo crisis of 1999 and the Libyan crisis of 2011. Between these two crises, moreover, fundamental divisions over Iraq in 2003 showed that the EU would find it hard to act in any unified or cohesive way.

Just one year after St Malo, the 1999 Kosovo War was the first real test case of Blair's Idealism, and it was also a test of European will. Blair was in many ways the prime mover in that conflict, but it was fought by NATO as a whole in its first ever military engagement. Ethnic Albanians – many, but not all of them, unarmed – were under military onslaught from the Serbs. What we now know to have been a genocide against them had begun, and events spurred Blair into action. Lasting 78 days in all, the war was fought exclusively from the air, since resistance to putting in ground forces (especially in the United States) was always very strong. We may never know exactly why Serbian strongman Slobodan Milošević backed down after two and a half months of bombing. Certainly, the West in general failed to appreciate the significance of Kosovo to him; any Serb nationalist had to be concerned with the area, since it has always been seen as the jewel in the Serbian crown. But it was probably a combination of factors that brought the war to an end. There were plans within NATO to insert ground forces eventually, and the threat of this ground offensive, combined with the withdrawal of Russian support from their fellow Slavs under Boris Yeltsin, was probably just as crucial as the bombing of Serbia itself. But Blair would emerge victorious from the war, and the whole experience cannot but have reinforced his idea that Britain could be a 'force for good' in the world. As Oliver Daddow notes,

> Kosovo helped mould the Prime Minister into the leader he was previously wary of becoming. Blair's fear that Kosovo could be his downfall was soon quelled by the international acclaim he received for his efforts in bringing at least a degree of peace and stability to the Balkans, and after this time we see a more confident, proactive leader genuinely committed to grounding British foreign policy in the theory of liberal interventionism.[64]

Overall, Kosovo is usually seen as a success, as Blair's 'good war'. From a European perspective, however, the great disappointment was that the EU was seemingly powerless to act to confront a crisis at the very heart of Europe, in the place where World War I had begun. One especially strong impetus behind the effort to create a cohesive EU foreign policy was the first Bosnian War from 1990 to 1995. The Europeans had been unwilling or unable to act against Milosevic, expecting the United States to once again act as a kind of 'globocop' many miles from its shores. A policy of 'rift and drift' had been the response in European capitals, and the war dragged on for five years. And yet here again was a second crisis in the former Yugoslavia, and Europe was paralysed again.

The attempt to reach unity was further ruptured by the war in Iraq in 2003, which split Europe down the middle and (as we indicate in the next chapter) forced Blair to choose between two circles. But in many ways,

Libya was an even greater disappointment for EU enthusiasts than Iraq. Together with the French, Britain led a movement of regime change to remove Libya's long-term dictator Muammar Ghaddafi in 2011. As with Kosovo, this was no EU operation by any stretch of the imagination, even though the involvement of the British and the French gave it that superficial appearance. As Menon notes,

> Less than 18 months after Lisbon came into force, the European Union stood on the sidelines and watched as France and the United Kingdom, acting within a NATO framework, intervened militarily on the Union's doorstep. Indeed, as the crisis in Libya escalated, no one apparently seriously considered intervention under the framework of the CSDP. The belated decision on 1 April 2011 to approve a military mission to support humanitarian assistance in Libya smacked more of face saving than effective intervention.[65]

The EU was apparently in the business of mopping up after a fight, but would take no part in the conflict itself, both because its member states could not agree and because of bitter internal rivalries within the Union itself. Indeed, one EU insider went so far as to proclaim the demise of European defence itself: 'the CFSP died in Libya – we just have to pick a sand dune under which we can bury it'.[66]

Summary and Conclusions

Britain's shift towards Europe after 1956 was the natural complement to its decreasing involvement in the Empire-cum-Commonwealth. What has been suggested in both this chapter and the last is that the major causes of this 'emptying out' of the Empire circle and the attendant 'infilling' of the European one were essentially *structural*: the emptying out and the infilling would have occurred anyway, whatever policy choices had been made by successive British governments. The shift in the focus of Britain's trading activity away from the Empire and towards Europe – which occurred over a decade before the United Kingdom's accession to the EC/EU – represented a fundamental change in Britain's material economic interests that no government, no matter how determined, could have resisted.

This is not to suggest, however, that domestic politics, policy calculations and policy decisions were unimportant in determining events in Europe after 1956. On the contrary, the precise institutional form which Britain's greater involvement would take, as well as the timing of that greater involvement, was always very much a matter for governmental decision. It was not really the British government's fault that, having decided that the United Kingdom's destiny lay inside the EU, its formal entry into 'Europe' should have been delayed for so long by an intransigent French president with a personality problem. All three of Britain's attempts to join the EEC between 1961 and 1972 were based on entirely rational assessments both of the strategic shifts in Britain's international position which were taking place and of the likely costs and benefits of British membership. Given that even the British government was capable of interpreting trade statistics, it became increasingly clear in the 1960s that Britain's primary material economic interests now lay in its close trading contacts with Western Europe, and this remained true decades later as trade within the EU had increased Britain's stake further. By the same token, however, the rise of the Eurosceptics – and ultimately, the narrowly won 2016 vote within an extremely divided Britain, unsure whether to respond to these structural imperatives or to the 'Brexit' camp's political determination to leave the EU – has shown that not everyone reacts in such a way to structural forces, as overwhelming as these forces may be.

Chapter 6

The Changing 'Special Relationship', 1956–2016

As was seen in Chapter 2, the 'special relationship' between Britain and the United States was forged during the vicissitudes of World War II. Yet as that chapter also showed, in the late 1940s that relationship received a severe buffeting. The abrupt termination of Lend-Lease in September 1945 seriously weakened an already overstretched British economy. The passage of the McMahon Act in August 1946 unilaterally ended five years of intimate Anglo-American nuclear collaboration and obliged the Attlee government to initiate its own independent programme of nuclear research. American diplomatic pressure was an added factor in provoking the British withdrawal from Palestine in May 1947.[1] And the US government's insistence on sterling's free convertibility in July 1947 produced a catastrophic run on the pound.[2]

Notwithstanding the considerable Anglo-American collaboration that took place both inside NATO after 1949 and under the auspices of the UN peacekeeping force in Korea after 1950, the 'special relationship' continued to experience traumas throughout the early 1950s. The exclusion of Britain from the ANZUS defence pact between the United States, Australia and New Zealand in September 1951 was interpreted in London as clear evidence of Washington's long-term intention to increase its influence in the Pacific at Britain's expense. Similarly, the US failure to join the Baghdad Pact in February 1955 was seen as an indication of America's refusal to underwrite an alliance which might enable Britain to preserve its political influence with existing client states in the third world. Suez was the final straw. Who *did* the Americans think they were? How on earth could Britain continue to enjoy a 'special relationship' with an 'ally' which had so malevolently ambushed British diplomacy in its hour of need?

The remarkable feature of Anglo-American relations in the years after 1956 was how quickly the 'special relationship' was restored. The first part of this chapter describes the rapid improvement in relations that occurred immediately after Suez, the decline that set in during the mid-1960s, the partial revival that was effected during the Reagan–Thatcher period after 1980 and the ups and downs of the relationship under John

Major, Tony Blair, Gordon Brown and David Cameron. The second part examines the major causal factors which underpinned these changes and suggests that the course of Anglo-American relations always depended primarily on the calculations of *realpolitik*. It also seeks to assess how far the 'special relationship' still existed in the early part of the 21st century.

There were at least four main phases in Britain's post-Suez relations with the United States. For almost a decade after Suez, strenuous efforts were made on both sides of the Atlantic to repair the damage that Eden's Egyptian adventure had wrought. The efforts were largely successful. By the early 1960s, with Britain's decolonisation programme well under way (a development vigorously applauded in Washington), London looked set to adopt a significant support role behind the United States in the latter's attempts to protect the global strategic interests of the West. However, this position did not survive the death of John F. Kennedy in November 1963 and the political demise of Harold Macmillan of the same year. By 1965 it was clear that Britain no longer possessed the physical capability to sustain an extensive global military presence: as London became increasingly unwilling to commit resources to out-of-NATO area operations, Britain quite simply became less *useful* to the United States. As a result, the 'specialness' of the 'special relationship' gradually faded, with Britain increasingly taking on the character of just another European ally. During the period after 1980, relations experienced something of a revival. The common commitment of Margaret Thatcher and Ronald Reagan to market economies at home and strong anti-communism abroad led to a resurgence in Anglo-American collaboration in a variety of diplomatic, economic and military contexts. To return to the heady days of the wartime special relationship was of course impossible. Nonetheless, under Thatcher the government loudly proclaimed its determination to preserve and strengthen Britain's ties with the 'Atlantic Circle'. After a brief period of *sang froid* under John Major vis-à-vis George H. W. Bush and Bill Clinton, the Clinton–Blair relationship post-1997 also re-established a close relationship between Washington and London, although this time it was initially commonalities between 'New Labour' and the 'New Democrats' – a kind of left-leaning approach rather than a rightward-leaning one – which drew the two together. Against all expectations, that relationship persisted after the departure of Clinton, as Blair forged strong links with George W. Bush. In the years since the 'Americanised' Blair left office, however, the closeness of that relationship has never quite been replicated. Steady (but rather uneasy) relations have been established, and the Americans have been especially concerned that Britain will turn away from its commitments to the EU and NATO, which it regards as pillars of Europe's defence against a resurgent Russia.

Phase 1: Repair, 1957–63

The political breach between London and Washington over Suez had undoubtedly been serious. The British in particular had been deeply wounded by the diplomatic humiliation which they had suffered at the hands of the Eisenhower administration. Yet the Soviet threat in Europe – underlined by the Soviet invasion of Hungary only a week before the Suez fiasco itself – and the continuing global threat of communist encroachment remained serious enough to merit a rapid restoration of bilateral relations. After all, the United States was still the world's leading capitalist power. And Britain, although its step was now clearly faltering, still possessed the ambition and the capabilities of a Great Power. As ever, classic *realpolitik* principle dictated that the common interests of both powers (above all else, preventing the spread of communism) would be better served by friendship and collaboration than by further discord and mutual recrimination.

The initial repair was effected by renewed cooperation in the military sphere. Throughout the 1950s – at a time when Britain's strategic air deterrent still relied totally on the RAF's increasingly outdated fleet of bomber aircraft – American (and Soviet) scientists had been making significant advances in the military application of ballistic missile technology. The Macmillan-Eisenhower meeting in Bermuda in March 1957 effectively gave Britain access to the fruits of the American research: some 60 Thor missiles were to be stationed in East Anglia under the joint ('dual-key') control of both British and American operational commanders. The US decision to share the new technology was an important symbolic concession: it not only indicated Washington's intention to heal the diplomatic rift over Suez, but also reaffirmed the fact that the Anglo-American partnership remained at the heart of the defence of Europe.

The need to repair bilateral relations was made even more urgent by the Soviet launch of Sputnik in October 1957. There was no telling what this (presumably temporary) Soviet victory in the space race might imply for the delivery of nuclear warheads. In any event, prudence suggested that the two great capitalist allies should pool their scientific knowledge in order to meet the new challenge. The outcome, in July 1958, was the repeal of the 1946 McMahon Act (which had abruptly terminated the intimate Anglo-American nuclear collaboration of the war years) and the signing of the Agreement for Co-operation on the Uses of Atomic Energy for Mutual Defence Purposes (which effectively restored the nuclear-sharing *status quo ante* of the pre-McMahon years).[3] To be sure, the treaty would probably not have been signed if Britain had not had something useful to offer as a result of having maintained its own independent nuclear research programme throughout the 1950s. Yet it was certainly of greater political import than its prosaic title might have suggested. Nuclear sharing would have been inconceivable without the high levels of mutual trust enjoyed by the political and military establishments of both countries: the smooth operation of the treaty's provisions in the years after 1958 served to reinforce that sense of trust and to maintain an 'island' of intimacy long after the 'special relationship' itself had ceased to have any real geostrategic significance.

The new post-Suez spirit of collaboration was not confined solely to nuclear weapons technology, however. In the immediate wake of Nasser's diplomatic victory over Britain and France, Eisenhower had offered to provide anti-communist regimes in the Middle East with any economic and military assistance which they might require in order to strengthen their resistance to either external or internal threat.[4] In July 1958, combined Anglo-American forces were urgently dispatched to the Middle East. The civil disturbances in Jordan and the Lebanon were both quickly suppressed and the authority of their respective governments accordingly restored. This was joint global policing *par excellence*, the two great Western allies acting in tandem to ensure that the Western sphere of influence in the Middle East would not be eroded by Soviet subterfuge and stealth: Suez was merely an unhappy memory now largely erased by the need to meet the undiminished and still ubiquitous challenge of Soviet expansionism.

The new convergence of interest and policy in the Middle East did not mean that Anglo-American relations were entirely free of discord, but those relations remained excellent. In June 1960, following three months of intensive negotiations, Washington agreed to supply the newly developed Skybolt missile system – capable of delivering nuclear warheads to Soviet bloc targets – to Britain's armed forces.[5] As far as London was concerned this was an even more important accord than the introduction of American Thor missiles in 1958: whereas Thor had been deployed under a dual-key arrangement, Skybolt (once it had been supplied) was to be solely at the disposal of Britain. If it were still needed, here was clear evidence that the 'special relationship' had indeed been restored. No other ally of the United States had even come close to achieving the kind of deal which Macmillan had secured over Skybolt. And with the reinvigoration of the Cold War, provoked by the erection of the Berlin wall in August 1961, close Anglo-American relations would perhaps become even more necessary.

Unfortunately, in November 1962, it was announced that Skybolt, the new symbol of Anglo-American nuclear cooperation, simply didn't work. In London, suspicions that had previously been suppressed began to surface. Perhaps the Americans had not really wanted to assist Britain's nuclear weapons programme in the first place and the whole

Skybolt deal had been a charade. Or perhaps Washington had had second thoughts about the British government's reliability and no longer wished to facilitate Britain's continued membership of the 'nuclear club'. Although the doubts seemed well founded, they were firmly swept away by the agreement reached between Kennedy and Macmillan at Nassau in December 1962. Under remarkably generous terms,[6] the United States agreed to supply the United Kingdom with the Polaris submarine-launched missile system. And, although the missiles were officially designated for NATO purposes, it was clear that in supplying Polaris the Americans were effectively enabling Britain to maintain its independent nuclear deterrent without having to incur the enormous (and possibly prohibitive) costs of a full research and development programme.

The Nassau agreement, moreover, had come in the wake of the Cuban missile crisis of October 1962, when the world had waited with bated breath to see if Khrushchev would accede to Kennedy's demand that Soviet missile installations be removed from Cuban soil.[7] There is some disagreement as to what the crisis implied about the character of Anglo-American relations. According to some accounts, the crisis revealed the effective demise of the 'special relationship' itself: Washington's persistent disregard of London's views demonstrated the irrelevance of Britain's 'world role' posturings in the post-Suez era of the two superpowers.[8] In contrast, however, more recent evidence seems to suggest that throughout the crisis Kennedy in fact solicited advice from Macmillan on a frequent and regular basis.[9] Viewed in this light, in the last quarter of 1962, the 'special relationship' was apparently in better shape than at any time since early 1946. The Americans were prepared not only to supply Britain with the latest nuclear weapons technology but also to consult closely with London in what had undoubtedly been the most threatening international crisis since 1945. Almost inevitably, however, this position was not to endure for long. Although during the course of 1963 British and American negotiators continued to collaborate intimately in their discussions with the Soviets over the Partial Test Ban Treaty,[10] from the end of 1963 onwards relations between London and Washington, though they remained friendly, undoubtedly entered a period of gradual but inexorable decline. It is the character of this decline which is now examined.

Phase 2: Decay, 1964–79

Very few of the major changes which occur in international politics are without deep historical roots. The decay in the special relationship after 1963 was no exception. Even though the Nassau agreement could reasonably be presented as an indication of the closeness of relations, the agreement had in fact been reached in the face of strong opposition from the 'Europeanist' lobby inside the US State Department.[11] This lobby – centred upon Under Secretary of State George Ball – was strongly opposed to the continued British possession of an independent nuclear deterrent for two main reasons: first, it would encourage nuclear proliferation and thereby threaten the stability of Soviet–US mutual deterrence; and second, it might serve to weaken the resolve of Western Europe to provide sufficient conventional forces for the effective operation of NATO's flexible response strategy, which was strongly favoured by the United States. The response of the Europeanist lobby in December 1963 was to persuade newly installed President Johnson to support their proposals for a multilateral force (MLF) which would incorporate Britain's nuclear deterrent into a combined Western European force. The British reaction to MLF, not surprisingly, was extremely cool. After all, the retention of the independent deterrent was still considered necessary for the maintenance of Britain's Great Power status. In the run-up to the October 1964 General Election, however, the MLF issue receded from prominence. Nonetheless, in November 1964, the new Labour government issued a series of counter-proposals for an Atlantic Nuclear Force (ANF) which would combine the entire nuclear forces of Britain and France with the submarine capabilities of the United States.[12] By this time, however, the Johnson administration had become less convinced of either the efficacy or the desirability of a unified European nuclear deterrent and it accordingly abandoned its plans for MLF. Having suggested ANF principally as a bargaining counter to prevent MLF, the Wilson government was in turn only too ready quickly to shelve its proposals.

If the diplomatic impasse over MLF and ANF had done little more than ripple the surface of Atlantic relations, much deeper – and far more disruptive – currents were soon to make themselves felt over Vietnam. Although the United States had been providing military assistance to the Ngo Dinh Diem regime in South Vietnam since 1961, during the course of 1964 American involvement had increased considerably. Indeed, at the beginning of 1965 the United States looked set to make further major deployments in order to resist the communist insurgency which was clearly being orchestrated from Hanoi. In an apparent attempt to emulate Attlee's visit to Washington in December 1950 – when the British premier had sought, unnecessarily, to dissuade Truman from using nuclear weapons in Korea – Wilson requested an urgent audience with Lyndon Johnson in order to counsel against deeper American involvement in South-East Asia. His approaches to the American President met with a rebuff, however, and he was sharply informed: 'I won't tell you how to run Malaysia and you don't tell us how to run Vietnam.'[13]

The real problem, of course, was that the differences between London and Washington over Vietnam ran much deeper than the contents of one irate telephone call between Wilson and Johnson. The Americans were desperate to receive international backing for their South-East Asian campaign: even a token British force would have constituted an important propaganda coup for the US administration. Unfortunately, the deep anti-American strain inside the Labour left, combined with Wilson's slender majority in the Commons, made it quite impossible for the Labour government seriously to consider sending a British contingent, no matter how small, to Vietnam in support of the American action. The Americans were understandably furious. Here was Washington's closest ally – which only two years earlier had been given the latest nuclear weapons technology at a knock-down price – refusing to lend even token assistance in a military campaign which the US administration deemed essential if the whole of South-East Asia was to be saved from communism. Secretary of State Dean Rusk was moved to observe that 'all we needed was one regiment ... don't expect us to save you again'.[14] By mid-1965 the 'special relationship' was certainly looking a lot less special than it had at Nassau.

An even more serious blow to the special relationship, however, came with the Wilson government's 1967 decision – clearly presaged in the 1966 Defence Review – to withdraw from East of Suez. The decision to reduce Britain's world role and to concentrate its defence efforts primarily within Western Europe inevitably meant that in future Britain would be far less able either to play the sort of anti-communist trouble-shooting role that it had performed in Malaya between 1948 and 1956 or to furnish the sort of continuous anti-Soviet presence which the Royal Navy had provided in the Indian Ocean throughout the post-war period. In a world still fraught (in American eyes) with communist danger, the British withdrawal from East of Suez was a serious abdication of responsibility. If the British were no longer available to patrol the South China Sea, the Indian Ocean and the Persian Gulf – and there was certainly no other Western nation ready to act as a satisfactory replacement – then the Americans would be obliged to undertake the task themselves. And although Wilson attempted to sweeten the pill by providing the United States with extensive naval facilities at Diego Garcia,[15] such a concession to the needs of global *realpolitik* did little to compensate Washington for the considerable extra expense that it would incur as a result of having to extend its own global naval commitments. Moreover, as far as the Americans were concerned, the timing of the British withdrawal – between 1968 and 1972 – could not have been worse, coming as it did when the morale-draining involvement in Vietnam was at its peak. For twenty years, the British presence east of Suez had lightened

Washington's burden in its efforts to make the world safe for capitalism and liberal democracy: with the British gone, the burden was inevitably increased and the Americans became commensurately more resentful. By reducing the potential for Anglo-American collaboration in out-of-NATO area operations, the British withdrawal from East of Suez had further weakened the special relationship, weakening Britain's ties with the residue of Empire *and* with the United States. It also paved the way for Britain's greater subsequent participation in the European circle, which itself served further to diminish – for policymakers in Washington – any 'specialness' that Britain might once have possessed.

After June 1970, Edward Heath's new Conservative government failed to make more than cosmetic adjustments to the deep defence cuts which had originally necessitated the withdrawal from East of Suez. In its desire to establish Britain's credentials as a 'good European', the Heath government then chose to ignore Henry Kissinger's somewhat extravagant plans to make 1973 the 'Year of Europe'. Worse still, in October 1973, Heath proceeded to make common cause with Britain's European partners in refusing base facilities to the American aircraft which were supplying Israel during the Yom Kippur War with the Arab states.[16] All of these developments, inevitably, did little to endear London to Washington. Britain was merely behaving like any other self-regarding West European state: incessantly complaining about the cost of deterring the Russians; relying on the Americans to do the job for it; and refusing to provide material assistance to the United States when it was really needed for fear of what the Arabs might do in retaliation. It simply was not good enough. Wilson had been right when he had observed in December 1964 that Anglo-American relations were by then merely 'close' as opposed to 'special'.[17] With the German Federal Republic now supplying the biggest European troop contingent to NATO[18] and with the NATO *Eurogroup* well established, Britain's relative importance to the United States in the security field was declining both inside and outside the NATO area of operations.

With Labour again in power from February 1974, London and Washington seemed to take increasingly divergent views of developments in world politics. Events that were viewed with alarm in Washington – such as the overthrow of the right-wing Salazar dictatorship in Portugal and the resultant revolutions in Angola and Mozambique in 1974–75 – were received with relative equanimity in London. In the Middle East, President Jimmy Carter's diplomacy between 1976 and 1979 was focused primarily on achieving a peace accord between Egypt and Israel; in contrast, the Callaghan government, along with its European partners, attached rather more importance to the fact that the Carter-sponsored peace process did almost nothing to alleviate the plight of the displaced Palestinians. In Latin America, the Americans were happy to provide financial and military assistance to the right-wing dictatorships in Chile under Pinochet after 1973 and in Nicaragua under Somoza until 1979. But London expressed rather more sympathy for the assassinated Chilean President, Salvador Allende – a Marxist – and for the avowedly socialist Sandinista resistance. By May 1979 Anglo-American relations were at their lowest ebb for over a generation. And although continued Anglo-American collaboration within NATO seemed assured, with the left clearly on the ascendant within the Labour Party, the prospects for anything resembling even the lukewarm relationship of the Wilson years seemed dim indeed. Yet much was about to change: in May 1979, Margaret Thatcher was elected Prime Minister with a sizeable majority in the House of Commons.

Phase 3: Revival, 1980–2007

It might have been expected that Margaret Thatcher would prove unable to halt the increasing tendency during the 1970s for London and Washington to adopt divergent positions on major international issues. British and American interests were slowly diverging, and an increasing policy divergence would naturally follow. Such expectations were soon confounded, however. Where Heath had been a self-avowed and highly committed European, the newly elected Prime Minister was an equally committed Atlanticist, resolute in her conviction that the maintenance of Britain's long-term security – the primary objective of UK foreign policy – lay in strengthening Britain's ties with the United States. From June 1979 onwards, the cultivation of Washington became a top priority.

In December 1979, the Thatcher Cabinet's efforts in this regard bore their first fruit when NATO foreign ministers resolved their internal differences over the deployment of cruise and Pershing II missiles in Western Europe. In January 1980, Britain announced its intention to allow 160 American-owned cruise missiles to be deployed in the United Kingdom.[19] This was an important symbolic affirmation of London's trust in Washington at a time when public opinion in Western Europe generally was becoming increasingly concerned about both the size and the character of American nuclear forces based in the European theatre. In July, agreement was reached over the purchase of the Trident I (C4) missile from the United States.[20] The new missile would replace the increasingly outdated Polaris system and provide for the continuance of the British independent deterrent well into the 21st century on terms equally favourable to those secured by Macmillan at Nassau. In January 1981, the task of promoting closer Anglo-American relations was rendered even easier when Ronald Reagan succeeded Jimmy Carter as President of the United

States. Henceforward, Thatcher's natural Atlanticist inclinations would be firmly underpinned by a shared Anglo-American 'new right' ideology. For both Reagan and Thatcher, the earthly salvation of all mankind, both at home and abroad, lay in the restoration of the market and the destruction of collectivism. Throughout the 1980s, this common ideological commitment to the rejuvenation of capitalism would be enough to ensure a remarkable degree of Anglo-American collaboration, even in situations where the immediate interests of London and Washington might appear – however temporarily – to diverge.

Thatcher and Reagan started as they meant to go on. In February 1981, Thatcher made a highly publicised and extremely successful visit to the United States. Apart from further advancing the closeness of her personal relationship with the President, the visit produced a vigorous public statement of Britain's approval of the Reagan plan for the creation of a 'rapid deployment force' (RDF), a highly mobile military force which could be sent as and when necessary to trouble spots anywhere in the world. Although Britain's contribution would be extremely limited, by expressing London's preparedness to contribute to RDF, Thatcher was providing precisely what Wilson had failed to give President Johnson in 1965; symbolic support and involvement in out-of-NATO-area operations. Thatcher's reward for backing RDF arrived swiftly, moreover. In October 1981 the Reagan administration announced that Trident II (D5) would become fully operational well ahead of its original target date and that Britain was welcome to purchase it as a replacement for Polaris instead of Trident I. After six months of assessment, in March 1982 a contract for the British purchase of Trident II was duly signed, again, on terms extremely favourable to Britain.[21]

But even greater American largesse was close at hand. At the end of March 1982, the Argentinians invaded and occupied the Falkland Islands. Thatcher's response was both decisive and determined. The Royal Navy declared an exclusion zone around the islands and a task force was urgently dispatched with orders to retake the islands. In terms of *realpolitik,* the United States was in a rather delicate position. First, if it followed Reagan's political instincts and sided with Britain, it risked damaging its good relations not only with Argentina, but also with the rest of non-communist Latin America, where US companies had substantial investments. Second, the dispute itself had come to a head at a time when Britain was making common cause *against* the United States by siding with a number of EU countries that were resisting American efforts to dissuade them from building a gas pipeline to the Soviet Union. In addition, the United States was under no legal obligation to assist a NATO ally in this sort of out-of-area operation. Throughout April, therefore, the US government attempted to act as a mediator between Buenos Aires and London, though with both General Galtieri and Thatcher immovable, US efforts were entirely unsuccessful. By May, however, in the absence of a diplomatic settlement, Reagan's policy came out decisively in favour of Britain. Public statements of support were backed by the provision of refuelling facilities at Ascension Island and by the supply of satellite intelligence to the British War Cabinet. This latter factor in particular was extremely important in securing an early British victory in the actual military campaign.[22] Crucially, however, what the Falklands episode had demonstrated was that, in a serious crisis, Britain could count on American support. Perhaps this was not quite a resurrection of the old wartime special relationship, but in the changed circumstances of the 1980s, in a world dominated by superpower *realpolitik*, it was a passable imitation.

The only major source of Anglo-American discord during Thatcher's first two periods of office was the Grenada affair of 1983. A former British colony and member of the Commonwealth, Grenada had been ruled until 1979 by a conservative, pro-Western government under Eric Gairey. In March 1979, however, the Gairey regime had been ousted in a coup by Maurice Bishop's New Jewel Movement (NJM), a Marxist–Leninist organisation which had close ties with the Castro regime in Cuba. In October 1983, on the pretext of protecting the safety of American citizens stranded in Grenada, US forces invaded the island, removed the remaining NJM leaders from power and installed a pro-Western provisional government which subsequently held elections and delivered Grenada from the Soviet-Cuban embrace that the NJM government had favoured. The American action – judging by the welcome the invading US troops received – was popular with most Grenadians. It was also approved by the majority of other Caribbean governments: the State Department had even managed to persuade several of them to contribute troops to the invading force so that (as in Lebanon) the force could be invested with the epithet 'multinational'.

In terms of its effects (eliminating an unpleasant bunch of Marxists) the Grenadian invasion was warmly welcomed in London. What rankled, however, was the precipitate manner in which Washington had acted. Grenada, after all, was part of the Commonwealth, and accordingly Her Majesty's Government could reasonably expect to have at least been informed of American plans and intentions prior to the invasion. Yet only hours before the US action, Foreign Secretary Howe had confidently told the Commons that in his view an American intervention was unlikely.[23] Notwithstanding the Thatcher government's resultant political and diplomatic embarrassment, however, Anglo-American relations were not seriously affected.

Britain also found itself in agreement with the Reagan administration on the great international moral issue of the mid-1980s – what to do about South Africa now that it was experiencing increasing civil disorder as a result of an upsurge in black political consciousness. In a situation where the rest of the Commonwealth, as well as the vast majority of other countries, were strongly in favour of economic sanctions against Pretoria, Britain and the United States rejected such punitive measures out of hand. London and Washington justified this position on the grounds that economic sanctions would do nothing to bring about internal reform in South Africa; indeed, they might damage the material position of the very people they were designed to assist. Critics, in contrast, argued that white South Africa had already retreated into its laager as far as it was possible to go and that the majority of blacks were quite happy to see their material position damaged in the medium term if it meant an end to apartheid. In any event, during the summer of 1986, the combination of British and American resistance effectively defeated a series of international moves to impose sanctions against South Africa. If such resistance perpetuated an outrageously unjust and inhumane system of government, then this was unfortunate but unavoidable. Reagan and Thatcher were in no doubt that South Africa was far too valuable a strategic resource to risk its loss to the Soviets in the bloody aftermath of a bloody revolution. A simple *realpolitik* principle was at work, which the West could ignore only at its peril: better the racist – but stanchly capitalist – tyranny you know than the anarchic, unstable and possibly pro-Moscow democracy you do not.

Thatcher also displayed her Atlanticist commitment in relation to Libya. Colonel Ghaddafi had been a thorn in the Americans' side for over a decade, and the final straw came in March 1986 when American intelligence services purportedly intercepted a series of communications between Tripoli and the Libyan People's Bureau in West Berlin which – at least to President Reagan's satisfaction – provided incontrovertible evidence of Libyan government complicity in the deaths of numerous American servicemen in the bombing of a Berlin night club.[24] The US administration, already involved in a naval confrontation with the Libyans in the Gulf of Sirte, swiftly decided to take punitive action against Libya and sought the British government's permission to use American F-III fighter aircraft stationed in Britain in order to effect a 'surgical strike' against Ghaddafi's capital.[25] With this permission readily given, on the night of 14–15 April American planes bombed selected targets in Tripoli and Benghazi.

Western reaction to the attack was perhaps more antipathetic than Thatcher had anticipated. The Labour Party, of course, fumed; but then that was entirely expected. More seriously, opinion polls showed that

almost two-thirds of the British electorate – partly concerned that inno-
cent civilians had been killed and partly fearful of Libyan reprisals to
come – disapproved of the British government's tacit involvement in
the American raid.[26] Meanwhile, Britain's EU partners were angry that
on the day before the raid took place Sir Geoffrey Howe had failed
to inform a meeting of European Foreign Ministers that Britain had
already acceded to the American request to use British-based aircraft
in the attack. Thatcher simply rode out the criticisms. She informed the
Commons that it would have been 'inconceivable' for the British government to have refused the American request for assistance when all else
had failed to subdue the Libyan 'mad dog'.[27] She emphasised the debt
that Britain owed to the United States as a result of services rendered
during the Falklands War. And she even suggested that from the humanitarian point of view the use of British-based F-111s had restricted Libyan
civilian casualties: long-range bombers flying from bases in the United
States would have been far less able to effect the sort of limited surgical
strike that the Americans had attempted to undertake.[28]

Yet Thatcher was not merely 'Reagan's poodle', as Denis Healey suggested at the time. In the summer of 1987 during the Iran-Iraq war, an
American request for minesweeping assistance in the Persian Gulf was
initially rejected by the British. This gave Thatcher the opportunity to
show that the poodle characterisation was not entirely fair. The fact that
she had starkly refused an American request for assistance – judging
intervention at that stage to be contrary to British interests – suggested
that she had gone along with US requests on previous occasions because
her analysis of the situation had been similar to that of the US government. In the 1987 Gulf crisis, on the other hand, the British government's
analysis had been at variance with that of the Americans, and the Cabinet
had accordingly been reluctant to provide backing for the American position even when explicitly requested to do so.

By the late 1980s, then, it was clear that Thatcher was not an automatic
supporter of American foreign policy in all of its out-of-area operations.
Crucially, what she shared with the key decision-makers in Washington
was a *convergence of view* of the nature of international politics and
of the character and seriousness of the global threats to Western interests. It was this more than anything else which produced the numerous examples of Anglo-American policy collaboration throughout the
1980s. Thatcher might not have restored the special relationship in
full – in the changed circumstances of the post-war world this was an
impossibility anyway – but she had without doubt established *a* special
relationship with Ronald Reagan's America. In spite of the reformist
Soviet leader Mikhail Gorbachev's *Perestroika* (economic reform) and
glasnost (political openness), the world was still a dangerous place in

which only resolute strategies of *realpolitik* would prevail against the ubiquitous Soviet threat. Reagan's America was still the main defender of the capitalist values and interests of the West. Even if Britain no longer possessed the capability to be America's universal number two, it could at least provide assistance with all the resources at its command in certain limited contexts. What was good for American foreign policy was good for the capitalist West. And what was good for the capitalist West was good for Britain. This was the essential logic underlying Thatcher's Atlantic circle foreign policy, so small wonder that she enjoyed a special relationship with Reagan.

The end of the Cold War happened much more slowly than many people remember. In order, the Soviet Union withdrew from Afghanistan (in 1989), the Berlin Wall came down (in the same year) and the Soviet Union itself ceased to exist (in 1991). But it all happened gradually, over the course of roughly two years. The end of the Cold War, as one might imagine, proved to be a turning point in the history of British foreign policy. For one thing, Britain no longer faced an international system in which there was a single visible threat to its security, and this scenario was soon replaced by a whole array of seemingly lesser threats. Idealists in particular originally envisioned that there would now be some sort of 'peace dividend'; with the Cold War over and done with, Britain and other states could now turn inward and address their own domestic issues, such as economic regeneration. In the United States, the neo-conservative writer Francis Fukuyama envisioned 'the end of history'. Ideas like capitalism and communism would cease to be motivating forces, he suggested, since the former had 'won' and the Soviet Union had ceased to exist altogether.

In 1990, Margaret Thatcher was forced to resign from the Leadership of the Conservative party (and hence from her position as Prime Minister) by Tory backbenchers, convinced that she would lose the next general election. That resignation produced a more visible change, perhaps, than did the gradual end of the Cold War. Gone was Thatcher's crusading rhetoric about restoring British greatness, to be replaced by something more fundamentally reactive. From 1990 to 1997, the government of John Major would preside cautiously over the end of the Cold War (somewhat like his Realist counterpart in the United States, George H. W. Bush). In Britain, this turn to a classically Realist approach in foreign policy was more traditional than not, dealing with a period of transformation and change by returning to what was most familiar and comfortable.

One of the clearest indications of this Realism in Major's case was the manner in which his government unambiguously distanced itself from calls for a humanitarian-inspired military intervention in the former

Yugoslavia. Yugoslavia disintegrated between 1991 and 1992 into older constituent parts such as Serbia, Bosnia and Montenegro, terminology which was familiar to most British people only from reading books about the World War I era (most assumed that these loyalties no longer exerted any meaningful pull). And yet these years saw the resurgence of genocide at the heart of Europe, and warlike instability in a region which many people had expected to be fundamentally peaceful after the end of the Cold War. Europe seemed to be increasingly in the grip of what the writer Robert Kaplan called 'ancient hatreds', a phrase which Major himself would use on the floor of the House of Commons.[29] War, it turned out, was not obsolete after all, and history had not quite ended.

After Bill Clinton came to office in America in January 1993, the Yugoslav issue created a major rift in the special relationship between the Americans (who saw the Serbs as the enemy) and the British (who tended to view the conflict in a more neutral or amoral way). Clinton's natural Idealist impulse – at least before the 'Black Hawk Down' incident in Somalia in 1993 – had been to strike the Serbs from the air, while keeping US ground forces out of the conflict. Clinton favoured a policy of 'lift and strike', in which the UN arms embargo placed on all parties (including the Bosnian Muslims) would be raised and America would strike the Serbs using airpower. But the Major government fundamentally disagreed. Foreign Secretary Douglas Hurd controversially articulated the Realism at the heart of British foreign policy in 1992, when he claimed that lifting the UN embargo would be like 'pouring fuel on the flames'. The British also had unarmed 'peacekeepers' on the ground in Bosnia – although there was really no peace to keep – and the UK government feared that air strikes would lead to their own people being taken hostage. The weak relationship between Bill Clinton and John Major was certainly not helped by the lack of any real chemistry between them – nor by the fact that Major signalled his support for Bush during the 1992 presidential election – but its more fundamental root cause was the clash between Major's Realism and Clinton's Idealism.

Nevertheless, for all of this caution, Douglas Hurd in particular – part of an explicitly Realist generation which had worked for (and greatly admired) Anthony Eden in the 1950s – envisioned an expansive role for Britain.[30] It was he who came up with the boxing metaphor 'punching above our weight' in international affairs. Like 'keeping a seat at the table', this has since become something of a cliché, but the phrase was relatively new when Hurd used it in a speech to Chatham House in 1993. That speech owed a great deal to the three circles idea, arguing that the UK could continue to play a strong role in the world by exploiting its seat on the UN Security Council and utilising its role in NATO. It could also keep its seat at the table by using its connections to both the New World and the Old. This last idea in particular would also soon come to animate a (New Labour) government which, on the face of it at least, had a completely different foreign policy philosophy from its predecessor.

After a period of UK foreign policy that some found stodgy, the rise to power of the youthful new Labour Party leader Tony Blair in 1997 seemed like a breath of fresh air. Much like Thatcher, Blair talked often of restoring Britain's place in the world. As we saw in the Introduction, he saw the UK as providing a kind of 'bridge' between the old world and the new, and essentially retained the Churchillian idea of the 'three circles' (although he saw the United States and Europe as the critical elements). He viewed Britain as 'equidistant' between the United States and the European Union (in a political sense, though obviously not in a literal or geographical one). He bathed in the aura of what became known as 'Cool Britannia'.[31] Although he was obviously closer to the political left than the right, some considered him the natural intellectual heir of Thatcher, a figure he has often said that he admired.

There is no doubt that – much like William Gladstone before him – Tony Blair was genuinely animated by a deep and abiding Christian faith, which made him an effective advocate for a morally Idealistic foreign policy. His genuine belief in doing 'what was right' was clear to all observers, and it played a strong role in his advocacy of interventions in Kosovo (in 1999), Sierra Leone (in 2000), Afghanistan (in 2001) and Iraq (in 2003). Stephen Dyson notes that Blair's personality traits, including his black-and-white moral beliefs and a conviction that he had a strong ability to control events, combined to create 'a consistently interventionist, proactive foreign policy strategy'.[32] His Idealism has also left its mark on subsequent administrations and on British military doctrine, which in 2016 almost always discusses UK values as well as interests in a way that it never did before 1997.[33] Doing what was morally right, rather than simply what was in Britain's national interests, was the critical thing.

Blair's pro-Americanism was also quite evident, and the 'special relationship' was arguably at its warmest during his Prime Ministership from 1997 to 2007. While he saw Britain as equidistant between Europe and the United States, in practice the pull of the latter was always somewhat greater for Blair. There were accusations at the time that he saw himself almost as a second US President alongside Bill Clinton, and he certainly 'Americanised' some aspects of British political life (such as announcing many policy changes from the doorstep of No. 10 rather than the floor of the House of Commons). This has continued in later years with the emergence of a formal *National Security Strategy* (NSS) and the creation of a National Security Council for decision-making, both modelled on their American equivalents. Blair almost became a 'US' decision-maker during the Kosovo crisis of 1999, most notably when he flew to Washington DC and tried (but failed) to convince Clinton and his inner circle of advisers to send ground forces into the region. On that occasion, Clinton's informal adviser Dick Morris came out firmly against putting 'boots on the ground'. When Blair noted that Britain no longer had enough troops to escalate the war in Kosovo in this way, Morris reportedly told him (something to the effect of) 'Oh, I get it Mr Prime Minister, you're willing to fight to the last American'.[34]

Blair even had his own doctrine, although he never referred to it explicitly as such.[35] At the Economic Club in Chicago in April 1999, Blair laid out his Idealist vision of the world. He argued that the international community can and should act to prevent major suffering and atrocities around the globe, even laying out the bases under which diplomatic and armed humanitarian intervention should occur. The speech was actually intended to put pressure on Clinton and the Americans to consider a ground invasion of the Serbian-controlled enclave of Kosovo – it is no accident that it was made in the United States – but it was remarkable for being so 'American' in style. As Steven Haines puts it,

> British leaders are not noted for such things. Indeed, one might even argue that the British are emotionally disinclined to be 'doctrinaire'.... Where are the Attlee, Churchill, Eden, Macmillan, Home, Wilson, Heath, Callaghan, Thatcher and Major doctrines? Nothing of the sort is ever referred to in accounts of British foreign policy.[36]

It could be argued, of course, that Churchill's three circles was a doctrine of sorts, but it might better be seen as a strategic framework (and indeed it is rarely, if ever, referred to as a doctrine). On the other hand, no American President since the end of World War II has ever left office without having a 'doctrine' associated with his name.

The 1999 Kosovo War was the first real test case of Blair's Idealism, and in many ways he was the prime mover in that conflict, fought by NATO as a whole in its first ever military engagement. Ethnic Albanians – many but not all of them unarmed – were under military onslaught from the Serbs. What we now know to have been a genocide against them had begun, and events like the Racak massacre spurred Blair into action. While the military campaign was directed by a coalition or 'committee' – and hence its strategic objectives and operational conduct both represented fuzzy compromises rather than any sort of clarity – Blair was very much the moral 'salesman' behind the war, taking the lead while President Clinton was preoccupied with domestic matters (most notably by the House's impeachment of the President arising from the Monica Lewinsky affair). Lasting 78 days in all, the war was fought exclusively from the air, since resistance to putting in ground forces (especially in the United States) was always very strong.

As we have noted already, it is unclear why Slobodan Milosevic eventually decided that he could not win the conflict. It should have been clearer than it was to the Western powers that he would cling to power, because any Serbian nationalist in that area regards Kosovo as 'holy ground'. Certainly, the bombing of Serbia itself helped to convince Milosevic that he had to back down, but the threat of the introduction of NATO ground forces – combined with the withdrawal of Russian support – probably made an overwhelming case. What is clear, however, is that victory in Kosovo helped to convince a young and inexperienced Prime Minister that Britain could prevail in international disputes. As Oliver Daddow notes, it also helped to produce "a more confident, proactive leader genuinely committed to grounding British foreign policy in the theory of liberal interventionism".

> Kosovo helped mould the Prime Minister into the leader he was previously wary of becoming. Blair's fear that Kosovo could be his downfall was soon quelled by the international acclaim he received for his efforts in bringing at least a degree of peace and stability to the Balkans, and after this time we see a more confident, proactive leader genuinely committed to grounding British foreign policy in the theory of liberal interventionism.[37]

Blair would later surprise observers by remaining close to George W. Bush after Clinton's departure (as noted earlier, he incurred the mockery of some in Britain by wearing a ten-gallon hat and cowboy boots to one meeting at Bush's Texas ranch, for instance). But added to his Idealism and pro-Americanism, his 'appetite for war' was also whetted by bitter experience. As a young candidate, he had been soundly beaten by his Conservative opponent in the 1982 Beaconsfield by-election, at a time when patriotic fervour was sweeping Britain and Margaret Thatcher was benefiting from a considerable rally-around-the-flag effect.[38] He lost in large part because he opposed the Falklands War, although his opposition may well have been only rhetorical (and he won a safe Labour seat the following year). As Max Hastings has suggested, Blair apparently took the lesson from his defeat in 1982 that the British people 'approve of war'.[39]

If this was the lesson drawn, however, then it was a shallow or inappropriate one. As subsequent experience was to show, the British people might approve of short, in-and-out commitments which conclude in victory – even if they are a long way from our own shores – but it does not like drawn-out wars with seemingly 'no end of sight' (to employ an old American phrase used of Vietnam). In Realist fashion, the British public also does not care for wars that cannot be justified by some abiding national interest. The UK public was not wildly enthusiastic about the Kosovo War and a very large minority were strongly opposed to the Iraq War, which was widely seen as an American venture into which Britain was reluctantly dragged using intelligence gleaned from what became known as the 'dodgy dossier'.

One important problem with this nexus of Idealism, pro-Americanism and hard-won experience as applied to Iraq and Afghanistan was that since the 1990s Britain had lacked the military resources to engage in overseas adventures in all but the smallest theatres. By this time, it had already become very much the junior partner in a whole host of US ventures, almost an inevitability when a nation in steep decline is paired with a government which gives absolute (and perhaps unquestioning) loyalty to the special relationship. In 1982, Britain had put together a naval task force which was in reality a collection of various *ad hoc* elements, some of which (like the aircraft carriers **HMS** *Hermes* and **HMS** *Invincible*) had been bound for the scrapheap or were about to be sold to Australia until just before the war. Focused on the Cold War conflict, the perplexed Americans saw this as a quarrel between friends, although they eventually (but very quietly) provided some logistical support to Britain in a war it was struggling mightily to fight on its own.

But if this lack of resources was beginning to bite by the early 1980s, it had become absolutely chronic by the late 1990s. Gordon Brown's commitment to fiscal 'prudence' as Chancellor of the Exchequer meant that the Blair government acquired a somewhat Janus-faced approach on Iraq and Afghanistan. There was a real conflict within the government between cutting back Britain's armed forces to what could actually be afforded and the impulse to return to the past. As Richard Dannatt has argued, Blair might articulate a broadly Idealist vision, but then the harder-edged Brown – ever a financial realist, if certainly not a Realist in the foreign policy sense – would refuse to pay for this vision.[40] As Ledwidge states, this 'stabbed in the back' thesis – the idea that politicians alone were responsible for underfunding of our efforts in Iraq and Afghanistan – is only partially correct because it lets Britain's generals conveniently off the hook. Nevertheless, the lack of resources was a major part of the problem.[41] There was a particular shortage of helicopters, reinforced military vehicles and body armour, and what was provided was never enough. All of this reflected not only penny-pinching in Whitehall but also procurement decisions which had been made ten years or more before, estimations which were made in the light of perceptions of what Britain would *probably* need from 2003 onwards. These estimations were based on a mixture of what it was thought would be needed to fight the old Soviet Union in Europe and perceptions that there would now be a 'peace dividend', not what would be required to confront Saddam Hussein or the Taliban in so-called small wars, low-intensity wars, 'wars among the people' or wars of counterinsurgency.[42]

Another major problem was the lack of any real strategy in Iraq and Afghanistan. Blair himself was exceptionally strong on moral and patriotic fervour, but he was something of a novice when it came to military strategy.[43] Arguably, Idealism leads to a commendable desire to 'do something' whenever we are confronted by a genocide or some other humanitarian disaster, especially in this age of the 24-hour news cycle. The do-something impulse is also in evidence whenever the bearer of an identifiable 'evil' (like Slobodan Milosevic or Saddam Hussein) is oppressing or killing his own people. But from the military-strategic perspective, the real question becomes 'do what?' Although we like to think that every difficulty has a solution, so-called 'wicked problems' involve issues that by their nature have *no* solution.

It was never really clear what Britain was doing in Iraq or Afghanistan, and only the most general guidance of the end-state sought was given.[44] In Afghanistan, for instance, what *was* the strategic objective? Was it to defeat the Taliban? Was it to eradicate their 'guests', Al-Qaeda? Was it perhaps to do both? Was this a counterinsurgency? Was this a war to win over the 'hearts and minds' of the local population, many of whom invoked the history (and mythology) of brutal British interventions in the past? Was 'Westernisation', including the building of roads, schools and hospitals, a goal? Or was merely maintaining the status quo or stabilising the situation what was sought? And was this even a 'war' in the conventional sense? There was a sense in both Britain and the United States that the goal posts were constantly shifting, and that when one strategic goal could not be met, it was simply replaced by another. The general policy itself – the desired end-state supposedly set down by politicians – was never clear, but then neither was the military strategy that was supposed to derive from it.[45]

But perhaps the most central problem of all from Britain's perspective was that old historical analogies did not seem to apply to Iraq and Afghanistan. The British had acquired a reputation for being 'good at counterinsurgency', especially as a result of past experiences in Malaya during the 1950s and Northern Ireland during the 1970s and 1980s. It was therefore expected that they would be equally good in Basra (in Iraq) and in Helmand Province (in Afghanistan).[46] The worth of these comparisons was always debateable, and the Americans would soon debate them explicitly: arguably Malaya was a brutal exercise in colonial policing of a sort that could not be put into practice today without a serious worldwide counter-reaction, while the decline of the Provisional Irish Republican Army had a lot to do with the collapse of its support in the face of colossal blunders like the 1993 bombing of Warrington and the 1998 Omagh bombing (both of which served to reinforce the need to find a political, negotiated solution). Nevertheless, it was to Basra and Helmand that the British troops were sent, and the initial expectation was that they would provide a highly skilled 'niche capability'.

The British interventions in Basra and Helmand are now almost universally seen as failures, even (and perhaps most of all) within the UK military itself. In particular, the book *British Generals in Blair's Wars* represented an especially damning indictment of the performance of British military leaders for their *own* failures, both individual and collective.[47] It may well be true that the British Army is more of a learning institution than its US counterpart, and the prerequisite for any form of learning from negative episodes is first accepting that failure has indeed occurred. But as Ledwidge sees it, in neither case – Basra or Helmand – was there a true insurgency to begin with, and the main effect of the presence of British troops was to *provoke* one. Unbeknown to many of those who arrived from the UK, for instance, Iraqi civilians had been attacked by the British military in a 1919–23 uprising in Iraq by a young Arthur 'Bomber' Harris, and Basra was a poor choice as the location for any attempt to win over the local population. Helmand was an even poorer choice, especially given that the 1880 Battle of Maiwand had occurred in that very area (something which is still recalled in Afghanistan, a country highly attuned to its own history of foreign invasion and occupation).[48] The British might (conveniently) have forgotten the darker aspects of their own history, but the Iraqis and the Afghans had not.

The July 2016 Chilcot Report[49] on Britain's involvement in the US-led decision to invade Iraq offered a measured but still devastating critique of the conduct of Tony Blair's whole approach to both the US and Iraq. While it stopped short of calling for the prosecution of Blair and his advisers – a measure that some of those directly affected, such as the families of slain servicemen, had recommended – the Report left the way open for such prosecutions to take place at some point in the future. It argued that the UK had deliberately exaggerated the threat posed by Saddam Hussein to Western interests, and that in any case the decision to side with the United States had been taken before diplomatic alternatives to a military invasion had been exhausted. Moreover, the troops had been sent into war without adequate equipment or preparation, and UK advice to the George W. Bush administration on the post-war situation was essentially ignored.[50]

The public response to the Iraq report from a tearful Tony Blair (speaking in the summer of 2016) was almost immediate. Apologising for the suffering of UK servicemen and -women but not for his original decision – which he said that he would make again, given the opportunity – Blair insisted that the invasion of Iraq had been justified in the light of the information available to him at the time. From his perspective, the whole viability of the special relationship (or British involvement within the Atlantic circle) seems to have depended upon the decision to side with the United States, and he pledged in a then-secret July 2002 memorandum to Bush that he would support the American government 'whatever'. Whether this was an *ex post facto* defence of his decisions at the time is unclear, but it is certainly consistent with his view that the relationship with the Americans was worth a very high price indeed. On the other hand, it is unclear whether siding with America was essential. Secretary of Defense Donald Rumsfeld famously said that the invasion would have gone ahead with or without UK support – just as Harold Wilson's refusal to provide British troops in Vietnam damaged but certainly did not destroy the special relationship (which has ridden out a variety of such differences). Indeed, as we have seen already, the 'special relationship' had survived Suez. There were many at the time, moreover – including large majorities in Britain and across Europe – who warned Blair that the decision on which he was embarking was simply wrong. But the British Prime Minister appears to have believed firmly that he knew better.

Whether Blair *should* have done what Harold Wilson did in 1966 is a historical and normative question upon which we will not dwell here. As we have already seen, that year and subsequent ones saw repeated US efforts to get Wilson to commit troops to the Vietnam War, all of which came to naught when the British Prime Minister simply turned them down. As we suggested earlier, the *sangfroid* caused by the Suez episode and by the withdrawal from East of Suez must have been a part of that. So too, though, was the fact that Wilson saw no national interest in putting British troops in harm's way, while for Blair getting rid of Saddam was a moral imperative. Suffice it to say here, though, that the 'special relationship' – arguably the strongest it had ever been from 1997 to 2007 – would have been gravely damaged had Blair not agreed to send UK troops into Iraq and Afghanistan.

Phase 4: Divergence Again, 2007–2016

Broadly speaking, the period since 2007 has seen a slight divergence in the objectives of Britain and the United States and some weakening of the special relationship. The brief ascendancy of Gordon Brown from 2007 to 2010 might be said to have changed relatively little about British foreign policy, but it did spell the end of the kind of crusading rhetoric for which Blair was known. Brown's experience as Chancellor of the Exchequer had been immense, and he seemed better prepared for the job than any Prime Minister since Eden. Deep down, Brown was the same kind of moral Idealist as Blair; like Woodrow Wilson, he was the son of a Presbyterian Minister and he saw politics in a moralistic way. But he had a 'dark side' – he supposedly wanted to annihilate his enemies, for instance, rather than simply defeat them[51] – and he lacked Blair's 'convivial' style.[52] He also lacked the kind of political skills that Blair put to such strong use, and often appeared awkward in social situations. He was not naturally given to the kind of jet-setting international exercises in persuasion that had been Blair's forté. As he was trained as an economist, it is also fair to say that foreign and defence policy was not really Brown's 'thing'.

It is always difficult to be the successor. Brown struggled to put his own individual spin on foreign policy, although some novelty was evident in his particular emphasis upon multilateralism in UK foreign policy (more a means than an end itself) and upon social justice (certainly an end, but a vague one). Brown's appetite for liberal interventionism was expected to be more lukewarm than Blair's had been – indeed, this would have been perfectly understandable given the failures in Iraq and Afghanistan – yet Brown actually expanded the UK's highly questionable presence in both Basra and Helmand. Most importantly, he remained strongly committed to Britain's relationship with the United States, at least rhetorically. In a speech in July 2007, for instance, he insisted that

> we will not allow people to separate us from the United States of America in dealing with the common challenges that we face around the world. I think people have got to remember that the special relationship between a British prime minister and an American president is built on the things that we share, the same enduring values about the importance of liberty, opportunity, the dignity of the individual.[53]

In another sense, however, the period after 2007 also signalled a somewhat weaker relationship with the US, as did the ascendancy of David Cameron as Conservative Prime Minister between 2010 and 2016. In both cases, the relationship was somewhat cooled by the personality mix, as it had been under Clinton–Major. Indeed, it can plausibly be argued that between 2007 and 2010 the 'chemistry' between Gordon Brown and George W. Bush (and then Barack Obama) was simply not what it had been between Reagan and Thatcher or between Blair and his US counterparts. Brown reportedly flew into rages behind the scenes – in one case, in front of Barack Obama – and was supposedly intolerant of criticism.[54] He also micro-managed in unhelpful ways; found it hard to make decisions; was far more intellectual and deliberative than the instinctive Blair had been; and was much more given to agonising about decisions he had already taken.[55] Brown was reportedly so troubled by British casualties that he would sink into the kind of funk reminiscent of

LBJ with regard to the latter days of Vietnam, for instance. In the end, though, he lost the 2010 election, and we will never know whether his foreign policies would have developed in a new direction or whether he would simply have continued the direction that Blair had already taken.

At the time of writing, there exists no published book-length treatment of David Cameron's foreign policies and very few major biographies, even though his administration came to power in 2010 and lasted five years.[56] This may be a function in large part of the fact that for its first four years, the Conservatives governed in coalition with the Liberal Democrats, and it is hence somewhat difficult to gauge Cameron's true foreign policy inclinations. Within this political climate, Cameron was forced to allow the House of Commons to play a rather more active role in foreign policy making than had historically been the case. Given the precarious advantage he enjoyed in the House, in 2013 Cameron submitted his policy on Syria, for example, to a full vote in a way that previous Prime Ministers had not. The House of Commons' decision to disallow bombing within Syria produced the highly inconsistent policy of Britain being able to bomb the followers of Islamic State within Iraq, but not when IS fighters crossed the border into Syria. The Conservatives' general election victory in May 2015, which allowed them to jettison their Liberal Democrat coalition partners, paved the way for a reversal of this policy – bombing of IS targets in Syria began in December 2015. The true character of the current Conservative government's foreign policy will presumably have revealed itself under Theresa May. As we saw in Chapter 5, however, Cameron often appeared buffeted by the forces in his own party, especially by those who favoured withdrawal from Europe.

There are, however, a number of accounts that emphasised Cameron's liberal interventionist impulses, especially when it came to Libya in 2011 and the war against Islamic State (or ISIS) after 2014.[57] Together with the French, Britain led a movement to institute regime change by removing Libya's long-term dictator Muammar Ghaddafi. While US forces were also integral to the effort, it has been argued that Barack Obama 'led from behind' on this issue. On the other hand, it remains true to say that French military involvement in bombing Libya was far greater than Britain's. As Ledwidge notes, British Eurofighters (Typhoons) had to be accompanied by Tornadoes whenever they went on a mission, because the latter could not aim their own bombs. British Army helicopters launched only 26 missions against Ghaddafi, while French helicopters mounted 200. 'By any standards the British military contribution to the Libya effort was little short of laughable', he argues. 'Libya was exactly the sort of mission for which an "expeditionary capability" should be designed. France has it and we do not.'[58]

Cameron's liberal interventionism was also in evidence with regard to ISIS, which uses the shock tactics of beheading and the indiscriminate killing of women and children to sell its message. In general, Cameron's response was similar to what might have been expected from Tony Blair, suggesting that there were significant continuities in Britain's 'ethically influenced' style of foreign policy between 1997 and 2016.[59] In truth, Cameron's approach encompassed an effort to blend Idealism and Realism that was somewhat closer to the former than the latter, resulting in a blend that was termed 'liberal Conservatism'.[60] As Daddow and Schnapper put it,

> the bounded liberal tradition defines the parameters of what the main parties of government have come to perceive as acceptable and unacceptable in British foreign policy conduct. As a direct response to the poverty of realism evident during the Major years, Blair and Cameron (albeit in slightly different ways) put principles back to the heart of UK foreign policy, settling on liberal interventionism as a way of embracing a 'modern' role for Britain in the world whilst harking back to the time-honoured principles of realist thought in international relations.[61]

In a rather strange way, the 'usual' pattern of US Idealism paired with British Realism has been reversed in recent years. Barack Obama as the US President was more given to Realism than its Idealist counterpart, while the opposite appeared to be true of David Cameron.

How did Cameron's foreign and defence policies affect the special relationship? Setting his professed ideology and his personal relationship with Obama aside, the strains in Anglo-US relations were all too evident between 2010 and 2016. Robert Gates – the former US Defence Secretary under both George W. Bush and Barack Obama – apparently spoke for the whole of the US government when he expressed grave concern about the cutbacks in UK defence that have been going on since 2010. Speaking in January 2014 on Radio Four's *Today* programme, Gates said that 'with the fairly substantial reductions in defence spending in Great Britain, what we're finding is that it won't have full-spectrum capabilities and the ability to be a full partner as they have been in the past' (by 'full-spectrum', he meant the ability to operate in all three environments of air, land and sea).[62] This was the first time since 1918, he noted, that Britain would not have an operational aircraft carrier and the first time since the Napoleonic wars that Britain's standing army had been so small. The Americans were clearly concerned that the UK would spend less than the allocated NATO total of 2 per cent of its national budget on defence, although this total has been met in recent budgets.

Set against these US concerns, Cameron apparently had an expansive view of Britain's position in the world, and the 2010 National Security Strategy promised that there would be 'no strategic shrinkage' in British foreign and defence policy. Nevertheless, he presided over very significant cuts to Britain's defence resources, signalling perhaps that Britain is no longer a power of the first rank; there is arguably a profound degree of wishful thinking in the 'no shrinkage' claim. We shall return to this theme in the final chapter, but for now it is sufficient to note that the Cameron government's foreign policy exhibited a somewhat Thatcherite Idealism, paired with the kind of deep defence cuts that Thatcher herself was forced by sheer economic reality to implement. Even today, Britain has not fully accommodated itself to the loss of Empire, perhaps, or at least has not properly adjusted to the reality of what it can actually do in the world.

Continuity and Change in Anglo-American Relations: Some Explanatory Factors

It is clear, then, that the special relationship underwent a number of important changes in the years after Suez. What is also clear, however, is that, even though the relationship certainly became less 'special' after 1963, relations remained sufficiently strong to provide both Thatcher and Blair with the firm diplomatic base they needed in order to reinvigorate London's links with Washington. What were the principal factors responsible for Britain's continued good relations with the United States? Why, within that framework of generally good relations, did the intimacy of Anglo-American cooperation vary over time? While it is not possible to answer these questions definitively, there are nonetheless several factors which were of such obvious and overriding importance that they merit review here.

Sources of Continuity

Four main factors underpinned the basic stability of Anglo-American relations in the years after 1956. The first was the continuing natural affinity which derived from a common language and a broadly similar culture.[63] This shared identity is something emphasised above all else by Constructivists (see Introduction). However, while similarities in language and culture were obviously relevant to the general feelings of mutual affect that were evident on both sides of the Atlantic, they were clearly neither a necessary nor a sufficient condition for close *governmental* relations. Indeed, although sentiment derived from cultural affinities was frequently employed in public in order to justify or legitimise policy choices that had already been made, the available evidence suggests that most decisions affecting mutual bilateral relations were based primarily on tough, self-interested calculation.[64]

It is in this context that a second, and certainly more important, factor underlying the continuity in Anglo-American relations immediately assumes relevance: the convergence of the two countries' economic interests (a factor emphasised by Realists). One aspect of this convergence was trade. British exports to the United States remained at substantial levels throughout the post-war period, apparently unaffected by the fundamental shift in exports away from the Empire and towards Western Europe which occurred after 1955.[65] Bilateral trade alone, however, was never sufficiently important to produce a special relationship between London and Washington: while, on average, some 14 per cent of British exports have been destined for the United States since the 1980s, only around 4 per cent of American exports in 2015 relied on markets in Britain.[66] The convergence of economic interest that really mattered was the mutual benefit which Britain and the United States derived from the preservation of the existing capitalist system of world trade. As relatively open economies with wide-ranging and diverse patterns of trade, Britain and the United States had a mutual interest, first, in preventing the 'loss' of any capitalist economies (together with their markets and raw material resources) to the rival 'socialist' camp; and second, in ensuring that the spectre of protectionism – which had surfaced so disastrously in the 1930s – was pushed further into the background by the progressive liberalisation of world trade. Even in the face of Britain's continuing relative economic decline, which was increasingly apparent to everyone after the mid-1950s, London and Washington retained both of these mutual interests, which they continued to attempt to maximise jointly, albeit increasingly in cooperation with other OECD countries, and especially with the so-called 'Group of 7'.[67]

Rather like cultural affinities, however, a mere convergence of general economic interests was not sufficiently significant to produce the sort of intimate relations enjoyed by London and Washington for much of the postwar period. Certainly from 1968 onwards, when Britain was obliged to abandon the Overseas Sterling Area, Britain was no more important to the United States as an economic partner than any of the other Group of 7 countries. A third, and crucial, source of stability in post-war Anglo-American relations was, in classic *realpolitik* fashion, a convergence of security interests (again, a factor which Realists above all else would stress). During the Cold War, it was of paramount importance to both countries that the Soviet Union should be prevented from making any incursion into Western Europe or extending its influence in the third world. And in the current era – especially since 9/11 – Britain and the United States have shared a determination to stamp out so-called 'Islamic' extremism, as manifested by groups like the Taliban, Al-Qaeda and ISIS. The searing experience of '7/7' 2005 – the day on which radical Islamists attacked the British transport system and took 52 lives – brought home to UK citizens the threat posed by international terrorism, much as the earlier experience had been a wake-up call for many Americans.

After 1956, it was less obvious (perhaps) why Britain should have attempted to play such a strong subsidiary role in support of the United States. For one thing, Suez itself had cruelly exposed the limitations of British power in the third world. For another, by the late 1950s formerly 'safe' British markets overseas were increasingly being eroded by American, Western European, Japanese and Chinese competition. In essence, the country could apparently do little to protect the global interests of Western capitalism. However, it was Britain's historical misfortune to be in possession of the remnants of an Empire which provided its government with a significant amount of political leverage in several strategically vital parts of the world: this uniquely qualified Britain to act as Washington's 'universal and indispensable number two'. Moreover, in spite of its veneer of altruism, the reasoning of British governments was firmly grounded in *realpolitik*. What London shared with Washington was a common commitment to Realism. In the face of the threat of communist encroachment and now global terrorism, British and American policymakers alike were convinced that the world was an extremely dangerous place in which narrow calculations about the relative benefits likely to accrue to individual countries were clearly outweighed by the overriding need to maintain the security of the West as a whole. It was this shared perception of common security interests – as much as any *objective* interest convergence – that lay at the heart of the close relations between London and Washington throughout the post-war period. Again, this is a factor emphasised by Constructivists, but it is championed by Cognitivists as well.

A fourth major factor underlying Britain's consistently close relations with the United States, at least after 1958, was nuclear sharing. The McMahon Act of 1946 had ended the vitally important atomic collaboration of the war years and obliged Britain to develop its own independent nuclear programme. The repeal of McMahon in 1958 and the subsequent signing of the Anglo-American treaty,[68] however, had effectively restored much of the old nuclear relationship. Not only could technical secrets once again be exchanged, but the path was now cleared for Britain to receive American nuclear hardware in the future – as the American decisions to supply first Skybolt and then Polaris were soon to demonstrate.

Of course, on both sides of the Atlantic an essential precondition for nuclear sharing had been a high level of mutual intergovernmental trust. Significantly, it seems that the very act of sharing itself served to increase that sense of trust still further.[69] Even as London and Washington gradually drifted apart politically in the late 1960s and 1970s, relations between them still displayed an intimacy in nuclear matters that neither country ever achieved with a third party. And in the context of more contentious policy areas, such as out-of-area operations, this intimacy undoubtedly helped to promote smoother bilateral relations than might otherwise have been expected. The crucial feature of Anglo-American nuclear sharing after 1958, however, was that it cemented the informal understanding between Britain and the United States regarding their respective roles in the international system. The United States would effectively help Britain to maintain its Great Power status by supplying it with an up-to-date independent nuclear deterrent, while London for its part would provide 'independent' support for the Americans in their efforts to keep the world safe for capitalism and liberal democracy. It was a convenient arrangement for both parties and it certainly helped to underpin the generally good relations which London and Washington enjoyed throughout the post-Suez period.

Sources of Change

While there were several factors encouraging stability in Anglo-American relations after 1956, there were also a number of forces at work that were conducive to change. As noted earlier, in the immediate wake of Suez the need to prevent the growing Soviet influence in Egypt from spreading to other parts of the Middle East led to such a rapid restoration of relations that within a year London and Washington were engaged in joint military action to protect pro-Western regimes in Jordan and the Lebanon. Once Britain's 'second wave' decolonisation programme got under way after 1956, an even more potent source of Anglo-American cordiality came into operation: strong American approval of the revised world role which the British government seemed poised to adopt. Successive US administrations had consistently voiced their suspicions of Britain's post-war imperial designs. The fact that London was now vigorously decolonising – which clearly demonstrated Britain's attachment to democratic ideals – was inevitably viewed with considerable favour in Washington. What pleased the Americans even more was that, notwithstanding the shedding of its colonial possessions, Britain still seemed to be committed to maintaining a military presence in enough strategic locations worldwide to enable Britain, should the need arise, to make a useful contribution to anti-communist trouble-shooting operations anywhere in the world.

This was exactly the sort of burden sharing that the Americans wanted. With Washington clearly the senior partner, the United States and Britain could face the threat of communist encroachment together, as joint protectors of the strategic interests of the West.

From 1964 onwards, however, this vision of renewed Atlantic collaboration gradually began to fade as a series of developments – largely outside the British government's control – started to weaken the close diplomatic ties between London and Washington. The first of these was a consequence of the United Kingdom's long-term relative economic decline. Throughout the post-war period Britain had achieved significantly lower growth rates than its major industrial competitors and by the mid-1960s the cumulative effects of this poor performance were becoming all too apparent. Successive governments were being plagued by endemic balance of payments crises and by persistent pressure to cut government expenditure. Against this background of relative economic decline, the cost of maintaining a widely dispersed overseas military presence was rising inexorably. The logic of the situation was inescapable. The British economy was increasingly incapable of supporting the sort of political and military world role to which its government aspired, and cuts would have to be made. The immediate consequence of the Wilson government's resultant decision to cut defence spending by withdrawing from East of Suez was that Britain simply became less useful to the United States in its efforts to resist communist expansionism in the third world. How could the Royal Navy help to protect democracy in Thailand, for example, if it had already evacuated Singapore? At the same time, moreover, Britain was being overtaken by what was then called West Germany as the main European contributor to NATO's conventional forces.[70] Both outside and inside the NATO context, therefore, Britain's significance as a military partner for the United States was in serious decline. In the harsh world of *realpolitik,* such a development was bound to produce a cooling in Atlantic relations, especially at a time when Britain was looking to strengthen its ties with the European Union.

A second major source of the decay in Anglo-American relations after 1963 concerned the political and economic changes that were occurring inside the United States itself. Not least among these was the gradual shift in the geographical locus of American economic activity – away from the industrial states of the eastern seaboard and towards the hi-tech sunrise states of the south and west. Beginning in the mid-1960s, this apparently autonomous shift in economic activity towards the west coast was reinforced by the dramatic growth over the next two decades of the Far Eastern economies of Japan, Taiwan, South Korea, Hong Kong and Singapore.[71] This expansion in turn created an awareness in Washington that US economic interests in this new Pacific Basin region were just as important, if not more important, than those in Western Europe. Moreover. this awareness was reinforced by the largely coincidental decline of the old east coast foreign policy establishment.[72] This process was accelerated in the late 1970s and 1980s by the retirement of a generation of politicians, administrators and military personnel who had established close personal and institutional links with Britain and Western Europe either during or immediately after World War II. Their successors were far less committed to the idea of the United States as a member of an *Atlantic* security community and concomitantly far more open to the idea of developing an alternative one in the Pacific, a development which has perhaps reached its nadir in recent years with the supposed 'Asian tilt' in the foreign policies of the Obama administration. This gradual change inevitably resulted in the United States adopting a more critical approach to its dealings with Western Europe. This in turn caused Washington to attach rather less importance to its links with London, and, not surprisingly, the Anglo-American relationship suffered accordingly.

A third factor was the United States' increasing concern with superpower relations during the Cold War. Until the mid-1960s, Washington had tended to conduct its negotiations with the Soviet Union mainly on a multilateral – rather than a bilateral – basis. The British Embassy in Moscow in particular had enjoyed intimate relations with its American counterpart and London had almost invariably been consulted when the United States administration was considering a major departure in its Soviet policy.[73] From 1964 onwards, however, the United States was far more inclined to restrict formal negotiations over such a vital area as arms control to the Soviet Union alone. How far this was the result of American as opposed to Soviet preferences is uncertain, but the outcome was the same. There was no place for Britain in either the anti-ballistic missile (ABM) treaty negotiations in 1971–72 or in the negotiations that led up to the Strategic Arms Limitation Treaties (SALT) of 1972 and 1979. On the contrary, the high table was reserved exclusively for the superpowers. As a mere Great Power in decline, Britain could not reasonably expect to be represented. Indeed, even Margaret Thatcher's resuscitation of Anglo-American collaboration in the 1980s could not win Britain a place at the Reykjavik Summit in 1986. As a result, London had no hand in the negotiations that laid the foundation for the subsequent US–Soviet agreement to eliminate medium-range nuclear missiles in Europe, or in the eventual ending of the Cold War.

Yet the personalities and beliefs of politicians who came in and out of office mattered as well (a factor that Cognitivists would emphasise). For instance, Margaret Thatcher did re-establish a more intimate relationship with the United States than that enjoyed by any Prime Minister since Harold Macmillan. This intimacy was partly a result of Thatcher's instinctive Atlanticism, but it was also partly a consequence of the close correspondence between the Reagan and Thatcher views both of the seriousness of Soviet-inspired threats to Western interests and of the concomitant need to resist them with determination; they shared a strong desire to prevent further encroachment by the 'evil Empire'.[74] Similarly, the ideological consonance between Blair and Clinton served to solidify Anglo-American cooperation, just as the frostier relations between Major and Clinton or between Brown and Bush did something to reduce this. Yet under Thatcher, the would-be special relationship was not quite the one-sided affair that it had frequently appeared to be for the previous 30 years. And when Blair sought to exercise an impact on US decision-making during the Kosovo affair of 1999, a somewhat similar effect was achieved.

Summary and Conclusions

One problem that confronts any analysis of Anglo-American relations in the post-war period is that the special relationship itself is susceptible to such a wide range of interpretations. It has variously been claimed that the relationship was always much more special for London than it was for Washington, an argument which was revived in 2016 as Theresa May failed to get through to President-elect Donald Trump on the telephone;[75] that, as an 'agreeable British myth to help cushion the shock of national decline', it never really existed at all;[76] that, on the contrary, it *did* exist until the mid-1960s, but faded as British and American interests diverged;[77] that in matters of military intelligence it survived throughout the post-war period;[78] that with regard to the crucial question of nuclear-weapons sharing it came fully to fruition only after 1958;[79] and that, having faded with the death of Kennedy and the resignation of Macmillan, it was revived on a tide of Thatcherism in the 1980s and perhaps Blair in the 1990s and the early part of the 21st century.[80] While all of these interpretations can plausibly be derived from the history of post-war Anglo-American relations, relations between London and Washington were remarkably good throughout the post-war period, though whether this closeness constituted something which was at any stage uniquely 'special' remains a matter for speculation. The United States, after all, has special relationships with Israel and Ireland as well.

The Suez affair exercised a double-edged effect on Anglo-American relations. The short-term effect, since it was primarily US pressure which had forced the abrupt Anglo-French withdrawal, was clearly deleterious. In the medium term, however, the fact that Suez subsequently served to enhance Soviet influence in Egypt caused London and Washington to recognise the importance of their mutual security interest in preventing Moscow's malign influence from spreading further. Combined with the added danger in Europe that seemed to be implied by the Soviet intervention in Hungary, this renewed awareness of common security interests enabled the British and American governments to effect a rapid repair to their mutual relations. The new closeness was symbolised by the nuclear sharing agreement of 1958 and subsequently reinforced by the excellent personal relations enjoyed by Prime Minister Macmillan and President Kennedy.[81]

Within two years of the signing of the 1962 Nassau agreement, however, the special relationship entered a long phase of decay. The new Labour government was less convinced of the enormity or the ubiquity of the Soviet threat outside Europe and accordingly was less prepared to provide automatic support for American efforts to defend what Washington still regarded as the global strategic interests of the West as a whole. The simultaneous attempts by the Wilson government to bring out-of-area operations more into line with the nation's straitened economic circumstances – moves which were not reversed by either the Heath or Callaghan governments – seriously reduced the United Kingdom's utility as a global military partner. This declining utility, together with the increasingly European focus of Britain's foreign policy, seemed to presage an inexorable divergence in British and American interests which would inevitably mean a further weakening of what remained of the 'special relationship'.

The revival phase in Anglo-American relations after 1979 and 1997 was predicated entirely on the election of leaders in the two countries who shared very similar ideological convictions. Under Thatcher, Britain was no better placed in economic terms to perform an active support role for American global policing than it had been in the days of Wilson, Heath and Callaghan. Thatcher, however, firmly shared Reagan's fears about the seriousness of the Soviet global threat and his conviction that it must be pre-empted where possible and confronted where necessary. Similarly, under Blair Britain's ability to influence global affairs had declined still further, but he nevertheless shared Clinton's conviction that both countries possessed a moral duty to stop suffering where they could. Even though the British government was now unable to provide the level of military support that it had in the 1950s, it could still bestow the appearance of 'multilateral' legitimacy on American-sponsored out-of-area operations. This was clearly valuable to Washington in its attempts to justify its own behaviour to world opinion. Yet it provided both Thatcher and Blair with the opportunity to burnish their credentials as the true 'heir' to the mantle of Winston Churchill. It remained to be seen, at the time of writing, whether a viable counterpart to the controversial Donald Trump would emerge in Britain.

Chapter 7

The International Economic Dimension

In some respects it might appear unnecessary to delineate a separate area of a nation's foreign policy and designate it as 'economic'. After all, not only are self-evidently political strategies frequently shaped by economic objectives and constraints, but decisions about economic policy are equally often guided by political criteria. In spite of the undoubted connections between 'the economic' and 'the political', there is still a distinctively economic area of British foreign policy which – if only because of its rather technical nature – merits separate investigation. As will be seen, in terms of foreign economic policy the post-war era can be conveniently partitioned into two distinct phases: from 1945 to 1968, when the 'reserve' role of sterling was finally abandoned; and from 1968 to the present day, when the role of free markets has expanded relative to the power of the state.[1] During the first phase, successive governments sought to restore Britain's prewar international economic position by continuing to play a *dominant* and would-be guiding role in the international financial system. During the second phase, a less ambitious and rather more *reactive* strategy was adopted, a strategy that was in reality far better suited to Britain's reduced economic circumstances.

This chapter is concerned with two main questions: (1) what were the major external economic policies that Britain actually pursued in the years after 1945; and (2) why were they followed? Before the relevant policy developments can be described, however, a preliminary distinction is necessary. There are in fact three separate (though, inevitably, interrelated) aspects of foreign economic policy.

1. *Trade policy* is concerned primarily with the question as to who Britain's major trading partners should be and the extent to which those partners enjoy free access to British markets.
2. *Overseas investment policy* is concerned with the extent to which British companies are allowed or encouraged to export capital in order to build up overseas assets which will act as a source of future invisible exports in the form of repatriated profits.
3. *Currency policy* is concerned both with the extent to which the government stimulates the use of sterling as an 'international currency'

and with the Treasury's efforts to influence the external value of the pound; that is, its price against other currencies.

Most of the discussion in this chapter focuses on the third aspect and to a lesser extent on the second. However, this is not at all to suggest that trade policy was unimportant in the post-war years. On the contrary, the promotion of Britain's export trade with the outside world was an important priority for governments of all political persuasions through-out the post-war era. The cursory treatment accorded to trade matters here largely reflects the sheer *continuity* of the trade policy which, within the limits imposed by Britain's membership of different international organisations, successive governments pursued for over four decades. This continuity stemmed mainly from the fact that all post-war governments maintained faith with the 'theory of comparative advantage': with the claim that trade stimulates economic growth by enabling different nation-states to specialise in producing those goods and services for which their natural factor endowments best qualify them.[2] As a result, successive governments consistently accepted that Britain, as a nation which traded a high proportion of its GDP,[3] should strive to follow the principles of what became the World Trade Organization (WTO)[4] by removing mutual restrictions on trade wherever possible and by avoiding the illusory temptations of protectionism.

In recent years we have seen an intensification of this strategy. The Cameron government, in office in coalition from 2010 to 2015 and on its own from 2015 to 2016 has aggressively pursued a trading strategy based on export promotion; in other words, it attempted to 'sell' British goods and services abroad in a rather aggressive way. Quite simply, export promotion is a particular strategy for attaining economic development. Cameron has been accused of following such a strategy 'obsessively', as if it were the only path to such development or to erasing the British balance of payments deficit, but it accords with a basically Realist strategy.[5]

IR theory has not yet been comprehensively applied to foreign economic policy, at least not in any fully satisfying way. Nevertheless, a Constructivist or a Cognitivist might note that there is nothing 'natural' or inevitable about such an approach. There are in fact a number of ways in which an international payments deficit can be addressed and potentially reduced. The bluntest instrument of all is *deflation*. While globalisation limits the extent to which a state can go it alone in the international economic system, it can still deliberately seek to reduce the level of overall economic activity within its borders – for example, by increasing taxes or cutting back public spending – in such a way that also reduces the demand for the importation of goods. An alternative is deliberate *devaluation* of the currency, of such a degree that imports become more expensive and exports cheaper. A third option is *mercantilism* or *protectionism*, by which the state uses trade tariffs or quotas to purposely keep out imports, and *export promotion* is yet a fourth. However, from a Realist point of view, such an approach does tally with the promotion of the national interest, and Cameron's foreign economic policies might be said to reflect the economic application of *realpolitik* within a liberal, free-trading network, but in a structure which decreasingly works to Britain's benefit.[6]

In truth, Cameron's approach followed long-running trends in Britain's post-war trade policy, whose central objective was to trade with as many foreign partners as possible (no matter what the political complexion of their governments) and to grant each partner access to British markets on conditions broadly similar to those enjoyed by British firms seeking market access abroad. While the Labour Party flirted with the idea of protectionism in the early 1970s and (as we shall see) deliberate devaluation of sterling was a feature of its policies in the 1960s, in the longer run, devotion to the principle of free trade has so far triumphed politically. The principles of reciprocity informed not only Britain's bilateral trading relations with a wide range of countries, but also its multilateral dealings with the Commonwealth in the 1950s, with the European Free Trade Agreement (EFTA) in the 1960s and with the European Community/Union after 1973. This political trend has further intensified since the 1980s and 1990s with the movement away from states and towards markets, a change fully endorsed by 'New Labour' under Tony Blair and adhered to by all British political parties in the years since.[7]

The overall continuity of Britain's post-war trade policy, then, was considerable. While there were obviously some shifts in policy as Britain's involvement with different countries and with different international organisations varied over time, such changes were not of sufficient importance to warrant detailed discussion here. By far the most significant aspects of Britain's post-war foreign economic policy were the developments in its 'currency policy' – developments which in turn affected the pattern of Britain's overseas investment. It is these changes which are now examined.

The Attempt to Preserve a Dominant World Financial Role, 1945–68

The main theme of this section is that there were significant parallels between the overextended *political* strategy that Britain pursued between 1945 and 1956 (discussed in Chapter 2) and the similarly overextended *economic* strategy that was pursued between 1945 and 1968. Just as the political strategy followed by successive British governments was not commensurate with Britain's depleted post-war resource base, so in the economic sphere London persistently attempted to project an economic role in the world which the domestic economy was not strong enough to support. As will be seen, the political strategy and the economic strategy had a common origin. They both derived from the post-war belief, widely held inside Cabinet and Whitehall, that Britain was still a Great Power and that its government should accordingly pursue foreign policies appropriate to that status. In the political sphere this meant a strategy designed to preserve British influence in all three of Churchill's 'circles'. In the economic sphere it meant a strategy designed to restore sterling to at least a semblance of the 'top currency' *reserve role* that it had enjoyed in the heyday of the Empire.[8]

This section is divided into two main parts. The first describes the major changes in Britain's currency policy that were made between 1945 and 1968. It tells the story of the progressive decline of sterling and (in the face of stubborn resistance from successive governments) the loss of its role as a reserve currency – a loss which was both a consequence and a symbol of Britain's declining status as a world power. The second part examines two alternative explanations (one Marxist, one non-Marxist) as to why successive governments sought for so long to maintain sterling's reserve role long after it had plainly outlived its usefulness.

The Decline of Sterling, 1945–68

Although it is possible to trace the decline of sterling as a major currency to at least 1914, the most useful place to begin for the purpose of the present exposition is September 1931, when Britain formally abandoned the Gold Standard. Under the Gold Standard (since 1925) the value of sterling had been tied to gold, and the values of most other currencies had been tied to sterling, the then 'top currency'. The main consequence of the abandonment was that the international financial system fragmented, splitting into a number of distinct 'currency blocs' based principally upon sterling, the dollar, the mark and the franc. Crucially, from the British point of view, the dominions of the Empire, together with several of the smaller European countries, continued to tie their currencies to the pound, forming an informal 'sterling bloc'. The independence and internal cohesion of this bloc was subsequently reinforced by Britain's abandonment of free trade in March 1932. Indeed, the coalition government's introduction of a general external tariff (from which imports from the Empire were to be excluded) accelerated the development of a *sterling currency area* in which the participant members traded freely with one another but hardly at all with the outside world.

The American-sponsored Bretton Woods Agreement of 1944 sought to ensure that the anarchic international economic conditions of the 1930s, in which trade between member states of different currency blocs was difficult, would not be repeated in the post-war era. Put simply, Bretton Woods provided the basis for a new liberal international economic order. The newly established International Monetary Fund would help member states to finance short-term balance of payments deficits, thus promoting international trade. The World Bank would provide long-term funding for economic development projects. And the soon to be created GATT would facilitate the progressive multilateral reduction of tariff barriers. The cornerstone of the new regime, however, was a system of fixed parity exchange rates in which the value of the dollar was pegged to gold (at $35 per ounce) and all other national currencies were tied to the value of the dollar. (The pound, for example, was set at $4.03.) The fixed parity system was intended to provide a much-needed stabilising mechanism for international trade: business certainty about the cost of imports and the value of exports would replace the high levels of uncertainty which had been associated with the fluctuating exchange rate anarchy of the 1930s.

From Britain's point of view, the crucial aspect of the Bretton Woods system was that its efficient operation required each participating state to hold *reserves* either of gold or of some 'hard' 'reserve' currency – reserves which each state could subsequently use if necessary to maintain its own currency's agreed par value. (For example, if a participating state experienced a balance of payments deficit – if the total value of its exports was less than the value of its imports – there would by definition be a lower demand for its currency. In these circumstances, the state's central bank would intervene in the currency markets, offloading some of its reserves in order to buy its own currency. This in turn would increase the demand for the currency and thereby restore its par value.) In deference to the United States' paramount position in the post-war economy, the dollar was designated as the major reserve currency. In recognition of Britain's continuing de facto economic dominance in the old 'sterling bloc' area and its still powerful (if relatively diminished) position in the world economy in general, sterling was also accorded the status of a reserve currency. Thus, although the post-Bretton Woods international order would undoubtedly be dominated by the United States, there would still be a special role for Britain: London would act as Washington's junior economic partner, giving strong diplomatic backing for American efforts aimed at expanding world trade and if necessary providing support for the dollar in times of crisis.

But if the foundations of the new world economic order – and Britain's place within it – were firmly in place by the end of the war, the war itself had affected Britain's international financial position in two important senses. On the credit side, the pre-war 'sterling bloc' had been transformed into the Overseas Sterling Area (OSA). As Strange observes, not only was the OSA 'almost a monetary union' in which the pound was employed as the major reserve currency, but the reserves of the OSA countries were held in a common pool in London under the control of the British government.[9] On the debit side, however, Britain emerged from the war with assets of £610 million in gold and foreign currency reserves but with liabilities in excess of £3,500 million. These liabilities were almost entirely debts owed to Commonwealth governments as a result of their material assistance during the war; debts which became known as the 'sterling balances'.

The incoming Attlee government was thus faced with some very hard choices. On the one hand, the size of Britain's debts, its small asset base and its projected balance of payments deficit of £1,000 million for 1945–47 all pointed to the conclusion that the United Kingdom could not possibly afford the luxury of maintaining sterling's position as a reserve currency. The Bank of England simply did not have access to sufficient foreign currency reserves to maintain international confidence in the pound – confidence which was crucial if sterling was to continue to play a role as a major international currency. On the other hand, however, in the mid-1940s it was still believed that Britain should preserve sterling's reserve role. There were four main benefits that were assumed to follow from the maintenance of this role. The first was a simple matter of status. Britain was the capitalist world's second most important power, and if it wished to be acknowledged as such internationally it must continue to play a major role in the international financial system. Second, sterling's reserve role was thought to be a necessary condition for the continued extensive use of the pound as an international transactions currency, a usage which was crucial to the invisible export-earning capacity of the City of London. Third, the fact that OSA governments held their reserves in London also meant that they were 'managed' in London and this in turn yielded valuable commission fees to financial institutions in the City. Fourth, it was widely recognised that Britain would be able to use the OSA to protect the overseas markets of British manufacturers. This possibility resulted from the fact that, through the Exchange Equalisation Account, the Treasury was able to determine the total number of pounds that could be exchanged for any other currency. This meant it could effectively ration the supply of *foreign* currency within the OSA and made it easier for businesses *inside* the OSA to purchase goods and raw materials from *other* OSA countries. This in turn provided relatively 'safe' markets for British manufacturers of both capital and consumer goods: deprived of foreign currency, importers in the dominions and colonies were obliged to buy from Britain (or from elsewhere in the OSA) or do without.

Thus the dilemma for the Attlee government was sharply focused. It wished to maintain sterling's reserve role status (and its corollary, the OSA) because of the considerable benefits that such status was assumed to bestow. Yet in 1945 Britain did not possess the financial wherewithal necessary to run a reserve currency. In the event, it was the Truman administration that came to Attlee's rescue. The 'American Loan' agreement of June 1946 provided Britain with a $3,750 million loan sufficient to preserve sterling's status as a reserve currency and hence to preserve the OSA itself. It also made it possible for the British government to press ahead with its domestic expansion of the welfare state and to maintain its global military capability. There were obvious benefits for both sides. The United Kingdom gained a welcome respite from what it was hoped would prove its temporary state of financial embarrassment and for the time being at least kept control of its protected markets in the OSA. The United States gained the promise of continued British military backing for its global struggle against communism. Washington also sought private assurances that in the near future sterling would be made freely convertible against the dollar, a development which would undoubtedly weaken Britain's hold over OSA markets and thereby increase the prospects for American export penetration. However, when the Attlee government duly abided by its tacit commitment (in July 1947), a disastrous run on the pound led to a rapid suspension of convertibility only one month later. Not wishing to witness a sterling crisis doing untold damage to the economy of its principal Cold War ally, the Truman administration accepted the swift ending of convertibility with relative equanimity. As a result – and more by luck than by judgement – the British government managed to preserve sterling's reserve role (courtesy of the American loan) *and* the integrity of the OSA and the 'safe' markets contained within it. Even when Dalton decided to devalue sterling in September 1949 (from $4.03 to $2.80) Washington continued to acquiesce, accepting that Britain's painful economic recovery could only be maintained if its exporters were allowed to benefit from the cheaper (and therefore more competitive) export prices that devaluation entailed.

If the 1940s had been characterised by the creation of a 'defensive' currency area safe for British exports, however, the 1950s witnessed a series of policy changes aimed at strengthening the international use of sterling as a transactions currency for worldwide financial operations.[10] Three institutional changes in particular contributed significantly to the revival of the City of London as a financial and commercial centre and thereby indirectly stimulated the growth of sterling's transactions role. In 1951, the City was reopened as an international market for foreign exchange dealing and for commodity trading. In 1954, various exchange controls were removed, thus allowing non-residents of the United Kingdom to deal more freely in sterling. And in 1958, the pound was made fully convertible. These changes certainly helped to maintain the international use of sterling as a reserve currency. More importantly still, they also allowed the City continuously to expand the range and sophistication of the services that it could offer the world financial and commercial community; as a result, there was a steady growth in Britain's 'invisible' export trade, without which the United Kingdom would have been in continuous balance of payments deficit since the early 1950s.

Yet in addition to the enormous benefits that this more liberal approach to Britain's currency policy bestowed in terms of the expansion of the City, there were also significant costs. Full convertibility in particular had two clearly damaging consequences. First, it reduced the 'safeness' of OSA markets for British exporters. With the pound freely convertible, OSA importers could now purchase goods or raw materials from *outside* the sterling area, using either dollars or some other convenient currency. Second, full convertibility rendered sterling increasingly vulnerable to speculative short-term capital movements. Foreign speculators could now buy sterling more easily, but they could just as easily *sell* it. And, given the peculiar psychology of market behaviour, this in turn increased the tendency for speculators simultaneously to sell sterling for no other reason than their collective expectation (which subsequently became a self-fulfilling prophecy) that the value of sterling was about to fall. The main consequence of this tendency during the late 1950s and 1960s was a long-running series of 'runs on the pound'. And in response to each of these crises the Bank of England was obliged – under the Bretton Woods fixed parity arrangement – to intervene in the currency markets in order to support sterling; each intervention thus constituted a drain on Britain's gold and foreign currency reserves.

The situation came to a head in October 1967 after a series of abortive attempts at crisis management by the Treasury. In the face of continuous foreign and domestic speculation against sterling, and a disastrous fall in Britain's reserves, the Wilson government announced a devaluation of the pound; a reduction in its fixed parity from $2.80 to $2.40. The devaluation had the desired effect of staunching the short-term speculative outflow. Yet it also had the effect of devaluing the OSA governments' sterling balances – the long-term interest-yielding debts owed by the Treasury – by the same 14 per cent. As a result, the consequences of devaluation were dramatic. Fearful that yet more devaluations would follow, overseas sterling holders, especially OSA governments, began to move their long-term funds out of sterling: they quite simply stopped using the pound as their main reserve currency. This development effectively signalled the de facto demise both of the OSA and of sterling as a major reserve currency – without any specific policy decision to that end being taken by the British government. London nevertheless recognised a *fait accompli* when it saw one, and immediately began with the OSA governments a series of negotiations which culminated in the Basle Agreements of September 1968.[11] These agreements resolved a number of technicalities over the legal status of the remaining sterling balances and effectively terminated the Overseas Sterling Area.

Although the ending of sterling's reserve role was lamented in some quarters as being yet another indication of Britain's 'descent from power', many observers took the view that the termination of the reserve role had come not a moment too soon.[12] Between 1945 and 1968 the continued existence of the OSA and of the reserve role had had three profoundly disturbing consequences for Britain's domestic economy. First, the lack of constraints on the export of capital to OSA countries had encouraged a massive outflow of private long-term capital from Britain as investors strove to take advantage of the higher profits that, in the 1950s and 1960s, were available in Australia, South Africa and the Middle East. According to Andrew Shonfield this 'leakage of capital' led directly to lower investment levels in Britain and indirectly contributed to Britain's relatively poor industrial performance throughout the immediate post-war period.[13] Second, the system of discriminatory exchange controls which made it difficult for OSA countries to trade outside the Sterling Area, and which accordingly preserved 'safe' overseas markets for British exports, was a decidedly double-edged weapon. By insulating British industry from the energising effects of foreign competition, it ensured that even the most lethargic and inefficient of producers could sell their goods in the 'soft' OSA markets. By thus encouraging British inefficiency, therefore, the OSA – rather like the Empire before it – both masked and contributed to Britain's long-term industrial decline.[14]

A third consequence of the maintenance of sterling's reserve role was that the interest rate policies necessary for its smooth operation exacerbated the damaging stop-go fluctuations of the British domestic economy (see Table 7.1). The core of the problem in this context was psychological. In order to sustain the pound's reserve status, successive governments had to maintain international confidence in sterling – the confidence both of foreign governments and of private investors. Unfortunately, whenever the British balance of payments ran into deficit, 'confidence' in (as well as 'real', trade-related demand for) the pound almost invariably declined, thereby draining Britain's foreign exchange reserves as the Bank of England intervened in the market to maintain sterling's parity with the dollar. The Bank of England's typical response (after consultation with the Treasury) as each crisis loomed was to raise interest rates in

Table 7.1 The 'Stop-Go' cycle of the UK economy during the 1950s and 1960s

Annual growth in	UK balance of UK industrial production (%)	Payments, current account (£ million)
1953–5 expansion	5.6	+ 145 to – 155
1955–8 stagnation	0.4	– 155 to + 336
1958–60 expansion	6.2	+ 336 to – 275
1960–62 stagnation	1.1	– 275 to + 101
1962–64 expansion	5.6	+ 101 to – 393
1964–66 stagnation	1.5	– 393 to – 61

SOURCE: E. A. Brett, *The World Economy since the War* (London: Palgrave Macmillan, 1985) p. 155.

London in order to attract short-term funds back into sterling. While this had the desirable consequence of relieving the pressure on the country's reserves, it also discouraged investment and inhibited economic growth at home by raising the domestic cost of borrowing. According to Brett, the alternate phases of growth and stagnation which characterised the British economy between the early 1950s and the late 1960s owed much to the currency policies of successive governments and their determination to preserve sterling's reserve status.[15] As Table 7.1 shows, during this period there were a series of expansionary phases in which the balance of payments shifted from a position of surplus to one of deficit. The resultant increase in interest rates, designed primarily to maintain international confidence in sterling, would then usher in a period of stagnation during which the balance of payments position would recover as a result of reduced demand for imports. Interest rates could then be relaxed, thus stimulating more investment activity and economic growth. However, the next balance of payments crisis – and the next run on the pound – would soon make itself felt.

Now, of course, it is easy to assert that many of the difficulties experienced by the British economy during the 1950s and 1960s were exacerbated – if not actually caused – by the attempts of successive governments to maintain sterling's international role. Unfortunately, it is far more difficult to demonstrate that the pursuit of the reserve role actually had an effect on anything at all. This said, the broad consensus of informed opinion seems to suggest that the attempts to preserve the reserve role did indeed have a continuously damaging effect on Britain's domestic industrial development. Yet such a conclusion immediately gives rise to an important question: why on earth did successive governments attempt to sustain sterling's reserve role – and its corollary, the OSA – when the consequences for the home economy appear to have been so consistently debilitating? It is this question that is now considered.

Explaining the Reserve Role Strategy: Marxist and Non-Marxist Interpretations[16]

The Marxist View

For Marxist scholars, the puzzle concerning the protracted efforts to preserve sterling's reserve role can best be resolved by posing a further question: given that Britain's foreign economic strategy after 1945 produced so little benefit for the British economy as a whole, who did benefit from it? In the opinion of many Marxists the main beneficiaries were in fact that fraction of the capitalist class known as *'financial capital'*: the bankers, insurers, currency dealers and commodity traders whose activities were concentrated in the City of London. In essence, Marxists argue, the reserve role was maintained because it was in the interests of financial capital that it be maintained and because financial capitalists were sufficiently dominant within the British policy-making process to ensure that their own interests prevailed.[17]

How, then, did this come about? In the Marxist view, one of the key sources of the dominance of financial capital was the peculiar historical evolution of the British state apparatus. In most advanced capitalist countries, one of the primary functions of the state is to encourage the process of capital accumulation; this, after all, is the central economic activity of the capitalist mode of production. As a result the capitalist state typically contrives to maximise the interests of 'industrial capital', the fraction of the capitalist class that comprises the owners and controllers of the means of production and distribution. In Britain, however, financial capitalists managed to retain their hold on the levers of political power for longer than was typically the case elsewhere. In so doing, moreover, they ensured that in Britain at least it was the interests of financial rather than industrial capital that dominated foreign economic policymaking well into the 20th century. This continued dominance of financial capital stemmed partly from the generalised informal influence that City interests were able to exert over the decision-making apparatus of the British state and partly from the high level of decision-making autonomy retained (in spite of its formal nationalisation in 1945) by the Bank of England. In the Marxist view, from the late 19th century onwards, the City and the Bank of England were able to use the Bank's institutional links with the Treasury in order to exercise 'structural power' – to pressure successive governments into pursuing foreign economic policies that were conducive to the interests of financial capital.[18]

Contemporary Marxist scholars identify two major policy consequences of the dominance of financial capital in Britain's foreign economic policymaking. One strand of Marxist opinion stresses the significance of the City's conviction during the 1950s and 1960s that the preservation of the OSA was essential for the maintenance of sterling's international transactions role. It was believed that without the transactions role the City's income from transactions fees would be seriously reduced. And, as a result, financial capital consistently exercised its 'structural power' over the political system by tacitly posing the threat of a disastrous 'flight of capital' from Britain if the reserve role were to be abandoned.[19] A second strand of Marxist opinion argues that, from the late 19th century onwards, the continued dominance of financial capital ensured that a central objective of Britain's foreign economic policy was the facilitation of capital exports. For Lenin, of course, this was what the Empire after 1870 had in any case been all about: the main purpose of the territorial acquisitions in Africa and the Far East in the late 19th century had been to resolve the crisis of capital over-accumulation at home by rendering the areas thus acquired safe for British capital exports. For contemporary Marxists, the OSA continued to perform a similar function in the post-war years: it remained an extremely congenial device for facilitating the export of capital to OSA countries where financial capitalists, together with large multinational industrial firms, could gain a higher return on their portfolio and direct investments.[20] And as long as the rate of profit remained higher in OSA countries than in Britain, financial capital had a clear incentive to ensure that the OSA itself was preserved. This, essentially, was why, in the face of the evident costs to the British economy as a whole, it did in fact survive for so long. According to the Marxist account, it was not until the late 1960s, when Britain's pattern of trade and investment had shifted 'naturally' towards Western Europe, that financial capital lost interest in the Sterling Area. The OSA, quite simply, was no longer required as a destination for British capital exports to anything like the extent that it had been in the past. The promise of profits from investment inside Europe clearly began to outweigh anything that the OSA had to offer. For the Marxists it was this autonomous change in the material interests of financial capital – away from the Empire and towards Europe – that led to the abandonment of the OSA and of sterling's reserve role. In short, financial capital was not only the chief beneficiary of the maintenance of the OSA, it was also the chief architect of its demise when the OSA was no longer needed.

The Non-Marxist View

The Marxists, then, emphasise the interests and the dominance of financial capital in their explanation of the survival of the OSA. The dominant non-Marxist view, associated most clearly with the writings of Susan Strange, is rather different. According to Strange, the OSA was perpetuated well beyond its useful life largely because the key decision-makers in the British foreign policy elite adhered to a faulty analysis of Britain's post-war economic position.[21]

Strange argues that the post-war strategy of attempting to re-establish and maintain sterling's role as a major reserve currency was the result of two assumptions, both of which were incorrect. The first was the conviction that Britain shared an identity of material interest with the world economy: that what was good for the world economy was good for Britain. For Strange, this belief had made perfectly good sense before 1914. When British manufacturers were (among) the most efficient in the world, it was certainly in Britain's interest for the government to underwrite an international financial system that was designed to liberalise and expand world trade. After 1945, however, with the dollar clearly enthroned as the top currency, the coincidence between British interests and those of the world economy was no longer so clear-cut. Britain desperately needed to modernise and rationalise its industrial base. Yet it was unable to follow the defensive protectionist policies that might have effected such a modernisation as long as it remained committed to a strategy of trade and currency liberalisation designed to benefit the world economy as a whole. The essential problem in this context was that the British government was suffering from what Strange calls 'top currency syndrome', a damaging hangover from the days when sterling *had* been the top world currency and when Britain's economic interests and those of the world economy *had* coincided.

A second false assumption that led to the strategy of attempting to restore and maintain sterling's 'master currency' status derived from the continuing belief that the material benefits of running a reserve currency significantly outweighed the increasingly evident costs. These benefits and costs were reviewed above and they need not be described here. Following Strange, however, it is worth re-emphasising the importance of the belief, held by successive governments, that sterling's reserve status was a necessary precondition for the successful operation and expansion of the City as a financial and commercial centre (which was itself considered essential to the British economy's overall health). It was only as the 'top currency syndrome' faded – a decline which was obviously accelerated both by decolonisation and the realisation that it would soon be necessary to withdraw from East of Suez – that it was recognised that for the City to thrive it was just not necessary to maintain sterling's reserve role; the two, quite simply, were unconnected.

Strange's central point, then, is that the British government's foreign economic policy between 1945 and the late 1960s was predicated on a faulty analysis of Britain's post-war economic position and capabilities. It was believed that Britain was still a great economic power and accordingly that the benefits of operating a reserve currency would outweigh the costs. However, the British economic recovery after the war was very slow in coming. And it was continually set back by balance of payments deficits which constantly weakened international confidence in sterling. In these circumstances the costs of running a reserve currency substantially outweighed the benefits. Unfortunately the 'top currency syndrome', born of earlier experiences in the heyday of the Empire, imposed on the key decision-makers an intellectual strait-jacket which took time to break down. As a result it was only acknowledged that the abandonment of the reserve role would be to Britain's distinct economic advantage when the damage had already been done.

But which of these explanations – the Marxist or the non-Marxist – is correct? Unfortunately this is not a question that can be answered easily, if at all. The analyses make rather different assumptions about the nature of political and economic power in advanced capitalist societies, about where it is located and how it is exercised.[22] As a result it is not possible to adduce any specific piece of 'critical evidence' that might enable the disinterested observer to decide between the alternative analyses that are provided: both accounts are consistent with most of the 'known facts'; and each is capable of explaining, within its own terms of reference, why it took so long for Britain to abandon the OSA and sterling's reserve role. Choosing between the explanations is really a matter of choosing between two different intellectual traditions, a choice which the reader has probably already made on the basis of a wide range of other considerations.

The Shift to a More Reactive Strategy since 1968

It was suggested in the previous section that the British government's efforts to play a major role in the international economic system between 1945 and 1968 were broadly unsuccessful. The benefits that were supposed to accrue from running a reserve currency failed to materialise because of the chronic weakness of the domestic economy, a weakness that was manifested in a series of balance of payments crises which progressively weakened sterling. This 'overextended' strategy of the early post-war years was brought to an abrupt end, however, with the termination of the OSA in 1968. It was replaced by a more flexible, reactive strategy that was much more suited to Britain's status as a 'major power of the second rank'.[23] Unfortunately, in terms of promoting the general health of the British economy and protecting its share of overseas markets, the foreign economic policies pursued after 1968 were not much more successful than those that had preceded it. As will be seen, some of the problems of the 1970s and 1980s, such as the implications of Britain's EU/EC membership for its balance of trade deficit, were partly self-inflicted. But the main factor underlying the lack of success of Britain's foreign economic policy after 1968 was the dramatic changes that were taking place in the global economy: changes that were well outside London's ability to control and to which successive governments were obliged to react on a more or less ad hoc basis. This section begins by reviewing the main policy developments that occurred during the two subphases (1968–79 and 1979–88) of the post-OSA era. It then seeks to identify the major factors that constrained British foreign economic policy after 1968 and which contributed to the continuing difficulties that it encountered.

Policy Developments after 1968

After 1968 Britain began to pursue a rather more 'self-sufficient' international economic strategy.[24] Without the burden of trying to maintain sterling's reserve role, the British economy should have been less vulnerable to the sort of speculative short-term capital movements which had continually provoked balance of payments crises and the need for stop-go since the early 1950s. The reason it should have been less vulnerable was simple: fewer people were holding sterling and therefore fewer could move out of it to cause a 'run on the pound'.

Unfortunately, two related changes in the world economy contrived to undermine the new strategy. The first of these was the downturn in the world economy which began in the late 1960s and the effects of which were beginning to be felt worldwide by the early 1970s. The downturn made it even more difficult for Britain's already hard-pressed exporters to maintain – let alone expand – their overseas market share, and this in turn exacerbated the country's continuing balance of payments problems. By far the most important development in the world economy after 1968, however, was the collapse in 1971 of the Bretton Woods system of fixed exchange rates. During the 1960s the American government had massively increased the supply of dollars by running a continuous budget deficit. (This deficit enabled successive administrations to finance both the Kennedy–Johnson social welfare reforms and the escalating war in Vietnam without a significant increase in taxation.) However, contrary to its implied obligations under the Bretton Woods agreement, the US Treasury did *not* acquire additional gold stocks to back this increase in dollars. The result was that an informal market for gold developed in which gold was traded for more than its 'official' (Bretton Woods) price of $35 per ounce.

As Strange observes, the United States could have progressively (and unilaterally) raised the price of gold from the late 1960s onwards, in line with the increase in the supply of dollars.[25] For a variety of reasons, however, it chose not to do so. Instead, in August 1971, the Nixon administration simply abandoned the gold–dollar link altogether, in effect 'floating' the dollar and allowing market forces to determine its price against gold.[26] This flotation of the dollar broke the back of the Bretton Woods fixed parity exchange rate system, ushering in an era of generally floating exchange rates in which market forces, rather than Central Bank agreements, would determine the price of each currency against all the others.[27]

As far as Britain was concerned, it was somewhat ironic that, having battled for so long and at such great cost to maintain sterling at $2.80, less than three years after the battle had been lost the entire fixed exchange rate system should have collapsed. In common with the other major industrial trading nations, however, Britain was not yet ready for a floating free-for-all. In December 1971, the Smithsonian Agreement led to a temporary realignment of exchange rates among the major currencies. Unfortunately lack of American commitment to the new parities caused the agreement to collapse within six months.[28] By way of a substitute, in April 1972, the EEC countries together with Britain established the 'snake-in-the-tunnel', the forerunner of the European Monetary System (EMS). Under this arrangement each member state agreed that its Central Bank would intervene in the foreign exchange markets in order to maintain its currency's parity value, and/or pursue appropriate interest rates policies whenever the currency's market value went beyond certain defined bounds (the 'tunnel').[29] However, each currency would be allowed to fluctuate – to 'snake about' – within these bounds without eliciting intervention. This, it was hoped, would bring a measure of stability to the foreign exchange markets, while at the same time permitting an acceptable degree of market flexibility. By June 1972, however, the Heath government had decided that participation in the snake was too much of a constraint on domestic economic policymaking – particularly in terms of the adjustments in interest rate policy that it promised to require – and as a result Britain withdrew from the snake arrangement altogether. In spite of the United Kingdom's membership of the EC after January 1973, Britain did not participate fully in the monetary arrangements of the Community.

From June 1972 until 1976 successive British governments opted for a strategy of unilaterally managed floating. In principle sterling was allowed to find its own market value against other currencies, though in practice the Bank of England consistently intervened in the markets to prevent the pound from falling too far. The objective of these interventions was to prevent a falling pound from giving a further boost to domestic inflation (a lower pound would mean essential imports would be more expensive, thus fuelling inflation). The main consequence of the interventions, however, was a continuing decline in Britain's gold and foreign currency reserves, even though in theory a floating exchange rate should have relieved the pressure on the reserves to a considerable extent.

By March 1976, in spite of heavy Bank of England interventions, the combined effects of speculative pressure and persistent trade deficits had caused the pound to fall below $2 for the first time. An important psychological barrier – for the international speculators – had been broken and sterling continued its downward spiral. The crisis continued throughout 1976 and by October sterling had fallen to $1.56, notwithstanding the announcement by a consortium of Central Banks that they would provide the Bank of England with a stand-by credit of $5.5 billion. At this point the Labour government entered into negotiations with the IMF for a $3.5 billion loan. The granting of the loan certainly helped sterling to recover – to $1.71 by December – but the domestic costs were substantial. The conditions of the loan stipulated that the British economy should be subject to a hefty dose of deflation. Interest rates were gradually increased and as a result unemployment, which was already growing, further accelerated. These costs were unavoidable, however. The loan had been necessary to prevent sterling from sinking even lower, which would undoubtedly have caused inflation to rise even higher. Fortunately the loan did enable the Callaghan government to maintain its earlier strategy of 'managed floating', providing it with access to sufficient reserves to keep sterling on a relatively even keel for the remainder of its period in office.

A Radical Change? The Thatcher Era, 1979–1990

Margaret Thatcher's government achieved office in May 1979, committed to an ideology of economic liberalism which prescribed that market forces must be given free rein.[30] The effects of this new, free market ideology were immediately felt in the field of foreign economic policy. Almost as soon as it came to power the new government abolished the few controls that still remained on foreign exchange dealings. Thatcher also initiated a series of discussions which led in October 1986 to the 'Big Bang' in the City of London, deregulating financial dealings and increasing both the competitiveness of the City and its attractiveness to foreign investors.

In relation to sterling, from May 1979 until early 1981 the Thatcher government adopted a genuinely floating exchange rate policy, with the Bank of England engaging in only minimal intervention in the foreign exchange markets. Unusually, during most of this two-year period, the pound floated upward rather than downward. This was partly because, with North Sea oil coming on stream, the pound was increasingly attractive to foreign speculators as a 'petrocurrency'. Yet it also resulted from the high interest rate policies that were pursued between 1979 and 1981. Here the Thatcher government encountered the contradiction that frequently besets interest rate policy. High interest rates have two major effects: internally, they restrict the expansion of the money supply and help to counter inflation; externally, they attract short-term capital movements from abroad and therefore (*ceteris paribus*) cause the exchange rate to rise. The high interest rate policies of the early Thatcher years certainly achieved their desired *internal* objective of reducing inflation. However they also had the undesirable *external* consequence of massively increasing the international value of sterling. This in turn effected a radical reduction in Britain's export competitiveness with devastating consequences for Britain's manufacturing base: it was only in 1987 that the official index of industrial production, which had fallen by over 20 per cent between 1979 and 1981, regained its May 1979 level.

From the beginning of 1981 onwards, therefore, the government began to recognise that it must act decisively to ameliorate the damaging consequences that an overvalued pound was having for Britain's manufacturing export performance. As a result, the management of the exchange rate once again became one of the government's clear policy objectives. Partly through Bank of England interventions and partly through a less doctrinaire interest rate policy, the exchange rate was gradually brought down from its peak of $2.40 in January 1981 to $1.54 in June 1983. Similar interventions and interest rate adjustments (though in the opposite direction) were employed in February 1985 when the exchange rate fell too low (to $1.08), thus threatening to give inflation an unwelcome boost in the run-up to the 1987 General Election. Interventionist policies were also pursued in 1985–86, following the 'Plaza Agreement' of September 1985, in which the 'Group of 7' top industrial nations agreed that joint measures should be taken to reduce the overvaluation of the dollar. Crucially, what all of these interventions demonstrated was that in spite of the flirtation with a freely floating exchange rate between 1979 and 1981, the Thatcher government in fact ended up pursuing a strategy of 'managed floating' similar to that which had been pursued by its predecessors between mid-1972 (when the Smithsonian Agreement collapsed) and May 1979.

By the late 1980s the Thatcher government's strategy of managed floating was achieving what appeared to be an optimal exchange rate level for sterling. The currency was fairly stable; it was sufficiently low against other currencies to prevent Britain's exporters suffering unduly; yet it was not so low as to threaten higher inflation through increased import costs. The fall in both the dollar and world-share values which began in October 1987 did not seriously damage the long-term position of sterling. However, in the months after October 1987, the Bank of England did participate in the extensive collaborative efforts of the major Central Banks, with the aim of preventing the dollar from 'sinking through the floor'. This participation, fully approved by the Treasury, indicated yet again that the days when the Thatcher government had been committed to the entirely free operation of market forces on the foreign exchanges were gone. In the context of currency policy at least, free market principles had proved to be a luxury that even the Thatcher government could not afford. It had accordingly been obliged to abandon them and revert to interventionism when external circumstances demanded it. From the vantage point of 1990, then, it appeared that the days of a free floating rate were over. In fact, in the longer term the reverse would prove to be the case. Thatcher saw herself as initiating a radical new policy of free markets and free trade. In fact, she merely intensified the whole shape and tone of British policy since 1945.

The Post-Thatcher Era

In the 1990s, the trend towards the free market was reinforced by what proved to be a disastrous experiment with managed rates. The three most significant developments in UK exchange rate policy during this period and since have been the decision to join (and then leave) the EMS between 1990 and 1992, the decision to make the Bank of England independent in 1998 and the refusal to join the 'euro' (or single European currency), which went online for nearly all members of the EU in 2000. Indeed, the crisis over the first was to exert a significant formative effect on the latter two.

Despite her commitment to market forces and in spite of her natural Euroscepticism, Thatcher eventually proved willing to manage the exchange rate through the European Exchange Rate Mechanism, which preceded the introduction of the euro.[31] She would be forced from power in 1990 shortly after this, but Britain under the more 'pro-European' John Major had now joined what was effectively a collectively managed system of exchange rates.[32] Successive governments had refused to become full members of the ERM, which came into force in March 1979. Their reasoning was simple: they were not prepared to countenance the accompanying loss of national decision-making autonomy that member-ship of the European system implied. But in 1990 Thatcher eventually bowed to political pressure. Under this 'supersnake' arrangement, each member state was committed to intervening in the foreign exchange markets and to pursuing interest rate policies which would maintain the value of its currency within a 2.5 per cent band either side of its collec-tively agreed parity.

In relatively short order, however, the UK was compelled to leave the European Monetary System in September 1992, as a result of what became known as 'Black Wednesday'. This was an episode of currency speculation which cost Britain an exorbitant amount of money. It has been estimated that it cost the government anywhere between £6 and £27 billion, all in a vain attempt to prop up sterling (although the Treasury estimated the cost to the taxpayer to be a 'mere' £3.4 billion). Interest rates were briefly raised to 15 per cent, but this did not put matters right either, and the UK was forced to withdraw from the ERM. All of this, of course, indicated just how weak the British state had become relative to international markets, and the event reportedly netted currency specu-lators like George Soros very handsome profits (Soros became known in financial circles as 'the man who broke the Bank of England'). The experiment with an ERM-managed exchange rate was over, blamed for creating – or at least exacerbating – a major recession in the UK.

The 1990–92 experience was to greatly strengthen pro-market ideas in Britain as well, contributing to the general trend already noted. Since 1992 UK exchange rate policy has always been one of free floating rates determined by the international market. In contrast to previous Labour leaders – who had, as we have seen, experimented with Keynesian tech-niques prior to 1968 – Tony Blair and Chancellor Gordon Brown very quickly made the Bank of England independent upon coming to office.[33] The decision was partly modelled on the American experience, since many believed at the time that US hegemony was in part a result of the independence of America's own Central Bank, the Federal Reserve. Announced only four days after Labour's landslide electoral victory in 1997, it has been suggested that the decision was taken unilaterally by Brown himself, perhaps as some sort of deal between Blair and the new Chancellor. Blair claims in his memoirs that the decision was his own,[34] although Brown's advisers – including a young Ed Balls, later the Shadow Chancellor – had argued for Bank independence some years before. It is still not entirely clear which version of the story is true. More generally, however, it was hoped that giving independence to the Bank would end the kind of 'boom and bust' economics which Brown and Blair had frequently attacked during the period when Nigel Lawson had been Chancellor of the Exchequer. It would also lower inflation and give the exchange rate a measure of stability, which would in turn encourage economic growth (or so the theory went). The Bank of England would no longer officially 'target' the exchange rate, although clearly this is part of monetary policy and impinges upon the setting of interest rates (which *is* officially part of its job).

Bank independence was certainly convenient in a political sense; for one thing, politicians could no longer be held responsible for high interest rates, as Major had been. Independence for the Bank of England was also designed to show that 'New Labour' could be trusted in British financial circles. 'Old Labour' was still associated with the 1976 bailout by the IMF, when the government was compelled to go 'cap in hand' to the international community. But Blair wanted to show that he was a new kind of Labour Prime Minister. As Yergin and Stanislaw put it:

> Blair's victory [in 1997] certainly amounted to a repudiation of the past – though not of the Thatcherite revolution. In the long run-up to the election, Blair and New Labour had campaigned as vigorously against their own past as they had against the Conservatives. New Labour rejected Old Labour, with its commitment to intervention and the expansive state. And by the time of its victory, New Labour had embraced the economics of Thatcherism, although projecting values of 'compassion', 'social democracy' and 'inclusiveness'.[35]

This was also in part a function of changed realities. As we shall see in the next section, given the globalisation of finance, it is unclear whether any British government could really 'manage' the value of its currency anymore.

The ERM issue also intensified Britain's ambivalent relationship with the European circle and in some ways magnified popular anti-EU feeling. For some observers, the ERM experience shows not only that exchange rates should not be used to target low rates of inflation, but also that entanglements with Europe are likely to leave their mark on a foreign economic policy which is supposed to be 'British'. In 2000, the euro or single European currency was introduced. However, the UK – even under the strongly pro-European Blair – chose to stay out of the Eurozone, and its future membership seems especially unlikely since the British people voted to leave the EU. Recurrent crises in the international system since this book first appeared in 1990 appear to have reinforced the British sense of deep ambivalence towards Europe, pushing David Cameron towards a position in 2015–16 where he was effectively compelled to announce a referendum on EU membership (a gamble which, as we have seen, the Prime Minister lost). As the work of Susan Strange shows, the emergence of the 'casino economics' and the obviously interconnected nature of the global economics has left states like Britain increasingly vulnerable to external shocks.[36] For their part, the 1997 Asian economic crisis and 2008 global economic crisis both increased concerns that Britain was no longer a 'sovereign nation', since both illustrated those interconnections only too well (and both showed the ability of financial developments to drive 'real world' economics). From the vantage point of 2016, moreover, the Greek economic crisis and pressures on the euro appeared to have vindicated anti-European circle beliefs, even if the 'true' interest of Britain suggested that the country was better off within that circle than out.

What can be said by way of summary of the developments in Britain's foreign economic policy after 1968, then? The main conclusion, unsurprisingly, is that, as in the period before 1968, policy continued to be heavily constrained by external factors. The shift to a strategy of 'managed floating' after 1971 was due entirely to the collapse of the Bretton Woods system of fixed parities, a collapse which was itself the sole responsibility of the US Treasury. In the years after 1971, although sterling was no longer employed as a major reserve currency, it was still widely used as a transactions currency. This was particularly the case after 1973 when London became the temporary repository for billions of the petrodollars that flooded the international money markets in the wake of the first OPEC 'oil shock'. Given Britain's continuing balance of payments problems during the 1970s (which arose from the British consumer's preference for foreign imported manufactures and the lack of competitiveness of British exports), sterling remained vulnerable to short-term speculative pressures which continued to act as a drain on Britain's foreign exchange reserves and provoked the 1976 sterling crisis. Thatcher's ideology-driven determination to allow these 'speculative pressures' free rein – to allow the pound to find its own market value – foundered because of the effects which the policy had on the domestic economy. The combination of high interest rates and free market forces drove sterling so high that British exporters could not compete in foreign markets. The decline of Britain's manufacturing base forced a reduction in interest rates and a return to 'managed floating' in early 1981. Nevertheless, under Tony Blair and Gordon Brown exchange rates were left to find their own level, even if it remains unclear whether or not the Bank of England is now 'manipulating' the exchange rate of sterling or not.

Some Explanatory Factors: The Major Constraints after 1968

Three major factors served to constrain British foreign economic policy-making in the years after the end of the Sterling Area: the increasing internationalisation of markets and of production; Britain's membership of the European Union; and the general crisis in the world economy.

The Internationalisation of Markets and of Production

Currency and commodity markets have always been to some degree international, with currencies and commodities being bought and sold by private individuals across national borders. After 1945 the extent of this internationalisation gradually increased. After 1980 it accelerated considerably. More currencies and more commodities were traded in more countries, and at significantly greater volumes, than ever before. After 1970, moreover, this internationalisation of currency and commodity markets was complemented by the increasing internationalisation of markets in government-issued stocks and in the shares of private sector companies. The deregulation ideology of the Thatcher and Reagan governments, the ingenuity and inventiveness of the financial dealers in devising new methods of speculation, and the revolution in communications technology: all of these factors contributed to the internationalisation of markets throughout the world. By the late 1980s, currencies, commodities, stocks and shares were being traded round the clock worldwide, with near-instantaneous information links connecting all the major financial centres: a truly global market had been created, if not with the complete approval of the major capitalist governments, then at least with their acquiescence. Developments in information technology after 1980 also served to reinforced the process of financial globalisation.

An analogous process was taking place after 1945 in patterns of manufacturing production. Multinational corporations (MNCs) were busily expanding and diversifying their activities across national frontiers. An MNC based in one country could readily circumvent tariff barriers by entering into a partnership with an existing corporation inside another 'host' country, or even by creating an entirely new subsidiary inside that host country. By this sort of institutional ploy, and by providing employment for the indigenous 'host' population, MNCs found that they could sidestep accusations that the domestic market was being swamped by foreign imports. The MNC also proved to be an extremely useful vehicle for transferring technology, capital and profits across national boundaries; and the complexity of the internal accounting procedures that were frequently employed made it extraordinarily difficult for national governments even to monitor such transfers, let alone control them.

Thus the fundamental consequence of the internationalisation of markets and of production was that it seriously impaired the decision-making autonomy of national governments, the British government included, in two senses. It meant, first, that individual governments found it increasingly difficult to intervene effectively in any given currency, commodity or stock market: there were simply too many other participants in each market to enable any one government to determine a particular market outcome. Acting on its own, even the US Federal Reserve would probably have been unable to support the dollar in the wake of the Wall Street 'crash' of October 1987: it required the assistance of other Central Banks in order to complete the task effectively. There is no telling what the Bank of England would have done if it had been obliged to cope alone with the effects of British budget and trade deficits of a magnitude comparable with those regularly encountered by the United States.

A second sense in which 'internationalisation' impaired the autonomy of governments was that it made it more difficult for them to constrain the behaviour of others. By the late 1980s, it was extremely hard to envisage, for example, how any British government – whatever its political complexion – could effectively reintroduce any sort of exchange controls on sterling. A large part of the problem was simple practicality: there was so much dealing in sterling going on overseas that it was completely outside the Bank of England's capability either to monitor or police it. As we have seen, the British government was clearly unable to support sterling after a major 'run on the pound' occurred in 1992, since currency speculators had become too powerful relative to the British state. Another aspect of the problem was that, even if the British government had attempted unilaterally to reimpose some sort of regulation on the financial markets, the costs would have been enormous: in all probability, foreign investors would have moved their funds out of London in droves, the City would have experienced a disastrous loss of confidence and sterling would have suffered a 'meltdown'. Such calamitous outcomes could not be seriously entertained. By 1992 if not well before, it had become clear that Britain would be confronted and constrained by the power of the international markets for the foreseeable future.

Britain's Membership of the European Union

In principle, British membership of the EU could have exerted a powerful constraining influence on Britain's currency policy and on its trade policy. In fact, though, *currency policy* remained largely unaffected. The exceptions were Britain's brief three-month involvement with the 'snake' in 1972 and the (much more notable, but slightly longer) foray into the European Monetary System between 1990 and 1992. Both cut against the grain, however, and proved to be temporary in nature.[37] After 1992 in particular, successive governments refused to be bound by Brussels in the realm of monetary policy. This had been true before 1990, and it would be reinforced as a 'lesson' by the EMS experience after the less-than-two-year experiment.

The effects of EU membership on Britain's *trade policy,* however, were rather more substantial. Although *all* intra-community barriers against the free movement of capital, labour and goods were not removed until 1992, from 1973 onwards London was bound by the terms of accession to allow virtually free access to manufactured imports from EU countries. Notwithstanding the fact that British exporters also enjoyed freer access to markets in Europe, Britain's trade deficit with the EU grew significantly after 1973. As Table 7.2 shows, in 1972 the United Kingdom had a visible trade deficit with European Union countries of £580 million, which constituted just under 42 per cent of its total visible deficit. By 1980 the EU deficit had grown to 54 per cent of the total deficit. Even taking account of the growing EU share of Britain's total trade, the visible deficits with the EU certainly worsened. As Table 7 also indicates, the main source of the increasing deficit was Britain's bilateral trade with Germany: this constituted some 18.1 per cent of the total deficit in 1972 but had grown to a massive 54 per cent by 1980. As the table shows, however, these figures have remained more or less stable since then (both the proportion of the debt going to Germany, and the proportion of debt going to the EU as a whole). As long as Britain remained inside the European Union, however, there was little or nothing that London could do – by way of changing its trade policy – either to remedy the imbalance with the EU in general or to reduce it. Membership of the European circle

Table 7.2 UK visible trade deficit with the EU 1972–2003 (£ million)

	1972	*1980*	*2003*
Total deficit (all countries) Germany:	– 1,302	– 6,288	– 47,290
imports from	841	5,778	33,433
exports to	589	4,218	20,656
Balance	– 252	– 1,500	– 12,777
Bilateral deficit as % of total deficit	18.1	24.8	27.0
EU*			
imports from	3,521	20,888	135,362
exports to	2941	17,479	109,807
Balance	– 580	– 3,409	– 25,555
EU deficit as % of total deficit	41.7	54.2	54.0
Trade with EU as % of total trade	30.9	43.8	55.3

*All EU figures refer the membership in that year.

SOURCE: *Annual Abstract of Statistics* (HMSO, various years).

was a constraint that would exist as long as Britain remained a member, but the weakness of the British economy meant that Britain might well be *worse off* outside the EU than it would be within it. By 2003, trade with the EU represented about 55 per cent of *all* Britain's trade. As the economist Martin Beck noted in 2015, while the last ten years have seen some reduction in the EU's importance as a market for British exports, 'the EU remains by far the UK's single most important export market'.[38]

The General Crisis in the World Economy

The most important constraint on British foreign economic policy after 1968, however, was almost certainly the continuing difficulties that were experienced by the entire world economy from the early 1970s onwards. In practical terms, the downturn – which was recognised worldwide in the wake of the 1973 'oil shock' – made it very difficult for British manufacturers to increase their share of overseas markets. This in turn perpetuated Britain's long-running balance of payments problems and thereby continued to exert downward pressure on the value of sterling throughout the 1970s.

However, the nature of the crisis itself was characterised very differently by different observers. In government circles during the mid-1970s there was a tendency to attribute the crisis almost entirely to the machinations of OPEC: by quadrupling the price of oil in October 1973, the oil-exporting nations had massively increased worldwide inflation and pushed the world economy into recession. The optimistic implication of this interpretation, however, was that, as the United Kingdom was expected to be a net oil exporter by 1980, Britain might well be able to turn the new situation to its advantage. Accordingly the main object of foreign economic policy in the 1970s was to hold the fort – to prevent anything too disastrous from happening either to sterling or to the balance of payments – until North Sea oil came fully on stream. Armed with its newly won oil revenues, the British economy could face the future with confidence.

Yet, as the 1970s progressed, and the global recession showed few signs of abating, rather more sophisticated analyses of the nature of the world's economic problems began to emerge. Milton Friedman and his monetarist acolytes argued that the core of the problem derived from a long history of too much government interference in market mechanisms and too much trade restraint. For Friedman, a return to free market economics, avoiding protectionism, reducing state economic activity and deregulating markets, would restore the world economy to equilibrium, thereby creating optimal conditions for sustained recovery and growth.[39] Marxist analysts, in contrast, tended to follow Mandel's claims in the late 1960s that the capitalist world economy had begun to suffer from a serious crisis of capital over-accumulation. Entrepreneurs' increasing inability to find profitable outlets for their previously accumulated capital had led to a fall in the overall rate of profit and this in turn had thrown the entire capital system into a state of disorganisation and crisis that would probably last until the early 1990s.[40]

The 'hegemonic stability' theorists offered yet another analysis.[41] Their basic assumption was that any liberal system of international trade and finance can only function effectively when it is sponsored and controlled by a dominant hegemonic power. Between about 1840 and 1914 the role of 'international hegemon' was performed by Britain; between 1945 and 1970, by the United States. In both cases, however, the very effort of performing the hegemonic role sapped the economic strength of the hegemonic power: capital exports, intended to strengthen the economic system, constituted a 'leakage of capital' which depleted the hegemon's industrial base; and the out-of-area military commitments necessary to support and maintain foreign governments sympathetic to the liberal international regime were extremely expensive. According to the hegemonic stability thesis, by the late 1960s the United States was beginning to lose its hegemonic status. The collapse of the Bretton Woods system was the first major sign of America's relative economic weakness. The rising economic strength of Germany and Japan was another. And the defeat in Vietnam showed that American military power was also on the wane. With the strength of its hegemon in serious decline, the world economic system was incapable of functioning effectively. From the 1970s onwards, with no single power in control, both international trade and the system of international finance slowly drifted into a state of confusion that was beyond the power of any one state to control. It was small wonder that the US – even with considerable support from Britain and other EU states – proved unable to avert the global economic crisis that struck the world economy in the wake of the 2007/08 'credit crunch'.

Whatever the relative merits of these competing characterisations of the world economic crisis, it was the Friedmanite model which guided Britain's external economic policy after 1976. For the Callaghan government (as noted earlier), the espousal of a strict monetarist domestic economic strategy and a managed floating exchange rate policy were the price that had to be paid for the IMF loan. For the Thatcher government after May 1979, however, tight money at home and a free-floating pound abroad were welcome ideological totems; indispensable elements in the new Tory strategy of exposing the British economy to the invigorating winds of international competition. For Thatcher, the long-running economic crisis of the 1970s had been the result of governments tampering with market mechanisms. Her government would follow Friedman's prescriptions: it would roll back the state, restore the market as the primary mechanism of distribution and deregulate wherever possible.

By the late 1980s, there were two broad sets of views as to how successful the Thatcher government's strategy of liberalisation had actually been. Government supporters emphasised the regeneration of British industry that the new competitive environment had made possible: the British economy had outridden the crises of the 1980s, and was set to surmount those of the 1990s, precisely because it had followed the principles of deregulation and market discipline. The government's critics were far less sanguine, however. In line with Susan Strange's exposition of *Casino Capitalism*, they inclined to the view that the deregulation of the financial sector under Reagan in the United States and under Thatcher in Britain had seriously exacerbated the *instability* of markets worldwide. In the late 1980s the prices of currencies, of commodities, of credit and of stocks and shares were fluctuating ever more violently as speculative funds were transferred in and out of different markets at an increasing velocity. In the view of the pessimists, the stock market crash and 'dollar slide' of October 1987 were merely the first indications that the international financial casino – thanks to deregulation – was now out of control. The world recession that followed the 2007/8 banking crisis appeared to provide a remarkably strong endorsement of the pessimists' views.

Summary and Conclusions

Britain's external economic policy in the post-war period can be divided into two distinct phases. During the first phase, between 1945 and 1968, the main focus of Britain's foreign economic relations was its currency policy. Successive governments sought both to preserve the integrity of the Overseas Sterling Area and to maintain sterling's attendant role as a reserve currency. The preservation of the OSA in turn provided implicit guidelines for the British government's overseas investment and trade policies. The continued existence of the OSA made it relatively easy for British investors to export capital to OSA countries where it could frequently earn a higher rate of return than was readily available in the United Kingdom. And London's ability to control the sterling reserves of OSA countries enabled it to 'ration' currency in such a way as to preserve 'protected' markets for British exports in the dominions and colonies.

Until the late 1960s, therefore, Britain's economic links with most of the old Empire 'circle' remained quite strong, supported quite explicitly by the external financial policy of successive governments. Two factors served to change this situation. The first, documented in Chapter 5, was the autonomous shift in Britain's trade, away from the Empire and towards Europe, which began in the late 1950s. The second was the growing realisation in the mid-1960s that the post-war strategy of continuing to operate a reserve currency had been fundamentally misconceived; that it had in all probability acted as a drain on the strength of the British economy for over twenty years. The devaluation crisis of October 1967 presented the Wilson government with an opportunity to abandon sterling's reserve role which it was in no position – and had no desire – to oppose. The reserve role, and the Sterling Area with it, were duly ended under the terms of the Basle Agreements in 1968. Depending upon which account was believed, it had taken so long to abandon the reserve role either because of the vagaries of 'top currency syndrome' (which induced the key decision-makers into making a faulty analysis of the costs and benefits of maintaining the OSA) or because of the predominant position within the British state apparatus of financial capitalists and their allies (who continued to derive enormous pecuniary advantage from the maintenance of the OSA until the mid-1960s).

Yet whatever the 'real' reason for the maintenance of the OSA, its termination certainly brought the overextension of Britain's external economic policy to an end. During the second phase of the post-war period (1968–88) the British approach was less ambitious and more flexible. Currency policy, especially after the introduction of a floating exchange rate in 1972, retained its central importance, though after 1973 (when Britain joined the EC) trade policy and overseas investment policy became less dependent on what was happening to sterling and more dependent on the collective rules of the European Community.

But was the more flexible post-1968 strategy any more successful than its predecessor in its ultimate objective of strengthening Britain's international economic position? For much of the 1970s the answer would appear to be 'no'. Foreign economic policy during that period mainly consisted in the government adopting (virtually unavoidable) remedial measures in response to the latest crisis either in the world economy (the collapse of Bretton Woods in 1971; the 'oil shocks' of 1973 and 1979) or at home (the persistent balance of payments problems up to 1976). Thatcher's experiment with a freely floating exchange rate in 1979–80 – informed by firm ideological commitment rather than the pragmatism of the Heath/Wilson/Callaghan years – made the position even worse. An overvalued pound, buoyed up by North Sea oil revenues, wrought havoc with Britain's manufacturing export trade. The position was certainly eased by the return to managed floating from 1981 onwards. Tony Blair clearly drew the lesson that the Thatcherite economic programme should be smoothed at the edges, not abandoned. But it was difficult to judge whether Thatcher, with her commitment to the restoration of market forces in both domestic and external contexts, had effected a genuine transformation in Britain's international economic position, or whether the apparent improvement in Britain's growth rate and balance of payments was the all too temporary consequence of the exploitation of North Sea oil.

What was certain about the post-1968 period, however, was that Britain's foreign economic policy was more heavily constrained by external factors beyond its control than ever before. To have attempted to insulate the British economy from the internationalisation of markets that has occurred since the 1970s would have been both ineffectual and – in terms of the adverse foreign reaction it would have provoked – counterproductive. To have attempted to reduce the visible trade deficit with the European Union would have been impractical and equally counterproductive in terms of the likely reaction of Britain's European partners. And there was certainly very little that Britain could do to pull the world economy out of the deep recession in which it had languished in the 1970s or away from the 'shocks' of 1997 or 2011. To be sure, the government could on occasion support multilateral efforts at crisis management. But multilateral cooperation of this sort barely scratched the surface of the core problems of the global economy: the US budget deficit; the trade deficits of Japan's major trading partners; the unpaid – and unpayable – third-world debts and the out-of-control 'casino' of the financial markets. Since 1945, and especially since 1968, Britain's international economic position had been in secular decline and its foreign economic policy had accordingly been subject to increasing external constraints. In 2016 – a quarter of a century since this book first appeared – it looked as though the next 25 years would yield more economic decline and ever more powerful constraints.

Chapter 8

British Defence Policy

Defence policy is that aspect of external policy concerned with maximising the nation-state's security interests. It consists in the construction of alliances and the development of military strategy designed to deter and/ or counter potential foreign aggression. To the extent that foreign policy generally is also concerned in part with security calculations, a number of defence-related themes have already been discussed in previous chapters. This chapter seeks to draw these different themes together by summarising the major changes that have characterised British defence policy since World War II and by outlining the main causal factors which provoked them. As will be seen, one especially significant development of this period was the shift away from the defence of the Empire circle that was associated with the 1968 decision to withdraw from 'East of Suez'. This shift enabled successive governments to concentrate their defence efforts in the combined European and Atlantic circles – areas where Britain's primary economic interests were increasingly located. Another significant development in recent years has been that Britain's participation in global defence affairs has become increasingly dependent on operating within bilateral coalitions or inside multinational alliances like NATO or the United Nations. We therefore focus on the ways in which coalitions and alliances have since become a central focus of British defence policy since the 1990s. Britain has, though, also maintained its own independent nuclear deterrent since the 1950s. Why did UK policymakers – working in an era of increasing austerity – feel that this was not only necessary but essential to Britain's defence, and does it remain so today?

The chapter also looks at how British defence policy today is shaped by an extremely precarious balance between needs and resources. This problem is then located historically by examining the increasingly laboured efforts after World War II to continue to project a global military role and the gradual contraction of that role since the 1960s in the face of mounting economic pressure. Since most of the developments have already been described in earlier chapters, there is a strong emphasis here on the successive defence reviews that Britain has undertaken since 1952; although big strategic statements may be a recent import from the United States, spending reviews have a much longer and more venerable history in British defence policy.

229

Military Strategy and Economic Necessity

One (very common) criticism of contemporary UK defence policy is that it is driven more by economic necessity than it is by genuine strategic need – even though British politicians are usually loath to admit this possibility. As Cornish and Dorman put it, 'UK governments have historically been wary of opening themselves to the charge that their approach to national defence policy has been "Treasury-led". In British political culture, the "Treasury-led defence review" has long been code for a range of policy errors and misjudgments,' such as a lack of military preparedness for the future.[1] In 2010, the Coalition government of David Cameron faced a crisis caused by a significant shortfall in the defence budget and spending projections inherited from the Blair and Brown governments (a '£38 billion black hole', according to Chancellor of the Exchequer George Osborne). This is not wholly unusual in an historical sense, since the government of one party usually leaves the succeeding one with a defence budget deficit. Nevertheless, the UK's 'adventures' in Iraq and Afghanistan proved amazingly costly to the Treasury, and in the face of the resultant crisis the Coalition adopted drastic measures: it announced in 2010 that the UK military would be cut by about 17,000 men and women by 2015. The Navy would lose 5,000 personnel, the Army about 7,000 and the Air Force around 5,000. The Army would be especially hard hit, losing 20 per cent of its personnel, while reservists – who are trained militarily but whose day job is outside the military itself – were to take up the resulting slack. Most controversially, with the withdrawal of Invincible-class carriers Britain would have no functioning aircraft carrier until 2020, rendering it all-but-incapable of performing another Falklands-type invasion. HMS *Ark Royal* would be scrapped. The famous Harrier jump-jet was to be decommissioned and sold off as well, and the scrapping of the RAF's brand new Nimrod MRA4 surveillance and reconnaissance aircraft – which would cost £200 million over the short term but was projected to save £2 billion over the next ten years – would also be undertaken.

Robert Gates, previously US Secretary of Defense under both George W. Bush and Barack Obama, epitomised the critical reaction to all of this in January 2014 when he told Radio Four's *Today* programme that 'with the fairly substantial reductions in defence spending in Great Britain, what we're finding is that it won't have full-spectrum capabilities and the ability to be a full partner as they have been in the past'.[2] This was the first time since World War I, he noted, that Britain would not have an operational aircraft carrier and the first time since the Napoleonic wars that Britain's standing army had been so small. The suggestion that Britain had abandoned its responsibility to share the burden of defending Europe clearly stung. In fact, though, these comments merely echoed the slightly more diplomatic remarks of Sir Nicholas Houghton, the British Chief of Defence Staff, who had also warned a few weeks earlier that cuts to defence spending would leave Britain with only a 'hollowed-out force' that could no longer compete in 'the Premier League of smart power'.[3] The tendency to put economics first can also lead to capabilities being cut simply because they *can* be, as opposed to reducing things which ought to be cut on strategic grounds (a practice known colloquially as 'cheese paring' or 'salami slicing').

Certainly, economic considerations are a very powerful input into defence policy, and may be the *most* powerful input for a middle-range power like Britain whose resources are quite limited. Economic constraints are one of the 'givens' or permanent features of British policymaking today, and as we shall see in this chapter the subtext of successive defence or strategic reviews under politicians of all parties since the 1940s has been the need to 'save money'. But it has not just been about this; the history of UK defence policy has also been all about trying to strike a *balance* or compromise between what is needed and what can be afforded. The need to save financial resources also has to be set against the effects that defence cuts have on friends and foe alike: friends may no longer feel that you are a 'reliable' partner if you cut too deep – hence the critical tones of Robert Gates's remarks – while adversaries may no longer be deterred militarily if you scale back too far. Moreover, the need to defend the security of the state itself from external threat is of course an absolutely critical consideration as well.

Before we go on, though, it is important to locate this story within the broader history of British defence policy since World War II and especially within the history of previous defence reviews. As Gill Bennett puts it, 'no matter how large the defence budget, there is always a big gap between commitments and spending, tremendous resistance to any reduction in either from the different branches of the armed services, and great determination by the Treasury to achieve substantial savings'.[4] The pressures that the current government faced did not begin in 2010, nor did they begin with the previous Labour government (although they have been exacerbated by commitments in Iraq and Afghanistan which were unusually extensive). Indeed, we need to go back at least as far as 1945, and to the decline of the Pax Britannica after the war, in order to understand the full story of how mounting economic pressures have tempered British ambitions in this sphere, and how initial political pressures to *increase* British involvement in the world warred with economic pressures to scale back.

Defence Policy in the Three Circles since 1945

For two decades after 1945, the British government continued to take the sort of 'wide view' of British security that had characterised the outlook of successive governments since the early 18th century: that the security of the homeland was intimately bound up with the security of Britain's overseas possessions. There was nothing mystical about this belief. It derived, quite simply, from the Realist world-view of the key decision-makers, from the conviction that, if London did not control the strategic bases and resource-rich territories of the Empire, then a potentially unfriendly power might – an eventuality that would seriously prejudice Britain's ability to prevail in any future war. In the immediate post-war years, this *realpolitik*-induced need to protect the security of the Empire was boosted by the emerging threat to Western interests posed by Soviet-style communism. What it meant in practice, as noted in previous chapters, was that London, in spite of its desire to reduce its overseas commitments if at all possible, found itself deploying military forces in almost every major theatre across the globe. As the February 1946 report on the defence estimates indicated, British forces in 1945–46 were not only concerned with administering the surrender and occupation of Germany, Austria, Italy and Japan: they were also providing assistance to the Greek government in its struggle to suppress a communist insurgency; attempting to keep law and order in Palestine; helping to maintain internal security and stability throughout the Empire; and safeguarding the global network of bases upon which Britain would rely in the event of any future global conflict.[5]

In the immediate post-war years, these responsibilities collectively imposed a considerable burden on Britain's defence budget. The Clement Attlee government was still obliged to maintain defence forces far in excess of those necessary for the immediate protection of the United Kingdom itself. In this situation, Britain's post-war 'Empire circle' defence policy was driven by two conflicting objectives. On the one hand, the desire to see pro-British – or at least pro-Western – regimes proliferate throughout the third world encouraged support for almost any friendly government threatened by communist encroachment. On the other hand, the wish to reduce the worrying overextension of Britain's armed forces also encouraged it to seek to cut back its overseas responsibilities wherever withdrawal seemed unlikely to provoke serious local instability. The cynic would undoubtedly conclude that the simultaneous pursuit of these two contradictory objectives was bound to produce an inconsistent and directionless series of ad hoc policy decisions. The more generous observer, however, would recognise the British government's inability to abandon either objective in the threatening conditions of the Cold War and would probably conclude that, all things considered, successive governments made a series of intelligent compromises which successfully held communism at bay for over 30 years without bankrupting the Treasury.

Of course, there were strategic blunders as well early on. In 1946 and 1947 Attlee's government rather foolishly allowed Rolls-Royce, the defence industry leader of its day, to sell Nene engines to the Soviet Union, an export decision firmly opposed by the Americans. Unfortunately, this enabled the Russians (experts in 'reverse engineering') to produce MiG aircraft that far outstripped British capabilities and helped the Soviets to 'catch up' in the nuclear arms race, at a time when delivery from the air was the system of choice for nuclear weapons.[6] Economic necessities seemed to dictate that the sales go ahead, but what would be the strategic costs? Just as damaging overall, perhaps, was the general failure to re-examine British strategy and commitments given that the UK planned to withdraw from places like India, Burma, Ceylon, Palestine, Turkey and Greece. What was Britain's role to be now, and how was it to be managed? Again, there was a strategic failure to rethink this, and UK policymakers fell back upon their 'wider view' that homeland security and the Empire – albeit in what might today be called its 2.0 or 3.0 version – were one and the same.

The war had stretched Britain's resources beyond their limit, and Clement Attlee had in many ways inherited a 'poisoned chalice' from Churchill in 1945: he faced the almost impossible task of defending a nation whose economy had been severely damaged by World War II and commitments abroad which Britain could no longer afford. Amazingly, the government began to feel pressure to *increase* British involvement in the periphery almost as soon as the war was over. In 1945–46 the War Office assumed control of the former Italian colonies of Somaliland, Libya and Eritrea in order to prepare them for independence in the early 1950s.[7] In 1948, British forces began extensive anti-insurgency operations in Malaya which were to last until 1958. In 1950, British forces joined the UN contingent which was fighting in Korea – a move that contributed to the near doubling of defence expenditure which subsequently occurred under the guise of the 1951–54 rearmament programme. Defence spending had reached a high of £5 billion in 1944, and almost inevitably it fell in the years after the war. But with the outbreak of the Korean War, planned expenditure was doubled to over £4,700 million, from 8 per cent of GNP to a whopping 14 per cent.

Winston Churchill and the 'Global Strategy' Paper of 1950

Spending on the Korean War in particular threw the Ministry of Defence (MoD) into what would later become an all-too-familiar crisis mode. The incoming Conservative government under Winston Churchill produced a 'Global Strategy' paper in 1952, widely seen as the first full-scale defence review of its kind, although there had in fact been less publicised reviews in 1947 and 1950. It would be followed, as we shall see, by many more, and it was spurred by the desperate need to put the UK's defence house in order – Britain, it was explicitly acknowledged, was simply doing too much with not enough. It was also prompted, as Baylis and Macmillan note, by the fact that 'Winston Churchill himself believed that insufficient account was being taken in current British (and Western) defence planning of the value of nuclear weapons'.[8] Of the two aims, however, economic necessity seems to have been the most critical. 'Reading the Paper one is left with the distinct impression that economic pressures were decisive in forcing a rethink of policy', they note.[9]

Yet the 1952 Paper – which was only declassified in 1993, and is not much read today – was first and foremost a rumination on nuclear strategy (again, this was one of Churchill's major concerns). To be sure, the Army and Navy were seen as playing too important a deterrent role for cutbacks to be feasible at this early point in the Cold War, but the Chiefs were quite prepared to countenance cuts in conventional forces within the RAF. The real reason that the Paper produced few savings was probably not simply that it superimposed a nuclear capability over conventional forces engaged around the globe, or because it failed to make hard but politically unpalatable decisions, or because the Chiefs were only interested in defending their own bureaucratic corners. A major problem was that the recommendations were not fully implemented in practice, and savings might therefore have been greater. The deeper problem, though, was that under Churchill British military forces would be stretched thinner as a whole string of new commitments were added in which all three services were involved. In 1953, for instance, British troops became heavily involved in the struggle against the Mau-Mau nationalist guerrilla movement in Kenya. And in the same year, Churchill's government bound itself by treaty to come to the aid of Libya in the event of it being attacked. Even as these new deployments were being made, however, existing commitments still had to be met. In 1954, at perhaps the peak of Britain's post-war involvement in the Empire circle, sizeable British forces were stationed in the Mediterranean (in Gibraltar, Malta, Libya and Cyprus); in West Africa (in the Gambia, Sierra Leone, Ghana and Nigeria); in the Middle East (in the Canal Zone, at the Gulf of Aqaba and in Muscat); in East and Central-Southern Africa (in Kenya, Somalia, Sudan, Rhodesia, Nyasaland and Tanganyika); and in the Far East (in Korea, Japan, Hong Kong, Malaya and Singapore).[10] As if these commitments were not enough, in September 1954 Britain extended its obligations still further by guaranteeing the security of the Philippines, Thailand, Malaya and Singapore under the terms of the (SEATO) Manila Pact.[11] And the process was taken even further in February 1955 with the signing of the Central Treaty Organisation (CENTO) Baghdad Pact, which committed Britain to the defence of Pakistan, Iran, Iraq and Turkey.[12] Finally, under the terms of the Simonstown Agreement of June 1955, the British government agreed to participate with Pretoria in joint naval operations to protect the shipping lanes around the Cape and in the Indian Ocean.[13]

Yet although these alliances against the ubiquitous communist menace clearly *extended* Britain's formal responsibilities, in another sense they also reflected the government's contrary objective of *reducing* its global commitments. Even before 1955, a Communist attack on any of the countries that were to become either CENTO or SEATO signatories would almost certainly have resulted in Britain coming to the aid of the non-communist victim, but any response would not have been met unilaterally by Britain alone; the United States was committed to share the burden and probably take the lead. Even while the Attlee government was increasing its activities in Malaya in the late 1940s, moreover, it was simultaneously withdrawing from India and from Palestine. And after the Korean War the process of withdrawal accelerated. Under the terms of the Canal Zone Agreement of October 1954, Britain undertook to remove its forces from Suez within two years. In 1956, the 'second wave' phase of decolonisation began with the granting of independence to Sudan. Within ten years, in the face of escalating indigenous demands for change, Britain had removed the imperial yoke from all of its major colonies. And although Britain's withdrawal from each colony was generally accompanied by the promise of future support, if necessary, to the newly independent government, the decolonisation process itself inevitably involved considerable reductions in the deployment of British forces overseas.

Harold Macmillan and the Sandys Review of 1957

A description of the Suez crisis under the short-lived prime ministership of Anthony Eden was provided in an earlier chapter, so we will not rehash it here. Suffice it to say that the gap between Britain's shrinking economic resources and its defence capabilities – as well as the UK's dependence upon the Pax Americana, of course – had been cruelly exposed by that crisis. Working under Prime Minister Harold Macmillan, Duncan Sandys arrived at the Ministry of Defence in 1957 determined to redress this imbalance between what was wanted and what could actually be delivered. Although Sandys was also motivated by the desire to upgrade Britain's defence technology to emphasise nuclear weapons over conventional ones – most controversially, his White Paper proposed to replace the use of fighter aircraft with surface-to-air missiles – *economic* constraints were a major factor in his reasoning as Britain's resources dwindled. Sandys was concerned that defence spending, which had increased during the mid-1950s before and after the Korean War for the reasons we have discussed, was simply spiralling out of control. Indeed, this factor was probably a good deal *more* important than technological considerations in the end. As Wyn Rees concluded:

> [I]n the provision of forces for the prevention of global war, the changes instituted by Sandys were due to fiscal constraint rather than strategic reassessment. Although the Chiefs of Staff now believed that global war was unlikely, Sandys did not heed the advice of the Air Ministry who advocated a medium bomber force of 200 aircraft and a variety of successor systems. Instead, Sandys chose to cut the V-force further, despite the warnings of the Air Ministry that it would lose ability to influence the United States. He also cut the level of fighter protection afforded to the United Kingdom and retained only a point defence system of the V-bomber bases. These cuts and the termination of the supersonic bomber programme were motivated above all by the need to save money.[14]

The Sandys Review – formally named *Outline of Future Policy* – introduced a number of significant changes, principally in the arenas of air and land but also with regard to the seas. As Rees points out, the Review of 1957 involved 'a series of painful cuts in the Army, Navy and Air Force at a time when they were recovering from the bitter experience of the Suez campaign', and so Sandys is not remembered with much fondness or affection today amongst those who can still recall him.[15] In addition to the shift towards nuclear technology – a major hit to the RAF, necessitating the cancellation of many aircraft – Sandys also reduced the Army in size to 162,000 men and made it an entirely volunteer force for the first time since World War II (National Service or conscription was to finally end in 1960). He also proposed a 'rationalisation' of the British defence industry, merging Britain's many defence businesses into bigger, more powerful companies and ensuring that only these companies could bid for MoD contracts.

Was the Sandys Review *only* a cost-cutting exercise in which the quality of nuclear deterrence was secondary? In one sense, the two goals were complementary. The move to a missile-based rather than aircraft-based system was supposed to achieve both strategic wisdom and increased economy simultaneously. Sandys hoped that he could reduce defence expenditure from 10 per cent of GNP to 7 per cent by 1962. Within the five-year period envisioned, the armed forces overall were cut from

702,000 personnel to 423,000, and the percentage of GNP devoted to defence spending did decline. Nevertheless, one could argue that no *real* reduction in Britain's overseas commitments resulted from all of this, and that Britain simply attempted to hang on to its existing defence policies and 'Empire circle' approach. After 1956, it was obvious that a fundamental reassessment of British foreign and defence policy would have to be undertaken. But there were *still* some very tough decisions about Britain's overstretched military resources to be made, and it was left to the Labour government which took power in 1964 to undertake these.

The Harold Wilson Government and the 'East of Suez' Retreat

The 1960s would see British defence enter a period of almost 'permanent defence review' as the UK struggled the make ends meet. Initially, the Labour government clung to the notion that the UK could have its cake and eat it. However, it gradually discovered that some sort of fundamental strategic retreat was all but inevitable. The crucial turning-point in 'Empire circle' defence policy – indeed, for British defence policy in general – was the decision that all British military forces would be withdrawn from 'East of Suez' by the end of 1971. The decision was announced by Prime Minister Harold Wilson in January 1968. That year there were still over 57,000 troops and 14,000 naval personnel permanently deployed east of the Suez Canal. Their purpose was not only to deter communist aggression in the Far East, but also to safeguard international commercial and trading routes.[16]

As we saw earlier, like many of his generation Anthony Eden had regarded the canal as the 'gateway to Empire', and this view was still a widespread one among the makers of British foreign and defence policy. But defending that gateway and maintaining forces of the size necessary to protect it was fast becoming a luxury that the hard-pressed Exchequer could no longer afford. The 1966 Defence Review had announced the government's intention to cut defence spending from 7 per cent to 6 per cent of Britain's GNP by 1969–70. The review had also intimated that the 'overstretch' of the country's defence forces would have to be eliminated in the near future: the situation in which London had been obliged to despatch emergency forces to eight trouble-spots around the globe in 1963, to sixteen in 1964, and to seventeen in 1965, could not be sustained much longer.[17] Under these circumstances, it was virtually inevitable that the government would soon seek to reduce the scope of Britain's defence efforts in order to concentrate on the one theatre – Western Europe and the North Atlantic – that was clearly of the most immediate relevance to the security of Britain itself.

Once the decision to withdraw from East of Suez had been taken, events moved rapidly. In December 1967, British forces withdrew from Aden, which became what we know today as the Arab Republic of Yemen. The election of a new Conservative government in June 1970 under Edward Heath made little difference, and by 1974 Britain's world role had been almost completely abandoned. Garrisons were still stationed in the remaining dependencies of Belize, Gibraltar, Hong Kong and the Falkland Islands; and a small force was still assisting the Sultan of Oman.[18] But plans to withdraw from Mauritius and Brunei (where the rump of the Brigade of Gurkhas was still deployed) were well advanced and negotiations had already been started with the South Africans with a view to terminating the 1955 Simonstown Agreement and abandoning the British base there. Indeed, the March 1975 Defence White Paper could justifiably refer, without pretence or affectation, to Britain's *'former* aspirations to a world-wide role'.[19] By the mid-1970s, the British government's defence policy – as with its foreign policy in general – had clearly shifted away from the Empire circle and towards Europe.

Why had it been necessary to end Britain's world military role?[20] As we have seen already, decolonisation was irresistible in the face of rising indigenous nationalism, and the increasingly European focus of Britain's trade had robbed the bases at Aden, Singapore, Simonstown and on the Gulf of their principal strategic *raisons d'être*. However the main reason underlying the decision to withdraw from East of Suez was *cost*. Britain could not afford to make an effective contribution to the defence of Western Europe *and* to maintain a powerful military presence in the Gulf and in the Far East; and if both tasks could not be accomplished properly because of scarce resources, it was far better to cut commitments and ensure that at least one was. Another element in the decision calculus was that, even if Britain itself could no longer participate effectively in the protection of Western interests East of Suez, it had friends (like Australia, New Zealand and the United States) who could be relied upon to step into the breach. Finally, it was increasingly recognised in the 1960s that, if war were to break out between East and West, then it would probably 'go nuclear' very quickly. In these circumstances, the strategic value of a global network of bases would be highly questionable: what would be the point of controlling bases and sea-lanes if the home territory and population had already been eliminated? And once this shift in perceptions *had* occurred, it became clear that a British withdrawal from East of Suez was not as strategically 'risky' as it might have appeared twenty years earlier. Although the Soviets would almost certainly attempt to increase their influence in the territories from which British forces had been withdrawn (as they did in Aden, with some success, between 1969 and 1986), the potential strategic costs of such developments would no longer be so great as to prejudice the security either of Britain or of its NATO allies.

With the withdrawal from East of Suez completed by 1971–72, the focus of British defence policy shifted firmly towards Europe and the Atlantic. The bulk of Britain's trade was with Europe. And the United Kingdom had slipped so far down the GDP 'league table' that it was clearly no longer anything more than 'just another European power'. In these circumstances the British government neither needed nor could afford to take the sort of world-view of British security interests which had characterised its defence policy for over two centuries. Although the threat of communist encroachment in the third world obviously still existed, the United States would simply have to continue the struggle alone; Britain no longer possessed the economic strength to assist in the task.

The Margaret Thatcher Years and the Nott Review of 1981

Successive governments had quietly accepted Britain's gradual decline in the world as an established fact, and had looked for ways to manage it. Margaret Thatcher took a different approach. For her, decline was not inevitable, since the tide could be reversed by a fundamental change of domestic policy. This position was closely linked in her radical world-view to the restoration of British 'greatness'. When Thatcher's government assumed office in May 1979, it consequently attempted a reversal of Britain's long-term relative economic decline using the harsh medicine of monetarism. Thatcher was committed to reducing public expenditure overall, a factor she believed had sapped British business of its vitality. But there was a complexity and perhaps even contradiction at the heart of all this. In the words of Andrew Gamble, she believed in both 'the free economy and the strong state'. This became somewhat confused in the public mind – her public dialogue emphasised simply a 'smaller' state – but a 'strong state' meant a revival of Britain's role in the world, and especially a revitalised defence budget.[21] In many ways, of course, Thatcher merely continued and intensified the James Callaghan government's 1977 commitment to increase the defence budget by 3 per cent per year in real terms in order to strengthen NATO's defences, and she continued economic policies favoured by Callaghan as well. But her fiery rhetoric captured the public imagination in a way that Callaghan's stolid, uninspiring speeches had not. Between 1979 and 1985, defence spending increased by 18 per cent in real terms, and the general trend as a proportion of GNP was upward as well.

Naturally, the real story was a bit more complex than this. Like many of its predecessors, the Conservative government inherited a significant budgetary shortfall from its predecessor. Thatcher's original Defence Secretary, Francis Pym – derided by Thatcher's supporters as a 'wet' at the time – had refused to implement an array of *cuts* to his budget. His replacement, John Nott, was considered more of a Thatcher loyalist, and it was he who spearheaded the 1981 Defence Review. This originally envisioned a range of cuts to conventional armed forces and equipment and like previous reviews, it stressed the need to make Britain's ambitions commensurate with resources while nevertheless raising defence spending overall.[22] As in the 1952 and 1957 reviews, nuclear technology – in this case, Trident, rather than the Blue Streak project abandoned in the late 1950s or the increasingly obsolete Polaris – was to be the main beneficiary while crowding out conventional spending. As Bennett notes:

> Although the cuts fell across the board, the Navy felt particularly hard done by. The operation of the strategic nuclear submarine force would remain its primary task, but there would be large reductions in the numbers of frigates and destroyers, and fewer aircraft carriers would be required. In practice, this meant getting rid of the aircraft carrier HMS *Hermes*, selling the *Invincible* to Australia, and scrapping the assault ships *Fearless* and *Intrepid*. Crucially, the listening ship HMS *Endurance* was to be withdrawn from the South Atlantic.[23]

The 1981 review proposed harsh reductions to the Navy's budget (a reduction of the number of destroyers and frigates from 59 to 42 was planned). In the event, though, the Falklands War of 1982 intervened. Between April and July of 1982, British forces re-invaded the Falkland/Malvinas Islands after the latter had been seized by Argentina's military dictator General Leopoldo Galtieri. As we have seen, the war was a classic case of mutual misperception, and each side fundamentally mis-perceived the intentions of the other.[24] But putting together the British Task Force proved costly. Moreover, the fact that Argentina still refuses to bring a formal end to hostilities – indeed, the democratically elected Christina Kirchner continued to 'sabre rattle' over this issue in 2014 – means that Britain has been forced to garrison the islands for an indefi-nite period, and it has become a long-running political and financial saga which (in Argentine eyes, at least) remains unresolved today.

Back in Britain, the Falklands invasion made John Nott's proposals difficult if not impossible to implement, since as Dorman notes 'the war was viewed by many within Whitehall and elsewhere as an indication that Nott's defence review had been wrong in its conclusions'.[25] In 1981, Nott had considered future out-of-area amphibious British operations like the one which the Navy undertook during the Falklands unlikely – little wonder that the Argentines shared this perception – and he had consequently pushed through plans to sell HMS *Invincible* and HMS *Hermes* (both of which ended up playing a pivotal role in the war, since through sheer luck they had not yet been decommissioned). Britain could certainly not afford to embark on a massively expensive rearmament programme designed to restore Britain's out-of-area capabilities to pre-1968 levels, but Margaret Thatcher did preside over large defence spending increases in the end, and the cuts that Nott had planned were essentially halved by his successor Michael Heseltine. She also took a much broader view of British security interests than her more 'European' predecessors. Reasoning along classic Realist lines, Thatcher insisted from the outset that the key feature of the contemporary international system was the global struggle between capitalism and communism. In Thatcher's view – and, even before the Falklands crisis, hers was the decisive voice in Cabinet – developments in every third-world theatre had a bearing on the global balance of power. And should anyone doubt that communism was on the march, the Soviet invasion of Afghanistan in December 1979 provided a clear illustration of the threat that Soviet adventurism posed.

For all her Realism, though, Thatcher was also motivated by a sort of conservative Idealism, a kind of fire-in-the-belly revulsion to communism itself and everything it stood for. For the 'Iron Lady', communism was as much a moral evil as it was a question of manipulating the balance of power. This wider view of the Thatcher government did not mean that British defence policy lost its European focus. Thatcher, after all, was almost obsessively concerned with the need to make economies in most (if not all) areas of government spending, and she spent much of her time in office trying to 'claw back' cash that Britain had contributed to the European Union and attempting to renegotiate the terms of membership.[15] While this shift in posture did not amount to Britain playing anything resembling an active world role in the 1980s, it was certainly associated with a more muscular role than that pursued in the 1970s. As already noted, Thatcher's approach also entailed a significant revival of the Atlanticist relationship; Thatcher and Ronald Reagan had a warm personal relationship, but they also they also held an ideological vision of foreign and defence policy that was strikingly similar.

To be sure, there were occasionally tensions within the Empire/ Commonwealth circle which pulled the US and British governments apart from one another and conflicted with the Atlantic circle. Perhaps the most significant of these came with the US invasion of Grenada in 1983, about which Thatcher was not consulted in advance. The Prime Minister considered this a considerable affront, since Grenada was (and remains) a member of the Commonwealth and a former British possession. The Reagan administration apparently believed (wrongly, as it turned out) that Cuba's Fidel Castro was attempting to establish Grenada as a communist stronghold, but from the British perspective the 'head of state' was still Queen Elizabeth. The US invasion was code-named 'Urgent Fury', and a British character in one of John Le Carré's novels would later joke that 'the fury was mainly ours'.[26]

To a lesser extent, the Falklands issue in 1982 had brought the two allies into potential conflict within the Empire circle as well. Both Argentina and Britain were allies of the United States, and one or two of Reagan's advisers (notably US Ambassador to the United Nations, Jeanne Kirkpatrick[27]) were more inclined to support the Argentines than the British in what the Reagan administration tended to see as a 'quarrel among friends' (Kirkpatrick was strongly countered by the more pro-British US Secretary of State Alexander Haig). In the event, however, there was probably never any real possibility of Reagan failing to side with Thatcher's government over the Falkland islands, and the US would in fact provide secret military support to Britain while maintaining the public pretence of impartiality.

These incidents were minor, moreover, when compared with the over-all revival of the Atlantic circle relationship during the 1980s. Following the Suez fiasco of 1956, the 'special relationship' had been strained under Harold Macmillan and John Kennedy during the Skybolt crisis in 1962, when the Americans refused to provide Britain with Polaris technol-ogy, and it had reached an all-time low when Harold Wilson refused to commit a single British troop to Vietnam (much to the outrage of President Lyndon Johnson and his advisers). It had been further strained by Britain's turn towards the European circle in the 1960s under Wilson and in the 1970s under the 'European' Edward Heath at a time when there were concerns in the US that Europe was not contributing enough, through NATO, to its own defence. But the closeness of the Thatcher–Reagan relationship re-established the Atlantic circle in both the public mind and among policymakers in Whitehall. Britain and the United States were real 'friends' again.

John Major, the End of the Cold War and the 1990 Review

Despite having won three General Elections in a row, in December 1990 a tearful Margaret Thatcher was forced from power by Conservative Party backbenchers and replaced as Prime Minister with the less charis-matic but workmanlike John Major. He had enjoyed a meteoric rise to power after not much more than ten years in the House of Commons. It was Major who would preside over much of the end of the Cold

War, as Eastern Europe escaped from the yoke of communist control and Mikhail Gorbachev's reformist policies (*Glasnost* and *Perestroika*) ultimately led – very much against their original design – to the dissolution of the Soviet Union itself. While Major (and indeed the West as a whole) was essentially a passive bystander to this implosion in the end, these were certainly very significant changes in the international system, and it was initially felt that there would now be a 'peace dividend' as swords were turned into ploughshares. Perhaps Western nations could turn away from external affairs and focus on more pressing domestic issues such as economic regeneration, a position staked out by President Bill Clinton during his successful run for the American presidency in 1992. This view was encouraged by many commentaries on foreign and defence policy on both sides of the Atlantic. Analysts like the American Francis Fukuyama, for instance, talked of 'the end of history': capitalism and liberal democracy had seemingly 'won', while communism had been permanently defeated. Whether this was true or not would be widely debated for years, and some would later claim that neither side actually 'won'.[28] What was soon clear to everyone, though, was that the Soviet Union was not there anymore. Change of some sort seemed inevitable.

Although all of this happened gradually – free movement between East and West Berlin was re-introduced in November 1989 but the Soviet Union did not dissolve until more than two years later, in December 1991 – it was still a comparatively sudden development which induced significant uncertainty in the West. The effect of the end of the Cold War on UK strategic thinking was not immediate, and this was perhaps not altogether surprising. On the one hand, a whole bureaucratic apparatus within British government had lost its original *raison d'être*. The major objective of the British intelligence bodies MI5 and MI6, as well as the recent mission of much of the MoD and FCO, had been the defeat of Soviet communism. Government organisations tend to resist change, however, and the uncertainty that the future brings tends to make those organisations highly risk-averse, clinging to established ways of doing things and reverting to tried-and-trusted bureaucratic routines. This trend was certainly visible in the United States, where the Realists George H. W. Bush and his CIA Director Robert Gates were slow to take Gorbachev seriously or to establish the kind of trust which the Soviet leader had enjoyed with the more Idealist Reagan. But this was also borne out in the Major government's response to events; like their American counterparts, both Major and his Foreign Secretary Douglas Hurd were cautious practitioners of *realpolitik*, who were disinclined to upend established policy before it was clear to them what was actually happening.

It had been nine years since the last defence review, and the Falklands issue had scuppered or diluted many of the Nott Review's initial recommendations. Here at last, though, was an opportunity for new thinking and for a complete overhaul of established organisations and procedures. With no enemy or adversary in sight, moreover, major cuts in defence spending were expected during the 1990 Review, *Options for Change*, which was set in train by then Defence Secretary Tom King. We should remember, though, that this review occurred in July 1990, right in the middle of these earth-shattering events but before the Persian Gulf War of 1991. While it might seem clear to us now, looking at events through the rear-view mirror as it were, history appears far less clear to the participants at the time. Some of the subsequent criticism of the review is rather unfair, in the sense that it assumes that the reviewers 'know' what is going to happen in the coming year. Secondly, the review also occurred not under the new government of John Major but during the last year of Thatcher's long prime ministership. Defence reviews usually take place under brand-new governments, as the successor grapples with the resource and spending problems left by the predecessor. This was not the case in the summer of 1990.

Nevertheless, the review was certainly occasioned by the need to capitalise on the changed relationship between Britain and the Soviet Union, even if the usual need to save money was very much the main driver behind this. In the event, *Options for Change* proved to be less radical than expected, but it still involved some of the deepest cuts to the armed services ever undertaken. Indeed, the Review would be lampooned by its critics as 'Options for Cuts'. The whole purpose of Britain's military strategy until this point had been the containment of the Soviet threat in Europe, and this was reflected in the way that the three services had deployed their resources: the Royal Air Force and Army held the line in Germany, while the Marines and Navy patrolled Scandinavia and the North Atlantic in general. *Options for Change*, though, began the process of pulling these forces back. It cut the size of Britain's military by about 18 per cent overall (it would now number about 255,000 personnel). There would also be major reductions in the size of each service. These cuts were so deep that they reduced the proportion of spending Britain devoted to defence to its lowest level since the 1930s (about 2 per cent of GNP). Again, the nuclear deterrent was retained, but conventional forces had to be cut back in order to maintain this.

For much of the post-war period, the UK had enjoyed a fairly 'balanced' force, with a reasonable mix of forces on land, in the sea and the air; now, 'the balance reflected inter-service politics and NATO command structures, as much as military logic', in the words of Lawrence Freedman.[29] Now the axe was falling somewhat indiscriminately on whatever could be cut. Perhaps the real failing of *Options for Change*, though, was that it assumed that a 'peace dividend' would obtain for the foreseeable future. The unspoken assumption was that with the Soviet threat gone, no new military challenges would rise up to replace it. This proved entirely mistaken.

The failing was revealed almost as soon as John Major became Prime Minister. For one thing, the pressure to take part in the Persian Gulf War of 1991 – to be a major part of the broad coalition against Saddam Hussein assembled by George H. W. Bush – proved irresistible. The Atlantic circle remained critical to Britain's security, and Major refused to jeopardise it (as Wilson had perhaps done in the Vietnam case). His instinctive Realism would be immediately apparent in the case of the former Yugoslavia, and he denied in the House of Commons that Britain could do anything to stop 'ancient hatreds'. Yugoslavia rapidly disintegrated between 1991 and 1992, years that saw the resurgence of genocide at the heart of Europe. Foreign Secretary Douglas Hurd – an experienced friend and admirer of the German-American Realist Henry Kissinger who had also worked under Anthony Eden during the 1950s – claimed that arming the Bosnians against the Serbs would be like 'heaping fuel on the flames'. This caused enormous controversy at the time, but in distancing themselves from calls for a humanitarian-inspired military intervention, Major and Hurd were expressing the tenets of classic Realism. Britain avoided taking an active role in ending the Yugoslav conflict, and it was largely left to Clinton and the Americans to do this. But Major could not avoid taking part in the humanitarian mission which followed the end of the war in 1995, and neither could he avoid Britain's continuing (and substantial) troop commitment to Northern Ireland. Major's government was 'unusually active' in the end. Indeed, a new era of military activism was beginning, in spite of Major's obvious intent to cut back Britain's role. Britain would soon become more militarily involved in the rest of the world than at any point in the post-World War II era, in spite of the hugely diminished resources necessary to do this.

Tony Blair, New Labour and the 1998 Review

John Major was replaced in 1997 by a Prime Minister who seemed to positively revel in the use of military power. We have already seen how the rise of New Labour pushed British foreign policy in an Idealist direction, and how Blair's deeply moralistic and especially Christian beliefs after his election to Downing Street in 1997 led him to champion not only the interventions during the Kosovo War of 1999 and in Sierra Leone in 2000 but also the invasions of Afghanistan in 2002 and Iraq in 2003 (despite the very deep unpopularity of the latter amongst the British people). We will not rehash that discussion here, and the reader is referred to previous chapter segments on Blair's foreign policies. However, it was initially expected that UK defence policy would be affected by this change of emphasis in at least one significant area: arms sales. For years, the British arms industry had sold its weapons to regimes which might be described as ethically or morally dubious. Tanks and water cannon, for instance, were sold to governments that seemed quite likely to use these weapons against popular protests by their own populations. As Jeevan Vasagar noted at the time, 'the sale of arms to foreign countries is big business – and Britain is the second biggest exporter of arms in the world. Two of the biggest buyers of British arms are Indonesia and Saudi Arabia, both with poor human rights records. The two account for 25 per cent of UK arms sales.'[30]

As Foreign Secretary, Robin Cook was a particularly strong advocate of ending arms sales to such regimes. But as the Bureaucratic Politics model would predict, the stances taken by individual ministers were strongly influenced by their respective bureaucratic positions, and the issue fell victim almost immediately to bureaucratic infighting. Viewed from the Foreign Office, Cook could see the larger diplomatic or 'soft power' benefits of living up to British values. But from their vantage points, both the Department of Trade and Industry (DTI) and the Treasury saw the issue in primarily economic terms. If we did not sell arms to these regimes, then others *would*, it was argued. This would cost UK jobs – itself a significant moral consideration – while leaving the overall human rights situation no better than it had been before. The argument was essentially that 'everybody loses' under this scenario, and unsurprisingly it won the day. A basically Realist approach to arms sales remained in place.

Arguably, there are a number of (recurring) reasons why UK defence reviews have tended to fail. Perhaps the most significant of these has been that events or circumstances frequently derail 'the best laid schemes of mice and men', as the Scottish poet Robbie Burns once put it. This was so in 1952, after which Churchill undertook various new commitments which made cuts to conventional forces difficult to achieve. It was also especially true of 1981, after which the Falklands War intervened and made John Nott's review look wrong-headed (it had tried to cancel much of the naval equipment that proved central to victory in that conflict). It was true of the 1990 review, after which the Persian Gulf War of 1991 made cuts to conventional forces more difficult politically and perhaps less sensible strategically. Instead, the UK's military attempted to do much more with a good deal less. But it was probably most apparent in the 1998 Strategic Defence Review, undertaken just one year into Blair's tenure. Understandably, the 1998 review did not envisage the events of 11 September 2001 or the subsequent wars in Iraq and Afghanistan. Nevertheless, the vast cost of those wars would exert a fundamental impact on UK defence policy, constraining the actions of later governments. Indeed, the period 1997–2010 saw the most intense period of military activism Britain has known since World War II, but that could scarcely have been predicted from Labour's strategy or its 1997 manifesto commitments.

The 1998 review was generally heralded as a success by critics at first, in the sense that it was the first real attempt by a UK government to seriously address the question of what the future might look like. In opposition, the Labour Party had criticised John Major for not having a clear view of what the post-Cold War landscape was likely to be and for lacking a view on how Britain's defence forces should be reshaped and reorganised in accordance with the 'new' threats involved. Although neither Tony Blair nor Gordon Brown was a specialist in foreign policy – both had in fact intended originally to focus on domestic affairs – they were intent on there being some sort of fundamental reassessment. In July 1998 Defence Secretary George Robertson unveiled the new document, heralded as 'radical' by Robertson himself while still retaining many of Britain's traditional commitments (notably Trident and the special relationship). The innovation came mostly in the means rather than the ends. The Strategic Review envisioned Britain employing a small, rapid expeditionary force, able to go anywhere on a moment's notice (if not to do anything). This employed a stronger role for the Navy and a lesser one for less mobile units, and in particular strengthened the case for fighter-laden carriers which could act as temporary 'bases' around the globe. New Labour therefore planned for the building of two huge, Queen Elizabeth-class aircraft carriers to replace the smaller, ageing Invincible-class carriers. This expeditionary force was expected to involve itself in short (often humanitarian) bursts of activity, but it was conceded that the forces could not stay where they were for very long for obvious economic reasons. Britain was no longer a superpower, but it could still be what Blair called 'a force for good' in the world.

Again, however, the whole exercise was at least partially overtaken by events. There were constant updates, and it frequently looked like events were driving the strategy rather than the other way round. After several updates – for instance, the *New Chapter* was designed to take account of 9/11 – the second Labour National Security Strategy of June 2009 identified the things which might end up threatening the United Kingdom, or what it called 'Threat Drivers' (these were identified as global trends, climate change, competition for energy, poverty, inequality and poor governance, and ideologies and beliefs). It also specified the likely 'Threat Actors' (states, failing or fragile states, terrorists, criminals and the hazards of nature). These issues were stated at such a high level of generality, however, that their utility as a guide to the future might be regarded as a 'kitchen sink' approach. It did not prioritise threats or assign them to particular 'tiers' (as the Coalition government's 2010 Strategy later would).

More particularly, it took time to change Britain's forces, far longer than a democracy often allows. Organisations move slowly, and so does the defence appropriations process. Indeed, it would not be until 2020 that the two carriers (after many delays) were finally scheduled to come online. In the meantime, Britain's interventions went ahead anyway, based on what we happened to have in the 'back shed'. As Jonathan Bailey puts it, there was a resultant mismatch of ends, ways and means. 'As a result of the SDR of 1998, the Labour government reconfigured the Armed Forces for short operations', he argues, 'not long before it would launch them on enduring and demanding ones'.[31] After 2003, the Blair government had even committed UK troops to two highly demanding theatres simultaneously: Afghanistan (mainly in Helmand Province) and Iraq (mainly in Basra), both tasks for which it was arguably ill-equipped.

The military invasions of both countries proved surprisingly swift, and had the wars simply ended there the story of the Blair and Brown governments might have been different. But of course, the conventional invasion was just the beginning, as both evolved into exercises in counterinsurgency for which neither Britain nor the United States was well equipped (recall that the 1998 document had envisioned relatively short interventions). For Britain, both wars also involved open-ended commitments of a type which had not been budgeted for in the 1998 review. British forces, of course, had a well-established reputation for being 'good at' beating insurgencies, derived most of all from the experience of the British Army in the 1970s and 1980s in Northern Ireland but also from more dimly recalled victories over insurgents in Malaya during the 1950s (which had inspired brief interest from the White House at the outset of its involvement in Vietnam). Why, then, did Britain's strategy fail?

Failure in both theatres had causes that were undoubtedly complex, and reasonable observers can (and do) disagree as to which were most central. Some blame the supposed 'hubris' of Tony Blair himself and a sense of pure overconfidence bred by success in other wars. Others trace the problem to Blair's supposed over-willingness to do America's bidding whatever the costs (what we might term the 'poodle factor') and it is certainly true that with the invasion of Iraq, Blair began to favour the US circle over the opposition of many within the European one. According to (retired British General) Christopher Elliott, on the other hand, British failure may have had more to do with organisational problems and the fact that UK forces were simply spread too thin to be effective. 'The British Army knew in its very DNA that an insurgency in Belfast less than ten years previously had only been contained by a permanent deployment of thirteen battalions of infantry', he noted, 'yet after the initial benign period the UK attempted to meet an even more violent challenge in Basra, a city three times the size, with only three. We were bound to fail, so who allowed that to happen?'[32] Sir Nicholas Houghton, on the other hand, has suggested that the failures can also be traced to an ignorance of the internal makeup of the countries we invaded and so of the battles that would likely be waged. 'One of the follies of the current age has been an unmatched ambition to change the world without bothering to under-stand it first', as Houghton put it in his annual CDS lecture in 2013.[33] It is certainly true that George W. Bush himself did not understand that Iraq was composed of Shia, Sunnis and Kurds (among other groupings) until this was pointed out to him by Iraqi immigrants to the United States, and many Britons – despite the UK's supposedly stronger grip on history – had forgotten about Britain's own (unsuccessful) adventures in Mesopotamia in the early part of the 20th century. Finally, failure may, in the end, have most to do with the fact that counterinsurgency itself is inherently difficult to do. John Nagl – the author of one very popular account of the subject assigned in several of the US War Colleges – is fond of saying that counterinsurgency works best 'on a peninsula against a visibly obvious ethnic minority, before CNN is invented'.[34] In other words, it worked well in Malaya but is much harder to do in places like Vietnam or Afghanistan, where it is difficult for soldiers on the ground to tell the difference between friend and foe, where the enemy force cannot easily be pinned down to a single area or denied the resupply of men and materials, and where 24-hour news teams are watching everything you do. The Malayan operation had often been brutal, involving the forceful separation of villagers from the communist guerrillas and their move-ment to what were euphemistically termed 'the New Villages'. One can only imagine what that would have looked like on CNN.

Whatever the causes of failure in these 'ethical wars', moreover, the cost to the British Exchequer proved enormous. By May 2014, the Royal United Services Institute calculated that the price tag for Britain's interven-tions in Iraq and Afghanistan had reached almost £30 billion.[35] Britain's contribution to the war in Afghanistan – even before it had withdrawn from the country – was just below £20 billion between 2006 and 2013 (or about £1,000 a year for every taxpayer in the UK, although this makes the assumption that the government was not simply borrowing the money). Between 2003 and 2009, the cost of UK intervention in Iraq was somewhat less, a relative 'bargain' at just below £10 billion. The Blair government's loyalty to the Bush administration had come at a very considerable cost not just in treasure, moreover, but in blood. Thanks to advances in the technology of healthcare and helicopter transportation, the number of fatalities among military personnel in Iraq and Afghanistan was not as high as in Vietnam (where 58,000 Americans lost their lives). Nevertheless, at the time of writing in early 2015, 179 British troops had died in Iraq and 453 more had died in Afghanistan, together with losses among the local populations which are simply incalculable and are ongoing at the time of writing. Given the human toll, it may seem inappropriate to focus on the cost to the UK taxpayer. But as mentioned at the beginning of this chapter, the wars nevertheless had a financial impact on UK defence policy because they left a very large 'black hole' at the heart of the Treasury's finances, which any incoming government – regardless of its coloration – was going to have to address after 2010.

The Coalition Government, 2010–2015

Like its predecessor, the Coalition government – with Conservative Party leader David Cameron as Prime Minister and Liberal Democratic Party leader Nick Clegg as his deputy – immediately launched a defence review upon coming to office in 2010. The *Strategic Defence and Security Review* (SDSR) of July 2010 was preceded by the publication (one day earlier) of the UK National Security Strategy (NSS). The NSS is self-consciously modelled on the US National Security Strategy – traditionally, Britain has issued no such 'grand' statement – and although the first one was introduced by the Blair government, the Coalition followed this practice and planned to institutionalise it. The Conservative government elected in May 2015 produced a further review, running on a five-year cycle.

The 2010 NSS in particular was lauded on a number of counts, not least because for the first time it identified three levels of threat (or 'tiers') on the basis of how likely the threat is judged to be and how severe it is thought likely to be in terms of its consequences for the United Kingdom. To make it into 'Tier One', a threat had to fulfil both of these criteria simultaneously. The NSS placed cyber warfare in the first tier, for instance, listing it as a major threat that might well have to be faced in the near future. It also listed terrorism as a first-tier threat, together with natural disasters like a major flood or flu pandemic and more traditional military crises that might lead to inter-state war and draw in Britain and its allies. Biological warfare, on the other hand, only made it into the second tier, presumably because it was considered less likely to occur than the earlier scenarios, even though the effects might be devastating.

Both the NSS and SDSR of 2010 were criticised on a variety of grounds, however. In essence, the NSS document of that year identifies what policymakers see as the key strategic threats confronting Britain.

One can argue that it is not especially 'British' to generate formal strategy documents of this kind given UK policymakers' usual reliance on pragmatism or 'muddling through'. It can also be argued that the NSS in any case represented a vague list of problems rather than a genuine strategy relating ends to means, and we shall examine such critiques in more depth in the final chapter. But the 2010 version laid out what the Coalition government saw as the main security demands being placed on Britain (the 'ends'), while the SDSR was supposed to lay out the resources available to meet these (the 'means').

There was symmetry and a logic to all this, but many critics saw the two documents as essentially unrelated. While it is fair to say that the history of British defence policy since the end of World War II has been all about this struggle to make the military means match the political ends – a struggle which is becoming progressively difficult with the passing of each generation – there does not appear to be a 'match' between the expansive ends sought since 2010 and the increasingly meagre means provided. While the Coalition said that there will be no 'strategic shrinkage' in Britain's role, it is hard to believe that more (or even the same) can be achieved with the pared-down force which has been provided. It was also true that the sheer force of events – not least in Libya in 2011 and in Iraq again against Islamic State from 2014 onwards – threatened to overtake the review almost immediately.[36] We will have more to say about the NSS and SDSR of 2010 in the concluding chapter, not least because both represent the most important attempts made in recent years at the UK governmental level to think about both strategy and resources. We will also defer discussion of the 2015 NSS – the most recent attempt to balance threats with resources – until the final chapter.

As with New Labour, the Coalition government explicitly included a 'moral' component in its foreign policy, and references are made in the 2010 document to 'ethical realism'. As we saw in an earlier chapter, David Cameron partly retained a focus on *realpolitik*, but attempted to marry this with a measure of idealism. We can criticise this move on a number of grounds – when push comes to shove, for instance, is UK defence policy to be driven by interests or by values? – and it might be seen as a rhetorical device rather than a substantive commitment. Nevertheless, Cameron was heir to the conservative idealism of Margaret Thatcher, whose foreign policies were motivated both by a hard-headed calculation of the national interest and by doing what she saw as the 'right thing', especially in the fight against communism and with reference to the Falkland Islands (which were of little strategic value to Britain).

Idealistic realism would find its most concrete expression in the operation to free Libya from its long-time dictator Muammar Ghaddafi in 2011 and the effort to prevent a predicted genocide within dissident areas.

With the United States hovering in the background – Barack Obama was later accused of 'leading from behind' on this issue – the British and French formed a temporary coalition to force Ghaddafi from power, outside of the remit of NATO. The war was waged almost entirely from the air and was self-consciously based upon what has become known as the 'Afghan model'. In Afghanistan, the anti-Taliban Northern Alliance, working on the ground, had initially been assisted by air power alone in 2002 as the Allies pounded any useful targets they could find within Afghanistan. Similarly, in Libya dissident groups working on the ground were assisted by Britain, France and the United States, which provided control of the air. This seemed to work. Politically, moreover, it also proved more palatable than putting 'boots on the ground', especially given the war weariness of post-Iraq, post-Afghanistan public opinion.

Within the highly constrained, post-East of Suez atmosphere, there were parallels with New Labour's approach not just in the ends sought but in the means used as well. It appeared that light expeditionary forces were Britain's 'thing' now, but in the absence of carriers, the Coalition was similarly forced to use other means to project power overseas. As we saw in a previous chapter, the newfound prime ministerial habit of submitting putative military interventions to Parliament for their approval may or may not become an established constitutional tradition – it is more in keeping with the US political system of separated powers, and may have been a product of the fact that Cameron lacked an overall parliamentary majority – but one effect of the vote against direct involvement in Syria has been to restrict British air operations against ISIS to Iraqi territory. The operations against Islamic State after 2014 – ongoing at the time of writing – involved flying UK Tornadoes to Cyprus and using the friendly bases there as a staging area. Currently, this is one of the very few options still available for the projection of British 'hard power' overseas.

The Unresolved Status of Britain's Bomb

The ghost of Ernest Bevin still haunts the corridors of Whitehall. As Foreign Secretary under Attlee, Bevin was instrumental in committing the UK to having its very own 'independent' deterrent, with 'a bloody Union Jack on top of it', as he so charmingly put it after an extended (and supposedly alcoholic) lunch in Whitehall.[37] But the commitment to nuclear weapons helped to unbalance commitments and resources. The new Conservative government agreed that Britain should develop its own independent deterrent force. Following a series of atomic tests in 1952–53, the RAF was supplied with nuclear bombs capable of being delivered by its ageing fleet of Canberra aircraft in 1954.[38] In March 1955, Defence Secretary Harold Macmillan announced that Britain's new V-bomber force was now nuclear-armed.[39]

Many defence reviews have stressed the utility and deterrent quality of Britain's nuclear capabilities, but have then shied away from the political pain associated with cuts to conventional forces. We have generally seen a refusal to choose between one or the other, and an unwillingness to accept the trade-offs that inevitably come with the vast cost of nuclear weaponry. We can see this in the 1952 'Global Strategy' Paper, as already noted. But it was also present in the Sandys and Nott reviews of 1957 and 1981 respectively, right up to the 1998 SDR and 2010 SDSR. The latter both essentially sidestepped the issue and left the nuclear debate to another day, even though sorting this issue out is probably central to resolving the budgetary debate.

Bureaucratic politics were also very much in evidence within UK nuclear policy, right from the start. Throughout the 1950s there was considerable rivalry between the RAF and the Royal Navy as to which service was best equipped to deliver nuclear warheads to enemy territory, for instance.[40] The Navy's case centred on the doubts that were increasingly being voiced about NATO's post-1956 threats of 'massive retaliation' which, it was argued, invited the Soviets to engage in a pre-emptive 'first strike' against the West's nuclear arsenals. Nuclear bombs stored at airfields in Western Europe were prime targets for such a first strike. What was needed was a 'second strike capability' which could plausibly threaten to hit back at Soviet targets even if Warsaw Pact forces launched a successful *blitzkrieg* – nuclear or otherwise – against Britain itself.[41] With developments in ballistic missile technology gradually weakening the RAF's case for a manned-aircraft delivery system, the Navy's case began to prevail. The decision to purchase Polaris – a submarine-launched ballistic missile system – from the Americans in December 1962 decided the matter. From the time that Polaris became operational in 1968, Britain's independent deterrent was based on a small submarine fleet which was permanently designated for NATO responsibilities but which could be withdrawn specifically for British use in an emergency. The secret 'Chevaline' upgrade of the Polaris warhead authorised by the Heath, Wilson and Callaghan governments during the 1970s continued the commitment.[42] And the Thatcher government's decision to purchase, first, Trident I (C4) and then Trident II (D5) – again from the Americans – in 1982 meant that Britain could expect to maintain a credible independent deterrent capability well into the 21st century.[43] But why had it been necessary for Britain to possess an independent deterrent in the first place? Why could not London have relied on the Americans to protect Britain, as well as the rest of Western

Europe, with their extended nuclear deterrent? Four factors seem to have been particularly significant, although, as is frequently the case, it is difficult to determine their relative importance. One factor, in the early 1950s at least, was the need for Britain to retain its prominent position in what was already an American-dominated alliance. As a government Global Strategy Paper argued in 1952, the United Kingdom could only expect to influence the development of American nuclear strategy if it possessed its own independent nuclear capability.[44] A second, and related, factor was the question of prestige. If Britain wished to retain its Great Power status and to continue to exercise influence in the international corridors of power, it had to have a share in the awesome destructive potential of the latest military technology. A fashionable pun of the mid-1950s was that nuclear weapons were 'great levellers' – both of buildings and of the power differentials between nation-states.[45] Nuclear weapons seemed to provide middle-range powers like Britain and France with the opportunity to achieve strategic equality with the two recently emerged superpowers. The attraction of thereby retaining a leading position in world diplomacy proved too much for both Labour and Conservative governments: the development of an independent nuclear capability accordingly became an important defence policy priority.

A third factor underlying the British decision to press ahead with its own independent deterrent was the implicit message that such a programme sent to the Kremlin. In the mid-1950s, it was entirely possible that Moscow simply found American threats of 'massive retaliation' non-credible; that the Soviets did not believe that Washington would unleash what would inevitably be a mutually fatal nuclear exchange merely because of a Soviet conventional incursion into Western Europe. In these circumstances, Britain's possession of an independent nuclear capability not only provided another decision centre that Moscow was now obliged to consider in its calculations about the credibility of NATO threats of 'nuclear punishment'; it also provided a Western punishment deterrent that was far more likely to be *used* if Moscow were to call Washington's bluff and to attempt to take advantage of its conventional superiority in Europe. A prime function of the independent deterrent in this sense was to make NATO's nuclear sword more *credible*.

The fourth main factor was that the independent deterrent provided an insurance policy against the possibility of future American withdrawal from NATO and/or loss of 'American will' in general. Such a withdrawal still looks like a distant possibility – the United States has often found that it can exercise greater influence within NATO than it can inside the often deadlocked UN Security Council – but from the vantage point of the 1940s and 1950s, it was nonetheless reassuring to NATO's European wing to know that, even if Washington were to decide at some future date that it no longer had any interest in defending Western Europe, the Europeans would still possess their own nuclear deterrent capability. Either alone, or in combination with the French *force de frappe,* the British deterrent would still provide a formidable counter-threat to any future Soviet challenge, and arguably continues to provide a hedge against (say) a nuclear-armed North Korea or Iran today. Some UK policymakers simply did not believe that – if push came to shove – the Americans would go to war over a tiny group of islands, and still do not believe that in the current strategic environment. If that is so, then having its own deterrent ensures that Britain is defended, regardless of US or NATO commitments or what US policymakers might decide to do in the heat of battle or the fog of war.

Regardless of why Britain developed an independent deterrent in the first place, can it continue to do so today? Trident may have been new technology in the 1970s, but it is certainly not any more; in fact, from the vantage point of 2016, it appears increasingly obsolete. One political strategy to deal with the existence and cost of nuclear weapons in Britain has been to simply pretend that they are not there. The 1998 defence review, for instance, deliberately did not 'factor in' the cost of updates to Trident, while the 2010 review essentially put off the question until an unspecified later date. Whether Britain can afford to replace its fleet of ageing weapons is an issue that cannot be held off for very much longer since it is surely central to both economy and strategy, and this is therefore a question to which we shall turn in the final chapter. Nuclear weapons are relatively cheap to maintain over the years, but the purchase cost of a new or updated system is very high. It can also be asked what the role of nuclear weapons *is* within Britain's current strategy, given that so few of the 'new', post-Cold War security threats identified by recent governments seem to have much to do with nuclear weapons or are amenable to being addressed by their threat or actual use. (Non-nuclear states, terrorists and insurgents pay relatively little attention to nuclear capabilities, for instance, while inanimate forces like floods and hurricanes cannot.) But we shall also return to this issue at the end.

Defence in an Era of Austerity

With unilateralism no longer on the 'menu of choice', British defence policy has nevertheless seen various governments favour one of our circles over the other. Is military power to be projected using the alliance with the United States or with Europe? Between 1945 and the mid-1960s, London continued to adhere to the traditional belief that British security required not only geostrategic stability in Western Europe but also the preservation of the Empire's global network of bases. The bases were considered essential both to the defence of the Empire itself and to the protection of the Western sphere of influence in the third world generally. By the mid-1960s, however, the burden of 'carrying two rifles instead of one' had proved too great. In order to prevent an unacceptable escalation in defence costs, successive governments between the mid-1960s and the late 1970s opted to concentrate the United Kingdom's defence efforts within the European theatre, where Britain's principal material interests were increasingly located. Notwithstanding the need to make limited deployments overseas, therefore, Britain effectively withdrew from its 'world role', increasingly defining itself as a European power with primarily European interests. During the 1980s, though, the pendulum swung back again towards the Atlantic circle, where it has arguably remained ever since (although Blair envisioned a Britain perched equidistant between Europe and the United States). Europe seems unable or unwilling to develop its own independent defence capability, while Britain's membership of the European Union looked increasingly precarious under David Cameron and appeared about to end after the 2016 referendum. At the same time, the 'special relationship' has remained reasonably strong since Thatcher, and Britain increasingly operates only in tandem with the United States and NATO. To be sure, the simple facts of Britain's long-term relative economic decline have ensured that there is no real prospect of London ever reacquiring the permanent out-of-area capability necessary for it to resume its former world role, and the strong suspicion remains that the UK can now only exercise a meaningful defence role in partnership with America.

An even broader issue is whether Britain should still be spending at such a high level on defence. The UK has the world's fourth or fifth largest defence budget relative to its gross national product, depending on how this is measured. Britain spent about 2 per cent of its GNP on defence in 2016. But the economy is not keeping up with this commitment. This raises a whole host of issues. First of all, it is difficult to know how much defence the country needs, since perceptions of threat can differ widely. Secondly, the 'guns versus butter' debate is highly relevant here. Oliver Wright, for instance, notes that the approximately £30 billion that the UK spent in Iraq and Afghanistan would pay for 1,464,000 more NHS nurses, 408,000 NHS consultants and 75 per cent of Britain's HS2 budget.[38] Defence does not produce quantifiable goods, and the larger the share of the budgetary pie that goes to it, the less is available to spend on domestic concerns like education and healthcare. Another issue is the question of whether defence spending not only 'crowds out' expenditure on worthy domestic causes, but might even erode the economic base on which an effective defence depends. Paul Kennedy for one argued in

The Rise and Fall of the Great Powers that defence spending is a leading cause of economic decline.[39] Being a superpower itself costs money, and maintaining overseas bases and the spending necessary to retain that status in general is not at all cheap. A fourth issue to consider is whether what we see today as a range of threats is really the absence of a single overriding threat. Some would argue that Britain has never been safer; in the absence of a Spanish Armada, a Napoleon, a Joseph Stalin or an Adolf Hitler, it can now afford to breathe a little easier and perhaps prioritise other issues. If that is so, is the defence community attempting to manufacture threats to Britain's defence in an era of relative peace and the absence of a direct security threat to the United Kingdom? Why has there not been a bigger 'peace dividend', if this is the case? Or does the UK defence community genuinely feel that Britain is objectively less safe than during the Cold War? We will return to these issues in the concluding chapter, since the answers will help to shape British foreign policy to come. Before we do so, however, we will return to the theoretical issues with which we began in the Introduction. How useful have the four theories that we identified there been in understanding the development of UK foreign policy?

Chapter 9

The Relevance of Foreign Policy Theory

In the introduction to this book it was indicated that the present study would seek to explain the major developments in Britain's post-war foreign policy at two different levels. On the one hand, it would examine the calculations that underpinned the foreign policy decisions of successive governments, paying particular attention to the 'Realist' world-views of the policymakers themselves. On the other, it would simultaneously attempt to identify the most significant underlying 'structural' factors that seem to have influenced Britain's changing international position, again making particular use of the Realist model.[1] Given this intrusion of Realism at both the decision-making and structural levels of investigation, it was acknowledged from the outset that the analysis provided in this book adopted a broadly state-centric, Realist approach, although the view taken was mostly implicit rather than explicit. It is clear from the foregoing chapters, however, that some of the other theoretical perspectives outlined in the Introduction have also proven useful. In these circumstances, the purposes of this chapter are to review the main theoretical perspectives that could have been used in order to analyse Britain's post-war foreign policy and to assess the relevance of each of these perspectives to the particular analysis conducted here. Not surprisingly, a substantial part of the discussion is devoted to an exposition of Realism, the approach that has featured most significantly in previous chapters.

The chapter itself is divided into two parts. The first provides a formal statement of the Realist model and outlines its main uses and limitations in the context of the present study. The second describes (in rather more detail than was possible in the Introduction) the 'Constructivist' approach to British foreign policy, examining the way in which each has provided additional insights into Britain's post-war foreign policy behaviour. At the decision-making level, it also examines the utility of 'Cognitivist' and 'Bureaucratic Politics' approaches, arguing that the latter in particular – although it was originally developed in the United States – has a resonance that applies to the United Kingdom as well.

Realist World-Views and the Realist 'Model'

One of the distinguishing features of the Realist approach to foreign policy analysis is that Realism is both an academic theory about the nature and workings of international politics and a way of characterising the world-views of the policymakers themselves. Realism consists of a set of propositions (specified below) that purport to describe and explain the foreign policy behaviour of nation-states. By extension, a 'Realist world-view' is an adherence on the part of the policymaker to the basic tenets of the theory, even though he (or she) may only dimly understand the full model itself, relying instead on a simplified version of it. Short definitions are easy to provide, however, so what precisely does Realism entail?

Modern Realist or 'power politics' thinking has a long pedigree. Derived from the writings of Thucydides, Machiavelli and Hobbes, among others, it has been reinforced by the researches of generations of diplomatic historians who have sought to analyse the motives and calculations underlying foreign policy strategy.[2] The foundation of Realism is the claim that the international state system is essentially anarchic: that there is no overarching authority that can adjudicate in important or serious disputes between nation-states and that, as a result, the nation-state must ultimately rely upon its own efforts and resources to sustain it in a dangerous and threatening world.

The recognition of the anarchic nature of the international system has led to the use by Realists of the 'Hobbesian analogy'. This device suggests that there is a strong analogy between the situation that confronts the nation-state (or bloc) in the international system and the situation that confronts the individual in Hobbes' State of Nature, where life is 'poor, solitary, nasty, brutish and short'. In both situations, the individual actor is in a continuing state of fear and uncertainty, unsure as to whether, and which, other actor(s) might launch an unprovoked and unanticipated attack. Thus, just as Hobbesian man is motivated by his desire for safety, for the satisfaction of his 'appetites' and for the enhancement of his reputation, so the nation-state is driven primarily by its need to promote its security, its material-economic well-being and its international reputation. Similarly, just as Hobbesian man can best reduce his overwhelming sense of fear by developing whatever power capability is available to him, so the nation-state (or bloc) can best protect its security and material interests by pursuing a strategy of either maximising its own power capabilities or seeking to avoid the development of any power preponderance elsewhere.[3]

There are, of course, a number of serious objections that can be raised against the use of the Hobbesian analogy in this way.[4] It has often been observed that states are unlike individuals in so many important ways that the attempt to draw an analogy between them is worthless. Unlike individuals, states vary enormously in the power capabilities at their disposal (compare, for example, the United States and Bangladesh). Unlike an individual whose interests are broadly unitary, states are usually composed of a variety of competing factions and groupings with an equally variegated set of contradictory interests and goals. And, unlike an individual whose allotted life-span is relatively short, most states endure for long periods of time. Similarly, it is often argued that, whereas Hobbes's model of the State of Nature refers to the 'war of all against all', in the international system stable and long-lasting alliances and informal understandings are frequently in evidence. All these differences, it is alleged, mean that the sorts of motivation and calculation that prevail in Hobbes's anarchical and dangerous State of Nature cannot be systematically transferred to an analysis of the international system, even though that system might appear to be just as anarchic and dangerous as its Hobbesian counterpart.

The Realists' response to these criticisms is to acknowledge freely that Hobbes's theoretical model of anarchy obviously cannot be applied mechanically to contemporary nation-state behaviour: of course there are significant imbalances of power across the state system; of course states frequently pursue contradictory goals; of course the life of the state is not 'short' (though, with the advent of nuclear weapons, the accuracy of this assertion is not as self-evident as it once was); and of course long-term alliances enable the boundaries of Hobbesian fear to be redrawn so as to exclude longstanding 'friends'. In the Realist view, however, these concessions do not in any sense diminish the value of the fundamental insight into international conflict that the Hobbesian analogy provides. It is simply not necessary, the Realist argues, to adopt the entire paraphernalia of the Hobbesian model to recognise the general applicability of the core of that model to the adversarial relationships between nation-states. Of course the condition of Hobbesian fear is clearly not particularly valuable for describing the post-war relationships between, say, Belgium and the Netherlands. However, it is axiomatic to the Realist position that the international system is divided into a complex network of overlapping and to some degree interlocking 'security complexes', any of which may at any time erupt into violent conflict.[5] It is in the context of these security complexes that the concept of Hobbesian fear is relevant as a means of characterising the relations between a range of nation-states (for instance, between the United States and China).[6] In each of these relationships, the intense mutual mistrust felt by the two sides produces mutual postures of confrontation, which in turn encourage further mutual antagonism – a vicious circle from which there is no easy release. As noted earlier, the fact that the boundaries of Hobbesian fear can be redrawn so as to exclude fellow members of one's own 'bloc' does not mean that those boundaries can be removed altogether. In the Realists' view, only the creation of an international Leviathan could achieve such a feat, and since this is neither practicable nor desirable (who would control it?) nation-states simply have to devise foreign policy strategies that enable them to cope with the problem of Hobbesian fear as best they can.

Six Realist Propositions[7]

Indeed, with the concept of Hobbesian fear very much in mind, Realism offers a series of propositions which apply to all potentially conflictual situations in international politics. The first of these is that *the character of international relations is shaped primarily by political factors: the fundamental driving force behind the foreign policies of all states is the search for national security.* This is not to say that motives of economic gain and personal or national glory do not also operate, neither is it to deny that the form that the search for security takes will vary enormously over time and from country to country. It is merely to suggest that, in conditions of Hobbesian fear, the security motive is invariably the dominant one in the determination of foreign policy strategies.

A second proposition that Realism makes is that in any given security complex *the need to prevent 'the other side' from becoming too powerful acts as a powerful stimulus to pre-emptive expansionism.* Such expansionism tends to take two forms. On the one hand, it can involve a direct pre-emptive strike against an opponent's military capabilities, similar to the attack that the United States launched on Iraq in 2003.[8] On the other, it can involve an attempt to wrest control of part of an opponent's territory or 'sphere of influence'. The principle at work in both cases is simple: 'Do unto others before they do unto you'. Consider two relatively powerful states, A and B, which are located in the same security complex. If A fears that B may achieve a position of military superiority in the future – which may damage A's interests – A will be strongly tempted to deprive B of part of something important now in order to prevent B from achieving superiority in the future. B, in turn, fearful that A may be about to engage in some sort of pre-emptive strike, will be tempted to launch its own. In such a situation of Hobbesian fear, both A and B are predisposed to engage in expansionism of some kind.

What is even more disturbing about this condition of Hobbesian fear, however, is that even self-avowed neutrals are endangered by it. A is well aware that B might attempt to strengthen its resource base (and therefore its power capabilities) by extending its sphere of influence into the territory of a neutral state, C. Thus A has a strong incentive to try to incorporate C into *its* sphere of influence before B does. According to Realists, *A*'s principal motive in seeking to dominate *C* may well be unrelated to any desire to exploit *C* economically. Rather, *A*'s primary motive in expansion and domination is a self-protective, defensive one, deriving from the anarchic nature of the international system. If *A* does not dominate *C*, then eventually *B* (or *D* or *E* ...) will, and *A*'s relative power position (plus, therefore, its security) will be accordingly diminished. In the Realist view, as long as there is more than one state in *A*'s position (and invariably there is), expansionism and domination – that is, imperialism – will be an inevitable feature of international politics.

A third basic proposition concerns the role of cooperation in international affairs. According to the Realist model, *patterns of international friendship and antagonism are determined by the convergence or divergence of material and/or security interests.* Where material interests converge (for example, where there is abundant mutually beneficial trade) or where security interests converge (for example, where there is a 'common enemy' or a 'common threat'), then states will enjoy good relations. Conversely, where material or security interests diverge, inter-state relations will be at best tense and at worst overtly conflictual. The crucial corollary to this claim is that *both the extent and the consequences of cooperation in international politics are subordinated to the calculus of* realpolitik. Cooperation between nation-states is only possible to the extent that it is underpinned by a prior convergence of material-security interests. However, such cooperation has no real autonomy. It will only endure so long as the convergence of material-security interests itself endures; if national interests – for whatever reason – subsequently diverge, then no amount of prior cooperation will improve the prospects for good mutual relations in the future. All of this means that, given that the material and security interests of states tend to shift over time, so patterns of interest convergence and divergence also undergo continuous transformation and change. Indeed, in the Realist view, convergences of interest between nation-states are rarely stable in the long term, and foreign policy makers must accordingly make contingency plans for the protection of the nation's material and security interests which recognise that current friends, partners and allies may not remain so in the future. In the harsh world of international politics, it is the nation's 'vital interests' that matter, not emotional attachments to friends or former allies who may well have outlived their usefulness.

Realism's fourth proposition is concerned with the question of peace and war. From the discussion above, it is obvious that, in those situations where nations' material and security interests converge, peace is likely to ensue between or among them. The Realist does not argue, however, that interest divergence necessarily leads to war. On the contrary, if conditions are right, interest divergence can also be consistent with the maintenance of international peace. The crucial condition for the Realist in this context is the 'balance of power' or, more correctly, the prevailing 'balance of power capabilities'. *In any given security complex, if power capabilities are relatively evenly distributed between (or among) the potential protagonists, then a balance of power can be said to exist between (or among) them. Such a balance, in turn, produces a position of mutual deterrence in which each party calculates that it would incur more overall cost than overall benefit if it were to engage in aggression.* In these circumstances, for the Realist, peace is the consequence of a military 'stand-off' which is itself the consequence of a balance of power. Should the balance for whatever reason be broken then the result is likely to be a military confrontation between or among the states (or blocs) involved in the particular security complex, with the attendant danger of outside intervention from states located in other security complexes. In any event, the outcome of any conflict (like all outcomes in international politics) will be determined by the existing balance of *realpolitik* resources. In the world of the Realist, national (or bloc) ascendancy derives fundamentally from superior military and/or economic capability combined with political will. The strongest, the best organised and the most determined prevail.

A fifth Realist assertion states that the *role of legal and moral considerations in international politics is an ineffectual one.* For the Realist, the frequent claims of statesmen that they are acting according to the precepts of international law or some other 'higher morality' are largely if not entirely fraudulent. Rather, law and morality are used principally as *ex post* justifications for decisions already arrived at on the basis of hard-headed *realpolitik* calculations. According to the Realist account, this is indubitably true with regard to those issues that concern the nation's vital interests (that is, those areas that directly affect either national security, the fundamental character of the domestic political order or the fundamental health of the economy). Whenever conflicts involving vital interests arise, states not only refuse to refer unresolved disputes to any international legal process: they regard themselves as being unconstrained by prior legal commitments and obligations. Legal rectitude is invariably subordinated to Realist calculations aimed at protecting the national interest.

There is, however, one set of circumstances in which the Realist does allow a minor role for international law. With regard to issues that do not concern vital interests, decision-makers can afford to be magnanimous. Accordingly, in 'areas that do not really matter' nation-states can contentedly sign bilateral treaties and multilateral conventions that constrain their behaviour; they can likewise refer unresolved disputes to judicial tribunals with the full intention of accepting the tribunals' rulings even if they turn out to be unfavourable. For the Realist, however, such actions do not in any sense represent a commitment to the higher principle of the legal regulation of nation-state behaviour. Rather, both treaty making and the acceptance of judicial rulings are cynically derived from a self-interested belief in the value of reciprocity ('I am prepared to do x and/or not to do y if you will do the same'); and for the Realist reciprocity is based on nothing more than a cost–benefit 'What is in it for us?' *realpolitik* calculation aimed at advancing the nation-state's material and/or security interests.

The sixth and final proposition at the heart of the Realist approach concerns the role of economic motivations and forces in the determination of foreign policy behaviour. According to the Realist, as noted earlier, *the sense of Hobbesian fear that pervades inter-bloc and interstate relations invariably relegates economic factors to a subsidiary role in comparison with the deep-seated political imperatives of maximising security.* This is not to imply that economic forces cannot play an important role in certain situations. For example, in the relations between the rich countries of North America and Europe and the poorer countries of Africa and Latin America, economic factors are of obvious importance. American and European corporations wish to operate in the poorer countries in order to make profits that can be repatriated to the metropolitan homeland: Western governments, thankful of anything that will strengthen their balance of payments position, thus pursue policies that facilitate both the extraction of this economic surplus from the poor 'periphery' and its transfer back to the prosperous 'centre'.

From Structural to Neoclassical Realism

International politics, then, is fundamentally conflictual in character. Realism considers that the achievement and maintenance of national security is the paramount foreign policy goal. Moreover, it argues that national interests can only be maximised by the pursuit of cautious, self-regarding foreign policy strategies that are alert to the threat posed by potential aggressors abroad. We should distinguish, however, between the Structural Realist view and the Neoclassical (or classical) Realist approach referred to in the Introduction. While both see conflict between states as a recurrent feature of history, they ascribe this to different causes. For the classical realists like Hans Morgenthau, these recurrent features are explained by the flaws of human nature, or what he called the *animus dominandi*; human beings being what they are, conflict between selfish interests is inevitable.[9] For Structural or Neo-Realists like Kenneth Waltz, on the other hand, the cause of conflict is the nature of the international system itself. The system is anarchical, meaning not that it is necessarily disordered – although this can be the case – but rather that it lacks a centralised authority; it is like a game being played without a referee, and there is therefore nothing to prevent conflict from taking place. No world government, 'leviathan', or centralised political authority exists in the international system, and none is likely to appear because states zealously guard their own sovereignty (to the extent that they can). Within this overarching structure, different systems are possible; for instance, a system may be multipolar, bipolar or unipolar (that is, characterised by many states, by two states or by just one). The actions of states – including their foreign policies – are in large part shaped by what kind of system happens to exist, not by any domestic factor (which was ruled 'extraneous' to the approach). The originator of this brand of Realism, Kenneth Waltz, also explicitly disavowed an ability to fully explain foreign policy using his model (implicitly recognising that lower-level factors were indeed significant), although he maintained that Neo-Realism explains 'the big, important things'.[10]

Neoclassical Realism – which the reader will recall was originally discussed in our Introduction – has emerged since the 1990s as an alternative to Structural Realism, and it allows for domestic factors to matter just as much as systemic or structural ones (which was what Hans Morgenthau originally intended). Overall, the Structural Realist model was seen as rather too strident,[11] and it has attracted few explicit advocates other than Waltz himself and his former student John Mearsheimer.[12] One central problem with the theory is that 'structure is everything'; states were seen as more or less interchangeable within Structural Realism, so that – had the two dominant states been Canada and France after World War II, for instance[13] – we should have expected the same intense Cold War rivalry that was observed between the United States and the old Soviet Union. For many observers, though, the *domestic* character of the Cold War bipolar system – especially the contrasting ideologies of the two countries – was most critical here. Rather than simply the fact that there were two 'Great Powers' – the so-called 'polarity' of the international system – clashing beliefs at the domestic level probably mattered just as much, if not more. Many Realists were also frustrated by Neo-Realism's supposed inability to 'explain' foreign policy – a deficiency that was increasingly questioned.[14] Writing in 1991, Jack Snyder captured this feeling well in his book *Myths of Empire*, when he argued that 'Realism must be recaptured from those who look only at politics between societies, ignoring what goes on within societies'.[15]

Out of this counter-reaction came Neoclassical Realism, which accepts that a range of factors at different levels of analysis matter and maintains that foreign policy explanations are indeed possible.[16] The Realist response has not been to disavow the importance of structure – this still plays a significant role – but this development has meant a return to 'Morgenthauish' emphasis on lower-level factors. As we saw in the Introduction, Neoclassical realism continues to focus on the use of military capabilities to maximise British power and national interests in an anarchical world. For its part, Britain continues to be concerned with its own interests and with the maximisation of these. At the same time, it is constrained by its own declining military and economic power and by its (very much reduced) resources generally.

In a structural sense, Neoclassical Realism accepts that the nature of the international system, and the degree of material power which a state has within it, sets the broad parameters of a government's foreign policy. Britain's ambitions, for instance, are constrained by its material capabilities, and since the decline of Empire foreign adventures or interventions have been both difficult to sustain and rarely undertaken. On the other hand, states do not just respond to external 'demands'; while they are constrained by the polarity of the system (or number of superpowers within it), they enjoy a certain freedom to manoeuvre in choosing how to respond. There thus exists only an imperfect correlation between structural imperatives and the manner in which states actually behave (that is, between the amount of power we have and the nature and content of our foreign policy).

Of course, we have seen how Britain has sometimes stretched its military resources almost to their limits, as happened in Iraq and Afghanistan under the leadership of Tony Blair (see Chapters 6 and 8). In other words, it is up to the 'agent' or state to decide how it responds to constraints, and internal or domestic factors (such as the balance of power between state and society, a general commitment to the spread of democracy or a desire to divert attention away from the domestic economy) may prompt a state to behave in ways that could not have been predicted by examining its material power or role within the international system alone, strictly construed. Neoclassical Realists focus on a variety of 'unit-level' or domestic factors which cause foreign policy to only broadly reflect structural demands or objective material power.[17] Nevertheless, this perspective is still broadly based upon the Rational Actor model. This seeks to understand foreign policy behaviour as the goal-directed consequence of rational calculation by decision-makers. But domestic factors will influence the process as well and may 'get in the way'. As Amelia Hadfield-Amkhan puts it in her own Neoclassical Realist formulation, 'the new tripartite methodology thus incorporates the pursuit of power as the independent variable, a specific foreign policy outcome as the dependent variable, and domestic contextual influences (such as the perception of the nation or national power) as the intervening variable'.[18]

The approach we have taken in this book is especially consistent with Neoclassical Realism. It is clear that British foreign policy has conformed to broadly Structural Realist convictions; as the 'objective' structure of the international system has changed, so Britain's role in the world has altered too. Britain was once the 'hegemon' of the international system, and the system became bipolar as a result of World War II. But we have seen the significance of lower-level factors in the foregoing analysis as well. The change in foreign policy has not happened overnight, and it has not happened in quite the way suggested by Waltz in *Theory of International Politics*.[19] In reality, decisions like the one to withdraw from 'East of Suez' are reached only slowly, and with a great deal of deliberation and political pain. Technically, those decisions might have been taken in 1945. But there have been a number of delaying factors or 'time lags' which have caused Britain to adapt only slowly to structural changes. Interests matter in this process, but ideas and identity clearly matter as well. And as the 2016 European referendum illustrates above all, domestic politics is irretrievably a part of the process of foreign policy choice.

To be sure, not everyone is a Realist nowadays. Of the many policymakers who are committed to a Realist world-view, few would articulate their Realist convictions in quite such a formalised way as we present here. As we have seen, there has also been a notable Idealist bent to much British foreign policy since the days of Tony Blair, an approach which was also (at least partially) evident under David Cameron. Rhetorically at least, the UK now stands for 'values' as well as 'interests', and this is enshrined in British doctrine. But it is clear that Realism has dominated British foreign policy thinking since the late 1930s, and that it has been what we have termed the 'default' approach. It has undoubtedly been based on a number of simplified propositions, all of them directly traceable to the Realist approach outlined above. The more important of these simplified propositions – the practical principles of *realpolitik* – are summarised in Table 9.1.

The crucial sense in which these propositions are relevant to the analysis of Britain's post-war foreign policy is the way in which they informed the policymakers' priorities. Successive British governments during the post-war period certainly made reasoned calculations about the probable costs and benefits of alternative foreign policy actions and about the likelihood that a given course of action would maximise British interests, and many of these calculations rested on Realist foundations: the policymakers' Realist beliefs resulted in their insistence, on the one hand, that the paramount foreign policy goal would be the maintenance of national security and, on the other, that this primary objective could only be achieved if Britain possessed a strong defensive capability. Even before World War II was over, the British Cabinet had been convinced

Table 9.1 Simplified *realpolitik* principles illustrative of the Realist policymaker's world-views

Principle	Examples of application of the principle in 20th-century British foreign policy
(a) In wartime	
1. My enemy's enemy is my friend. If enemy A starts to fight enemy B, befriend whichever of the two represents the more distant threat in order jointly to eliminate the more immediate threat. However, prepare for renewed conflict with your newfound ally once the common threat has been eliminated.	Churchill's approaches to Stalin after the German invasion of the Soviet Union in June 1941. Even before the end of the war, Churchill was preparing to meet what he regarded as the inevitable post-war Soviet challenge to Europe's geostrategic stability.
(b) In peacetime	
2. If war seems imminent but you are militarily unprepared for it, play for time by using whatever diversionary tactics can be improvised.	Chamberlain's acquiescence to Hitler's demands to annex the Sudetenland in 1938 can be interpreted as following this proposition. However, the historical record (see Chapter 1) seems to contradict this interpretation.
3. Potential aggressors will remain unmoved by generous attempts to understand past injustices; by reasoned arguments about mutual interests in avoiding war; or by patient efforts aimed at securing an equitable compromise. Potential aggressors can only be deterred by firm and unambiguous threats, backed, if necessary, by credible military force.	(i) The creation of NATO in 1949 constituted a clear deterrent threat intended to thwart what were presumed to be Soviet designs on Western Europe (ii) The Anglo-French intervention at Suez was in part intended to deter Egypt from taking any further aggressive action against Western interests in that country.

4. Avoid situations where a potential aggressor possesses a preponderant military capability. Counter any significant military imbalance either by forming an alliance with a powerful state which shares your own security fears or by increasing your own military capability.

(i) The 1951–54 rearmament programme, initiated by Labour but continued by the Conservatives, aimed to reduce the alarming conventional imbalance between Soviet and NATO forces in the European theatre.

(ii) NATO's 3 per cent per annum increase in real defence spending 1979–84, to which Britain adhered, was intended to reinforce the credibility of NATO's anti-Warsaw Pact deterrent posture.

5. Since international politics, like nature, abhors a vacuum, retain control of overseas possessions for as long as possible. However, once effective control has either been lost or is about to be lost, a rapid withdrawal combined with the installation of a friendly government is preferable to a protracted withdrawal, because the latter is likely to strengthen the hand of indigenous forces antagonistic to your interests.

(i) The 'first-wave' decolonisations in India and Palestine in 1947–48.

(ii) The 'second-wave' decolonisations in Malaya, Africa and the Caribbean after 1956.

6. If you are forced to withdraw from potentially useful strategic locations because of commitments elsewhere, ensure that the territory thus vacated becomes part of the sphere of influence of your firmest and most trustworthy ally.

(i) The Attlee government's announcement in 1947 that it would no longer underwrite the anti-communist regimes in Greece and Turkey, on the understanding that under the newly proclaimed Truman Doctrine the Americans would take over these responsibilities.

(ii) The Labour government's granting of base facilities to the Americans at Diego Garcia after 1975 was intended to assist the US Navy in its efforts to police the Indian Ocean, following the Royal Navy's withdrawal in the early 1970s.

that the Soviet Union was pursuing an aggressive *realpolitik* strategy designed to erode the international position of the Western democracies. Moreover, from the mid-1940s through to the end of the Cold War, the Soviets did little to disabuse Britain's policymakers of this conviction. As far as successive British governments were concerned, the Soviet Union's enormous military capability, its growing influence in the third world and its expansionist ideology combined to constitute a profound Realist threat to Western interests that demanded a determined Realist response. Although London could afford to be distinctly 'un-Hobbesian' in its approach to its current friends, adopting a broadly cooperative posture towards them in matters of mutual economic benefit, the first priority of Britain's post-war foreign policy was always to ensure that the Soviets would never be tempted to take direct military action against Britain or its allies.

What the analysis presented in preceding chapters sought to demonstrate is that this world-view profoundly affected the development of Britain's post-war foreign policy. In the European and Atlantic 'circles' it played a crucial role in the creation of NATO in 1949. In the Empire circle – in a series of moves designed to inhibit communist encroachment in the Far East – it led Britain into Korea in 1950 and subsequently into SEATO in 1954 and CENTO in 1955. And as late as the 1980s it was also partly responsible for the firmly anti-Soviet posture adopted by the Thatcher government during the so-called 'Second Cold War'. In addition to providing valuable insights at the decision-making level of analysis, moreover, the Realist model has also been used in the present study to highlight the major 'structural' factors that affected Britain's post-war foreign policy. The main contribution of general Realist ideas in this regard derives from its assertion that the external behaviour of any nation-state depends fundamentally on the pattern of its economic and security interests: when these interests change, adjustments in foreign policy are likely to follow.

In this context the pattern of Britain's external trade can be regarded as a plausible indicator of where Britain's major overseas economic interests lie: an increase in trade with a given country over time can be considered to indicate a growing convergence of economic interests; a decline, to indicate a growing divergence. Using these notions, the Realist model provides a fairly compelling (if partial) explanation for the major strategic shift in Britain's post-war foreign policy strategy, away from the Empire-cum-Commonwealth and towards Western Europe, that occurred in the 1960s. The argument upon which this conclusion is based can be summarised as follows. In the 1940s and 1950s Britain's intimate military and political ties with the Empire circle were underpinned by its extensive trading relationship with Empire and Commonwealth countries.

(In 1955, for example, over half of British exports went to Empire circle destinations.) During the late 1950s and the 1960s, however, the focus of Britain's export trade experienced a marked and autonomous shift towards Western Europe: between 1955 and 1965 Western Europe's share of Britain's export trade rose from a third to a half; the Empire circle share fell from a half to a third over the same period. In different historical circumstances the effects of these changes might have been limited. By 2015, more than half of Britain's trade was within the European circle. The fact that Britain's economic interests were rapidly shifting towards Europe provided the British government with a powerful stimulus to concentrate more of its foreign policy and defence efforts in the European circle. In Realist terms, both the downgrading of the Empire and the higher priority accorded to Europe that occurred in the 1960s were the result, at least in part, of earlier and continuing shifts in Britain's material economic interests.

The Limitations of the Realist Model

Despite the extensive use that has been made of the Realist model in foreign policy analysis generally, the model itself is by no means immune from criticism. Indeed, as a characterisation of the world-views of Britain's post-war foreign policy makers, Realism can be subjected to two main criticisms. First, it could be argued, Realism's initial description of world politics as an essentially conflictual system populated by interest-maximising, self-regarding nation-states is wrong, or at least exaggerated. For one thing, there is far less conflict and far more cooperation about than the Realist model anticipates.[20] For another, the Realist's emphasis on the pattern of diverging and converging state interests significantly underemphasises the extent to which certain sub-national groupings in different countries (for example, 'financial capital') can share common interests that transcend national boundaries. 'Realist world-views' have not fully accorded with 'reality', and it may well be that their analysis of world events – and therefore, presumably, their policies – have in some sense been faulty. But if policymakers *believe* that international politics is a *realpolitik* game, whether or not it 'really' is, they will frame their policies on the basis of that belief. The claim that the policymakers' world-views did not reflect 'the way things really were' – though it may be correct – is thus irrelevant to the sort of decision-making analysis presented here. This leads us in a Constructivist and Cognitivist direction, as we shall see below.

A second way of criticising the use that the foregoing analysis has made of Realism is to suggest that Britain's post-war foreign policy makers may not actually have held Realist world views at all; indeed, we have seen that Idealism has come back into vogue since the days of Tony Blair. This criticism alludes in part to a more general accusation that is frequently levelled at the Realist model: that it is so amorphous and flexible that supporting evidence for *realpolitik* calculation can be found in almost every decision-making situation. Indeed, the argument continues, the present analysis has consistently found evidence of such calculation in foreign policy decision-making simply because it has consistently looked for it: if the analysis had searched for evidence of something else, it might have found that instead. One response to this criticism is to argue (1) that the mere fact that an analyst finds something, for example *realpolitik* calculation, almost every time s/he looks for it cannot be taken as evidence that the phenomenon in question does *not* exist; and (2) that accordingly it is incumbent upon the critic to demonstrate that the policymakers' world-views were based on something other than Realism.

Such a response, however, does not demonstrate definitively that Realism did indeed constitute the default 'world-view' of Britain's post-war foreign policy makers. Moreover, it has to be admitted that the analysis presented here has not provided such a demonstration. It is certainly the case that most of Britain's post-war foreign policy makers behaved *as if* they adhered to a Realist world-view. But we simply do not know what goes on inside policymakers' heads, even though we can make informed inferences on the basis of their spoken and written comments. In practical terms, what all of this means is that, at worst, the present study has provided a series of *metaphorical* explanations for the foreign policy decisions of successive post-war British governments: it has 'explained' those decisions 'as if' they were (generally) based on the Realist calculations of the policymakers. At best, it has provided a set of falsifiable *causal* explanations (that posit causal connections between the policymakers' Realist world-views and their policy decisions) that are in principle testable but which still await definitive confirmation because the necessary empirical evidence has yet to be assembled.[21]

The most important criticism that is made of Realism (both as structural theory and in its Neoclassical variation) is that it is *non-falsifiable*. It is alleged that, because of the flexible way in which the theory is formulated, no empirical evidence could ever be adduced that could not somehow be interpreted as being consistent with it; to the extent that Realism offers a 'true' analysis of international politics, it is an analysis that is true by definition – not one that has been rigorously tested against the available empirical evidence. And yet – while many Realist propositions are *not* falsifiable – a similar limitation also applies to almost all theories in the social and physical sciences.[22] Indeed, the analytic core of most theories is couched in an abstract language that is rarely susceptible to empirical testing. What matters is that the theory generates at least some propositions that are capable of being tested. The way that Realism has been employed as a mostly structural theory in the present analysis belies the accusation that Realism offers little more than sophisticated tautology. The substantive argument advanced earlier – that the changing pattern of Britain's economic interests in the 1950s and 1960s provided the main impetus behind the British government's strategic shift towards the European 'circle' during the 1960s and 1970s – certainly involved a non-tautological hypothesis that was in principle capable of being falsified. The statistical evidence that was reported regarding the changes that occurred in Britain's overseas trade after 1955 provided empirical corroboration for the hypothesis that changing national interests were at the root of the changes in Britain's foreign policy strategy. In short, the foregoing analysis did treat Realism as a falsifiable structural theory: it simply established that one of Realism's key falsifiable predictions was supported by the available empirical evidence.

Realism, then, though it has certain limitations, has undoubtedly provided valuable explanatory insights into Britain's post-war foreign policy. What of the other theoretical perspectives that were reviewed earlier, though? The reader should recall from the Introduction that while Neoclassical Realism is an approach which emphasises the role of *interests* (the British national interest, constrained by its power), Constructivism stresses the impact of *identities* (our collective images about ourselves and other nations) and Cognitivism focuses on idiosyncratic *ideas* (individual-level psychological perceptions of, and beliefs about, the world) that policymakers hold. Bureaucratic Politics, or the other hand, looks at how the operation of *institutions* frames the debate and at how 'pulling and hauling' between the representatives of different organisations shapes the selection of foreign policy options.[23] As noted above, although Realism has been the dominant theoretical perspective employed in the present study, the discussion has also been informed by several other approaches: at the structural level, by the Constructivist perspective and at the decision-making level, by the Cognitivist and Bureaucratic Politics approaches. How far can such explanations 'round out' the spare emphasis on objective structural factors? The fact that British decision-makers may only have *perceived* that Realism provided the best approach – regardless of whether it really does or not – suggests the significance of approaches based upon the role of ideas, and it is to such approaches that we turn next.

The Contribution of Other Theoretical Approaches

The Constructivist Approach

A social constructivist account of British foreign policy would stress Britain's sense of collective *identity*.[24] The fact that Britain 'sees itself' in the way that it does is critical to this approach. The past is very much a part of Britain's identity,[25] for instance, and has left it with a distinctive kind of 'imperial hangover'. The UK, according to this view, is still a major player in international politics, and can never perform the kind of role that (say) neutral Switzerland adopts vis-à-vis the rest of the world. This is because Britain does not see itself as a neutral or passive actor in shaping events; instead, it views itself as a major participant, and has 'constructed' an identity for itself which continues to emphasise this (even in the face of 'real' decline).

Although it was articulated as long ago as 1970 – and in fact, as Chancellor of the Exchequer Roy Jenkins had argued in a public speech in 1967 that the devaluation of that year and the withdrawal East of Suez meant that 'we are recognising that we are no longer a Superpower'[26] – there has been a general refusal in many quarters (and across the political parties that have held high office) to accept the 'power of the second rank' thesis articulated in this book.[27] The reader should note, for instance, the claim enshrined in the 2010 National Security Strategy that there will be 'no strategic shrinkage' in foreign policy, a belief which belies Britain's relatively minor capacity to act in both the Libyan crisis of 2011 and in the war against the so-called 'Islamic State' after 2014. But if we want to explain British actions abroad, we must focus on *ideational* rather than simply material factors. We must look at why the UK thinks it is 'different' from other states, both in its own eyes and in the views of others, and we must consider in particular the fact that it still considers itself 'exceptional'. According to social constructivists, it is the British sense of identity – its own self-image, as well as its images of others as 'friends' or 'foes' – which shapes what we think our national interests are in the first place. As emphasised in the Introduction, according to this view identities tell us *who* we are, as well as *how* we ought to behave in the world. We live by the ideas that we create.[28]

In applying this approach, consider again the Falklands War of 1982 between Britain and Argentina.[29] Arguably, Realism offers only a weak explanation for the British re-invasion, as David McCourt suggests.[30] After all, there was no vital national interest at stake for Britain in that crisis – the islands were of little economic value, for instance – and nor was Britain's physical security threatened by the invasion.[31] This is a case where constructivism or some other idea-based approach should apply, where the pure appearance of things mattered more than reality. The conflict over the Falklands took the form of a 'war of narratives' to define what was happening; while Argentina tried to portray Britain as a colonial power, Britain chose and was able to play what can be termed a *status quo-oriented power* role, with a large stake in the norms of international order, and the capacity and right to remove Argentina by military means… Importantly, the *status quo* oriented role Britain tried to play was meaningful because it was accepted by important Others in the international community'.[32] McCourt therefore claims that it was Britain's role within the international system that mattered, rather than any domestic or 'sub-systemic' factor.

The application of Constructivism to British foreign policy may be criticised on a number of grounds, of course. Just as there are different kinds of Realism, so there are different types of Constructivism. While this is not the place to dive extensively into the key debates, one key distinction is between unit and structural-level approaches.[33] Structural-level constructivism is associated in particular with Alexander Wendt, who argues that identities are derived mainly from the international system.[34] This does not sit especially well with the approach adopted here, however, since Britain's identity in the world seems to have come mostly from domestic sources. A second criticism is that Britain does not have one identity but several, so that policymakers must effectively choose between them.[35] This makes us wonder what use we might make of any notion of 'collective identity'. A third criticism is that there are profound limits to an approach which focuses only on identity and on the construction of reality, both because (a) objective interests play a powerful constraining role and (b) the individual construction of reality matters as well. This approach arguably emphasises the ideational world too much at the expense of the objective interests. Equally, it may not delve deep enough, in the sense that (unlike Cognitivism) it does not examine perceptions and beliefs which are not collectively shared. Fourth, like Realists, Constructivists are also open to the criticism that their approach is a non-falsifiable 'grab bag', a general approach from which one can take what one wants rather than a testable theory *per se*. Fifth, there may be ways of incorporating identity within existing models that emphasise interest; for instance, as Hadfield-Amkhan argues in an avowedly Neoclassical Realist account, identity may be treated as an 'intermediary variable' between interest and policy.[36] Finally, it should be emphasised that Constructivism has not yet developed into a normative approach to policymaking in the way that *realpolitik* has, with the result that it lacks the kind of explanatory reach that we have claimed for Realism in this book. There is as yet no '*konstructpolitik*', a practical guide which might tell the Constructivist policymaker what approaches are most consistent with the overall theory.

But identity clearly matters, whether it comes from domestic sources or anything else. At the very least, Constructivism adds something useful to a nakedly Realist account of British foreign policy. It looks 'behind' national interests to examine why a state like Britain views its own interests in the way that it does. From this perspective, Realism is itself a social construction, a way of looking at the world that is not necessarily correct. In that sense, much of the foregoing analysis might be seen as entirely *consistent* with Constructivist views. Objectively, perhaps, Britain ceased many years ago to play a world role, but that is not is not usually how it views itself. As we shall see in the next section, perception matters a great deal in international relations, just as much perhaps as any 'objective' reality.

The Cognitivist Approach

In order to fully understand the Cognitivist and Bureaucratic Politics approaches to decision-making, we first need to understand the 'Rational Actor' model that each is *reacting* to. The Rational Actor approach seeks to understand foreign policy behaviour as the goal-directed consequence of rational calculation by decision-makers, calculation that aims in some sense to maximise the national interests of the nation-state which the decision-makers represent.[37] Not surprisingly, according to this model it is the policymakers' decision calculus that is the stuff of foreign policy analysis. What were the major aims of a particular foreign policy decision? Why was this option chosen from among the available alternatives? What calculations were made about the intentions and capabilities of military rivals or enemies? What assumptions were made about the likely behaviour of other nation-states? While these questions offer only a glimpse into the kind of elements that might enter into a full analysis of foreign policy based on the Rational Actor model, they do indicate where the analyst should look both for 'explanatory factors' and for evidence: at the decision-makers themselves, at their sources of information, at their purposes, intentions and beliefs, as revealed both in personal memoirs and in official minutes, memoranda and briefing papers.

While neither the Cognitivist nor the Bureaucratic Politics approach completely abandons this Rational Actor approach, both stress its limitations (each is an 'imperfectionist' approach in this sense). As we saw early on, Cognitivists focus on psychology, on the beliefs, personalities and mindsets of leaders. If we want to understand why Britain acts as it does in relation to the rest of the world, we need to delve into individual decision-making episodes. In particular, we ought to look at the cognitive beliefs and past experiences of particular decision-makers, and not just at *socially shared* conceptions about what Britain is or ought to be doing. Eden may have viewed Britain's role rather differently from the way Attlee viewed it, for instance, and it is almost certain (as we saw in Chapter 6) that Major viewed Britain's foreign policy role in a different way from Blair.

The Cognitive approach emphasises the psychological imperfections of human beings, especially our tendency to undertake an array of cognitive short cuts; indeed, some recent research suggests that we may be born 'hard wired' with a tendency to make the errors which result from these.[38] Individual-level *ideas* and perceptions of the world matter, but these can prove impervious to change. Rather than slavishly following the dictates of the Rational Actor approach, we have a tendency to ignore evidence which does not 'fit' our existing beliefs, for instance.[39] We often discard or downplay information that cannot be assimilated within our existing 'world-views' or that suggests we are wholly wrong. Cognitive dissonance theory suggests that we see what we *want* to see, for instance, while schema theory contends that we see what we *expect* to see.[40] Such an approach differs from Structural Realism in emphasising that 'objective' factors do not automatically exert an impact on decision-making, and they are especially useful in explaining the 'lag' between objective changes and their subjective interpretation.

It is not our intention here to adjudicate between these approaches, but suffice it to say we can see evidence of both wishful thinking and 'seeing what you expect to see' in the previous chapters, although we have not explicitly referred to the psychology of decision-making in the main body of the text. If we return to the central theme of this book – Suez as a major 'turning point' in British foreign policy – we can see that this is relevant to the foregoing. As we saw in Chapter 4, during the Suez affair in 1956 Prime Minister Anthony Eden and his colleagues ignored evidence that the United States would not support Britain's venture (along with France and Israel) into Egypt. President Dwight Eisenhower had made it perfectly clear to British decision-makers that the US did not favour such an action, but the UK government chose to listen to more 'ambiguous' signals that Secretary of State John Foster Dulles was sending. In the end, however, a historical analogy – Iran in 1953 – proved to exert an especially powerful effect on British minds. The latter suggested that the United States would 'come in line', as they had done in 1953 under Eisenhower (the same president, only three years before). Eden clearly did not want the Americans to withdraw their support, but nor did he expect them to. Analogies frequently lead us astray, however, since we do not appreciate the differences between situations. Equally, we seem to use analogies over and over again, since they give us a way to make sense of a very complex and uncertain reality.[41] As we saw in Chapter 6, the Malayan and Northern Ireland analogies also had a pervasive effect on the British intervention within Helmand Province, Afghanistan, because they suggested a supposed ability to 'do' counterinsurgencies.

More generally, it is clear that emotion plays a powerful role in decision-making as well, as illustrated again by Thatcher's handling of the Falklands issue in 1982. At a very deep level, the Prime Minister was quite clearly offended by the Argentine seizure of what she regarded as British property, and felt a powerful sense of empathy with the islanders themselves. While the bureaucratic intervention of Admiral Henry Leach was important – as we shall see in the next section – he was in a sense knocking at an open door, since Thatcher seemed to have already determined (on the grounds of 'patriotism') that a Task Force should be sent to re-establish British control. The case also illustrates the importance of misperception in foreign policy decision-making.[42] As Lebow notes, the case featured a kind of 'double misperception': decision-makers in London did not expect the Argentines to seize the islands in the first place, and General Galtieri equally did not anticipate such a strong British response.[43] The Nott review of 1981 had effectively sent the message that Britain did not 'care' about the Falkland islands, and the Argentines underestimated the patriotic fervour that their forcible seizure would cause in London. This is somewhat ironic, since the Argentine generals seem to have been amply aware of the effect that this would have in Buenos Aires.

The Bureaucratic Politics Approach

Like the Cognitivist approach, the Bureaucratic Politics view of foreign policy analysis questions the Rational Actor model and notes its limitations. Briefly stated, it makes two central assumptions: first of all, that nation-states are not necessarily unitary actors; and, second, that policy may be the result more of a political compromise among competing bureaucratic and political elites than of a rational attempt by decision-makers to maximise the attainment of a defined and agreed set of goals.[44] Thus the Bureaucratic Politics model is concerned to establish, for example, how far different factions within government seek to effect foreign policy decisions commensurate with their preferred goals; how the different administrative departments and different factions within them vary in importance; what strategies are pursued by particular factions and groupings in order to ensure that *their* conception of 'departmental' or 'national' interest prevails. The Bureaucratic Politics model, in short, focuses on a much wider set of actors and influences than the Rational

Actor model would seem to allow – though, significantly, the evidential base required for the application of both models is broadly the same.

While the Rational Actor and Bureaucratic Politics approaches are separate models – in the theoretical literature the distinction between them is almost axiomatic – in fact the distinction can be pressed too far. As Freedman has noted, most contemporary narrative analysis of British foreign policy actually uses a mixture of both models.[45] Despite being conceptually distinct, the two models are in fact mutually compatible and can be jointly applied to the same empirical materials without serious difficulty or contradiction. In particular, the Bureaucratic Politics approach retains the rationality assumption but merely moves it downwards in the ladder of analysis, treating organisations as rational and self-interested rather than states. Advocates of this approach, though, are concerned to examine the inter- and intra-departmental manoeuvring that precedes the taking of a given decision, as different factions jockey to ensure that the policy which is finally selected accords as closely as possible with their own preconceptions of what the national interest is.

In the preceding discussion of Realism, the present study made indirect and implicit use of the Rational Actor model in the context of a changed international structure: although the policy priorities and calculations of Britain's policymakers were bounded by their Realist world-views, they in general followed a rational calculus in arriving at their policy decisions. Put simply, it has been argued that the retreat from Empire and the move towards the EU was a rational response to the changed situation in which Britain found itself in the 1950s and 1960s. The world role and the intimate connection with the Empire circle had been established at a time when Britain was one of the world's richest states and when the Royal Navy really did rule the waves. The post-war world was very different, however, and there was virtually nothing that successive governments could do to change it. The two superpowers could not be magically demoted, and the rising tide of indigenous nationalism in the colonies could not be reversed by parliamentary fiat. The problems of the ailing British economy, moreover, seemed to defy all efforts to remedy them. In this new situation, old solutions promised scant return. To have attempted to repress indigenous nationalism throughout the whole of British Africa and the Caribbean – along the lines pursued in Malaya and Kenya – would have been far beyond the physical capabilities of Britain's armed forces.

Although the present study has not accorded much explicit emphasis to the Bureaucratic Politics model, this should not be taken to imply that the interplay of bureaucratic pressures were unimportant in the determination of Britain's post-war foreign policy. On the contrary, there were a number of occasions when such pressures achieved prominence in the policy process, although we will provide only a few examples here. The Attlee government's decision to embark on a massive rearmament programme in December 1950, for example, was influenced to a considerable – and unusual – degree by the advice proffered by the Joint Chiefs of Staff regarding the seriousness and the imminence of the Soviet threat to British security. Throughout the debate on the acquisition of Britain's 'independent nuclear deterrent', moreover, there was tremendous factional rivalry among the three service ministries as to what sort of delivery system the deterrent should use, a competition that was duly won by the Royal Navy in December 1962 when Macmillan and Kennedy struck their deal over Polaris.

This kind of bureaucratic infighting has probably always been evident, but it has become even more noticeable since the emergence of the Royal Air Force (RAF) after World War I. Lord Hugh Trenchard's new body had to fight for its survival against two older services intent on taking their power back. The emergence of the new airforce increased the amount of bureaucratic infighting within the Ministry of Defence by one third almost at a stroke, because there was now a 'third force' competing for scarce resources.[46] According to Ledwidge, inter-service rivalry in Britain has become 'truly toxic', moreover.[47] He singles out the RAF – obsessed, as he sees it, with its own survival – for particular criticism, but does not exempt his own former service (the Navy) or the Army. 'Whilst the RAF is the most regular and long-standing offender', he contends, 'it is not the only service that places its welfare and survival above national interests'. The Army in particular insisted on going to Helmand in 2006 in order to justify its own (substantial) budget, while the Navy – facing very substantial cuts under the Nott defence review – had done much the same thing during the 1982 Falklands War (when Sir Henry Leach, First Lord of the Admiralty, made extraordinary efforts to persuade Margaret Thatcher that the Navy could send a Task Force 8,000 miles to retake the islands). Arguably, each capitalised on an event to press the case for what its organisation 'could do', and such bodies can come to genuinely believe the arguments that they use to justify their own cause. In 1942, for instance, the Navy was still convinced that battleships could not be destroyed by aircraft. Just as the Air Force has long claimed that carriers are a waste of money because they are vulnerable to bombers, so the Navy had come to believe (before the destruction of HMS *The Prince of Wales* by Japanese bombers during World War II) that its ships were invulnerable to attack from the air and were hence 'superior' to planes.

Bureaucratic Politics was very much in evidence during the first Wilson government in the 1960s, when the three services resisted the inevitable cuts which accompanied the 'East of Suez' withdrawal, and this debate re-ignited before and after 2010. In the late 1950s and early

1960s, the RAF needed a long-range strike and reconnaissance aircraft, and its preferred solution was the highly advanced TSR2. The plane was way ahead of its time, the envy of the Americans at a time when Britain had a 'real' aircraft industry. It would be blighted by cost overruns and technological delays from the start, however, and the TSR2 project was eventually cancelled in 1965 in favour of the purchase of F-111s from the United States 'off the shelf'. While at first blush this might seem like a comprehensively rational decision, the real picture was much more murky. The F-111 option was supposed to be much cheaper, but this project also repeatedly ran into costly overruns, and this option too was eventually abandoned. The cancellation of the TSR2, moreover, was to have momentous economic consequences internally, for it would signal the beginning of the end for the British aircraft industry. Many of those who had manufactured the TSR2 in Britain would soon join the 'brain drain' to America, where bigger salaries and more reliable jobs were to be had. Put simply, a long-term technological capability had been sacrificed for short-term economic gain.

From the start, bureaucratic rivalries and inter-service haggling were a central feature of TSR2's existence. Denis Healey – Britain's Defence Secretary for much of the 1960s – has suggested that the RAF was originally given the TSR2 project in the 1950s as a kind of bureaucratic 'compensation' for losing nuclear weapons delivery to the Navy, since nuclear submarines were thought to provide a better second-strike capability than the RAF-operated V-Bombers (which could potentially be taken out from the air).[48] Whether this was true or not is unclear, but it certainly accords with the manner in which the Chiefs approached the TSR2 issue from then on. The Navy was (equally strongly) wedded to its (equally expensive) CVA-01 carrier. As Chairman of the Defence Staff (CDS), Lord Louis Mountbatten (a former head of the Navy) realised that Britain could not afford both in an era of increasingly limited resources, and he decided that TSR2 would have to go. Determined to kill off the plane project, he enraged the Chief of the Air Staff, Sir Charles Elsworthy, by siding against TSR2 in private and in favour of the Navy's own pet project, the aircraft carrier.[49] Mountbatten wanted the RAF to settle for the Blackburn Buccaneer, which was cheaper and far less advanced but which was compatible with the Navy's aircraft carriers. But the Royal Air Force's position was that Britain did not need expensive and vulnerable aircraft carriers; overseas bases could be used instead. It argued that the UK needed to retain the ability to deliver nuclear weapons by air, something that would require the powerful long-range capabilities of a TSR2.

The Treasury, from its 'perch' in the government, was as always concerned about spiralling costs. Its principal interest was in cutting back the cost of TSR2, something which became increasingly easier to do with delay after delay. The Ministry of Aviation and the Board of Trade, on the other hand, were concerned that buying a plane *overseas* might inflate the already precarious balance of payments deficit.[50] As the infighting and jostling continued, Mountbatten even appears to have suggested to representatives of other countries (including potential buyers of the aircraft like Australia) that the TSR2 would never go into service! As Sir Frank Cooper later noted, 'Mountbatten actively discouraged [Air Chief Marshal Frederick] Scherger – his Australian opposite number'.[51] Together with the equally sceptical Sir Solly Zuckerman, the government's Chief Scientific Adviser, Mountbatten engaged in what Cooper calls back-stage 'clandestine operations'. Although it seems that the Australians already had doubts about TSR2, this must have been the final nail in the coffin. This tactic was, moreover, quite useful to the bureaucratic knife fighter – a skill at which Mountbatten was highly adept – since it could now be argued that no one else in the world was buying the aircraft, adding to the perception that TSR2 was simply not cost effective in an era when Britain could no longer afford to develop an aircraft which did not sell overseas. Had the Australians actually bought the plane, it might have provided 'a powerful, and perhaps decisive, counterweight' to the critics.[52] But as Damien Burke notes, 'it is particularly shameful that the behaviour of all three branches of the armed forces conspired to cause such damage to the nation's defence, with single-Service needs being put above all else, regardless of the consequences'.[53] Oddly enough, following cancellation everything was destroyed apart from one or two TSRs that would go to air museums. All the rest were scrapped or used for target practice on Army shooting ranges. The RAF were initially asked to take on the US F-111s instead, and when that purchase was cancelled in 1968, it was ironically left with the Buccaneers it had opposed all along.

Students of Bureaucratic Politics often worry that the main result might be that policy choices end up with 'the least common denominator' (that thing which keeps everyone minimally satisfied but doesn't really represent what anyone actually *wanted*). Just as damaging, perhaps, is a situation where nothing gets done because each organisation cancels out the others. Most ironically, perhaps, nobody got what they wanted in this case, since the CVA-01 carrier would itself fall victim to wrangling between the Navy, the Treasury and a vengeful RAF. As Jackson and Bramall note, 'the Carrier battle, which opened shortly afterwards, was a brutal gladiatorial contest in which the Navy and Air Force were fighting each other for their lives'.[54] One reason that the Navy had been opposed to the TSR2 was that the initial cost estimates for their carrier depended on them using the same planes as the RAF; thus the existence of the

TSR2 directly threatened the CVA-01. But with the TSR2 gone, the path was clear for the carrier. The Navy argued that the CVA-01 was needed because planes were getting bigger and heavier, so much so that this factor was rendering the ageing *Ark Royal* and *Eagle* obsolete.[55] But again, cost became an issue in the 'East of Suez' era. The Treasury insisted that cutback after cutback be made, with the result that the CVA-01 ended up being a much smaller vessel than originally intended.

And the RAF was not done attacking the whole project, either. It argued – successfully as it turned out – that Australia and other islands could be used as land bases for their aircraft instead. As Childs notes, 'many Navy veterans still believe the RAF cheated in making its arguments in the 1960s that its land-based aircraft could do the job of the carriers, by producing maps that showed Singapore 400 miles closer to Australia than it really is'.[56] Variations on that story have the RAF moving Australia by as little as 200 or as much as 1,000 miles.[57] It has never been clear whether this is true or not – the story is, perhaps, an apocryphal exaggeration of the inter-service rivalry which blighted UK defence policy then and now – but if true it would certainly accord with the claim that aircraft carriers were not needed and that relatively cheap land bases would do just as well. When CVA-01 was cancelled in 1966, the First Sea Lord Sir David Luce and the Navy Minister Christopher Mayhew both resigned in furious protest.

The debate about planes and carriers has continued to the present. Ironically, in the 1960s it was the Conservative Party which had acceded to various service demands and Labour which sought to cut these back, while the reverse became true of the period after 2010. But the Navy and RAF have not fundamentally changed their positions, in part because their bureaucratic interests have not really changed in the intervening years; the Cold War has been and gone, but organisational interests are far more durable, transcending the coming and going of particular events and personalities. Not coincidentally, the TSR2 and CVA cancellation recall the more recent debate over planes, carriers and cash. By the 1998 review, the Navy was again in the bureaucratic ascendant, in part because its vision of a long-range expeditionary capability dovetailed rather nicely with Tony Blair's notion of making Britain 'a force for good' in the world. Possessing the ability to 'go anywhere and do anything' would be integral to that vision, and the navy had long advocated the kind of long-range capabilities that would allow that to happen. The RAF position was again that the UK could do without costly carriers, which would also be vulnerable to anti-ship missiles and would therefore require escorting ships and submarines to defend them. But the navy position won the day, and the construction of the massive HMS *Queen Elizabeth* is the result (essentially the carrier that the navy has wanted all along). A second carrier, HMS *Prince of Wales*, is supposed to be in the pipeline as well, but there seems little prospect (at the time of writing) of it ever being used.

The 1960s debate also recalls the recent scrapping of nine brand-new Nimrod reconnaissance aircraft that had cost £3.6 billion and the cancellation of the Harrier jump-jet after 2010. The newly minted planes were literally broken up in their hangers, never to be used in combat or as anything else. The cancellation of the Nimrod – which occurred as part of the Cameron government's substantial package of defence cuts – was projected to pay for itself in about twenty years; until then, it would actually *cost* money to cancel, and in the meantime Britain would lack the capabilities that the Nimrod delivered. Instead, it was hoped that Allies could perform the long-range reconnaissance functions that the Nimrod was supposed to provide. As Matt Cavenagh, who served as a government adviser before 2010, notes:

> The optimal approach would be for each [service] to recommend cuts as well as enhancements, and for all their recommendations to be put into a joint or central strategic decision-making process, with all agreeing to abide by the outcome. But of course the best strategy for each – and what is clearly expected of them by their service and their peers – is to refuse to recommend any cuts, to fight for their service and, where necessary, brief against the others.[58]

Cavenagh cites the decision to do away with the Harrier jump-jet after 2010 as a classic case of 'inter-service haggling'. From a strategic point of view, the cancellation made little or no sense, since it left the UK military building aircraft carriers for which there will be no actual aircraft until 2020. It also made little economic sense because it did not save much money, not least since it was tied to a huge investment in Rolls-Royce engines already agreed to. Potentially, about £500 million paid by the Ministry of Defence to Rolls-Royce to develop vertical take-off engines similar to those using in the Harrier had been wasted.[59] Moreover, Britain may be confronted by a crisis well before 2020 which forces it to purchase more expensive carrier-based aircraft from a friendly nation 'off the shelf'. As Cavenagh puts it, the Harrier decision makes little sense from the perspective of either economics or strategy 'until you realize that it saves face for both the chief of the Naval Staff, who gets to keep the carrier, and the chief of the Air Staff, who gets to keep the Tornado'.[60] In spite of the long-running series of cost-cutting 'defence reviews' (see the previous chapter), and notwithstanding the ending of Britain's role 'East of Suez', moreover, the proportion of national GDP devoted to defence remained remarkably stable (around 5–7 per cent) throughout much of the post-war period, and has only recently fallen to a more realistic level (around 2 per cent). The stability of this figure was testimony to the tenacity of both the service chiefs and the defence industry lobby in persuading a succession of governments that Britain's security relied upon the continuation of a strong – and up-to-date – military capability.

Summary and Conclusions

Foreign policy research – indeed, social research of any sort, is rarely conducted in a theoretical vacuum. What this chapter has endeavoured to show is the extent to which the narrative account of Britain's post-war foreign policy provided in the previous chapters can be guided by different theoretical considerations. This is not to say that any of the theories described in this chapter have been systematically tested against Britain's post-war foreign policy experiences. Rather, the different theories have been used to inform description and explanation, to provide guidelines and signposts as to which observations are important and which are not.

What is clear from the foregoing discussion is that each of the theoretical approaches identified earlier has made some sort of contribution to the analysis present here. Indeed, although each perspective has been presented as a discrete position, the ideas summarised under the different headings are in many ways quite compatible with one another. In particular, the reader should note that the default belief in Realism among policymakers which we have emphasised here is quite compatible with Cognitivism, and an emphasis on structure is quite compatible with developments in Realist theory since 1990. Equally, Britain's sense of identity as a major player in the world has greatly delayed a 'rational' response to the UK's much reduced circumstances, as Constructivism has noted. Bureaucratic Political factors, especially the lobbying of various organisations to maintain defence spending on their own pet projects, have traditionally reduced the ability to adapt to changed conditions as well.

Chapter 10

British Foreign Policy in the 21st Century

At the time of writing, Britain appears to have cut off one of its own major strategic choices: namely, the historical move towards Europe, which had been motivated in large part by the economic interests that derive from trade. Only time will tell what results from the 'Brexit' vote, of course, but from our own perspective the referendum decision that the UK should leave the EU may prove to be a strategic error even more serious than Anthony Eden's at Suez (examined in depth in previous chapters). Eden's foray into latter-day gunboat diplomacy failed to achieve its own objectives and accelerated the loss of Empire, but it did not pose the existential threat to the UK's future that Brexit did. Cameron's error was much more egregious. Eden failed in 1956 to understand how Britain's strategic position had changed. Cameron, however, was much better informed and understood the strategic position very well. He knew that Britain possessed vital interests within each of Churchill's 'three circles': in the Commonwealth and the third world; in the special relationship with the United States; and, especially, in Europe. He also knew that for over 40 years Britain's European strategy had been predicated on its membership of the EU, and that continued membership of the EU was clearly the best way of maximising Britain's economic and political interests in Europe and beyond. Cameron gambled (recklessly in our view) that a referendum on EU membership would produce a Remain outcome when any competent political analyst could have told him that UK public support for the EU was strongly moved by external 'shocks' like the 2007/8 credit crunch and the Eurozone crisis after 2009. It was (at least in retrospect) sheer folly to call a referendum when the EU itself was suffering from the continuing effects of the Euro crisis and the world's worst refugee crisis since World War II. Cameron's successor, Theresa May, faces an even more limited menu of choice as a result. 'Equally, the ascendancy of Donald Trump to the US presidency potentially threatens a global economic system which has existed since the end of WWII'.

This book began with Winston Churchill's famous 'three circles' speech of October 1948. The three circles leitmotif continues to animate most underlying thinking about Britain's role today, as the 'Britain as a bridge', 'pivot', 'hub' or the 'centre of a networked world' notions used by much later politicians show. We have used the three circles as an organising device in this book, and as we saw early on, it remains relevant today as a simplifying tool among both those who study British foreign policy and those who actually make it.[1] Can Britain ultimately continue to 'punch above its weight', given the realities of economic decline, changes in the international structure of power since 1945 and continued economic pressure on Britain's military and diplomatic resources? Or will Britain's foreign policy die the death of a thousand (defence) cuts, in an age of deepening austerity? In this final chapter, we will re-visit the overall question of Britain's role in a world, which has obviously changed very substantially since the days of Empire and the Cold War.

Rather surprisingly perhaps, there has been relatively little debate or discussion about Britain's role in the world in recent years. We have to go back to the Thatcher years to find a major debate about whether Britain's decline is reversible, though her governments were unusual in the sense that they actually sought to stem the tide of British decline. All of those before (and all of those since) have essentially accepted that decline as an established fact to be managed, to the extent that this is possible, and then proceeded to shape foreign and defence policy around it. This has sometimes been an explicit admission – as we saw in Chapter 8, it was acknowledged as early as 1975 in Roy Mason's review, and arguably in Harold Wilson's 1968 East of Suez speech – and sometimes not. Sometimes governments seem to go into psychological denial about this, as arguably happened with Blair and with Cameron's 'no strategic shrinkage' claim. But in the years since Thatcher left office, it has rarely been addressed.

Perhaps as a consequence of this, there has also been little intellectual progression or hard thinking done about Britain's place in the world since the 1980s. With the brief exception perhaps of the 1998 *Strategic Security Review*, British governments have rarely considered what Britain's place in the world is or ought to be, and they have often been unrealistic about this (Suez, Iraq and Afghanistan being only the most obvious examples). They have also mostly clung to Churchill's three circles image, offering their own minor twists rather than re-conceptualising the metaphor itself. Even the Blair government – which did some of the hard thinking initially about the post-Cold War era – still clung to the three circles notion, seeing Britain as a vital 'pivot' between the old world and the new, between the European and Atlantic circles.

So what is British foreign policy likely to look like in the future, under the Conservative government of Theresa May and beyond? In Chapter 8 we briefly discussed the Coalition government's identification of likely threats and its downsizing of the military's capabilities. In this chapter, we will use the 2010 and 2015 National Security Strategy (NSS) and

Strategic Defence and Security Review (SDSR) as convenient pegs upon which to hang our discussion of the future, not least because they both raise questions with which it is rather fitting to end this book. What is Britain's role today, and what is it likely to be in the years to come? We live in a post-imperial, post-Cold War era, so what is Britain trying to do now? What *should* it try to do? Should UK foreign policy be about the projection of power, or values, or both? What threats is Britain likely to face, and how are these to be addressed? These are big questions, and it is clear that we cannot address them all within a single chapter. Nevertheless, we can suggest the flavour of future policy, focusing both on the things that may change and the factors which will probably stay the same.

The Future of British Foreign Policy: Continuity and Change

It is clear that British foreign policy in the future will continue to be constrained by all of those 'givens' that we discussed in Chapter 1, such as the country's geostrategic location, imperial history, exceptionalist mentality and not least of all the fact of relative economic decline. Certainly, there will be a continuity in the sense that the future will tend to look (roughly) like the present – at least on the assumption that Scotland does not secede from the union and that the territorial integrity of the UK remains intact. In a perfect world, a new set of challenges like that which accompanied the end of the Cold War would lead in short order to wholesale changes in the way that Britain conducts itself in foreign and defence policy. A calm and deliberative government would realise that the world had been transformed. Politicians would accept this, putting the nation's interests before short-term calculation or what works 'electorally'. Like the politicians, service chiefs would recognise this as well, and accept cuts and other adjustments accordingly. Rationality would rule the day, and commitments would be neatly realigned with resources, as most of us think they should.

In the real world, of course, this seldom happens – and for many reasons. For one thing, governments are slow to change in a bureaucratic sense, and incrementalism means that things at 't2' tend to look very similar to the situation at 't1'. Squabbles between the armed services also make change difficult. So too do domestic political commitments which impinge on foreign and defence policy (such as the promise to build aircraft carriers in particular shipyards). It is also clear that these historical constraints will not permit Britain to be 'another Switzerland' – a neutral state which generally stays out of global-strategic affairs or restricts itself purely to the defence of its own shores. The psychological hangover of

Empire is still very real in Britain, and it prevents its policymakers from seeing the UK as 'just another country' (this is the sense of exceptionalism which we have discussed at various points already). The 2010 NSS document commits Britain to remain a 'global player', if not a 'power of the first rank'. This kind of commitment is likely to continue, at least rhetorically, because it is far easier to assert it in a post-imperial state than to retreat inwards.

At the same time, we are bound to see some elements of change. The challenge is fundamentally one of the imagination, of imagining future threats that might one day materialise but are not yet present. No one has a crystal ball, and no one can know exactly what threats will materialise or how foreign and defence policy should be shaped to respond to them. History does not always move in a linear fashion, moreover, and the existence of what Nicholas Taleb (after Karl Popper) has called 'black swans' means that we cannot always assume that the future will be an extrapolation of the present.[2] Nevertheless, it does seem clear that several elements or factors are likely to dominate the future of British foreign policy: (1) continued uncertainty about strategic ends, in which 'new' threats mix with 'old' and *realpolitik* vies with *idealpolitik*; (2) an enhanced role for the NATO alliance and for temporary coalitions, especially with France; (3) reliance on a small and shrinking expeditionary military force, in which the role of the 'Afghan model' is especially prominent; and (4) a greater role for 'soft power' as opposed to hard military resources. The first factor has to do with the *ends* of British foreign policy, while the last three all concern *ways and means*. We look at each in turn.

1. Continued Uncertainty about Strategic Ends.

We now see the notion of 'threat' in a much broader way than we used to during the Cold War. Since 1990 there has been a slow-burning but nevertheless very marked willingness to reconceptualise the notion of threat itself, embracing a much broader and inclusive definition. In both British policymaking and strategic/security studies as a field, there has traditionally been a bias towards military strategy, such as 'counting missiles' and a seemingly endless examination of the causes of war. But both the 1998 SDR and the 2010 National Security Strategy, as well as many academic discussions of the notion of threat in textbooks, show that this has gradually changed since the end of the Cold War.

In academic circles, Barry Buzan and his followers have analysed 'securitization', the process by which an issue or problem comes to be seen as a genuine threat and 'a matter of security'. According to Buzan, issues become securitised when they are not merely politicised, but when a consensus emerges that this is 'an emergency'. Some 'securitization bids' fail (e.g. Vietnam and Iraq outside the US, 'global warming' within the US, asteroid attacks), while others succeed (e.g. 'Cold War' or 'War on Terror'). Security studies today are about 'existential threats', a definition well captured by Paul Williams, who sees security as the 'alleviation of threats to cherished values' (an inclusive definition that covers all bases).

Within policymaking circles, we now see what Buzan has called a broadened agenda of 'referent objects'. It is not so much that military issues have disappeared, since state-on-state war remains a possibility. It is more that attention has shifted to economic, social and environmental issues in the absence of a direct state-on-state threat. Economic security, environmental security, food and water security, health security, women's issues, immigration, genocide, natural disaster, terrorist attacks on individuals or groups of citizens, biological attacks and transnational crime are all treated today as major threats. In reality, these were mostly old issues that had lain dormant or been obscured by the East–West conflict, but they have come (back) to the fore since the end of the Cold War and the NSS of 2010 and 2015 both reflect these new realities.

As we saw earlier, Britain has a long tradition of 'muddling through' – a term often associated with the political scientist Charles Lindblom in America, but which actually seems to have come originally from Winston Churchill. Britain has typically eschewed grand policy statements while quietly pursuing an approach in the *realpolitik* tradition. As Peter Hennessy suggests, while generalisations or stereotypes can be misleading, we are essentially a 'back of the envelope' nation, understated, pragmatic and ad hoc.[3] We recoil almost instinctively from a term like 'strategy'. Critics have therefore questioned whether we really need 'grand declarations' like the 1998 *Strategic Defence Review* or the 2010 National Security Strategy (such things, it is quietly claimed, are necessary for relatively young nations like the United States, but not for more confident ones with a longer history and deeper traditions). Some critics see the introduction of such statements of purpose and of an actual National Security Council under David Cameron[4] as part of the 'Americanisation' of British politics, beginning in earnest under Prime Minister Tony Blair. This is a variation on the 'no strategy please, we're British!' type of argument.[5] It may be seen as having deeper roots than this, though, since the adoption of an Atlantic relationship as one of the three circles both during and after World War II set Britain on a 'road of convergence' with its American cousins. Blair certainly embarrassed many British observers by wearing a cowboy hat and boots at George W. Bush's ranch, but the British also have an appetite for all things American.[6]

It should be readily apparent that strategy is essential, though, because it provides a way of linking ends, ways and means. How can we know what kind of military forces are required, for instance, if we do not know what we are trying to achieve with those forces? What threats face Britain today, and how should those be addressed? A whole range of definitions have been offered for strategy over the years. What strategy is *not* is fairly clear to most people. For instance, President Obama was caught by an open mike in 2014 stating that his foreign policy was 'don't do stupid shit' (a seeming reference to Bush's invasion of Iraq, and a justification for his own preference for Realism). Critics have noted, however, that failing to do *x* or *y* is not a strategy. What does the term mean, then, in a *positive* sense? At a minimum, strategies explicitly state what our goals and objectives are, and then relate these to the means and resources available. Since the 2015 NSS – much like its predecessor – talks mostly about the former (focusing on threats) but not the latter, it is probably fair to conclude that it too is not a fully worked-out strategy. As Patrick Porter notes, 'strategy is the orchestration of ways, ends and means. It is a balancing act: the balancing of resources with commitments, power with interests ... it is a theory of how to cause security.'[7]

For some reason, strategy has always been done rather badly in the UK, and the 2010 National Security Strategy document has been held up by Porter and others as a case in point. Nonetheless, the National Security Strategies of 2010 and 2015 both offer an especially handy peg upon which to hang the next discussion, not least because these documents deal with the issue of likely threats. The 2010 review was entitled *A Strong Britain in an Age of Uncertainty*,[8] and it provides 'a nice strategic essay', as RUSI Director Michael Clarke has put it. For the first time in twelve years, it identified an array of contemporary threats to Britain's security values and interests. It also attempted to prioritise these in a way that previous strategy documents had not. Most notably, the 2010 version divided threats into three 'tiers' for the first time, suggesting both that particular threats were more likely to occur than others *and* that these would have a damaging impact on UK interests. As we saw in Chapter 8, to make it to the top a threat had to be considered both likely *and* especially harmful in its effects. The NSS placed cyber warfare in the first tier, for instance, listing it as a major threat that we might well have to face in the near future. It also listed terrorism as a first tier threat, together with natural disasters like a major flood or flu pandemic and more traditional military crises that might lead to inter-state war and draw in Britain and its allies. Biological warfare, on the other hand, only made it into the second tier, presumably because it was considered less likely to occur than the earlier scenarios, even though the effects might be devastating.

The 2015 review – *A Secure and Prosperous United Kingdom* – was a relief to many observers in the defence sector, some of whom had wrongly expected more cuts in spending similar to the 8 per cent reduction seen in 2010 (and perhaps the cancellation of more programmes like the Nimrod and Harrier). For the first time, it also combined the NSS and SDSR in a single document. Moreover, it was broadly similar to its predecessor, placing six core threats in tier one – terrorism, international military conflict, cyber attacks, a public health crisis, major natural hazards and an incident involving instability overseas (see Table 10.1).

Table 10.1   Tiered threats in NSS 2015

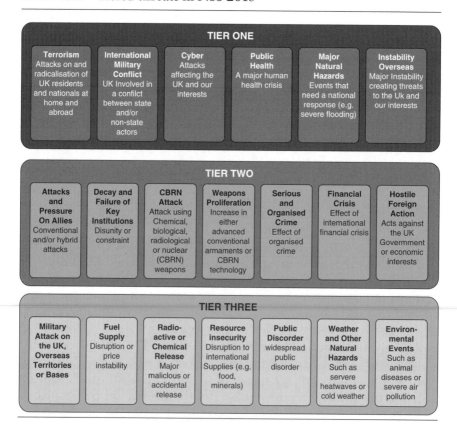

TIER ONE					
Terrorism Attacks on and radicalisation of UK residents and nationals at home and abroad	**International Military Conflict** UK Involved in a confilct between state and/or non-state actors	**Cyber** Attacks affecting the UK and our interests	**Public Health** A major human health crisis	**Major Natural Hazards** Events that need a national response (e.g. severe flooding)	**Instability Overseas** Major Instability creating threats to the Uk and our interests

TIER TWO						
Attacks and Pressure On Allies Conventional and/or hybrid attacks	**Decay and Failure of Key Institutions** Disunity or constraint	**CBRN Attack** Attack using Chemical, biological, radiological or nuclear (CBRN) weapons	**Weapons Proliferation** Increase in either advanced conventional armaments or CBRN technology	**Serious and Organised Crime** Effect of organised crime	**Financial Crisis** Effect of international financial crisis	**Hostile Foreign Action** Acts against the UK Government or economic interests

TIER THREE						
Military Attack on the UK, Overseas Territories or Bases	**Fuel Supply** Disruption or price instability	**Radio- active or Chemical Release** Major maliclous or accidental release	**Resource insecurity** Disruption to international Supplies (e.g. food, minerals)	**Public Discorder** widespread public disorder	**Weather and Other Natural Hazards** Such as servere heatwaves or cold weather	**Environ- mental Events** Such as animal diseases or severe air pollution

Source: UK Parliament, available at http://researchbriefings.files.parliament.uk/documents/ CBP-7431/CBP-7431.pdf.

Of course, it can be questioned whether any formal strategy document can really 'guide' policymaking well on anything like a day-to-day basis. Some critics have concluded that the predictive sections in 2010 NSS and 2015 NSS simply list problems and likely future threats, and therefore do not genuinely 'shape policy'. For instance, in 2012 the Joint Committee on the National Security Strategy – composed of members of the House of Commons and the House of Lords – was especially critical of the 2010 NSS in this regard when it argued that there was no evidence that the document had actually influenced decisions made since the SDSR.[9] As we have seen in this book already, the course of events can sometimes overcome the best laid plans (recall, for instance, the way that the 1981 Nott Review was essentially superseded by the Falklands War). It could also be argued that the 2015 NSS is not really a 'strategy' at all, since it talks mostly about ends rather than means, and does not devote more than a few pages to the latter. The Joint Committee also criticised the 2010 claim that the UK would not lose its influence on the world stage in coming years as 'wholly unrealistic in the medium to long term', but it also argued that there was no 'overarching strategy' within the document designed to guide decision-making.

It all depends on what is considered to constitute a 'strategy' in the first place. It could be argued that the 2010 NSS and SDSR in particular were out of step with one another, or at least that Britain's strategy is mismatched to the available resources, and that the 2015 document does little to remedy this defect. The previous point could be addressed by arguing that the two documents *together* represent a strategy, of course. Returning to Porter's definition, a strategy is 'the orchestration of ways, ends and means', so that the NSS (ends) and SDSR (ways and means) – originally a single document – might be considered a strategy if read concomitantly. That route out, though, leaves us with the question of whether the two actually 'match' one another or fit together. As Matt Cavenagh notes, the concomitant SDSR in 2010 was 'an opportunity to achieve the kind of radical reform which is necessary but difficult in the course of normal business', but he argues this was a 'missed opportunity'.[10] The planners got only four months to set their house in order, an almost impossible timeframe given the scale of the problems. What we got in the end was a rushed spending review, not a genuine strategic review – and even on those terms, Cavenagh argues, it 'failed'.[11]

Nevertheless, even though it might not represent a fully worked-out strategy, the items listed in Table 10.1 do seem to provide a reasonable list. It does not make the mistake of ruling out inter-state war (conflict *between* states) altogether. In recent years it has become fashionable to focus on intra-state conflict (wars *inside* states) to the exclusion of more traditional forms of conflict. But the 2014–15 crisis over Russia's incursion into neighbouring Ukraine offered a potent reminder of the fact that war between advanced industrialised states is not obsolete. It remains unclear, of course, what role (if any) nuclear weapons and the conventional NATO deterrent played in all of this. Russian leader Vladimir Putin seemed unlikely to go 'beyond Ukraine' because of these two factors, and the extent to which he ever planned to is still unclear – although he may well not have dared to act as he did had Ukraine not given up its own weapons voluntarily some years before the crisis occurred. If we look at the 2010 NSS, we can see that the possibility of 'an international military crisis between states' was one of the contingencies planned for in the first tier, which in light of later events looks rather prescient. The authors of the NSS may well have had something much bigger in mind, of course, such as a truly worldwide war. But they at least allowed for crises like that in Ukraine to play a major role in British policymaking.

Britain continues to place its faith in Trident and in an independent nuclear deterrent – though the debate about its future is likely to intensify in the coming years, since it is coming to the end of its life and is so expensive to replace. As we saw with the 1952, 1957 and 1981 defence reviews in previous chapters, one could argue that nuclear weapons reduced the need for conventional forces and justified cuts in the latter. On the other hand, it could be countered today that neither terrorists nor those who engage in cyber warfare (both in the 'first tier') can be deterred in any meaningful way by the possession of nuclear weapons, and that the latter are unusable in any case. Of course, 'using' them was rarely the point, since their main purpose was to prevent war from breaking out in the first place.

If one looks at the 'first tier' threats identified in the 2015 NSS, only one of the top six seems to have anything to do with nuclear weapons. Natural disasters and public heath crises are inanimate forces, and are hence by their nature non-deterrable. Terrorists and those who engage in cyber warfare are in principle deterrable, but arguably neither can actually be deterred in any way by the possession of nuclear weapons. The logic of deterrence during the Cold War suggested that 'rational' states could be deterred, and that peace and stability would be the inevitable result between nuclear-armed states in an era of 'mutually assured destruction'. But what if the adversary is neither rational (as opposed to being willing to die for an ideological cause) nor a state? The most recent NSS does not clearly integrate these issues within the discussion and effectively puts the central questions off until later, perhaps because dealing with them now would have re-opened debates that tore the country apart during the early Thatcher years in the 1980s.

'Tier two' and 'tier three' of the NSS identify a range of threats as well, but they fare no better in the sense of finding things that could be deterrable via the possession of nuclear weapons. Looking at tier two, here again only two of the seven threats mentioned – conventional attacks on Allies and chemical, biological or radiological attacks on the UK – might conceivably be deterred by Britain's possession of nuclear weapons. Tier three, meanwhile, lists seven threats, but only two of these – a military attack on the UK or a deliberate chemical or radioactive release – could be deterred by nuclear capabilities, while the latter might even be encouraged by Britain's nuclear capabilities. Since having nuclear weapons may thus potentially deter only one of the six threats considered to be most likely and most grave in their effects in tier one, two of the seven threats in tier two and two of seven threats in tier three, the UK may well want to revisit the question in the future of whether they are worth their very substantial cost and whether the UK government's strategy is really matching up ways, ends and means. Are they still useful in the defence of the realm, or are they being retained (rather like James Bond) because they confer a psychological status upon Britain that it lost, in objective terms, many years ago? Of course, the July 2016 House of Commons vote to update Trident may resolve things, at least in the short term.

2. The (Strange) Rebirth of the NATO Alliance.

NATO is likely to be at the heart of UK foreign policy in the 21st century, so a brief reminder of its origins and the way that the UK's defence role has developed within it is in order. Lord Ismay famously said of NATO that its real purpose during the Cold War was to 'keep the Russians out, the Americans in, and the Germans down'. In 1990 and 1991 as the Cold War dragged to an end, NATO looked like an organisation whose days were numbered. The Russians no longer seemed like a threat to anyone, the Americans were expecting a well-earned peace dividend and the Germans had been reunited as a single nation. Using remorseless Neorealist logic, John Mearsheimer predicted that NATO would soon cease to exist, since it had obviously served its purpose. Today, however, NATO not only still exists but appears to be undergoing an entirely new role in life as an agency for humanitarian intervention. The UK, moreover, plans to engage only in military operations that are sanctioned by either the United States or NATO (and preferably both).

After 1945, against the background of the ever-present Soviet threat, Britain's post-war defence policy sought to provide the military underpinning for the three-circle strategy which it had already decided would guide its foreign policy in general. Given that the British government wished to preserve its influence in each of the three circles, it would only be possible to meet the Soviet challenge if its limited military capabilities were distributed judiciously. In the event, through NATO, London was able to combine its security interests in the European and Atlantic circles by drawing the United States into the defence of Western Europe. The *quid pro quo* of greater US involvement, however, was that in order to *keep* the Americans in Europe, Britain was obliged to enter into an open-ended military commitment on the continent of Europe, a development unknown in peace-time since the Hundred Years War. Yet in the Empire circle, too, Britain remained heavily committed. So long as large parts of the Empire remained – even after the loss of India in 1947 – they had to be protected. This in turn required the maintenance of a significant out-of-area capability which would permit the rapid deployment of troops, air squadrons and naval forces to almost any part of the world.

By the mid-1960s, the United Kingdom's heavy NATO commitments, its continuing efforts to project a world role for the sake of British interests in the Empire, and the costs associated with the independent deterrent had all combined to overstretch Britain's military forces. After the withdrawal from East of Suez, a residual capability sufficient for minor emergencies was retained, but British defence efforts were concentrated almost exclusively in Europe, where Britain's primary economic interests had been increasingly located since the late 1950s. But then, in the 1990s, the Cold War was over, and predictions of the imminent demise of NATO were rife. In a famous (or perhaps infamous) argument, Mearsheimer suggested in 1990 that we would 'soon miss the Cold War', on the grounds that it had imparted a simplicity and directness to strategic affairs that made dealing with threat a comparatively straightforward (if not always entirely comforting) matter. Neorealists claim that multipolar systems are inherently less 'stable' than bipolar ones, and that war on a world scale becomes far more likely when the international system is dominated by more than two great powers. To the extent that this is what we are seeing today, Britain is by extension living under a sword of Damocles, according to this grim view of the world. Or at least, as the 2010 NSS suggests, we face an extraordinary array of complex threats nowadays which had no parallel during the days of the Cold War.

But NATO has not only persisted after the end of the Cold War in the face of predictions of its decline, it has actually thrived. What Mearsheimer and others missed is the extraordinary capacity of organisations to continue to exist, even when their original *raison d'être* – in this case, defeating the Soviet Union and global communism – has long gone. It is difficult to abolish institutions. They do not simply 'close up shop' or dissolve when their original reason for existing disappears. Instead – much like cockroaches after a nuclear strike – they tend to survive external shocks, morphing into something their creators never intended. Although we have seen NATO go through repeated 'identity crises' since the end of the Cold war, its continued utility to leaders like Clinton and Blair – especially when the US Security Council seems to be in a permanent state of deadlock, and the EU has failed to develop its own independent defence capability – quickly became clear.

One solution that UK policymakers have increasingly embraced is acting in tandem with other nations (either in informal coalitions or as part of NATO) rather than unilaterally. Moreover, for Britain working with organisations like NATO after the Cold War or constructing bilateral coalitions like the UK–French collaboration during the Libyan revolution which brought down Ghaddafi in 2011 also quickly became what Christopher Elliott has called 'a fact of life', as the UK's resources dwindled.[12] As we have seen, one consequence of decline 'after Suez' has been the necessity to work within both the European and Atlantic circles, and it is in NATO that the two come together. UK policymakers have increasingly been forced to act in tandem with other nations (either in informal coalitions or as part of the NATO alliance or UN) rather than unilaterally. Burden sharing is obviously cheaper, since it allows states to spread out the costs of military ventures.

To be sure, the Kosovo War in particular illustrated the difficulties of working within an alliance to achieve a military objective, whether that goal be humanitarian or anything else. Splits, cracks and leaks within the coalition threatened to reduce its effectiveness, and differences between the NATO Supreme Allied Commander (SACEUR) Wesley Clark and British Commander General Sir Mike Jackson laid bare the fact that even close partners can perceive threat very differently (they had clashed over whether to take Pristina airport in Kosovo before the Russians did, but Jackson felt that forcing the issue would start 'World War III' and countermanded Clark's orders). Political sensitivities can also limit the effectiveness of NATO, and some nations may be unwilling for domestic reasons to participate in certain ventures (such as providing basic rights). Operating within NATO can also lead to the 'too many cooks' problem. Clark was famously frustrated by the fact that every single one of the (then 19) members of NATO had to sign off on every target before it could be hit from the air, a cumbersome process which has been called 'war by committee'. Moreover, working in coalitions places a premium on joint training and what military people like to call 'interoperability' (the degree to which different military machines mesh together and are compatible). They make a unified command structure necessary or at least highly desirable, together with compatible standard operating procedures (SOPs) and rules of engagement. Intelligence sharing is needed in coalitions, but partners may not entirely trust one another (leading to an increased risk of 'friendly fire' incidents, for instance).

On the other hand, acting within coalitions or alliances provides increased political legitimacy and increased firepower. Burden sharing is cheaper and reduces 'free riding' (about which the US has complained frequently since the end of the Cold War). Allies can also provide missing or 'niche' capabilities, offering military services and comparative advantages which are not readily available elsewhere. Moreover, by the late 1990s it was unclear whether cash-strapped Britain had any real alternative to ventures like this. 'The UK no longer has the capability to fight a major inter-state war, and has not had it for at least a decade', argues Hew Strachan.[13] Given that the 'menu of choice' has been significantly narrowed, Britain's military future is likely to involve mainly multilateral commitments within the Atlantic circle, involving a particular emphasis on NATO but also on the United Nations. As David Kirkpatrick notes, 'today the UK is committed to join collective military operations in defence of the NATO group of nations and in support of UN-authorized actions to promote global peace and security, and it does not plan to engage in any major operation without the active participation of the United States of America'.[14] This seems unlikely to result in Britain becoming 'the 51st State', at least not in any formal sense; but it does seem likely that in the future it will involve some level of enhanced integration and operational compatibility with American forces.[15]

Britain retains its 'seat at the top table' in large part through its security relationship with the United States, and to a lesser extent because the ossified nature of the UN Security Council, frozen in time as if this were the mid-1940s, gives the UK a large measure of status as well. Within its hard power capabilities, though, nuclear weapons have also played a critical role, in the sense that they are often seen as imparting 'great power status' on their possessors (and perceptions are everything in international relations, as we have seen). In the short term at least, Britain will be able to continue to 'project power' despite its ever-weakening economic base and despite the precarious balancing act between needs and resources that it has engaged in since World War II – not least because it has these three factors of its security relationship with the United States, its UN Security Council seat and its nuclear deterrent in its favour. It will probably be some years before Britain is compelled to be 'just another country', defending its homeland but little else. In the medium to long term, though, things will probably get much more difficult.

While Britain may be in the process of leaving the European Union, the latter never became a serious security actor in its own right, and the UK remains strongly committed to NATO membership. And even if they are not multilateral, any future military interventions are likely to be *at least* bilateral. The model for this is of course the UK–French collaboration over Libya in 2011. More broadly, the so-called 'Afghan model' – in which air power is used to assist a force already on the ground, without the actual use of UK troops – is likely to be the first option of choice, at least for the foreseeable future. This is often a popular option because the precision of air strikes has increased greatly, while committing ground troops is often unpopular. It becomes a problem, however, where no friendly force can be identified on the ground or the friendly forces are too weak militarily to benefit from the air strikes. In 2015 during the attacks on Islamic State, for instance, it was unclear whether any ground forces in Syria or Iraq were in a position to benefit from US and UK aerial bombardment, or whether those that did benefit might actually be allies of the West.

3. Reliance on an Ever-Shrinking Military Force.

The fact that British policymakers no longer intend to undertake major operations in the absence of US support – a claim denied in the 2010 NSS, but something which has not genuinely been attempted since the fiasco of Suez[16] – has meant that military compatibility between the two nations (or 'interoperability') has become increasingly important. If all goes as planned, 'Force 2020' will look like that depicted in Figure 10.1. But is today's British military still up to the job of helping to police the world? Some have argued, as we have seen, that the cuts have gone too deep. The cutbacks which occurred after 2010, moreover, seem unrelated to the expansive aims (or list of threats) outlined in the NSS that year or in 2015.

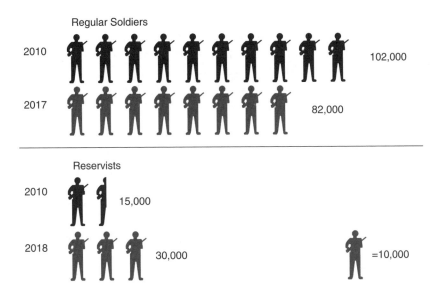

Army 2020 restructure

Regular Soldiers

2010   102,000

2017   82,000

Reservists

2010   15,000

2018   30,000   =10,000

Figure 10.1   Army 2020 Restructure

Britain now has a small expeditionary force, especially an expeditionary Army. It will also one day have an expeditionary Navy – once the *Queen Elizabeth*-class carriers are commissioned (assuming that the Treasury approves the building of a second carrier) and after 2020, when the fighters the ships will carry are expected to come online. As Clarke suggests, this will still be a 'go anywhere' and perhaps 'do anything' kind of military, with both blue- and brown-water capabilities (the military jargon for having the ability to operate in both oceans and smaller rivers and other bodies of water). But according to the projections of Force 2020, it will not be the kind of army that can sustain large, extended commitments like the Afghanistan intervention or a military that has the resources to stay anywhere for very long. Short-term, 'in-and-out' operations in tandem with the United States (like the Persian Gulf War of 1991 or the Kosovo War of 1999) are what Britain is now best equipped to do, as the 1998 SDR envisioned. This will continue to be a constraint in the future, in the sense that more extended commitments will be difficult to sustain.

In spite of the chaotic debate about the aircraft carriers and the evident desire of many politicians to cancel any new ones if they could, all may well work out for the best in the end, in the sense that the 1998 SDR – which emphasised expeditionary capability – may well prove a better guide to future needs than its 2010 or 2015 counterparts. As Christopher Parry has noted:

> With the introduction of the *Queen Elizabeth*-class carriers in the latter years of this decade, the UK will be able to deploy more versatile, capable and responsive maritime power projection, theatre-entry and littoral manoeuver capabilities, in operations that are likely to range from humanitarian relief to high intensity conflict. This oceanic and littoral capability will be complementary to and congruent with that of the US, able to work as the lead or framework element in European or ad-hoc coalitions, and have a sustainable composite capability that can undertake national tasks with confidence.[17]

The current NSS claims that Britain still has the capacity to act alone, if need be. However, unilateral action seems rather unlikely, not least because most commentators believe that Britain now lacks the capability to launch that type of military operation. Indeed, the UK struggled to put together an operational Task Force for the Falklands back in 1982, being forced to press aircraft carriers into service that the Nott Review had planned to sell off, while undefended civilian ships like the *QE2* were used to transport military personnel. Arguably even this was unilateralism only in name, since the projection of British military power so far from home required the tacit (but, at the time, unacknowledged) participation of the United States. The latter had to appear 'neutral' for political reasons, since both Britain and Argentina were then allies in the Cold War. We now know, though, that the Americans secretly provided a great deal of operational and tactical backup. As in World War II, Britain did not act alone.

At the same time, Britain's role in the European (or at least EU) circle remains fraught with uncertainty. The June 2016 referendum on EU membership narrowly rejected Britain's involvement in the European circle, but the immediate future was unlikely to involve the UK's participation in a joint European defence force or European army in any case, for at least two reasons. First of all, at the time of writing the British government seems likely to bow to the results of the 2016 referendum, which committed it to withdrawing from the EU altogether. The other (more formidable) barrier is that the EU itself has repeatedly failed to develop its own independent defence capability, not least because the member states regard this as a low priority in a time of austerity but also due to seemingly insurmountable considerations of national sovereignty (see Chapter 5). While Britain did get involved in EU peacekeeping operations, the European Union generally borrowed its equipment and resources from NATO in order to do this.

As we saw in Chapter 5, this is all a far cry from the heady days of the St Malo Declaration in 1998, which increased UK–French security collaboration. The Common European Foreign and Security Policy (CFSP) and the Common Security and Defence Policy (CSDP) of the EU have so far been limited to things like peacekeeping missions. The Clinton administration worried that an independent EU defence capability might crowd out NATO's role, and Secretary of State Madeleine Albright famously developed 'the three Ds', which referred to 'no diminution of NATO, no discrimination and no duplication'. US policymakers probably need not have worried, though, because in an age of austerity member states have placed domestic concerns ahead of foreign and defence issues. This is an area, of course, where IR theory can help us make sense of the present and what the future is likely to look like. Realists would argue that the EU will never develop a genuinely 'common' defence capability because states fear one another too much in a Hobbesian world, while Liberals would argue that a common capability will eventually result from the 'spillover' of cooperation on economic and other domestic issues in a Kantian world.

Yet we can also question whether 'the system' is capable of moving fast enough to keep up with changing threats. In an ideal world, an altered set of challenges like that which accompanied the end of the Cold War would lead in short order to wholesale changes in the way that Britain conducts itself in foreign policy, but sadly (and as we have seen already) this is not entirely how governments work. As Clarke notes, we have seen the 'salami slicing' of military budgets in recent defence reviews, and the result of the current cuts is an 'odd-looking' force structure that seems to have little to do with the NSS.[18] The suspicion remains that some things have been cut simply because they *can* be – an order of Chinook helicopters, for instance, was cancelled in 2010 even though the RAF needed them – while other 'sacred cows' of Whitehall remain because they are better defended politically. Projects that carry what economists call 'sunken costs' tend to be especially resistant to change, not least because failing to continue to invest in them implies considerable waste ('we've put so much into this') as well as an admission of failure in some sense ('why did we do this in the first place?'). Still other commitments which derive from the era of Gordon Brown, such as building the aircraft carriers HMS *Queen Elizabeth* and the (still putative) HMS *Prince of Wales*, seem to have been retained in the 2010 and 2015 NSS/SDSR simply because, in the words of Chancellor of the Exchequer George Osborne, 'we could not get out of the contract' and because cancellation would also have been more expensive than the alternative.[19] Apart from the economic costs involved – the *Queen Elizabeth*-class carriers are the largest ever built for the British Navy – the political costs of cancellation were immeasurable, with shipyards in Appledore, Birkenhead, Govan, Portsmouth, Rosyth and the Tyne all reportedly involved in the construction process.[20]

Chapter 2 of *Securing Britain in an Age of Uncertainty* deals with the contribution of the British military to our overall security, listing seven tasks that the military should be expected to undertake:

1. Defending the UK and its overseas territories
2. Providing strategic intelligence
3. Providing nuclear deterrence
4. Supporting civil emergency organisations in times of crisis
5. Defending interests by projecting power strategically and through expeditionary interventions
6. Providing a defence contribution to UK influence
7. Providing security for stabilisation.

Given the cuts to naval power and the fact that the *Queen Elizabeth*-class carriers are not expected to go fully online until 2020 – as well as continued uncertainty that the HMS *Prince of Wales* will even be built – how is the UK military expected to provide point five, for instance? And if those carriers were only retained because of prohibitive cancellation costs, where does that leave the Royal Navy? How is it supposed to go about 'defending interests by projecting power strategically and through expeditionary interventions', if it cannot move aircraft overseas? The same issue applies in the case of number one. How are overseas territories like the Falklands to be defended in the absence of a single operational carrier? Of course, UK Tornadoes can fly to friendly bases around the world – during the 2014 humanitarian crisis in Iraq, for instance, British aircraft were deployed to Cyprus – but UK forces are currently highly dependent on such bases in order to function overseas.

One can argue, of course, that there has *always* been a mismatch between ambitions and resources in the post-World War II era within British foreign and defence policy (one of the themes of this book). For instance, defence spending as a proportion of GNP and the physical size of the military itself were much higher in the 1950s than during the early part of this century, and yet the demands placed on the British military during the latter – especially during Britain's involvement in the Iraq and Afghanistan wars – were much *greater* than during the former (something which makes little sense on the face of it). In 1953 the armed forces numbered 865,000, but by 2008 that number had been cut to only 182,000, despite the fact that military activism in previous years was higher than at any time since the Korean War. The UK military was certainly under-resourced during the last Blair government relative to the commitments the Prime Minister was willing or able to make, and we have repeatedly noted that Britain has been similarly strapped for cash and resources for much of the post-war period. But none of this gets recent reviews off the hook for failing to make '2 + 2=4'. As Andrew Dorman argues:

> the principal problem with the NSS/SDSR is that the government continues to have eyes that are too big for its stomach. In other words, it still wants two-plus-two to equal five. Unfortunately it does not, except perhaps in a post-modern world. If strategy is the bringing together of ends, ways and means, this Review has failed.[21]

The overall consequence of the mismatch in the NSS/SDSR context, moreover, is that when the statement of threats is placed against the resources available, the effect is that there is a somewhat 'schizophrenic' quality when they are read together: the first part of the 2015 document is aspirational and freethinking, while the second is conservative with a small 'c' and concerned mainly with 'what can we cut?' 'Do more', suggests the first; 'you'll have less', says the second. But *can* Britain do more with less?

The answer depends in part on whether you think the United Kingdom has never been safer – one position in the current debate – or whether you believe that we now face a complex array of threats that ought to make its citizens pine for the days of the Cold War. States can of course deal more or less comfortably with having fewer resources if their needs are not great. From the first perspective, the absence of any remotely credible threat from mainland Europe means that the United Kingdom is safer than it has been for several centuries. At various times in its history, Britain was threatened by Spain, France and then Germany, but the prospect of any of them invading us today is slim to say the least. The NATO security umbrella, moreover, provides a good 'insurance scheme' in the event of bad weather, as does the possession of a nuclear deterrent against the kind of threats that can actually be deterred.

The opposite sins of paranoia and complacency are relevant here, but in truth Britain's security position probably lies somewhere on a spectrum between danger at one extreme and safety at the other. Readers must decide for themselves where they think this exact point lies, but it should be noted that both positions are in many ways equally compelling in the absence of advance information about how things will really turn out. Working under conditions of uncertainty – again, no one has a 'crystal ball' and no one can say definitively what the future will bring – the 2015 NSS is surely correct in highlighting this factor. From the vantage point of 2016, it seems unlikely that state-on-state war is obsolete, but it is also true that an individual's statistical chances of dying in a terrorist attack are far smaller than the probability s/he will be hit by a car tonight while the driver is checking cellphone messages, or that s/he will one day die of cancer or some other common illness. As Daniel Kahneman notes, we tend to judge risk and probability not by how statistically likely it is, but by how cognitively available it appears (how recent a similar case is, and in general how readily it springs to mind).[22] Worryingly, the planners of British foreign policy are just as susceptible to these cognitive 'quirks' – the tricks our brains play on us when we think about probability – as is the man or woman in the street. As noted earlier, UK policymakers may also want to revisit the nuclear question in the future, looking at whether nuclear weapons are worth their very substantial cost and whether ways, ends and means are really being matched up. Are such weapons still useful in the defence of the Realm, or are they being retained mainly because they confer a psychological status upon Britain that it lost, in objective terms, many years ago?

4. A Greater Role For 'Soft Power'?

From the previous discussion, the reader might be forgiven for thinking that British foreign and defence policy in the future will be driven by purely *military* capabilities, high-end or otherwise. But this is probably not the case, in the sense that (as many inside the UK military acknowledge themselves) some of the threats we have discussed may be far better addressed by *non-military* actors and capabilities. Most obviously, while one can in a metaphorical sense 'wage war' on climate change, it is not clear that soldiers can address this issue in any meaningful sense, or that economic insecurity, gender issues or epidemics are susceptible to military solutions. Even unconventional warfare – especially tasks involving counterinsurgency, which aim to win over the 'hearts and minds' of potentially hostile populations – seems ill-suited to the uniformed military. Other examples are more ambiguous, since it is conceivable that conflicts over scarce resources like water might be a cause of conventional war in the future, and military peacekeepers are useful across a whole series of humanitarian issues. At the very least, however, it is clear that military solutions alone will not suffice to address the full range of 'new' issues, and that other tools (such as diplomacy) may be more effective.

In the future, Britain's foreign policy may also be increasingly driven by 'soft' power, as opposed to the ability to use hard power or traditional 'kinetic' force. States which lack conventional or 'hard' power often turn to its soft variety. Joseph Nye – the originator of the term, who has refined its meaning in a series of books and articles – defines soft power as 'the power to attract'.[23] We often describe conventional power as 'the ability of A to get B to do what B would not otherwise do'. One obvious means of doing this is simple coercion: through conventional hard power, we can force B to do what A wants. But what if it were possible to get B to want what we want through non-coercive means, because (for instance) B respects A and shares his/her values? This is the essence of soft power, the appeal that certain nations may be said to possess and the use of this to achieve strategic ends. It does not matter whether these things are based upon myth, though it helps if there is an element of reality to them. For instance, the United States has an appeal which stems in part from the values it stands for (or is said to stand for). Hollywood projects an image of America as populated by wealthy, attractive people, and many immigrants come to the United States because they already share the beliefs in free-market capitalism and democracy which are said to underpin the American way of life.

In the British case, the UK is associated with a range of desirable things as well, such as a parliamentary system of democracy based on the towering Houses of Parliament, a sense of 'fair play' in legal and political affairs, free healthcare, good manners and punctuality, Jane Austen, William Shakespeare and Charles Dickens, the Premier League, what the poet William Blake called the 'green and pleasant land' of England, the British Museum, and the stable banking institutions of the City of London. Americans often think of the TV series *Downton Abbey* when they think of Britain, for instance, even though in reality that programme – although there are certainly a number of timeless themes to it – tells the story of a way of life that has largely disappeared, and did so a long time ago. These 'attractive' things are part of our stock of soft power, and Nye's theories suggest that this can be used to get things that we want. Conversely, when we think of Britain we do not generally think of military coups, torture or genocide (although in reality, British policymakers sanctioned at least some of these things during the days of Empire). Again, however, reality matters much less than perception; trains may not run on time at all; people may have 'bad teeth'; NHS queues may be endless; some of the contents of the British Museum may have been stolen; the crowds at Premier League games may be full of 'hooligans'; and banks may go bust even in London. But soft power relies on the positive, the things we can use to 'get our way'.

In 2012 Britain topped a noted 'league table' of soft power.[24] How might soft power be *used* in British foreign policy, though? Here things get a good deal vaguer, since soft power is inherently difficult to measure, and its precise effects are difficult to prove.[25] However, it is argued that the City of London attracts capital because of the reputation of the British people as 'trustworthy', for instance. Moreover, London attracts a huge amount of tourism, and the educational system attracts future world leaders and opinion leaders from around the globe. This then translates into influence over the rest of the world. Britain is supposedly able to get what it wants through the use of diplomacy, because the nation is respected as 'fair' and even-handed. It can also set the agenda on occasion in a way that hard power could not, as when Tony Blair used Britain's soft power to mobilise the international community against Milošević in 1999.

Conclusion

Arguably, the British should resist the temptation to fall back solely on pragmatism or a policy of muddling through, even though this may be the 'traditional' British way of doing things.[26] Whatever the future holds, it is clear that there will always be a need for *strategy*. This term is often misunderstood by politicians, who tend to equate it with 'policy'.[27] The military sense of this phrase, in contrast, sees policy as setting political direction, while strategy is about the ends and means by which we achieve these political objectives. But it also tends to be misunderstood, on the other hand, as a purely military thing. This is understandable given the root meaning of the word in the Greek term for 'generalship'. Carl Von Clausewitz famously described strategy as 'the use of engagements for the object of war'. For Basil Liddell Hart, it was 'the art of distributing and applying military means to fulfill the ends of policy', and for Colin Gray it is 'the theory and practice of the use, and threat of use, of organized force for political purposes'.

Strategy certainly involves both the use of force and the threat of its use. More generally, though, it involves using *all* the resources at the state's disposal, both military and non-military, hard and soft power and war-fighting capabilities and diplomacy to attain political ends. It also involves weighing the ends against the means. As Lawrence Freedman notes of strategy:

> One common definition describes it as being about maintaining a balance between ends, ways and means. The balance requires not only finding how to achieve desired ends but also adjusting ends so that realistic ways can be found to meet them by available means ... By and large, strategy comes into play where there is actual or potential conflict, where interests collide and forms of resolution are required. This is why a strategy is much more than a plan. A plan supposes a sequence of events that allows one to move with confidence from one state of affairs to another. Strategy is required where others might frustrate one's plans because they have different and possibly opposing interests and concerns.[28]

One of the real problems in assessing the likely future of British foreign and defence policy, however, is of course that no one really knows what our strategic *needs* will be a few years hence. Since (as already noted) no one has a crystal ball, we can only estimate (or 'guesstimate') what future threats Britain will face. Organisations like the Development, Concepts and Doctrine Centre (DCDC) (based at the UK Defence Academy in Shrivenham) do a good job of extrapolating and projecting what those needs are likely to be, but 'strategic shocks' may intervene to reverse or alter statistical trends. Just as generals are often accused of fighting the last war, so the bureaucratic and political time lag in adapting our capabilities may mean that we are never entirely ready or prepared for future threats.

In the end, it is also never clear how much security or how much defence is 'enough', since this is highly dependent on our psychological perception of threat. As Robert Jervis notes – using a metaphor employed by Arnold Wolfers originally – even a burning building leaves a menu of choices. For one thing, not everyone runs out of a building on fire, not least because firemen often run *in*. And in politics, perceptions differ markedly. World War II offers us some compelling examples. 'For Churchill, the house was burning soon after Hitler took power in Germany; for Chamberlain, this was the case only after March 1939; and for others there never was a fire at all.'[29] The world in which states and non-state actors must operate is often a violent one, but it is also an uncertain arena about which reasonable people can and do entirely disagree.

Notes

Introduction

1 Oliver Daddow, 'Britain, the World and Europe' in Bill Jones and Philip Norton (eds), *Politics UK*, 7th edn (New York: Routledge, 2010); see also Derek Harvey, 'Perspectives on the UK's Place in the World', Europe Programme Paper 2011/01, Chatham House, London, December 2011, available at http://www.chathamhouse.org/sites/files/chathamhouse/public/Research/Europe/1211pp_harvey.pdf.

2 Daddow, 'Britain, the World and Europe', p. 29.

3 Anyone who has taken the approximately eight-hour flight from London's Heathrow to New York's Kennedy airport and compared it to the roughly two-hour train journey from London St Pancras to Paris can readily attest to the disparity in distance!

4 Harvey, 'Perspectives on the UK's Place in the World', p. 7.

5 Ibid, p. 8.

6 It influences both theory and action, in other words. On the linkage between the two, see for instance Nicolas Guilhot, *The Invention of International Relations Theory* (New York: Columbia University Press, 2011) and Patrick James and Jarrod Hayes, 'Theory as Thought: Britain and German Unification', *Security Studies*, vol. 23, no. 2 (2014).

7 William Wallace, 'The Collapse of British Foreign Policy', *International Affairs*, vol. 82, no. 1 (2005), p. 53.

8 See Christopher Hill, *The Changing Politics of Foreign Policy* (London: Palgrave Macmillan, 2002).

9 The latter is now colloquially known simply as '7/7'.

10 See F. S. Northedge, 'Britain as a Second-Rank Power', *International Affairs*, vol. 46, no. 1 (1970) pp. 37–47 and Corelli Barnet, *The Audit of War: The Illusion and Reality of Britain as a Great Nation* (London: Macmillan, 1986).

11 David McCourt, *Britain and World Power Since 1945: Constructing a Nation's Role in International Politics* (Ann Arbor, MI: University of Michigan Press, 2014). McCourt sees the persistence of Britain's activity in the world as a function of widespread expectations about the role it ought to play.

12 In a strict geographic sense, England itself is not an island but part of an archipelago, but Britain is effectively a 'world island'. See Andrew Gamble, *Between Britain and America: The Future of British Politics* (London: Palgrave Macmillan, 2003), p. 34.

13 Robert Kaplan, *The Revenge of Geography: What The Map Tells Us About Coming Conflicts and the Battle Against Fate* (New York: Random House, 2012).

14 This decision was subsequently reversed, when the House of Commons voted to intervene after all in a decisive vote of 397–223 in December 2015.

15 For the view that consultation has already become an established norm or convention, see James Strong, 'Why Parliament Now Decides on War: Tracing the Growth of the Parliamentary Prerogative through Syria, Libya and Iraq', *British Journal of Politics and International Relations,* doi: 10.1111/1467-856X.12055, 2014.

16 For sophisticated discussions of the relevant issues, see Anthony Giddens, *Central Problems in Social Theory: Action, Structure and Contradiction in Social Analysis* (London: Macmillan, 1979; Alexander Wendt, 'The Agent-Structure Problem in International Relations Theory', *International Organization,* vol. 41, no. 3 (1987), pp. 335–70; Alexander Wendt, *Social Theory of International Politics* (New York: Cambridge University Press, 1999).

17 There are 'hard' and 'soft' varieties of Euroscepticism in Britain. Advocates of the hard version favour complete withdrawal from the EU, while its soft advocates merely want to slow the pace and extent of political integration. See Aleks Szczerbiak and Paul Taggart, 'Comparative and Theoretical Perspectives', in Szczerbiak and Taggart (eds). *Opposing Europe? The Comparative Politics of Euroscepticism* (New York: Oxford University Press, 2008).

18 See, for instance, Jamie Gaskarth, *British Foreign Policy: Crises, Conflicts and Future Challenges* (London: Polity Press, 2013) and McCourt, *Britain and World Power Since 1945,* both of which are broadly 'constructivist' in focus.

19 See for instance Gideon Rose, 'Neoclassical Realism and Theories of Foreign Policy', *World Politics,* vol. 51, no. 1 (1998), pp. 144–72.

20 Wendt, *Social Theory of International Politics.* For an analysis of a major episode in British foreign policy from a constructivist perspective, see David McCourt, 'Role-Playing and Identity Affirmation in International Politics: Britain's Reinvasion of the Falklands, 1982', *Review of International Studies,* vol. 37, no. 4 (2011), pp. 1599–1621.

21 One especially classic statement of this approach is Robert Jervis, *Perception and Misperception in International Politics* (Princeton, NJ: Princeton University Press, 1976).

22 See Amelia Hadfield-Amkhan, *British Foreign Policy, National Identity, and Neoclassical Realism* (Lanham, MD: Rowman & Littlefield, 2010), especially pp. 23–65.

23 See in particular Graham Allison and Philip Zelikow, *Essence of Decision: Explaining the Cuban Missile Crisis,* second edition (New York: Longman, 1999). Here we have combined what they call 'Model II' and 'Model III', which deal with 'outputs' and 'resultants' respectively.

24 In the United States, the Rwandan genocide of 1994 seems to have been the historical analogy of choice within the Barack Obama administration.

25 For an introduction, see for instance John Bew, *Realpolitik: A History* (Oxford, UK: Oxford University Press, 2016).

26 In Realism, this term denotes the absence of government, but not necessarily disorder.

27 See   http://www.publications.parliament.uk/pa/cm201012/cmselect/ cmdfence/761/761we05.htm.

28 The classic studies of foreign policy making in Britain remain William Wallace, *The Foreign Policy Process in Britain* (London: Royal Institute of International Affairs, 1976) and Michael Clarke, 'The Policy Making Process', in Michael Smith, Steve Smith and Brian White (eds), *British Foreign Policy: Tradition, Change and Transformation* (London: Unwin Hyman, 1988), pp. 71–96, although these are a bit dated nowadays. A useful and more recent addition is John Dickie, *The New Mandarins: How British Foreign Policy Works* (New York: I.B. Tauris, 2004). Two classic texts covering the substance of Britain's post-war foreign policy from World War I until the early 1970s are F. S. Northedge, *Descent From Power: British Foreign Policy 1945–1973* (London: George Allen & Unwin, 1974) and Joseph Frankel, *British Foreign Policy 1945–1973* (London: Oxford University Press, 1973). More recent additions to the literature include Mark Curtis, *The Ambiguities of Power: British Foreign Policy Since 1945* (London: Zed Books, 1995), Robert Self, *British Foreign and Defence Policy Since 1945: Challenges and Dilemmas in a Changing World* (London: Palgrave Macmillan, 2010), Brian White, 'British Foreign Policy: Continuity and Transformation', in Ryan Beasley, Juliet Kaarbo, Jeffrey Lantis and Michael Snarr (eds), *Foreign Policy in Comparative Perspective: Domestic and International Influences on State Behavior* , 2nd edn (New York: CQ Press, 2012), Gaskarth, *British Foreign Policy* and McCourt, *Britain and World Power Since 1945*.

29 See for instance Peter Hennessey, *Cabinet* (Oxford: Wiley-Blackwell, 1986).

30 It is so new, in fact, that few studies of its operations or effectiveness have so far been conducted, but see for instance the report by King's College London's institute of Government at http://www.instituteforgovernment.org.uk/ publications/national-security-council.

31 The first National Security Strategy document appeared in 2008 under the Labour government.

Chapter 1

1 See for instance Andrew Rothstein, *British Foreign Policy and Its Critics, 1830–1950* (London: Lawrence & Wishart, 1969), Philip Reynolds, *British Foreign Policy In The Interwar Years* (London: Longman, 1956), John Clarke, *British Diplomacy and Foreign Policy, 1782–1865: The National Interest* (London: Unwin Hyman, 1989), C. J. Lowe, *The Reluctant Imperialists: British Foreign Policy, 1878–1902* (New York: Macmillan, 1969), Muriel Chamberlain, *Pax Britannica?: British Foreign Policy, 1789–1914* (London: Longman, 1988), Paul Doerr, *British Foreign Policy, 1919–1939* (Manchester: Manchester University Press, 1998) and Michael Dockrill and Brian McKercher (eds), *Diplomacy and World Power: Studies in British Foreign Policy, 1890–1950* (Cambridge: Cambridge University Press, 1996).

2 For a brief review, see John Mackintosh, 'Britain in Europe: Historical Perspective and Contemporary Reality', *International Affairs*, vol. 45, no. 2 (1969), pp. 246–58.

3 Jeremy Paxman, *Empire* (London: Penguin Books, 2011), p. 168.

4 See for instance Eric Hobsbawm, *The Age of Revolution: Europe 1789–1848* (Weidenfeld & Nicolson, 1995); John Eatwell, *Whatever Happened to Britain?* (London: BBC, 1982); Andrew Gamble, *Britain in Decline: Economic Policy, Political Strategy and the British State*, second edition (London: Macmillan, 1985).

5 Paul Kennedy, *The Rise and Fall of British Naval Mastery* (New York: Humanity Books, 2006).

6 Eric Hobsbawm, *Industry and Empire: From 1750 to the Present Day* (New York: W.W. Norton, 1999), pp. 2–3.

7 Eatwell, *Whatever Happened To Britain?*

8 Hobsbawm, *Industry and Empire*, p. 27.

9 Gamble, *Britain in Decline*, p. 4.

10 Paul Kennedy, *The Rise and Fall of British Naval Mastery*, pp. 150–51.

11 Zimbabwe only gained full independence relatively recently, in 1980.

12 See Gamble, *Britain in Decline*, pp. 3–44.

13 Sir Eyre Crowe, 'Memorandum on the Present State of British Relations with France and Germany' (1 January 1907) cited in Graham Spry, 'Canada, the Emergency Force and the Commonwealth', *International Affairs*, vol. 33, no. 3 (1957), p. 290.

14 It has sometimes been argued that Realism is itself a morally based foreign policy strategy, since beneath the surface of the balance of power strategy lurks what is in fact a moral objective: the maintenance of global peace and stability. On the other hand, it often requires the violation of moral precepts in an immediate sense, as when US President Richard Nixon and his National Security Adviser Henry Kissinger supported Augusto Pinochet's Chile during the Cold War in full knowledge of the appalling human rights violations Pinochet was committing at home.

15 Crowe, 'Memorandum on the Present State of British Relations with France and Germany'.

16 Michael Howard, *Splendid Isolation* (New York: Macmillan, 1970).

17 See Thomas Magstadt, *An Empire If You Can Keep It: Power and Principle in American Foreign Policy* (Washington, DC: CQ Press, 2004), Chapter 2.

18 Robert Kaplan, *The Revenge of Geography: What The Map Tells Us About Coming Conflicts and the Battle Against Fate* (New York: Random House, 2012), pp. 30–31.

19 Henry Kissinger, *Diplomacy* (New York: Simon and Schuster, 1994), pp. 161–62.

20 Chamberlain, *Pax Britannica*, p. 142.

21 See for instance Marvin Swartz, *The Politics of British Foreign Policy in the Era of Disraeli and Gladstone* (New York: St Martin's Press, 1985), pp. 123–44.

22 Robert Pearson and Geraint Williams, *Political Thought and Public Policy in The Nineteenth Century: An Introduction* (London: Longman, 1984), p. 57.

23 Roy Jenkins, *Gladstone* (London: Macmillan, 1995).

24 Mackintosh, 'Britain in Europe', p. 248.

25 For a detailed analysis of the British government's military objectives during this period, see V. H. Rothwell, *British War Aims and Peace Diplomacy 1914–1958* (Oxford: Clarendon Press, 1971).

26 David Thomson, 'General De Gaulle and the Anglo Saxons', *International Affairs*, vol. 41, no. 1 (1965), p. 11. After 1918 the need to maintain a strong France became a basic axiom of Britain's European policy.

27 Mackintosh, 'Britain in Europe', p. 247.

28 W. L. Wright, 'Truths about Turkey', *Foreign Affairs*, vol. 26 (1948), pp. 349–59.

29 Peter J. Beck, 'A Tedious and Perilous Controversy: Britain and the Settlement of the Mosul Dispute, 1918–1926', *Middle East Studies*, vol. 17, no. 2 (1981), pp. 256–76; Robert W. Olson and Nurham Ince, 'Turkish Foreign Policy from 1923–1960: Kemalism and its Legacy, a Review and Critique', *Oriento Moderno*, vol. 57, no. 1 (1997), pp. 227–41.

30 Bernard Porter notes that during the 19th century Latin America was very much part of the United Kingdom's 'informal' empire. There was a greater degree of British capital penetration in Argentina, for example, than in many of Britain's actual colonies. See Porter, *The Lion's Share: A Short History of British Imperialism*, 2nd edn (London: Longmans, 1984), chapter 1.

31 Mackintosh, 'Britain in Europe', p. 249. For a detailed analysis see Bradford Perkins, *The Great Rapprochement: England and the US 1895–1914* (London: Victor Gollancz, 1969).

32 Nicholas Mansberg, 'Britain, the Commonwealth and the Western Union', *International Affairs*, vol. 24, no. 4 (1948), pp. 491–504.

33 In fact, France and Russia already possessed sufficient capability to outweigh the Royal Navy in the late 1880s. See Porter, *The Lion's Share*, pp. 123–25.

34 Keith Wilson, 'British Power in the European Balance 1906–14', in David Dilks (ed.), *Retreat from Power: Studies in Britain's Foreign Policy of the Twentieth Century, Volume I, 1906–1939* (London: Macmillan, 1981) p. 26.

35 Henry Kissinger, *A World Restored: Metternich, Castlereagh and the Problems of Peace, 1812–22* (London: Weidenfeld & Nicolson, 1957); Kissinger, *Diplomacy*.

36 Quincy Wright provides an admirable summary. See Quincy Wright, *A Study of War*, vol. II (Chicago: Chicago University Press, 1942) especially pp. 727–8.

37 David Dilks, 'Introduction', in Dilks (ed.) *Retreat from Power*, pp. 19–20.

38 See Porter, *The Lion's Share*, pp. 239–51.

39 On the dismemberment of the Ottoman Empire after 1918, see R. R. Kasliwal, 'The Foreign Policy of Turkey Since 1919', *Indian Journal of Political Science*, vol. 7 (1946), pp. 38–97.

40 On the new Soviet government's approach to the post-war settlement, see J. M. Thompson, *Russia, Bolshevism and the Versailles Peace* (Princeton, NJ: Princeton University Press, 1966).

41 M. Kajima, *The Emergence of Japan as a World Power 1895–1925* (Rutland, Vermont: Tuttle, 1978).

42 For a discussion of these treaties, see H. M. Swanwick, *Collective Insecurity* (London: Jonathan Cape, 1937), pp. 53–59.

43 H. A. L. Fisher, *A History of Europe, Volume II: From the Early Eighteenth Century to 1935* (London: Fontana, 1975), p. 1275. Cited in Porter, *The Lion's Share*, p. 249.

44 C. E. Callwell, *Field Marshall Sir Henry Wilson* (London: Cassell, 1927), pp. 240–41, cited in *The Lion's Share*, p. 252.

45 In 1922 Britain's armed forces personnel numbered 200,000. It was not until 1937 – in Duff Cooper's 1937 Army Estimates – that serious reform was considered. Hore-Belisha introduced further changes in 1938. See Liddell Hart, *The Defence of Britain* (London: Faber & Faber, 1939), especially pp. 251–309.

46 Paxman, *Empire*, p. 230.

47 On the British experience in Iraq, see for instance Toby Dodge, *Inventing Iraq: The Failure of Nation Building and a History Denied* (New York: Columbia University Press, 2003); Christopher Catherwood, *Churchill's Folly: How Winston Churchill Created Modern Iraq* (New York: Carroll and Graf, 2004); and William Polk, *Understanding Iraq* (New York: Harper, 2005), pp. 67–101.

48 On the background to this propaganda, see Philip Taylor, 'Publicity and Diplomacy: The Impact of the First World War upon Foreign Office Attitudes towards the Press', in Dilks (ed.), *Retreat from Power*, pp. 42–63.

49 Cited in Porter, *The Lion's Share*, p. 255

50 See Hersch Lauterpacht, *The Function of Law in the International Community* (London: Oxford University Press, 1933).

51 The three major League institutions were the Council, the Assembly and the Permanent Court of International Justice, which were intended to constitute, respectively, an embryonic supranational executive, legislature and judiciary. For a definitive review of the operations of the League, see F. P. Walters, *A History of the League of Nations* (London: Oxford University Press, 1960).

52 Ibid., chapters 3–6.

53 Graham Allison and Philip Zelikow, *Essence of Decision: Explaining the Cuban Missile Crisis*, 2nd edn (New York: Longman, 1999).

54 For details, see Walters, *League of Nations*, pp. 465–99 and 623–91.

55 Vansittart, a confirmed Realist of long standing, was Permanent Undersecretary at the Foreign Office between 1930 and 1938. He was reportedly ousted at Eden's instigation and replaced by Sir Alexander Cadogan, who remained in office until 1946: John Colville, *The Fringes of Power: Downing Street Diaries 1939–1955* (London: Hodder & Stoughton, 1985), p. 162.

56 For a detailed analysis of British policy during the Abyssinian crisis, see Norton Medlicott, 'The Hoare-Laval Pact Reconsidered', in Dilks (ed.), *Retreat from Power*, pp. 11–38.

57 C. J. Bartlett, *The Global Conflict: The International Rivalry of the Great Powers, 1880–1970* (London: Longman, 1984), pp. 182–83.

58 Ruth Henig (ed.), *The League of Nations* (Edinburgh: Oliver & Boyd, 1973), p. 117.

59 Bartlett, *The Global Conflict*, p. 175.

60 Ibid., p. 176.

61 Norton Medlicott, 'Britain and Germany: The Search for Agreement 1930–37', in Dilks (ed.), *Retreat from Power*, pp. 78–101.

62 Bartlett, *The Global Conflict*, p. 176.

63 Ibid., p. 177.

64 Medlicott, 'Britain and Germany', p. 92.

65 Chamberlain's commitment to appeasement eventually got too much even for Eden, who resigned in February 1938 over Chamberlain's efforts to conciliate Mussolini over the latter's African policy: Eden was by then convinced of the need to resist aggression – or the threat of it – with force. See Bartlett, *The Global Conflict*, pp. 207–8.

66 William Wallace, *The Foreign Policy Process in Britain* (London: Royal Institute of International Affairs, 1976), p. 75. For a critique of Henderson's diplomacy, see Sir Charles Webster, 'Munich Reconsidered: A Survey of British Policy', *International Affairs*, vol. 37, no. 2 (1961), pp. 137–53.

67 Bartlett, *The Global Conflict*, p. 197.

68 Sir Keith Feiling, *The Life of Neville Chamberlain* (London: Macmillan, 1947), p. 401, cited *in The Global Conflict*, p. 202.

69 Webster, 'Munich Reconsidered', p. 149.

70 The definitive work is E. L. Woodward, *British Foreign Policy in the Second World War* (5 vols) (London: HMSO, 1970–76). See also Christopher Thorne, *Allies of a Kind: The United States, Britain and the War Against Japan, 1941–42* (London: Hamish Hamilton, 1978); A. P. Adamthwaite, *The Making of the Second World War* (London: George Allen & Unwin, 1977); Elisabeth Barker, *Churchill and Eden at War* (London: Macmillan, 1978); David Dilks (ed.), *The Diaries of Sir Alexander Cadogan 1938–45* (London: Cassell, 1971); Michael Howard, *The Mediterranean Strategy in the Second World War* (London: Weidenfeld & Nicolson, 1968).

71 McNeill, *Survey*, p. 139.

72 Ibid., p. 668.

73 Sir Henry Tizzard's 'Scientific and Technical Information Mission' first went to Washington in August 1940. See Baylis, *Anglo-American Defence*, p. 5. Baylis also notes that British participation in nuclear research on the Manhattan Project was euphemistically recorded officially as involvement in 'Tube alloys' research.

74 Colville, *Fringes of Power*, p. 331.

75 This 'mixing up' had been anticipated by Churchill in the Commons on 20 August 1940. See Baylis, *Anglo-American Defence*, p. 4.

76 Ibid., p. 15.

77 The worst disaster was probably the ill-fated Arnhem expedition of September 1944.

78 The definitive work on the subject is William Roger Louis, *Imperialism at Bay: The United States and the Decolonisation of the British Empire, 1941–45* (London: Oxford University Press, 1977).

79 McNeill, *Survey*, p. 453.
80 Ibid., p. 524.

Chapter 2

1 The problems of the British economy in the immediate post-war years are discussed in more detail in Chapter 7.
2 *CMND 6707, Statistical Materials Presented During the Washington Negotiations* (HMSO, 1945) pp. 5–8.
3 William McNeill, *Survey of International Affairs 1939–46*, p. 676.
4 Bernard Porter, *The Lion's Share*, pp. 260–61.
5 For a review of the debate in the 1980s, see Andrew Gamble, *Britain in Decline: Economic Policy, Political Strategy and the British State* (London: Macmillan, 1985); David Coates and John Hillard (eds), *The Economic Decline of Modern Britain: The Debate Between Left and Right* (Brighton: Wheatsheaf, 1986).
6 *Monthly Digest of Statistics No. 49* (HMSO, January, 1950), p. 89. The annual deficits reported here are the published monthly averages multiplied by 12.
7 *CMND 6743, Statement Relating to Defence* (HMSO, February, 1946).
8 *CMND 7327, Statement Relating to Defence* (HMSO, February, 1948).
9 Ibid., p. 62.
10 A good example of the 'turning point' thesis can be found in Christopher Mayhew, 'British Foreign Policy Since 1945', *International Affairs*, vol. 26, no. 4 (1950), pp. 477–86.
11 Several of the subsequent departures both from the tacit agreements made at Yalta and from the more explicit declarations made at Potsdam are catalogued in Anne Whyte, 'Quadripartite Rule in Berlin', *International Affairs*, vol. 23, no. 1 (1947), pp. 30–41.
12 Arnold Toynbee, 'A Turning Point in the Cold War?', *International Affairs*, vol. 26, no. 4 (1950), p. 459.
13 Repayments of the loan were not to begin until December 1951. They would then be paid in 50 annual instalments at 2 per cent interest with no interest payable if Britain's trade balance fell below the 1936–38 level. McNeill, *Survey*, p. 683.
14 Ibid., pp. 652–53.
15 Cited in McNeill, *Survey*, p. 731.
16 Cited in Bartlett, *The Global Conflict*, p. 263.
17 Geoffrey Warner, 'The Truman Doctrine and the Marshall Plan', *International Affairs*, vol. 50, no. 1 (1974), p. 83.
18 Mayhew, 'British Foreign Policy', p. 480.
19 'Containment', of course, was identified most closely with George Kennan, a senior policy adviser within the US State Department, although he always objected that his original notion had been 'militarized' in a way that he never intended.

20 Reynolds attributes this remark to Paul Hoffman, one of the Marshall Aid administrators. See David Reynolds, '"A Special Relationship"? America, Britain and the International Order since the Second World War', *International Affairs*, vol. 62, nol. 1 (1986), p. 8.

21 The calculations underlying British decisions over the Brussels Treaty are discussed in John Baylis, 'Britain, the Brussels Pact and the Continental Commitment', *International Affairs*, vol. 60, no. 4 (1984), pp. 615–30.

22 Bartlett, *The Global Conflict*, p. 275.

23 A. H. Head, 'European Defence', *International Affairs*, vol. 27, no. 1 (1951), pp. 1–9. See also Michael Dockrill, 'The Foreign Office, Anglo-American Relations and the Korean War, June 1950–June 1951', *International Affairs*, vol. 62, no. 3 (1986), pp. 459–78; Peter Truscott, 'The Korean War in British Foreign and Domestic Policy, 1950–52' (PhD dissertation, Exeter College, Oxford, 1984), p. 24.

24 Bartlett, *The Global Conflict*, pp. 280–81.

25 The rearmament package was intended to cost some £4,700 million over the period 1951–54 (Truscott, 'The Korean War', pp. 108–10). This included a quadrupling of expenditure on military hardware by 1953–54 (CMND 8146, Defence Programme Statement Made by the Prime Minister in the House of Commons, January 29th 1951 (HMSO, 1951)).

26 The Federal German Republic achieved independence in September 1949.

27 The signatories were France, the Federal German Republic, Italy, Belgium, Luxembourg and the Netherlands.

28 The phrase 'Third World' was not itself widely used until the 1960s.

29 The Elbe was assumed to constitute the West German border and the Rhine the French border.

30 Anglo-American policy towards the oil states during the 1930s and 1940s is discussed in Sir Arthur Hearn, 'Oil and the Middle East', *International Affairs*, vol. 24, no. 1 (1948), pp. 63–75.

31 Bartlett, *The Global Conflict*. p. 272.

32 The British did ask Eisenhower and the CIA to topple Mohammed Mossadegh, the elected Iranian leader, but from that point on it was essentially an American operation. See Stephen Kinzer, *All the Shah's Men: An American Coup and the Roots of Middle East Terror* (New York: John Wiley, 2008). American compliance in 1953 may later have played a role in convincing the British that the Americans would 'go along' – despite all evidence being to the contrary – during the Suez affair of 1956.

33 Bartlett, *The Global Conflict*, p. 272.

34 The express reason for the Soviets' action was the Americans' refusal to allow the People's Republic of China a seat at the UN.

35 Kenneth Younger, 'Public Opinion and British Foreign Policy', *International Affairs*, vol. 40, no. 1 (1964), p. 26.

36 CAB 128/18 CM (50) 79, (11 Nov. 1950) cited in Truscott, 'The Korean War', p. 18.

37 Bartlett, *The Global Conflict*, p. 298.

38 Note from Dean Acheson to Ernest Bevin (10 July 1950) cited in Truscott, 'The Korean War', p. 3.

39 Ibid., p. 4.

40 Bartlett, *The Global Conflict*, p. 299.

41 This was certainly what Truman – according to his memoirs – told Attlee at their meeting in Washington in December 1950. See Truscott, 'The Korean War', p. 38.

42 Kenneth Younger, then Minister of State at the Foreign Office, observed: 'We were simply resigned to the fact that MacArthur had gone mad and was totally out of control'. See Truscott, 'The Korean War', pp. 58–59.

43 Ibid., p. 68.

44 Ibid., p. 14.

45 Ibid., pp. 14–16.

46 Nicholas Henderson, 'Britain's Decline: its Causes and Consequences', *The Economist* (2 July 1979), p. 34.

Chapter 3

1 Bernard Porter, *The Lion's Share*, p. 240.

2 John Darwin, 'Imperialism in Decline? Tendencies in British Imperial Policy between the Wars', *Historical Journal*, vol. 23, no. 3 (1980), pp. 657–79.

3 Anthony Howard, *RAB: The Life of R. A. Butler* (London: Jonathan Cape, 1987), pp. 57–58.

4 Y. Krishan, 'Mountbatten and the Partition of India', *History*, vol. 68, no. 1 (1983), pp. 22–37.

5 Ibid, p. 22.

6 I. A. Talbot, 'Mountbatten and the Partition of India: A Rejoinder', *History*, vol. 69, no. 1 (1984), pp. 29–35.

7 In 1922 there were some 48,000 Jews in Palestine. By 1948 the figure had increased to 640,000. See Sir Alan Cunningham, 'Palestine: The Last Days of the Mandate', *International Affairs*, vol. 24, no. 4 (1948), pp. 481–90.

8 Ritchie Ovendale, 'The Palestine Policy of the British Labour Government 1945–1946', *International Affairs*, vol. 55, no. 3 (1979), pp. 409–31.

9 Quoted in Michael Howard, *The Continental Commitment: The Dilemma of British Defence Policy in the Era of Two World Wars* (Harmondsworth: Penguin, 1974), p. 14.

10 T. H. Silcock, 'Policy for Malaya, 1952', *International Affairs*, vol. 28, no. 4 (1952), pp. 445–51.

11 CMND 9688, Memorandum of the Secretary of State for War Relating to the Army Estimates 1956–57 (HMSO, February 1958).

12 C. W. Greenidge, 'The Present Outlook in the British West Indies', *International Affairs*, vol. 25, no. 2 (1949), pp. 175–81.

13 Southern Rhodesia did not achieve legal independence – as Zimbabwe – until 1980.

14 Martin Wight, 'Brutus in Foreign Policy: The Memoirs of Sir Anthony Eden', *International Affairs*, vol. 36, no. 3 (1960), p. 309.

15 There is now an extensive literature on Suez. Keith Kyle, *Suez: Britain's End of Empire in the Middle East* (London: Weidenfeld & Nicolson, 1991) is

perhaps the most detailed, but see also Scott Lucas, *Divided We Stand: Britain, the US and the Suez Crisis: Britain, the United States and the Suez Crisis* (London: Hodder and Stoughton, 1991) and Anthony Gorst and Lewis Johnman, *The Suez Crisis* (London: Routledge, 1997).

Also useful are J. T. Henderson, 'Leadership Personality and War: The Cases of Richard Nixon and Anthony Eden', *Political Science*, vol. 28, no. 2 (1976), pp.141–64; Gill Bennett, *Six Moments of Crisis: Inside British Foreign Policy* (New York: Oxford University Press, 2013), Chapter 2 (pp. 37–64); Bertjan Verbeek, 'Do Individual and Group Beliefs Matter? British Decision-Making During the 1956 Suez Crisis', *Cooperation and Conflict*, vol. 29, no.4 (1994), pp. 307–332; Jonathan Pearson, *Sir Anthony Eden and the Suez Crisis: Reluctant Gamble* (London: Palgrave Macmillan, 2002); Bertjan Verbeek, *Decision Making in Great Britain During the Suez Crisis: Small Groups and a Persistent Leader* (London: Ashgate, 2003); Robert McNamara, *Britain, Nasser and the Balance of Power in the Middle East, 1952–1967* (London: Routledge, 2003); Lord Owen, 'The Effect of Prime Minister Anthony Eden's Illness on His Decision-Making During the Suez Crisis', *QJM: An International Journal of Medicine*, vol. 98, no. 6 (2005) pp. 387–402; *The Economist*, 'The Suez Crisis: An Affair to Remember', 27 July 2006; Nigel Ashton, 'Hitler on the Nile? British and American Perceptions of the Nasser Regime, 1952–1970', in Lawrence Freedman and Jeffrey Michaels (eds), *Scripting Middle East Leaders: The Impact of Leadership Perceptions on US and UK Foreign Policy* (New York and London: Continuum, 2013). Accounts of Suez can also be found in David Dutton, *Anthony Eden. A Life and Reputation* (London: Arnold, 1997) and D. R. Thorpe, *Eden: The Life and Times of Anthony Eden, First Earl of Avon, 1897–1977* (London: Chatto & Windus, 2003).

16 This theme is developed in F. S. Northedge, 'Britain as a Second-Rank Power', *International Affairs*, vol. 46, no. 1 (1970), pp. 37–47.

17 Doreen Warriner, 'Land Reform in Egypt and its repercussions', *International Affairs*, vol. 29, no. 1 (1953), pp. 1–10.

18 William Roger Louis, 'American Anti-colonialism and the Dissolution of the British Empire', *International Affairs*, vol. 61, no. 3 (1985), p. 413.

19 Ibid.

20 Geoffrey Warner, '"Collusion" and the Suez crisis of 1956', *International Affairs*, vol. 55, no. 2 (1979), pp. 226–39.

21 Reynolds, 'A Special Relationship', p. 10.

22 John Baylis, *Anglo-American Defence Relations 1939–1984*, 2nd edn (London: Macmillan, 1984), p. 73.

23 Anthony Howard, *RAB*, pp. 239–41.

24 Wight, 'Brutus', p. 306.

25 William Wallace, *The Foreign Policy Process in Britain* (London: Royal Institute of International Affairs, 1976), p. 75.

26 Sir Anthony Eden, *The Memoirs of the Right Hon. Sir Anthony Eden: Full Circle* (London: Cassell, 1960), p. 579.

27 David Sanders, *Lawmaking and Co-operation in International Politics: the idealist case re-examined* (London: Macmillan, 1986), ch. 5.

Chapter 4

1 William Wallace, *The Foreign Policy Process in Britain*, p. 82.
2 Wight, 'Brutus in Foreign Policy', p. 305; Elisabeth Monroe, 'British bases in the Middle East – assets or liabilities?', *International Affairs*, vol. 42, no. 1 (1966), pp. 25–27.
3 Graham Spry, 'Canada, the UN Emergency Force and the Commonwealth', *International Affairs*, vol. 33, no. 3 (1957), pp. 289–300.
4 This reasoning had already been articulated in the early 20th century. See, for example, Leopold Amery, *My Political Life (Volume 1): England Before the Storm, 1896–1914* (London: Hutchinson, 1953).
5 Indeed, in 1955 serious consideration had been given to consolidating the Commonwealth by increasing its membership from eight (United Kingdom, Canada, New Zealand, Australia, South Africa, India, Pakistan, Ceylon) to thirteen, through the creation of new dominions in the Caribbean, in West Africa, in the Rhodesias and Nyasaland, in East Africa and in Greater Malaya. See C. E. Carrington, 'A New Theory of the Commonwealth', *International Affairs*, vol. 31, no. 2 (1955), pp. 137–148.
6 Wight, 'Brutus in Foreign Policy'; CMND 150, Memorandum of the Secretary of State for War Relating to the Army Estimates 1957–8 (HMSO, April 1957).
7 For a summary of the changed establishment position, see Earl of Home, 'Interdependence: The British Role', *International Affairs*, vol. 37, no. 2 (1961), pp. 154–60.
8 For review, see R. I. Rotberg and Ali Mazrui (eds), *Protest and Power and Black Africa* (New York: Oxford University Press, 1970), especially sections 4–6.
9 This view was by no means confined to the British popular press. In July 1960, for example, the US representative on the UN Security Council (Henry Cabot Lodge) observed that the Soviet Union was 'evidently seeking to bring the Cold War to the heart of Africa' (*Keesings Contemporary Archive*, 1960, p. 17648).
10 For a detailed description of the process of social mobilisation, see Karl Deutsch, 'Social Mobilisation and Political Development', *American Political Science Review*, vol. 55, no. 3 (1961), pp. 494–512.
11 As Porter so succinctly puts it: 'colonialism was breeding its own antidote'. See Porter, *The Lion's Share*, pp. 322 ff.
12 Deutsch, 'Social Mobilisation', pp. 495–97.
13 For a review of the impact of social mobilisation on political developments throughout the third world generally, see Samuel Huntington, *Political Order in Changing Societies* (New Haven: Yale University Press, 1968).
14 In Mozambique and Angola the settler regimes were also in the fortunate position of receiving the full backing of the Salazar dictatorship in Lisbon: it was only when Salazar was ousted in an army coup in 1974 that independence was secured.
15 Iraq had also been a signatory to the pact, though it abrogated the agreement in 1958.

16 CMND 2902, *Statement on the Defence Estimates 1966 Part II: Defence Estimates 1966–67* (HMSO: Feb. 1966).

17 Wallace, *Foreign Policy Process*, pp. 138–39.

18 Ibid, pp. 119–20. For useful analyses of the East of Suez decision-making, see Gill Bennett, *Six Moments of Crisis: Inside British Foreign Policy* (New York: Oxford University Press, 2013), Chapter 4 (pp. 95–121) and Saki Dockrill, *Britain's Retreat from East of Suez: The Choice Between Europe and the World?* (New York: Palgrave Macmillan, 2002).

19 Ibid, p. 136.

20 Alistair Buchan, 'Britain and the Indian Ocean', *International Affairs*, vol. 42, no. 2 (1966), pp. 184–193.

21 CMND 2901 *Statement on the Defence Estimates 1966 Part I: The Defence Review* (HMSO: Feb. 1966).

22 CMND 3540, *Statement on the Defence Estimates 1968* (HMSO: Feb. 1968).

23 CMND 3701, *Supplementary Statement on Defence Policy 1968* (HMSO: July 1968).

24 In 1965 the United States devoted 7.6 per cent of GNP to defence expenditure. The UK figure was 5.9 per cent. The comparable figures for Britain's major competitors were as follows:

France	5.5%	Netherlands	4.0%	Denmark	2.9%
Sweden	4.4%	Italy	3.4%	Austria	1.3%
FRG	4.4%	Belgium	3.0%	Japan	0.9%

Source: Charles Lewis Taylor and Michael C. Hudson, *World Handbook of Social and Political Indicators*, 2nd edn (New Haven: Yale University Press, 1972), pp. 34–36.

25 Wallace, *Foreign Policy Process*, p. 134.

26 Michael Howard, 'Britain's Strategic Problem East of Suez', *International Affairs*, vol. 42, no. 2 (1966), pp. 179–83; CMND 2592: *Statement on the Defence Estimates 1965* (HMSO: Feb. 1965).

27 The 20-year UK–Libya Treaty of Friendship and Alliance had been signed in July 1953.

28 The 1953 Treaty was terminated by an Exchange of Notes in January 1972.

29 The Foreign Office and the Colonial Office were merged in 1968 to form the Foreign and Commonwealth Office.

30 Ghana experienced coups in 1972, 1978, 1979 and 1982; Nigeria in 1975, 1983 and 1985.

31 Treaties were signed with Bahrain in August 1971, with Qatar in September and with the United Arab Emirates in December. Note that it was partly these commitments – as well as the need to protect Western shipping – that led to the renewed British naval presence in the Gulf in the late 1980s, as the spill-over from the Iran-Iraq war threatened the security of Western shipping in the region.

32 CMND 4890, *Exchange of Notes between … the United Kingdom … and … Malaysia regarding Assistance for the Malaysia Armed Forces and the Arrangements for a United Kingdom Force in Malaysia* (1 Dec. 1971).

33 Ibid.

34 CMND 3231, *Exchange of Notes between the Government of the United Kingdom and the Government of the United States of America concerning the availability for defence purposes of the British Indian Ocean Territory* (30 Dec. 1966).

35 CMND 6413 *Exchange of Notes between ... the United Kingdom ...and ... the United States of America concerning a United States Navy Support facility on Diego Garcia, British Indian Ocean Territory* (25 Feb. 1976).

36 Training agreements were signed with Zambia, Cyprus and Botswana in 1968; with Nigeria in 1969; with Malawi in 1970; with Malaysia and Kenya in 1973; and with Zimbabwe in 1980.

37 There are now a number of good studies on the Falklands episode. See, for instance, Richard Ned Lebow, 'Miscalculation in the South Atlantic: The Origins of the Falklands War', *Journal of Strategic Studies* vol. 6, no. 1 (1983), pp. 5–35; William Furlong and Craig Albiston, 'Sovereignty, Culture and Misperceptions: The Falklands/Malvinas War', *Conflict*, vol. 6, no.5 (1985), p. 139–75; Lawrence Freedman, 'Intelligence Operations in the Falklands', *Intelligence and National Security*, vol. 3, no. 1 (1986), pp. 309–335; Lawrence Freedman and Virginia Gamba-Stonehouse, *Signals of War: The Falklands Conflict of 1982* (London: Faber and Faber, 1990); Max Hastings and Simon Jenkins, *The Battle For the Falklands* (New York: Norton, 1984); David McCourt, 'Role-Playing and Identity Affirmation in International Politics: Britain's Reinvasion of the Falklands, 1982', *Review of International Studies*, vol. 37, no. 4 (2011), pp. 1599–1621; Martin Middlebrook, *The Falklands War* (London: Pen and Sword, 2012); Naval Postgraduate School, *The Falklands War: Causes and Lessons* (New York: Pennyhill Press, 2014) and Bennett, *Six Moments of Crisis: Inside British Foreign Policy*, Chapter 6 (pp. 149–172). Lawrence Freedman has put together two especially useful documentary collections, *The Official History of the Falklands Campaign: The Origins of the Falklands War: Volume One* (Government Official History Series) (London: Routledge, 2006) and *The Official History of the Falklands Campaign: War and Diplomacy: Volume Two* (Whitehall Histories) (London: Routledge 2006).

38 CMND 8288, *The United Kingdom Defence Programme: The Way Forward* (HMSO: 1981).

39 Lebow, 'Miscalculation in the South Atlantic: The Origins of the Falklands War', p.5.

40 There is no direct evidence to support the view that Thatcher's stance was a calculated 'diversionary' move to increase her own domestic popularity. The effects of the Falklands War on the government's popularity are the subject of some contention. See, for example, David Sanders, Hugh Ward and David Marsh, 'Government Popularity and the Falklands War: A Reassessment', *British Journal of Political Science*, vol. 17, no. 2 (1987), pp. 281–313.

41 *The Telegraph*, 'Britain to Send More Troops to the Falklands to Counter "Heightened" Invasion Threat from Argentina', 24 March 2015, accessed at http://www.telegraph.co.uk/news/worldnews/southamerica/falklandislands/11491135/Britain-to-increase-Falklands-garrison.html.

42 *CMND 9543, Joint Declaration of the Government of the United Kingdom ... and the Government of the People's Republic of China on the question of Hong Kong* (19 Dec. 1984).

43 The literature on this subject is voluminous. Probably the most authoritative work is still Ernest Mandel, *Late Capitalism* (London: New Left Books, 1975).

44 Moreover, the complex internal and external accounting procedures used by contemporary multinational corporations make systematic profit-tracing an almost impossible exercise anyway.

45 It can of course be argued that some third-world politicians corruptly welcome foreign multinational investment for their own private gain. However, such an argument does not confront the crucial question as to the balance of cost and benefit that accrues from the activities of multinational corporations in third-world countries.

46 This is generally achieved by examining over time movement in the relative prices of raw materials as against manufactures. See, for example, Michael Beenstock, *The World Economy in Transition* (London: George Allen & Unwin, 1983), p. 101.

47 The phrase 'emptying out' is derived from Northedge. See F. S. Northedge, 'Britain as a Second-Rank Power', *International Affairs*, vol. 46, no. 1 (1970), p. 40.

Chapter 5

1 The original 'six' of the EU were France, the Federal Republic of Germany, Italy, Belgium, the Netherlands and Luxembourg. The EEC became the EU in 1993.

2 Advocates of the 'hard' version favour complete withdrawal from the EU, while its 'soft' advocates merely want to slow the pace and extent of political integration. See Aleks Szczerbiak and Paul Taggart, 'Comparative and Theoretical Perspectives' in Szczerbiak and Taggart (eds.), *Opposing Europe? The Comparative Politics of Euroscepticism* (Oxford: Oxford University Press, 2008).

3 Brian Wheeler and Alex Hunt, 'The UK's EU Referendum: All You Need To Know', *BBC News*, 24 June 2016. Available at http://www.bbc.com/news/uk-politics-32810887.

4 Leaving the EU involves the invocation of Article 50 of the Treaty of Lisbon, which lays down the conditions for exit, although at the time of writing it was unclear what exactly the British process would involve since the Article had never been used before.

5 During the Cold War, these were an important complement to its closer economic and political ties with Western Europe.

6 A good general introduction to the EU is Michelle Cini and Nieves Pérez-Solórzano Borragán (eds), *European Union Politics*, 4th edn (Oxford: Oxford University Press, 2013).

7 The Council of Europe was loosely based on an idea mooted by Churchill in September 1945. The original members were Britain, France, Belgium, the Netherlands, Luxembourg, Sweden, Norway, Denmark, Ireland and Italy. They were subsequently joined by Iceland, West Germany, Greece, Turkey and Austria.

8 See, for example, Altiero Spinelli, *The Eurocrats. Conflict and Crisis in the EEC* (trans. C. Grove Haines) (Baltimore: Johns Hopkins Press, 1966).

9 Some useful overviews of EU integration theory are Michael O'Neill (ed.), *The Politics of European Integration: A Reader* (London: Routledge, 1996), Ben Rosamond, *Theories of European Integration* (The European Union Series) (Basingstoke: Palgrave Macmillan, 2000) and Antje Wiener and Thomas Diez, *European Integration Theory* (Oxford: Oxford University Press, 2009).

10 CMND 13, *Agreement concerning the Relations between the United Kingdom and the European Coal and Steel Community* (21 Dec. 1954). This in many respects unique agreement in fact gave the UK government and industry direct access to the High Authority and, therefore, to the decision-making structure of the ECSC itself.

11 This is not to say, however, that Whitehall was entirely unaware of the changes that were under way. The shift in the pattern of Britain's external trade was certainly anticipated by Sir Frank Lee, then Permanent Undersecretary at the Board of Trade.

12 An additional reason for Britain's lack of interest in the EEC at this stage was the belief – widely held in British foreign policy circles – that French opposition would prevent the plans for the proposed EEC from coming into fruition. It was only after Suez had 'bounced' the French into the EEC and Euratom ventures that the British realised that they would indeed have to face a de facto customs union among the Six.

13 David Coombes, *Politics and Bureaucracy in the European Community: A Portrait of the Commission of the EEC* (London: George Allen & Unwin, 1970), p. 75.

14 This phrase comes from John Dumbrell, *A Special Relationship: Anglo-American Relations from the Cold War to Iraq*, 2nd edn (Basingstoke: Palgrave Macmillan, 2006), pp. 49–74.

15 Peter Calvocoressi, *World Politics since 1945*, 4th edn (London: Longman, 1982), pp. 167–68.

16 CMND 2108 *Polaris. Sales Agreement between the Government of the United Kingdom ... and the Government of the United States of America* (4 June 1963).

17 Wallace, *The Foreign Policy Process*, pp. 85–86.

18 Alan Campbell, 'Anglo-French Relations a Decade Ago: A New Assessment (1)', *International Affairs*, vol. 58, no. 2 (1982), pp. 237–53.

19 CMND 5179, *Treaty concerning the Accession of ... the United Kingdom ... to the European Economic Community and the European Atomic Energy Community including the Act concerning the conditions of Accession and the Adjustment to the Treaties ...* (1 Jan. 1973).

20 The Warsaw Treaty Organisation was created in 1955. Its members were the USSR, Poland, the German Democratic Republic, Hungary, Czechoslovakia, Romania and Bulgaria.

21 Sanders, *Lawmaking and Cooperation*, pp. 21–27.

22 CMND 4705, *Long-Term Economic and Trade Agreement between the Government of the United Kingdom ... and the Government of the Polish People's Republic* (21 April 1971).

23 CMND 5016, *Long-Term Economic and Trade Agreement between the Government of the United Kingdom ... and the Government of the Hungarian People's Republic* (21 March 1972); CMND 5074, *Long-Term Economic and Trade Agreement between the Government of the United Kingdom ... and the Government of ... Czechoslovakia* (27 June 1982); CMND 5106, *Long-Term Economic and Trade Agreement between the Government of the United Kingdom ... and the Socialist Republic of Romania* (15 June 1972).

24 Colville, *The Fringes of Power*, p. 683.

25 *The Oxford Dictionary of Quotations* (Oxford University Press, 1985) attributes the phrase to Theodore Roosevelt (p. 408).

26 The actual figures were: in favour, 48 per cent; opposed, 26 per cent; don't know, 26 per cent. See Younger, 'Public Opinion and British Foreign Policy', p. 31.

27 For a provocative – and entertaining – view of the decline, see Corelli Barnet, *The Audit of War: The Illusion and Reality of Britain as a Great Nation* (London: Macmillan, 1986).

28 This tendency is documented extensively in Peter Willetts, *The Non-Aligned Movement: The Origins of a Third World Alliance* (London: Frances Pinter, 1978).

29 The OSA itself is discussed in detail in Chapter 7.

30 For more detailed statistical breakdown, see the first edition of David Sanders, *Losing an Empire, Finding a Role* (Basingstoke: Macmillan, 1990), pp. 152–53.

31 Jonathan Lynn and Anthony Jay, *Yes, Prime Minister: The Diaries of the Right Hon. James Hacker, Volume II* (London: BBC Books, 1987).

32 France (after 1966) and the Irish Republic were not full NATO members.

33 There were nine such decisions in 1974 and 10 in 1975. See, for example, CMND 6258, *Decisions of the Representatives of the Governments of the Member States of the European Coal and Steel Community meeting in Council, opening, allocating and providing for the allocation of Tariff Quotas and opening Tariff Preferences for certain Steel Products originating in Developing Countries* (2 Dec. 1974).

34 A 2:1 majority voted in favour of continued membership of the Community in June 1975 (67.2 per cent Yes; 32.8 per cent No).

35 See Helen Wallace, 'The British Presidency of the European Community's Council of Ministers: The Opportunity to Persuade', *International Affairs*, vol. 64, no. 4 (1986), pp. 583–99.

36 For details, see Jan-Erik Lane and Svante O. Ersson, *Politics and Society in Western Europe* (London: Sage, 1987).

37 Joseph Frankel, 'Conventional and Theorising Diplomats: A Critique', *International Affairs*, vol. 57, no. 3 (1981), p. 547.

38 Wallace, 'The British Presidency of the European Community's Council of Ministers', p. 585.

39 See, for example, Leon Lindberg, *Political Dynamics of European Economic Integration* (London: Oxford University Press, 1963).

40 See Chapter 6 for a fuller discussion of the two positions.

41 Quoted in Wallace, 'The Collapse of British Foreign Policy', p. 3.

42 Ibid, p. 55.

43 Like military people, the politicians of the EU are especially fond of acronyms.

44 Robert Dover, 'The EU's Foreign, Security, and Defence Policies', in Michelle Cini, *European Union Politics*, 2nd edn (Oxford: Oxford University Press, 2007), p. 238.

45 Alastair Shepherd, 'Blair, Brown and Brussels: The European Turn in British Defence Policy', p. 40 in David Brown (ed.), *The Development of British Defence Policy: Blair, Brown and Beyond* (Farnham: Ashgate, 2010).

46 Benjamin Pohl, 'The Logic Underpinning EU Crisis Management Operations', *European Security*, vol. 22, no. 3 (2013) p. 311.

47 Menon, 'European Defence Policy from Lisbon to Libya', p. 82.

48 Ibid, p. 83.

49 Cited in Steven Haines, '"A World Full of Terror to the British Mind": The Blair Doctrine and British Defence Policy', p. 63 in David Brown (ed.), *The Development of British Defence Policy: Blair, Brown and Beyond* (Farnham: Ashgate, 2010).

50 See Michael Wilkinson and Rosa Prince, 'When Will an EU Referendum Be Held?'. *The Telegraph*, 28 June 2015, accessed at: http://www.telegraph.co.uk/news/newstopics/eureferendum/11324069/When-is-the-EU-referendum.html.

51 Poland's accession had been part of the 2004 enlargement of the European Union, during which Cyprus, the Czech Republic, Estonia, Hungary, Latvia, Lithuania, Malta, Slovakia and Slovenia also joined.

52 Alberto Nardelli and George Arnett, 'Today's Key Fact: You Are Probably Wrong about Almost Everything', 29 October 2014 accessed at http://www.theguardian.com/news/datablog/2014/oct/29/todays-key-fact-you-are-probably-wrong-about-almost-everything.

53 See for instance David Charter, *Europe: In or Out? Everything You Need to Know* (London: Biteback, 2014) and Hugh Dixon, *The In/Out Question* (London: Createspace, 2014).

54 The notion of 'soft power' is the invention of Joseph Nye. See, for instance, Nye, *Soft Power: The Means of Success in World Politics* (New York: Public Affairs, 2004.).

55 'Transcript: Albright Press Conference at NATO's Headquarters, December 8 2008', *USIS Washington File*, accessed at http://fas.org/man/nato/news/1998/98120904_tlt.html; see also Madeline Albright, *Madame Secretary* (New York: Miramax, 2003).

56 Lord Gladwyn, 'Western Europe's Collective Defence', *International Affairs*, vol. 51, no. 2 (1975), p. 168.

57 Douglas Hurd, 'Prospects for Europe: Political Co-operation', *International Affairs*, vol. 57, no. 3 (1981), p. 383. It is also worth noting that the Single European Act of 1986 extended EPC still further. The aim before 1986 was to provide a consultative framework that could be used if the political will was there: after 1986, consultation through EPC became a legal requirement.

58 James Eberle, John Roper, William Wallace and Phil Williams, 'European Security Cooperation and British Interests', *International Affairs*, vol. 60, no. 4 (1984), p. 546.

59 Evan Luard, 'A European Foreign Policy?', *International Affairs*, vol. 62, no. 4 (1986), p. 576.

60 Hurd, 'Prospects for Europe', p. 386.

61 For details of these matters, see Geoffrey Edwards, 'Europe and the Falkland Islands Crisis 1982', *Journal of Common Market Studies*, vol. 22, no. 4 (1984), pp. 295–313.

62 Greece became a full EC member in January 1981, Spain and Portugal in January 1986.

63 Luard, 'A European Foreign Policy?', p. 580.

64 Oliver Daddow, '"Tony's War"? Blair, Kosovo and the Interventionist Impulse in British Foreign Policy', *International Affairs*, vol. 85, no. 3 (2009), pp. 547–60.

65 Menon, 'European Defence Policy from Lisbon to Libya', p. 75.

66 Quoted in Ibid, p. 76.

Chapter 6

1 A large part of the problem, in fact, was Washington's refusal to assist Britain's efforts to pacify the growing intercommunal conflict. See Bradford Perkins, 'Unequal Partners: The Truman Administration and Great Britain', in William Roger Louis and Hedley Bull (eds), *The Special Relationship: Anglo-American Relations Since 1945* (Oxford: Clarendon Press, 1986), pp. 43–65; Ritchie Ovendale, 'The Palestine Policy of the British Labour Government, 1947: The Decision to Withdraw', *International Affairs*, vol. 56, no. 1 (1956), pp. 73–93.

2 Susan Strange, *Sterling and British Policy* (London: Oxford University Press, 1971) p. 62.

3 *CMND 537, Agreement between the Government of the United Kingdom ... and the government of the United States ... for co-operation on the uses of atomic energy for mutual defence purposes* (3 July 1958).

4 Baylis, *Anglo-American Defence*, p. 95.

5 Ibid., pp. 97–101.

6 The precise details of the financial charges to be made by Washington were given in Article XI of *CMND 2108* (6 April 1963). As *The Times* defence correspondent observed on 27 January 1983, this constituted 'a bargain that for most of its life has cost the Government less than 2% of its defence

budget'. Cited in Alistair Home, 'The Macmillan Years and Afterwards', in Louis and Bull (eds), *The Special Relationship*, p. 98.

7 See Graham Allison, *Essence of Decision: Explaining the Cuban Missile Crisis* (Boston, MA: Little, Brown, 1971) and the successor edition authored with Philip Zelikow.

8 See, for example, John Mander, *Great Britain or Little England* (London: Penguin, 1963), p. 21. Cited in Baylis, *Anglo-American Defence*, p. 106.

9 Home, 'Macmillan Years', pp. 92–93.

10 Ibid., p. 100. The Partial Test Ban Treaty itself was signed in August 1963.

11 Ibid., pp. 95–96.

12 Baylis, *Anglo-American Defence*, p. 147.

13 Cited in Ibid., pp. 154–55.

14 Cited in Ibid., p. 155.

15 *CMND 6413* (25 Jan. 1976).

16 David Watt, 'Introduction: The Anglo-American Relationship', in Louis and Bull (eds), *The Special Relationship*, p. 13.

17 Cited in Baylis, *Anglo-American Defence*, p. 151.

18 Reynolds, 'A "Special Relationship"?', p. 13.

19 Baylis, *Anglo-American Defence*, p. 182.

20 Ibid., pp. 182–83.

21 Baylis, *Anglo-American Defence*, p. 184. See *CMND 8517, The British Strategic Nuclear Force* (HMSO: March 1982).

22 Admiral Sir James Eberle, 'The Military Relationship', pp. 157–88, and Ernest May and Gregory Treverton, 'Defence Relationships: American Perspectives', in Louis and Bull (eds) *The Special Relationship*, pp. 175–76.

23 Baylis, *Anglo-American Defence*, p. 192.

24 *The Times*, 16 April 1986.

25 The British government's permission was necessary under the terms of the 'Truman-Attlee Understandings' of 1951. See Baylis, *Anglo-American Defence*, p. 186.

26 Two polls conducted in by-election constituencies (Ryedale and Derbyshire West) immediately after the Libyan bombing indicated that 61 per cent of the sample disapproved of the British government's decision to allow US bombers to fly from British bases (*Guardian*, 30 April 1986).

27 'Mad dog' was the deliberately provocative phrase used by President Reagan to describe Colonel Ghaddafi on 9 April. (See the *Observer*, 20 April 1986.)

28 *Guardian*, 21 April 1986, p. 17. Cynics noted that the 'surgical strike' had not been carried out particularly accurately. Most of the Libyan casualties were civilian. Colonel Ghaddafi himself – the presumed target of the attack – was unharmed.

29 Robert Kaplan, *Balkan Ghosts: A Journey Through History* (London: Pan Macmillan, 1993).

30 In the 1990s BBC series *The Search For Peace*, for instance, Hurd gazes admiringly at a bust of Eden, describing the latter as 'pure silver'.

31 Although John Major held the Prime Minister's position for seven years to Blair's ten, the latter's foreign policy has provoked a good deal more interest among academics than the former, which may reflect the fact that

Major's approach conformed more obviously to established traditions. See for instance Richard Little and Mark Wickham-Jones, *New Labour's Foreign Policy: A New Moral Crusade?* (Manchester: Manchester University Press, 2000), John Kampfner, *Blair's Wars* (New York: Free Press, 2004), Paul Williams, *British Foreign Policy Under New Labour, 1997–2005* (Basingstoke, Hampshire: Palgrave Macmillan, 2005), Stephen Dyson, *The Blair Identity: Leadership and Foreign Policy* (Manchester: Manchester University Press, 2009), Oliver Daddow and Jamie Gaskarth (eds), *British Foreign Policy: The New Labour Years* (Basingstoke, Hampshire: Palgrave Macmillan, 2011) and Oliver Daddow, *New Labour and the European Union: Blair and Brown's Logic of History* (Manchester: Manchester University Press, 2011).

32 Dyson, *The Blair Identity*, p. 2.

33 Yee-Kuang Heng, '"What Did New Labour Ever Do for Us?" Evaluating Tony Blair's Imprint on British Strategic Culture', *British Journal of Politics and International Relations*, vol. 14, no. 4 (2012), pp. 556–75.

34 A Dick Morris-type figure uses this phrase in the movie, *The Special Relationship*, which uses actors to reconstruct the relationship between Clinton and Blair. The phrase captures the essence of much US criticism at the time.

35 Steven Haines, '"A World Full of Terror to the British Mind": The Blair Doctrine and British Defence Policy', pp. 63–65 in David Brown (ed.), *The Development of British Defence Policy: Blair, Brown and Beyond* (Farnham: Ashgate, 2010).

36 Ibid., p. 63.

37 Oliver Daddow, '"Tony's War"? Blair, Kosovo and the Interventionist Impulse in British Foreign Policy', *International Affairs*, vol. 85, no. 3 (2009), pp. 547–60.

38 Max Hastings, *The Falklands Legacy*, documentary first broadcast on BBC2, 27 April 2012, available at http://www.dailymotion.com/video/x1da9iv_bbc-the-falklands-legacy-with-max-hastings-pdtv_tech.

39 Ibid.

40 Richard Dannatt, *Leading From the Front* (London: Bantam Press, 2010).

41 See Frank Ledwidge, *Losing Small Wars: British Military Failure in Iraq and Afghanistan* (London: Yale University Press, 2011), pp. 118–19.

42 The phrase 'wars among the people' comes from General Sir Rupert Smith, *The Utility of Force: The Art of War in the Modern World* (New York: Knopf, 2007).

43 Thatcher arguably got away with this in 1982, in part because of a fair measure of luck or happenstance (not least when British ground forces were quickly able to disembark from transport ships without being challenged from the air by French-made fighter jets).

44 See in particular Ledwidge, *Losing Small Wars*, pp. 109–34.

45 The operational and tactical difficulties were also significant, not least in Afghanistan, which (in part because of its rugged terrain, tribal traditions and lack of a strong central government) has a justified reputation as 'the Graveyard of Empires'.

46 See Chapter 2 for a discussion of the Malayan insurgency.

47 Jonathan Bailey, Richard Iron and Hew Strachan (eds), *British Generals in Blair's Wars* (London: Ashgate, 2013). See also Christopher Elliott, *High Command: British Military Leadership in the Iraq and Afghanistan Wars* (London: Hurst and Co., 2015).

48 Ledwidge, *Losing Small Wars*, p. 17. See also Jack Fairweather, *The Good War: Why We Couldn't Win the War or the Peace in Afghanistan* (London: Jonathan Cape, 2014).

49 Sir John Chilcot is a former civil servant who had been tasked in 2009 with the job of finding out how and why Britain became involved in the conflict in Iraq, initiated in 2003 when George W. Bush invaded that country.

50 'Chilcot Report: Key Points from the Iraq Inquiry', *The Guardian*, 6 July 2016. Available at https://www.theguardian.com/uk-news/2016/jul/06/iraq-inquiry-key-points-from-the-chilcot-report.

51 Tom Bower, *Gordon Brown: Prime Minister* (London: Harper Perennial, 2007), p. viii.

52 Steve Richards, *Whatever It Takes: The Real Story of Gordon Brown and New Labour* (London: Fourth Estate, 2010), p. 131.

53 Speech given on 14 July 2007, Washington DC, in a talk with journalists.

54 Anthony Seldon and Guy Lodge, *Brown at 10* (London: Biteback, 2011).

55 Andrew Rawnsley, 'Where Did It All Go Wrong?', *Dispatches,* broadcast on Channel 4, 9 June 2008, accessed at https://www.youtube.com/watch?v=A00f18HgKKI.

56 This omission will soon be at least partly corrected, with the imminent publication of Anthony Seldon and Peter Snowdon, *Cameron at 10* (London: Biteback, 2015).

57 See for instance Oliver Daddow and Pauline Schnapper, 'Liberal Intervention in the Foreign Policy Thinking of Tony Blair and David Cameron', *Cambridge Review of International Affairs*, vol. 26, no. 2 (2013), pp. 330–49

58 Frank Ledwidge, *Punching Below Our Weight: How Inter-Service Rivalry has Damaged the British Armed Forces* (Kindle E-Book: Yale University Press, 2012).

59 Jonathan Gilmore, 'Still a "Force for Good"? Good International Citizenship in British Foreign and Security Policy', *British Journal of Politics and International Relations*, vol. 17, no. 1 (2015), pp. 106–29,

60 Klaus Dodds and Stuart Elden, 'Thinking Ahead: David Cameron, the Henry Jackson Society and British Neo-Conservatism', *British Journal of Politics and International Relations*, Vol. 10, no. 3, 347–363, 2008.

61 Daddow and Schnapper, 'Liberal Intervention in the Foreign Policy Thinking of Tony Blair and David Cameron', p. 333.

62 Jonathan Beale, 'Military Cuts Mean "No US Partnership", Robert Gates Warns Britain', 16 January 2014, *BBC News* website. Available at http://www.bbc.co.uk/news/uk-25754870.

63 On both the similarities and differences of the British and American political cultures, see Gabriel Almond and Sidney Verba, *The Civic Culture* (Boston, MA: Little, Brown, 1965).

64 This is certainly the case for those periods where the official records have been opened. See, for example, Ritchie Ovendale, 'The Palestine Policy of the

British Labour Government, 1945–46', *International Affairs*, vol. 55, no. 3 (1979), pp. 409–31; Ritchie Ovendale, 'Britain, the US and the Cold War in SE Asia 1949–50', *International Affairs* vol. 58, no. 3 (1982), pp. 447–64.

65 The United States has become even more important as a trade partner for the United Kingdom. British exports to the United States increased from 6.3 per cent of total United Kingdom exports in 1955 to 14.4 per cent of total exports in 1984. This amount has remained quite stable in the years since. In March 2016, for example, exports to the US were about 14.2 per cent of the total (Source: first edition and HM Revenue and Customs, Overseas Trade Statistics).

66 United States exports to the United Kingdom constituted 4.5 per cent of all United States exports in 1952; 5.5 per cent in 1960; 5.5 per cent in 1970; 5.3 per cent in 1980; and 5.2 per cent in 1986. In 2015 it was approximately 3.7 per cent of all exports (Source: *United Nations Yearbook of International Trade Statistics*, various years; United States Census Bureau, 2015).

67 The G7 group comprises the United States, the United Kingdom, France, Italy, Germany, Japan and Canada, which together account for the majority of the world's wealth.

68 *CMND 537*.

69 Andrew Pierre, *Nuclear Politics: The British Experience with an Independent Strategic Force, 1939–70* (London: Oxford University Press, 1972), p. 144.

70 Reynolds, 'A "Special Relationship"?', p. 13.

71 Michael Clarke, 'American Reactions to Shifts in European Policy: The Changing Context', in John Roper (ed.), *The Future of British Defence Policy* (Aldershot: Gower, 1985), pp. 83–84.

72 Sir Michael Howard, 'Afterword: The "Special Relationship"', in Louis and Bull (eds), *The Special Relationship*, p. 391.

73 On the extent of this consultation, see, for example, Harold Macmillan, *Riding the Storm, 1956–1959* (London: Macmillan, 1971).

74 The 'evil Empire' was one of President Reagan's favourite terms for the Soviet Union, although he later abandoned it as relations with Gorbachev thawed.

75 Watt, 'Introduction: The Anglo-American Relationship', p. 7.

76 Max Beloff, 'The Special Relationship: An Anglo-American Myth', in Martin Gilbert (ed.), *A Century of Conflict 1850–1950: Essays for A. J. P. Taylor* (London: Hamish Hamilton, 1966), pp. 151–71.

77 Reynolds, 'A "Special Relationship"?', pp. 13–18.

78 Eberle, 'The Military Relationship', p. 154; May and Treverton, 'Defence Relationships', pp. 168–69.

79 Margaret Gowing, 'Britain, America and the Bomb', in Dilks (ed.), *Retreat from Power*, Vol. 2, p. 137.

80 This seems most closely to accord with Thatcher's own view. In December 1979 she referred to the Anglo-American relationship as 'the extraordinary alliance'. Cited in Baylis, *Anglo-American Defence*, p. 182.

81 Horne, 'Macmillan Years', pp. 90–92. Horne quotes Joe Hersch's comment that Macmillan was 'one of the few living British politicians who can manage to sound convincingly patriotic without sounding anti-American' (p. 91).

Chapter 7

1 Susan Strange, *The Retreat of the State: The Diffusion of Power in the World Economy* (Cambridge: Cambridge University Press, 1996) and Robert Gilpin, *Global Political Economy: Understanding the International Economic Order* (Oxford: Princeton University Press, 2001).

2 For a concise review of this theory, see John Ravenhill (ed.), *Global Political Economy*, 4th edn (Oxford: Oxford University Press, 2014), p. 104, Robert Gilpin, *The Political Economy of International Relations* (Princeton, NJ: Princeton University Press, 1987) and James Alt and Alec Chrystal, *Political Economics* (Brighton: Wheatsheaf Books, 1983).

3 In 1950, for example, Britain's overall trade volume (exports plus imports divided by two) constituted some 20.0 per cent of national GDP. Source: Annual Abstract of Statistics, 1952. In 1975, the equivalent figure was 20.9 per cent. The West German figure for 1975 was 19.5 per cent, the French figure 15.8 per cent and the United States figure 6.8 per cent. Source: United Nations Statistical Pocket/Second Edition, *World Statistics in Brief* (New York: United Nations, 1977).

4 The WTO replaced the General Agreement on Tariffs and Trade (GATT) in 2005. The latter had been in existence since 1944.

5 View, 'Trade No Longer Follows the Flag, Prime Minister', *The Financial Times*, 3 November 2015; see also Richard Tyler, 'Cameron Presents UK Firms with £30bn Export Challenge', *The Daily Telegraph*, 10 November 2011, accessed at http://www.telegraph.co.uk/finance/yourbusiness/8881338/Cameron-presents-UK-firms-with-30bn-export-challenge.html.

6 Mercantilism might be said to have the strongest parallels with Realism, as the late Robert Gilpin suggested. Politically, however, protectionism is unpalatable for Conservatives, and a policy which maximises (or seeks to maximise) the national interest within a liberal, free trading system has much more appeal.

7 See Daniel Yergin and Joseph Stanslaw, *The Commanding Heights: The Battle for the World Economy* (New York: Touchstone Books, 2002), pp. 330–33.

8 The technical aspects of the discussion that follows are largely derived from Susan Strange's *Sterling and British Policy* (London: Oxford University Press, 1971). The reader familiar with this study will realise the considerable debt that the present chapter owes to the late Professor Strange's work.

9 Strange, *Sterling*, pp. 56–57.

10 Strange, *Sterling*, pp. 64–69.

11 *CMND 3834, Sterling. Exchange of Notes and Letters concerning the Guarantee by the ... United Kingdom and the Maintenance of the Minimum Sterling Proportion by certain Overseas Sterling Area Governments (the Sterling Area Agreements)* (25 Sept. 1968).

12 Strange, *Sterling*, passim.

13 See, for example, Andrew Shonfield, *British Economic Policy Since the War* (Harmondsworth: Penguin, 1958).

14 For a development of this theme, see Porter, *The Lion's Share*, passim.

15 E. A. Brett, *The World Economy Since the War* (London: Macmillan, 1985).

16 Contemporary scholars of international political economy (IPE) can be divided into Mercantilists/Economic Nationalists, Liberals and Marxists. See for instance Gilpin, *The Political Economy of International Relations*.

17 As in many areas of academic debate, there is (strictly speaking) no single 'Marxist view' concerning the role of financial capital in the formation of British foreign economic policy. The characterisation provided here is a simplified amalgam of several works: Frank Longstreth, 'The City, Industry and the State', in Colin Crouch (ed.), *State and Economy in Contemporary Capitalism* (London: Croom Helm, 1979), pp. 157–90; Grahame Thompson, 'The Relationship between the Financial and Industrial Sector in the United Kingdom Economy', *Economy and Society*, vol. 6, no. 3 (August 1977), pp. 235–83; Geoffrey Ingham, *Capitalism Divided? The City and Industry in British Social Development* (London: Palgrave Macmillan, 1984); and Steven Kettell, *The Political Economy of Exchange Rate Policy-Making: From the Gold Standard to the Euro* (London: Palgrave Macmillan, 2004).

18 See for example, Bob Jessop, 'The Transformation of the State in Post-War Britain' in R. Scase (ed.), *The State in Western Europe* (London: Croom Helm, 1980), pp. 23–93.

19 Ingham, *Capitalism Divided?*

20 Whether or not there was an explicit 'alliance' between financial capital and multinational industrial capital in this context remains a matter for debate. See, for example, the exchanges between Overbeek and Minns: Henk Overbeek, 'Financial Capital and the Crisis in Britain', *Capital and Class*, vol. 11 (1980), pp. 99–120; Richard Minns, 'A Comment on "Financial Capital and the Crisis in Britain"', *Capital and Class*, vol. 14 (1982), pp. 98–110.

21 Strange, *Sterling*, passim.

22 In Lukes's terms, while the Marxists take a three-dimensional, 'radical' view of power, Strange takes a one-dimensional, 'liberal' view. See Stephen Lukes, *Power: A Radical View* (London: Macmillan, 1975).

23 The government-sponsored Duncan Report used this phrase in 1969. See *CMND 4107, Report of the Review Committee on Overseas Representation 1968–9* (HMSO 1969).

24 Brett, *World Economy*, p. 157.

25 Susan Strange, *Casino Capitalism* (London: Basil Blackwell, 1986) p. 68.

26 This move – though costly to the world economy – was enormously beneficial to the United States. Although the dollar–gold link had been broken, most other countries continued to hold the bulk of their reserves in dollars, thus ensuring that the value of their currencies was still defined in dollar terms. This effectively gave the American government 'unlimited reserves of dollars' (Strange, p. 9): the dollar was the standard against which all other currencies were valued and yet the United States government was free to determine how many dollars it wished to print. The resultant dollar flood was largely responsible for the worldwide inflation crisis of the 1970s. The OPEC 'oil-shock', often blamed for the downturn in the world economy after 1973, was merely a symptom of an inflation that had already begun, not a cause of it.

27 Floating exchange rates confer both costs and benefits on different national economies. The major cost is the uncertainty which floating rates engender for importers and exporters: an exporter may find that the price he receives for a particular commodity falls alarmingly if, for some exogenous reason, the value of his own currency rises. Similarly, an importer may find that the cost of a particular good rises alarmingly, purely as a consequence of an autonomous fall in the value of his own currency.

28 Strange, *Casino Capitalism*, p. 39.

29 Raising interest rates (in Britain, via the Bank of England's minimum lending rate) is another way of checking a declining currency. The rise in interest rates attracts short-term funds back into the currency, thereby raising its value. The problem is that raising interest rates also has domestic economic consequences (raising the cost of borrowing and therefore reducing both consumer demand and investment) which may damage the government's domestic economic strategy.

30 Observers remain divided as to just what Thatcher's legacy has been. See for instance Peter Riddell, *The Thatcher Era and its Legacy* (Oxford: Wiley-Blackwell, 1991), Andrew Gamble, *The Free Economy and the Strong State: The Politics of Thatcherism*, 2nd edn (London: Palgrave Macmillan, 1994) and Hugo Young, *One of Us: The Life of Margaret Thatcher* (Palgrave Macmillan, 1989).

31 Helen Thompson, *The British Conservative Government and the European Exchange Rate Mechanism, 1979–1994* (London: Routledge, 1996).

32 See Philip Inman, 'Black Wednesday 20 Years on: How the Day Unfolded', *The Guardian*, 13 September 2012, accessed at http://www.theguardian.com/business/2012/sep/13/black-wednesday-20-years-pound-erm.

33 BBC news website, '1997: Brown Sets Bank of England Free', accessed at http://news.bbc.co.uk/onthisday/hi/dates/stories/may/6/newsid_3806000/3806313.stm.

34 See Tony Blair, *A Journey* (New York: Random House, 2010).

35 Yergin and Stanislaw, *The Commanding Heights*, p. 330.

36 Strange, *Casino Capitalism*.

37 We will not labour these points, since both have already been described earlier in this chapter.

38 Quoted in Peter Spence, 'British Reliance on Trade with the EU Falls to an All-Time Low', *The Telegraph*, 9 June 2015, accessed at http://www.telegraph.co.uk/finance/economics/11661581/Trade-deficit-shrinkage-set-to-boost-UK-growth.html.

39 See, for example, Milton Friedman, *Prices of Money and Goods across Frontiers: The Pound and the Dollar over a Century* (London: Trade Policy Research Centre, 1980).

40 Ernest Mandel, *Late Capitalism* (London: New Left Books, 1975).

41 See in particular Charles Kindleberger, *The World in Depression 1929–1933* (London: Allen Lane, 1973) and Robert Gilpin, *War and Change in World Politics* (1981). For a Liberal critique, see Robert Keohane, *After Hegemony* (Cambridge, MA: Harvard University Press, 1984).

Chapter 8

1 Paul Cornish and Andrew Dorman, 'Fifty Shades of Purple? A Risk-Sharing Approach to the 2015 Strategic Defence and Security Review', *International Affairs*, vol. 89, no. 5 (2013), p. 1183.

2 Jonathan Beale, 'Military Cuts Mean "No US Partnership", Robert Gates Warns Britain', 16 January 2014, BBC News website. Available at http://www.bbc.co.uk/news/uk-25754870.

3 Caroline Wyatt, 'Top General Warns Over "Hollowed-Out" Armed Forces', BBC News website, 19 December 2013. Available at http://www.bbc.co.uk/news/uk-25440814.

4 Gill Bennett, *Six Moments of Crisis: Inside British Foreign Policy* (Oxford: Oxford University Press, 2013), p. 163.

5 CMND 6743, Statement Relating to Defence (Feb. 1946).

6 Jeffrey Engel, '"We are Not Concerned Who the Buyer Is": Engine Sales and Anglo-American Security At the Dawn of the Jet Age', *History and Technology*, vol. 17, no. 1 (2000), p. 43–67.

7 See D. C. Cumming, 'British Stewardship of the Italian Colonies', *International Affairs*, vol. 29, no. 1 (1953), pp. 11–21.

8 John Baylis and Alan Macmillan, 'The British Global Strategy Paper of 1952', p. 200 in *Journal of Strategic Studies*, vol. 16, no. 2 (1999), pp. 200–226.

9 Ibid., p. 218.

10 CMND 9075, Statement on Defence, 1954 (HMSO, Feb. 1954); CMND 9072, Memorandum of the Secretary of State for War relating to the Army Estimates 1954–55 (HMSO, Feb. 1954).

11 CMND 265, South East Asia Collective Defence Treaty, 8 Sept. 1954.

12 CMND 9859, Pact of Mutual Co-operation between His Majesty the King of Iraq and the President of the Republic of Turkey (Accessions: United Kingdom 5 April 1955; Pakistan 23 Sept. 1955; Iran 3 Nov. 1955).

13 CMND 9520, Exchange of letters with the Government of the Union of South Africa on the transfer of the Simonstown Naval Base and arrangements for its future use (30 June 1955).

14 Rees, 'The 1957 Sandys White Paper', p. 218.

15 Ibid., p. 215.

16 CMND 1936, Statement on Defence 1963 (including memoranda to accompany the Navy, Army and Air Estimates 1963–4) (HMSO, Feb. 1963), p. 15.

17 CMND 2901, Statement on the Defence Estimates 1966, Part I, The Defence Review (HMSO, Feb. 1966).

18 CMND 5976, Statement on the Defence Estimate, 1975 (HMSO, March 1975).

19 Ibid., p. 13.

20 On the decisions involved in the withdrawal from 'East of Suez', see Saki Dockrill, *Britain's Retreat from East of Suez: The Choice Between Europe and the World?* (New York: Palgrave Macmillan, 2002).

21 Andrew Gamble, *The Free Economy and the Strong State: The Politics of Thatcherism* (London: Macmillan, 1988).

22 Andrew Dorman, 'John Nott and the Royal Navy: The 1981 Defence Review Revisited', pp. 98–99 in *Contemporary British History*, vol. 15, no. 2 (2000), pp. 98–120.

23 Bennett, *Six Moments of Crisis*, p. 164.

24 Richard Ned Lebow, 'Miscalculation in the South Atlantic: The Origins of the Falklands War', *Journal of Strategic Studies,* vol. 6, no. 1 (1983), pp. 5–35.

25 Dorman. 'John Nott and the Royal Navy', p. 114.

26 John Le Carré, *A Delicate Truth* (London: Penguin Books, 2013), p. 90.

27 As an academic, Kirkpatrick had controversially defended dictatorship. In his memoirs, long-time British Ambassador to the United States Nicholas Henderson savaged Kirkpatrick in a typically British way, describing her as 'more fool than fascist'. See Henderson, *Mandarin: The Diaries of an Ambassador 1969–1982* (London: Weidenfeld & Nicolson, 1994).

28 Richard Ned Lebow and Janice Gross Stein, *We All Lost the Cold War* (Princeton, NJ: Princeton University Press, 1995).

29 Lawrence Freedman, *The Politics of British Defence, 1979–1988* (London: Palgrave Macmillan, 1999), p. 14.

30 Jeevan Vasagar 'British Policy on Arms Sales', 15 July 2000, *The Guardian*. Available at http://www.theguardian.com/world/2000/jul/25/qanda. jeevanvasagar.

31 Jonathan Bailey, 'The Political Context: Why We Went to War and the Mismatch of Ends, Ways and Means', p. 20 in Bailey, Richard Iron and Hew Strachan (eds), *British Generals in Blair's Wars* (Farnham, Surrey: Ashgate, 2013).

32 Christopher Elliott, *High Command: British Military Leadership in the Iraq and Afghanistan Wars* (London: Hurst and Company, 2015), p. 21.

33 Quoted in Elliott, *High Command*, p. 13.

34 John Nagl, *Learning to Eat Soup with a Knife: Counterinsurgency Lessons from Malaya and Vietnam* (London: University of Chicago Press, 2002). The Nagl quote comes from Fred Kaplan, in (for instance) Mark Thompson, 'The Pied Piper of the Insurgency', *Time*, 2 January 2013. Available at http://nation.time.com/2013/01/02/the-pied-piper-of-the-insurgency/.

35 Oliver Wright, '"Costly Failures": Wars in Iraq and Afghanistan Cost UK Taxpayers £30bn', *The Independent*, 27 May 2014. Available at http://www.independent.co.uk/news/uk/politics/costly-failures-wars-in-iraq-and-afghanistan-cost-uk-taxpayers-30bn-9442640.html.

36 Matt Cavenagh, 'Missed Opportunity: How Failures of Leadership Derailed the SDSR', p. 10 in *The RUSI Journal*, vol. 156, no. 5 (2011), pp. 6–13.

37 Peter Hennessey (ed.), *Cabinets and the Bomb* (Oxford: Oxford University Press, 2007), p. 5. This volume provides an especially worthwhile collection of UK government documents for researchers interested in this topic.

38 The National Health Service (NHS) in Britain provides largely free healthcare to UK citizens, while HS2 refers to a high-speed railway linking various UK cities.

39 Paul Kennedy, *The Rise and Fall of the Great Powers* (London: Vintage, 1989).

Chapter 9

1 See David Sanders and Geoffrey Edwards, 'Consensus and Diversity in Elite Opinion: The Views of the British Foreign Policy Elite in the Early 1990s', *Political Studies*, vol. 42, no. 3 (1994), pp. 413–40. This 1990 survey found that 'of all Britain's international engagements, the EC was clearly seen as the most important, a view that extended to generally favourable attitudes towards France and Germany in both defence and economic matters' (p. 440) – a finding which is consistent with the position taken here.

2 Thucydides, *The History of the Peloponnesian War* (translated by R. Crawley) (London: Everyman's Library, 1952); Niccolo Machiavelli, *The Prince* (translated by G. Bull) (Harmondsworth: Penguin, 1961); Thomas Hobbes, *Leviathan* (Harmondsworth: Pelican, 1968). There are many sources that describe the Realist approach, but for concise summary statements, see Martin Wight, *Power Politics*, revised edition (London: Bloomsbury, 1995) and John Baylis, Steve Smith and Patricia Owens (eds), 'Realism', in *The Globalization of World Politics: An Introduction to International Relations*, sixth edition (Oxford: Oxford University Press, 2013).

3 Kenneth Waltz, *Theory of International Politics* (Reading, MA: Addison-Wesley, 1979).

4 See, for example, Hedley Bull, 'Society and Anarchy in International Relations', in Herbert Butterfield and Martin Wight (eds), *Diplomatic Investigations: Essays on the Theory of International Politics* (London: George Allen & Unwin, 1966), pp. 35–50.

5 On the notion of 'security complex', see Barry Suzan, *People, States and Fear: The National Security Problem in International Relations* (Brighton: Wheatsheaf Books, 1983).

6 These are also known as 'security dilemmas'. See Robert Jervis, 'Cooperation under the Security Dilemma', *World Politics*, Vol. 30, No. 2 (1978), pp. 167–214.

7 A full or 'definitive' list of 'Realist propositions' would be difficult to provide. The propositions summarised here are a revised and extended version of those developed in Trevor Taylor, 'Power Politics' in Trevor Taylor (ed.), *Approaches and Theory in International Relations* (London: Longman, 1978), pp. 122–40.

8 Note that there is a distinction made in the IR literature between 'pre-emptive' and 'preventive' attacks. The latter are designed to address threats which are far in the distance and will exist at some point in the future, while the former deal with threats that are immediate and imminent. By this criterion, the 2003 invasion of Iraq was a preventive, rather than pre-emptive, war.

9 See Hans Morgenthau, Kenneth Thompson and David Clinton, *Politics Among Nations*, 7th edn (New York: McGraw-Hill, 2005).

10 Waltz, *Theory of International Politics*, p. 121. See also Waltz, 'International Politics Is Not Foreign Policy', *Security Studies*, vol. 6, no. 1 (1996), pp. 54–55.

11 For the most important set of critiques, see Robert Keohane (ed.), *Neorealism and its Critics*, New York: Columbia University Press, 1986).

12 See for instance John Mearsheimer, *The Tragedy of Great Power Politics,* updated edition (New York: W.W. Norton, 2014).

13 This is admittedly a 'miracle counterfactual' since it is unlikely to have happened at all, but the example is utilised here in order to illustrate the logic of the approach.

14 Colin Elman, 'Horses for Courses: Why Not Neorealist Theories of Foreign Policy?', *Security Studies*, vol. 6, no. 1 (1996), pp. 7–53.

15 See Jack Snyder, *Myths of Empire: Domestic Politics and International Ambition* (London: Cornell University Press, 1991), p. 19.

16 See, for instance, Gideon Rose, 'Neoclassical Realism and Theories of Foreign Policy', *World Politics*, vol. 51, no. 1 (1998), pp. 144–72, Fareed Zakaria, *From Wealth to Power: The Unusual Origins of America's World Role* (Princeton, NJ: Princeton University Press, 1998) and Jeffrey W. Taliaferro, Steven Lobell, and Norrin Ripsman, 'Introduction: Neoclassical Realism, the State, and Foreign Policy', in Taliaferro, Lobell and Ripsman (eds), *Neoclassical Realism, the State, and Foreign Policy* (New York: Cambridge University Press, 2009).

17 See Amelia Hadfield-Amkhan, *British Foreign Policy, National Identity, and Neoclassical Realism* (Lanham, MD: Rowman & Littlefield, 2010), especially pp. 23–65.

18 Ibid., p. 5.

19 Waltz did allow that some states might fail to perceive or correctly interpret structural constraints, but claimed that such countries would quickly 'fall by the wayside'. See Keohane, *Neorealism and its Critics*, pp. 136 and 291.

20 See, for example, Hedley Bull, *The Anarchical Society: A Study of Order in World Politics* (London: Macmillan, 1977).

21 On the general relationship between theory and evidence, see A. F. Chalmers, *What Is this Thing Called Science?*, 2nd edn (Milton Keynes: Open University Press, 1986). Note, however, that Chalmers' references to philosophical 'Realism' do not refer to the kind of Realism discussed here.

22 See Imre Lakatos, 'Falsification and the Methodology of Scientific Research Programmes', in Imre Lakatos and Alan E. Musgrave (eds), *Criticism and the Growth of Knowledge* (Cambridge: Cambridge University Press, 1974), pp. 132–35.

23 The phrase 'pulling and hauling' comes from Graham Allison and Philip Zelikow, *Essence of Decision: Explaining the Cuban Missile Crisis*, second edition (New York: Longman, 1999). The original edition was written by Allison alone and published in 1971.

24 Although this approach is relatively new at the time of writing, some attempts have already been made to describe the history and practice of British foreign policy from this perspective. See in particular Jamie Gaskarth, *British Foreign Policy: Crises, Conflicts and Future Challenges* (Cambridge: Polity Press, 2013).

25 See for instance William Wallace, 'Foreign Policy and National Identity in the United Kingdom', *International Affairs*, vol. 67, no. 1 (Jan. 1991), pp. 65–80.

26 Quoted in John Campbell, *Roy Jenkins* (London: Vintage, 2015), p. 309. This was a rare public recognition by a major politician that Britain's position had greatly declined.

27 F. S. Northedge, 'Britain As a Second-Rank Power', *International Affairs*, vol. 46, no. 1 (1970), pp. 37–47.

28 Alexander Wendt, *Social Theory of International Politics* (Cambridge: Cambridge University Press, 1999).

29 See for instance Nora Femenia, *National Identity in Times of Crisis: The Scripts of the Falklands-Malvinas War* (Lommack: Nova Science Publishers, 1996).

30 David McCourt, 'Role-Playing and Identity Affirmation in International Politics: Britain's Reinvasion of the Falklands, 1982', *Review of International Studies*, vol. 37, no. 4, pp. 1599–1621, October 2011. McCourt actually argues that a constructivist, identity-based approach is insufficient in the case study, and proposes a perspective based upon what he calls 'roles'.

31 Ibid., pp. 1599–1600.

32 Ibid., p. 1600.

33 For a more detailed analysis, see David Patrick Houghton, 'Reinvigorating the Study of Foreign Policy Decision-Making: Towards a Constructivist Approach', *Foreign Policy Analysis*, vol. 3, no. 1 (2007), pp. 24–45.

34 Wendt, *Social Theory of International Politics*.

35 Wallace, 'Foreign Policy and National Identity in the United Kingdom'; see also McCourt, 'Role-Playing and Identity Affirmation in International Politics'.

36 Hadfield-Amkhan, *British Foreign Policy, National Identity, and Neoclassical Realism*, p. 5.

37 The most impressive applications of the Rational Actor model have undoubtedly been undertaken in the field of Game Theory. For a wide-ranging application see Glenn Snyder and Paul Diesing, *Conflict Among Nations: Bargaining, Decisionmaking and System Structure in International Crises* (Princeton, NJ: Princeton University Press, 1977).

38 See in particular Kenneth Payne, *The Psychology of Modern Conflict: Evolutionary Theory, Human Nature and a Liberal Approach to War* (Basingstoke: Palgrave Macmillan, 2015), pp. 67–69, and Michael Petersen, 'Evolutionary Political Psychology: On the Origin and Structure of Heuristics and Biases in Politics', *Advances in Political Psychology*, Vol. 36, no. 1 (2015), pp. 45–78.

39 See Leon Festinger, *Theory of Cognitive Dissonance* (Stanford, CA: Stanford University Press, 1957); Festinger, Henry Riecken and Stanley Schachter, *When Prophecy Fails: A Social and Psychological Study of a Modern Group that Predicted the Destruction of the World* (New York: Harper & Row, 1964); and Carol Tavris and Elliot Aronson, *Mistakes Were Made (But Not By Me): Why We Justify Foolish Beliefs, Bad Decisions, and Hurtful Acts* (New York: Harcourt, 2007).

40 One approach is purely cognitive, the other partly emotional.

41 See in particular Yuen Foong Khong, *Analogies at War: Korea, Munich, Dien Bien Phu and the Vietnam Decisions of 1965* (Princeton, NJ: Princeton University Press, 1992) and David Patrick Houghton, *U.S. Foreign Policy and the Iran Hostage Crisis* (New York: Cambridge University Press, 2001).

42 Robert Jervis, *Perception and Misperception in International Politics* (Princeton, NJ: Princeton University Press, 1976).

43 See especially Richard Ned Lebow, 'Miscalculation in the South Atlantic: The Origins of the Falklands War', *Journal of Strategic Studies*, Vol. 6, no. 1 (1983), pp. 5–35.

44 The best-known study using the Bureaucratic Politics approach is the famous work by Allison and Zelikow, *Essence of Decision*. See also Priscilla Clapp, Morton Halperin and Arnold Kanter, *Bureaucratic Politics and Foreign Policy*, 2nd edn (Washington, DC: Brookings Institution, 2006).

45 Lawrence Freedman, 'Logic, Politics and Foreign Policy Processes: A Critique of the Bureaucratic Politics Model', *International Affairs*, vol. 52, no. 3 (1976), pp. 434–49.

46 Lewis Page, *Lions, Donkeys and Dinosaurs: Waste and Blundering in the Military* (London: Arrow Books, 2007). See also Anthony Cumming, *The Battle for Britain: Interservice Rivalry between the Royal Air Force and the Royal Navy, 1909–1940* (Naval Institute Press, 2015).

47 Frank Ledwidge, *Punching Below Our Weight: How Inter-Service Rivalry has Damaged the British Armed Forces*, E-Book (Yale University Press: Kindle Edition, 2012).

48 Denis Healey, interviewed in the documentary *TSR2: The Untold Story* (Impact Image Films, 2005).

49 Damien Burke, *TSR2: Britain's Lost Bomber* (Ramsbury, Wiltshire: The Crowood Press, 2010), p. 271.

50 Saki Dockrill, *Britain's Retreat From East of Suez: The Choice Between Europe and the World* (New York: Palgrave Macmillan, 2002), p. 89.

51 Sir Frank Cooper, 'TSR2 and Whitehall', in 'TSR With Hindsight', *RAF Historical Journal*, Issue 17B, 1998, p. 40. This issue is available at http://www.raf.mod.uk/rafcms/mediafiles/EEA483B3_5056_A318_A825FD4682E-DACAB.pdf.

52 Philip Strickland, 'Politics Over Strategy – Australia's Rejection of the TSR2', 'TSR With Hindsight', *RAF Historical Journal*, Issue 17B (1998), p. 46. Available at website given in previous note.

53 Burke, *TSR2*, p. 296.

54 Bill Jackson and Edwin Bramall, *The Chiefs: The Story of the United Kingdom Chiefs of Staff* (London: Brassey's, 1992), p. 366.

55 See for instance Anthony Gorst, 'CVA-1', in Richard Harding (ed.), *The Royal Navy 1930–1990: Innovation and Defence* (New York: Routledge, 2004).

56 Nick Childs, 'The Aircraft Carrier That Never Was', *BBC Magazine*, 3 July 2014. This is available at http://www.bbc.co.uk/news/magazine-28128026.

57 The story is repeated, for instance, in Rowland White, *Phoenix Squadron* (London: Bantam Press, 2009), p. 31, Sharkey Ward, *Sea Harrier Over The*

Falklands: A Maverick At War (London: Leon Cooper, 1992), pp. 10–11, and in Sir Raymond Lygo, *Collision Course: Lygo Shoots Back* (Lewes, Sussex: The Book Guild 2002), pp. 285–86.

58 Matt Cavenagh, 'Missed Opportunity: How Failures of Leadership Derailed the SDSR', p.8 in *The RUSI Journal*, vol. 156, no. 5 (2011), pp. 6–13.

59 Thomas Harding, 'Defence Jobs at Risk as MoD Drops Jump Jet Fighter Engine', *The Daily Telegraph*, 5 August 2009, available at http://www.telegraph.co.uk/news/uknews/defence/5978437/Defence-jobs-at-risk-as-MoD-drops-jump-jet-fighter-engine.html.

60 Cavenagh, 'Missed Opportunity', p. 9.

Chapter 10

1 The European circle remains a relevant choice to make, although it will be much harder after the Brexit vote to actually make that choice.

2 Nicholas Naseem Taleb, *The Black Swan: The Impact of the Highly Improbable*, 2nd edn (New York: Penguin Books, 2010).

3 Peter Hennessy, *Muddling Through: Power, Politics and the Quality of Government in Postwar Britain* (London: Victor Gollancz, 1996), pp. 13–14.

4 As the reader will recall from the Introduction, this was introduced as recently as 2010.

5 See Duncan Depledge and Klaus Dodds, 'No "Strategy" Please, We're British', *RUSI Journal*, vol. 159, no. 1 (2014), and Patrick Porter, 'Why Britain Doesn't Do Grand Strategy', *RUSI Journal*, vol. 155, no. 4 (Aug 2010).

6 As Jonathan Freedland notes, Britain 'does not keep its distance from the US … we import Americana by the crateload every day of the week – into every aspect of our lives, from the way we shop, dress and talk to the food we eat and the laws we make'. See Freedland, *Bringing Home The Revolution: How Britain Can Live the American Dream* (London: Fourth Estate, 1998), p. 4.

7 Porter, 'Why Britain Doesn't Do Grand Strategy', p. 6.

8 See the 2010 UK National Strategy at https://www.gov.uk/government/news/national-security-strategy.

9 See for instance the Joint Committee official report, available at http://www.publications.parliament.uk/pa/jt201012/jtselect/jtnatsec/265/26502.htm.

10 Matt Cavenagh, 'Missed Opportunity: How Failures of Leadership Derailed the SDSR', *The RUSI Journal*, vol. 156, no. 5 (2011), pp. 6–13.

11 Ibid.

12 Christopher Elliott, *High Command: British Military Leadership in the Iraq and Afghanistan Wars* (London: Hurst and Company, 2015), p. 33.

13 Hew Strachan, 'Capability as a Balancing Act: The UK's Dilemma', *RUSI Journal*, vol. 153, no. 3 (June 2008).

14 David Kirkpatrick, 'Dilemmas in UK Defence Policy', *RUSI Defence Systems*, 16-19, Summer 2012, p. 16.

15 Ibid.

16 Even during the 1982 Falklands War, the British received secret logistical support from the US.

17 Christopher Parry, 'The United Kingdom's Future Carriers: What Are They Good For?', *RUSI Journal*, vol. 157, no. 6 (December 2012), p. 9.

18 Michael Clarke, interview and Michael Codner, 'Introduction', p. 2 in Codner and Clarke (eds), *A Question of Security: The British Defence Review in an Age of Austerity* (London: I.B. Tauris, 2011).

19 George Osborne, quoted in an interview on the BBC's *The Andrew Marr Show*, 17 October 2010. See British Forces News, 'National Security Strategy Details Threats to the UK 18.10.10', available at http://www.youtube.com/watch?v=xza4LEaucIs.

20 See BBC News website, 'Whisky Toast for Royal Navy Ship in Rosyth', 30 June 2014, available at http://www.bbc.com/news/uk-scotland-edinburgh-east-fife-28087653.

21 Andrew Dorman, 'Making 2+2=5: The 2010 Strategic Defence and Security Review', *Defence and Security Analysis*, vol. 27, no. 1 (2011), pp. 77–87.

22 Daniel Kahneman, *Thinking, Fast and Slow* (London: Penguin Books, 2012).

23 See for instance Joseph Nye, *Soft Power: The Means of Success in World Politics* (New York: Public Affairs, 2004).

24 *The Independent* website, 'Britain is Now Most Powerful Nation on Earth', 18 November 2012. Accessible at http://www.independent.co.uk/news/uk/home-news/britain-is-now-most-powerful-nation-on-earth-8326452.html.

25 A Realist would argue that 'soft power' is merely a rationalisation for the lack of power, and it remains to be seen whether this argument is borne out in the future in the British case.

26 Hennessey, *Muddling Through*.

27 Hew Strachan, 'The Lost Meaning of Strategy', *Survival*, Vol. 47, no. 3 (2005), pp. 33–54.

28 Lawrence Freedman, *Strategy: A History* (New York: Oxford University Press), p. xi.

29 Robert Jervis, *Perception and Misperception in International Politics* (Princeton, NJ: Princeton University Press, 1976), p. 20.

Bibliography

Adamthwaite, A. P., *The Making of the Second World War* (London: George Allen & Unwin, 1977).

Albright, Madeleine, *Madam Secretary* (New York: Miramax, 2003).

Allison, Graham, *Essence of Decision: Explaining the Cuban Missile Crisis*, 1st edn (Boston, MA: Little, Brown, 1971).

Allison, Graham and Philip Zelikow, *Essence of Decision: Explaining the Cuban Missile Crisis*, 2nd edn (New York: Longman, 1999).

Almond, Gabriel and Sidney Verba, *The Civic Culture* (Boston, MA: Little, Brown, 1965).

Alt, James and Alec Chrystal, *Political Economics* (Brighton: Wheatsheaf Books, 1983).

Amery, Leopold, *My Political Life (Volume 1): England Before the Storm, 1896–1914* (London: Hutchinson, 1953).

Ashton, Nigel, 'Hitler on the Nile? British and American Perceptions of the Nasser Regime, 1952–1970', in Lawrence Freedman and Jeffrey Michaels (eds), *Scripting Middle East Leaders: The Impact of Leadership Perceptions on US and UK Foreign Policy* (New York and London: Continuum, 2013).

Bailey, Jonathan, Richard Iron and Hew Strachan (eds), *British Generals in Blair's Wars* (London: Ashgate, 2013).

Bailey, Jonathan, 'The Political Context: Why We Went to War and the Mismatch of Ends, Ways and Means', p. 20 in Bailey, Richard Iron and Hew Strachan (eds), *British Generals in Blair's Wars* (Farnham, Surrey: Ashgate, 2013).

Barker, Elisabeth, *Churchill and Eden at War* (London: Macmillan, 1978).

Barnet, Corelli, *The Audit of War: The Illusion and Reality of Britain as a Great Nation* (London: Macmillan, 1986).

Bartlett, C. J., *The Global Conflict: The International Rivalry of the Great Powers, 1880–1970* (London: Longman, 1984).

Baylis, John, 'Britain, the Brussels Pact and the Continental Commitment', *International Affairs*, vol. 60, no. 4 (1984), pp. 615–30.

Baylis, John, *Anglo-American Defence Relations 1939–1984*, 2nd edn (London: Macmillan, 1984).

Baylis, John and Alan Macmillan, 'The British Global Strategy Paper of 1952', *Journal of Strategic Studies*, vol. 16, no. 2 (1993), pp. 200–226.

Baylis, John, Steve Smith and Patricia Owens (eds), 'Realism', in *The Globalization of World Politics: An Introduction to International Relations*, 6th edn (Oxford: Oxford University Press, 2013).

Beale, Jonathan, 'Military Cuts Mean "No US Partnership", Robert Gates Warns Britain', 16 January 2014, BBC News website.

Beck, Peter J., 'A Tedious and Perilous Controversy: Britain and the Settlement of the Mosul Dispute, 1918–1926', *Middle East Studies*, vol. 17, no. 2 (1981), pp. 256–76.

Beenstock, Michael, *The World Economy in Transition* (London: George Allen & Unwin, 1983).

Beloff, Max, 'The Special Relationship: An Anglo-American Myth', in Martin Gilbert (ed.), *A Century of Conflict 1850–1950: Essays for A. J. P. Taylor* (London: Hamish Hamilton, 1966).

Bennett, Gill, *Six Moments of Crisis: Inside British Foreign Policy* (New York: Oxford University Press, 2013).

Bew, John, *Realpolitik: A History* (Oxford, UK: Oxford University Press, 2016).

Blair, Tony, *A Journey* (New York: Random House, 2010).

Bower, Tom, *Gordon Brown: Prime Minister* (London: Harper Perennial, 2007).

Brett, E. A., *The World Economy Since the War* (London: Macmillan, 1985).

Buchan, Alistair, 'Britain and the Indian Ocean', *International Affairs*, vol. 42, no. 2 (1966), pp. 184–93.

Bull, Hedley, 'Society and Anarchy in International Relations', in Herbert Butterfield and Martin Wight (eds), *Diplomatic Investigations: Essays on the Theory of International Politics* (London: George Allen & Unwin, 1966), pp. 35–50.

Bull, Hedley, *The Anarchical Society: A Study of Order in World Politics* (London: Macmillan, 1977).

Burke, Damien, *TSR2: Britain's Lost Bomber* (Ramsbury, Wiltshire: The Crowood Press, 2010).

Buzan, Barry, *People, States and Fear: The National Security Problem in International Relations* (Brighton: Wheatsheaf Books, 1983).

Callwell, C. E., *Field Marshall Sir Henry Wilson* (London: Cassell, 1927).

Calvocoressi, Peter, *World Politics Since 1945* (London: Longman, 1982).

Campbell, Alan, 'Anglo-French Relations A Decade Ago: A New Assessment', *International Affairs*, vol. 58, no. 2 (1982), pp. 237–53.

Campbell, John, *Roy Jenkins* (London: Vintage, 2015).

Carrington, C. E., 'A New Theory of the Commonwealth', *International Affairs*, vol. 31, no. 2 (1955), pp. 137–48.

Catherwood, Christopher, *Churchill's Folly: How Winston Churchill Created Modern Iraq* (New York: Carroll and Graf, 2004).

Cavenagh, Matt, 'Missed Opportunity: How Failures of Leadership Derailed the SDSR', *The RUSI Journal*, vol. 156, no. 5 (2011), pp. 6–13.

Chalmers, A. F., *What Is this Thing Called Science?*, 2nd edn (Milton Keynes: Open University Press, 1986).

Chamberlain, Muriel, *Pax Britannia? British Foreign Policy, 1789–1914* (London: Longman, 1988).

Charter, David, *Europe: In or Out? Everything You Need To Know* (London: Biteback, 2014).

Childs, Nick, 'The Aircraft Carrier That Never Was', *BBC* Magazine, 3 July 2014.

Cini, Michelle and Nieves Perez-Solorzano Borragan (eds), *European Union Politics*, 4th edn (Oxford: Oxford University Press, 2013).

Clapp, Priscilla, Morton Halperin and Arnold Kanter, *Bureaucratic Politics and Foreign Policy*, 2nd edn (Washington, DC: Brookings Institution, 2006).

Clarke, John, *British Diplomacy and Foreign Policy, 1782–1865: The National Interest* (London: Unwin Hyman, 1989).

Clarke, Michael, 'American Reactions to Shifts in European Policy: The Changing Context', in John Roper (ed.), *The Future of British Defence Policy* (Aldershot: Gower, 1985).

Clarke, Michael, 'The Policy Making Process', in Michael Smith, Steve Smith and Brian White (eds), *British Foreign Policy: Tradition, Change and Transformation* (London: Unwin Hyman, 1988).

Coates, David and John Hillard (eds), *The Economic Decline of Modern Britain: The Debate Between Left and Right* (Brighton: Wheatsheaf, 1986).

Codner, Michael and Michael Clarke (eds), *A Question of Security: The British Defence Review in an Age of Austerity* (London: I.B. Tauris, 2011).

Colville, John, *The Fringes of Power: Downing Street Diaries 1939–1955* (London: Hodder & Stoughton, 1985).

Coombes, David, *Politics and Bureaucracy in the European Community: A Portrait of the Commission of the EEC* (London: Allen and Unwin, 1970).

Cooper, Sir Frank, 'TSR2 and Whitehall', in 'TSR With Hindsight', *RAF Historical Journal*, Issue 17B (1998).

Cornish, Paul and Andrew Dorman, 'Fifty Shades of Purple? A Risk-Sharing Approach to the 2015 Strategic Defence and Security Review', *International Affairs*, vol. 89, no. 5 (2013), pp. 1183–1202.

Cumming, Anthony, *The Battle for Britain: Interservice Rivalry between the Royal Air Force and the Royal Navy, 1909–1940* (Naval Institute Press, 2015).

Cumming, D. C., 'British Stewardship of the Italian Colonies', *International Affairs*, vol. 29, no. 1 (1953), pp. 11–21.

Cunningham, Sir Alan, 'Palestine: The Last Days of the Mandate', *International Affairs*, vol. 24, no. 4 (1948), pp. 481–90.

Curtis, Mark, *The Ambiguities of Power: British Foreign Policy Since 1945* (London: Zed Books, 1995).

Daddow, Oliver, ' "Tony's War"? Blair, Kosovo and the Interventionist Impulse in British Foreign Policy', *International Affairs*, vol. 85, no. 3 (2009), pp. 547–60.

Daddow, Oliver, 'Britain, the World and Europe', in Bill Jones and Philip Norton (eds), *Politics UK*, 7th edn (New York: Routledge, 2010).

Daddow, Oliver and Jamie Gaskarth (eds), *British Foreign Policy: The New Labour Years* (Basingstoke, Hampshire: Palgrave Macmillan, 2011).

Daddow, Oliver, *New Labour and the European Union: Blair and Brown's Logic of History* (Manchester: Manchester University Press, 2011).

Daddow, Oliver and Pauline Schnapper, 'Liberal Intervention in the Foreign Policy Thinking of Tony Blair and David Cameron', *Cambridge Review of International Affairs*, vol. 26, no. 2 (2013), pp. 330–49.

Dannatt, Richard, *Leading From the Front* (London: Bantam Press, 2010).

Darwin, John, 'Imperialism In Decline? Tendencies in British Imperial Policy between the Wars', *Historical Journal*, vol. 23, no. 3 (1980), pp. 657–79.

Depledge, Duncan and Klaus Dodds, 'No "Strategy" Please, We're British', *RUSI Journal*, vol. 59, no. 1 (2014), pp. 24–31.

Deutsch, Karl, 'Social Mobilisation and Political Development', *American Political Science Review*, vol. 55, no. 3 (1961), pp. 494–512.

Dickie, John, *The New Mandarins: How British Foreign Policy Works* (New York: I.B. Tauris, 2004).

Dilks, David (ed.), *The Diaries of Sir Alexander Cadogan 1938–45* (London: Cassell, 1971).

Dixon, Hugh, *The In/Out Question* (London: Createspace, 2014).

Dockrill, Michael and Brian McKercher (eds), *Diplomacy and World Power: Studies in British Foreign Policy, 1890–1950* (Cambridge: Cambridge University Press, 1996).

Dockrill, Michael, 'The Foreign Office, Anglo-American Relations and the Korean War, June 1950–June 1951', *International Affairs*, vol. 62, no. 3 (1986), pp. 459–78.

Dockrill, Saki, *Britain's Retreat from East of Suez: The Choice Between Europe and the World?* (New York: Palgrave Macmillan, 2002).

Dodds, Klaus and Stuart Elden, 'Thinking Ahead: David Cameron, the Henry Jackson Society and British Neo-Conservatism', *British Journal of Politics and International Relations*, vol. 10, no. 3 (2008), pp. 347–63.

Dodge, Toby, *Inventing Iraq: The Failure of Nation Building and a History Denied* (New York: Columbia University Press, 2003).

Doerr, Paul, *British Foreign Policy, 1919–1939* (Manchester: Manchester University Press, 1998).

Dorman, Andrew, 'John Nott and the Royal Navy: The 1981 Defence Review Revisited', *Contemporary British History*, vol. 15, no. 2 (2001), pp. 98–120.

Dorman, Andrew, 'Making 2+2=5: The 2010 Strategic Defence and Security Review', *Defence and Security Analysis*, vol. 27, no. 1 (2011), pp. 77–87.

Dover, Robert, 'The EU's Foreign, Security and Defence Policies', in Michelle Cini, *European Union Politics*, 2nd edn (Oxford: Oxford University Press, 2007).

Dumbrell, John, *A Special Relationship: Anglo-American Relations from the Cold War* (Basingstoke: Palgrave Macmillan, 2006).

Dutton, David, *Anthony Eden. A Life and Reputation* (London: Arnold, 1997).

Dyson, Stephen, *The Blair Identity: Leadership and Foreign Policy* (Manchester: Manchester University Press, 2009).

Eberle, James, John Roper, William Wallace and Phil Williams, 'European Security Cooperation and British Interests', *International Affairs*, vol. 60, no. 4 (1984), pp. 545–60.

Eberle, James 'The Military Relationship', in Louis and Bull (eds) *The Special Relationship: Anglo-American Relations Since 1945* (Oxford: Clarendon Press, 1986).

Eden, Sir Anthony, *The Memoirs of the Right Hon. Sir Anthony Eden: Full Circle* (London: Cassell, 1960).

Edwards, Geoffrey, 'Europe and the Falkland Islands Crisis', *Journal of Common Market Studies*, vol. 22, no. 4 (1984), pp. 295–313.

Eatwell, John, *Whatever Happened To Britain?* (London: BBC, 1982).

Elliott, Christopher, *High Command: British Military Leadership in the Iraq and Afghanistan Wars* (London: Hurst and Co., 2015).

Elman, Colin, 'Horses for Courses: Why Not Neorealist Theories of Foreign Policy?', *Security Studies*, vol. 6, no. 1 (1996), pp. 7–53.

Engel, Jeffrey, ' "We Are Not Concerned Who the Buyer Is": Engine Sales and Anglo-American Security At the Dawn of the Jet Age', *History and Technology*, vol. 17, no. 1 (2000), pp. 43–67.

Fairweather, Jack, *The Good War: Why We Couldn't Win the War or the Peace in Afghanistan* (London: Jonathan Cape, 2014).

Feiling, Sir Keith, *The Life of Neville Chamberlain* (London: Macmillan, 1947).

Femenia, Nora, *National Identity in Times of Crisis: The Scripts of the Falklands-Malvinas War* (Lommack: Nova Science Publishers, 1996).

Festinger, Leon, *Theory of Cognitive Dissonance* (Stanford, CA: Stanford University Press, 1957).

Festinger, Leon, Henry Riecken and Stanley Schachter, *When Prophecy Fails: A Social and Psychological Study of a Modern Group that Predicted the Destruction of the World* (New York: Harper & Row, 1964).

Fisher, H. A. L., *A History of Europe, Volume II: From the Early Eighteenth Century to 1935* (London: Fontana, 1975).

Frankel, Joseph, *British Foreign Policy 1945–1973* (London: Oxford University Press, 1973).

Frankel, Joseph, 'Conventional and Theorising Diplomats: A Critique', *International Affairs*, vol. 57, no. 2 (1981), pp. 537–44.

Freedland, Jonathan, *Bringing Home The Revolution: How Britain Can Live the American Dream* (London: Fourth Estate, 1998).

Freedman, Lawrence, 'Logic, Politics and Foreign Policy Processes: A Critique of the Bureaucratic Politics Model', *International Affairs*, vol. 52, no. 3 (1976), pp. 434–49.

Freedman, Lawrence, 'The War of the Falkland Islands, 1982', *Foreign Affairs*, vol. 61, no. 1 (1982), pp. 196–210.

Freedman, Lawrence, 'Intelligence Operations in the Falklands', *Intelligence and National Security*, vol. 3, no. 1 (1986), pp. 309–35.

Freedman, Lawrence, *The Politics of British Defence, 1979–1988* (London: Palgrave Macmillan, 1999).

Freedman, Lawrence, *The Official History of the Falklands Campaign: The Origins of the Falklands War: Volume One* (Government Official History Series) (London: Routledge, 2006).

Freedman, Lawrence, *The Official History of the Falklands Campaign: War and Diplomacy: Volume Two* (Whitehall Histories) (London: Routledge, 2006).

Freedman, Lawrence, *Strategy: A History* (New York: Oxford University Press, 2013).

Freedman, Lawrence and Virginia Gamba-Stonehouse, *Signals of War: The Falklands Conflict of 1982* (London: Faber and Faber, 1990).

Friedman, Milton, *Prices of Money and Goods across Frontiers: The Pound and the Dollar over a Century* (London: Trade Policy Research Centre, 1980).

Furlong, William and Craig Albiston, 'Sovereignty, Culture and Misperceptions: The Falklands/Malvinas War', *Conflict*, vol. 6, no. 2 (1985), pp. 139–75.

Gamble, Andrew, *Britain in Decline: Economic Policy, Political Strategy and the British State*, 2nd edn (London: Macmillan, 1985).

Gamble, Andrew, *The Free Economy and the Strong State: The Politics of Thatcherism*, 2nd edn (London: Palgrave Macmillan, 1994).

Gamble, Andrew, *Between Britain and America: The Future of British Politics* (London: Palgrave Macmillan, 2003).

Gaskarth, Jamie, *British Foreign Policy: Crises, Conflicts and Future Challenges* (London: Polity Press, 2013).

Giddens, Anthony, *Central Problems in Social Theory: Action, Structure and Contradiction in Social Analysis* (London: Macmillan, 1979).

Gilmore, Jonathan, 'Still a "Force for Good"? Good International Citizenship in British Foreign and Security Policy', *British Journal of Politics and International Relations*, vol. 17, no. 1 (2015), pp. 106–29.

Gilpin, Robert, *War and Change in World Politics* (Princeton, NJ: Princeton University Press, 1981).

Gilpin, Robert, *The Political Economy of International Relations* (Princeton, NJ: Princeton University Press, 1987).

Gilpin, Robert, *Global Political Economy: Understanding the International Economic Order* (Oxford: Princeton University Press, 2001).

Gladwyn, Lord, 'Western Europe's Collective Defence', *International Affairs*, vol. 51, no. 2 (1975), pp. 166–74.

Gorst, Anthony and Lewis Johnman, *The Suez Crisis* (London: Routledge, 1997).

Gorst, Anthony, 'CVA-1', in Richard Harding (ed.), *The Royal Navy 1930–1990: Innovation and Defence* (New York: Routledge, 2004).

Gowing, Margaret, 'Britain, America and the Bomb', in Dilks (ed.), *Retreat from Power*, Vol. 2 (London: Macmillan, 1981).

Greenidge, C. W., 'The Present Outlook in the British West Indies', *International Affairs*, vol. 25, no. 2 (1949), pp. 175–81.

Guilhot, Nicolas, *The Invention of International Relations Theory* (New York: Columbia University Press, 2011).

Hadfield-Amkhan, Amelia, *British Foreign Policy, National Identity, and Neoclassical Realism* (Lanham, MD: Rowman & Littlefield, 2010).

Harding, Thomas, 'Defence Jobs at Risk as MoD Drops Jump Jet Fighter Engine', *The Daily Telegraph*, 5 August 2009.

Haines, Steven, ' "A World Full of Terror to the British Mind": The Blair Doctrine and British Defence Policy', in David Brown (ed.), *The Development of British Defence Policy: Blair, Brown and Beyond* (Farnham: Ashgate, 2010).

Hart, Basil Liddell, *The Defence of Britain* (London: Faber & Faber, 1939).

Harvey, Derek, 'Perspectives on the UK's Place in the World', Europe Programme Paper 2011/01, Chatham House, London, December 2011.

Hastings, Max and Simon Jenkins, *The Battle For the Falklands* (New York: Norton, 1984).

Hastings, Max, *The Falklands Legacy*, documentary first broadcast on BBC2, 27 April 2012.

Head, A. H. 'European Defence', *International Affairs,* vol. 27, no. 1 (1951), pp. 1–9.

Hearn, Sir Arthur, 'Oil and the Middle East', *International Affairs*, vol. 24, no. 1 (1948), pp. 63–75.

Henderson, Nicholas, 'Britain's Decline: Its Causes and Consequences', *The Economist*, 2 July 1979.

Henderson, J. T., 'Leadership Personality and War: The Cases of Richard Nixon and Anthony Eden', *Political Science*, vol. 28, no. 2 (1976), pp. 141–64.

Henderson, Nicholas, *Mandarin: The Diaries of an Ambassador 1969–1982* (London: Weidenfeld & Nicolson, 1994).

Heng, Yee-Kuang, ' "What Did New Labour Ever Do for Us?": Evaluating Tony Blair's Imprint on British Strategic Culture', *British Journal of Politics and International Relations*, vol. 14, no. 4 (2012), pp. 556–75.

Henig, Ruth (ed.), *The League of Nations* (Edinburgh: Oliver & Boyd, 1973).

Hennessey, Peter, *Cabinet* (Oxford: Wiley-Blackwell, 1986).

Hennessy, Peter, *Muddling Through: Power, Politics and the Quality of Government in Postwar Britain* (London: Victor Gollancz, 1996).

Hennessey, Peter (ed.), *Cabinets and the Bomb* (Oxford: Oxford University Press, 2007).

Hill, Christopher, *The Changing Politics of Foreign Policy* (London: Palgrave Macmillan, 2002).

Hobbes, Thomas, *Leviathan* (Harmondsworth: Pelican, 1968).

Hobsbawm, Eric, *The Age of Revolution: Europe 1789–1848* (London: Abacus, 1988).

Hobsbawm, Eric, *Industry and Empire: From 1750 to the Present Day* (New York: W.W. Norton, 1999).

Home, Alistair, 'The Macmillan Years and Afterwards', in Louis and Bull (eds) *The Special Relationship: Anglo-American Relations Since 1945* (Oxford: Clarendon Press, 1986).

Home, Earl of, 'Interdependence: The British Role', *International Affairs*, vol. 37, no. 2 (1961), pp. 154–60.

Houghton, David Patrick, *U.S. Foreign Policy and the Iran Hostage Crisis* (New York: Cambridge University Press, 2001).

Houghton, David Patrick, 'Reinvigorating the Study of Foreign Policy Decision-Making: Towards a Constructivist Approach', *Foreign Policy Analysis*, vol. 3, no. 1 (2007), pp. 24–45.

Howard, Anthony, *RAB: The Life of R. A. Butler* (London: Jonathan Cape, 1987).

Howard, Michael, 'Britain's Strategic Problem East of Suez', *International Affairs*, vol. 42, no. 2 (1966), pp. 179–83.

Howard, Michael, *The Mediterranean Strategy in the Second World War* (London: Weidenfeld & Nicolson, 1968).

Howard, Michael, *Splendid Isolation* (New York: Macmillan, 1970).

Howard, Michael, *The Continental Commitment: The Dilemma of British Defence Policy in the Era of Two World Wars* (Harmondsworth: Penguin, 1974).

Howard, Michael, 'Afterword: The "Special Relationship"', in Louis and Bull (eds), *The Special Relationship: Anglo-American Relations Since 1945* (Oxford: Clarendon Press, 1986).

Huntington, Samuel, *Political Order in Changing Societies* (New Haven: Yale University Press, 1968).

Hurd, Douglas, 'Prospects for Europe: Political Co-operation', *International Affairs*, vol. 57, no. 3 (1981), pp. 383–93.

Ingham, Geoffrey, *Capitalism Divided? The City and Industry in British Social Development* (London: Palgrave Macmillan, 1984).

Inman, Philip, 'Black Wednesday Twenty Years on: How the Day Unfolded', *The Guardian*, 13 September 2012.

Jackson, Bill and Edwin Bramall, *The Chiefs: The Story of the United Kingdom Chiefs of Staff* (London: Brassey's, 1992).

James, Patrick and Jarrod Hayes, 'Theory as Thought: Britain and German Unification', *Security Studies*, vol. 23, no. 2 (2014), pp. 399–429.

Jenkins, Roy, *Gladstone* (London: Macmillan, 1995).

Jervis, Robert, *Perception and Misperception in International Politics* (Princeton, NJ: Princeton University Press, 1976).

Jervis, Robert, 'Cooperation under the Security Dilemma', *World Politics*, vol. 30, no. 2 (1978), pp. 167–214.

Jessop, Bob, 'The Transformation of the State in Post-War Britain' in R. Scase (ed.), *The State in Western Europe* (London: Croom Helm, 1980).

Kahneman, Daniel, *Thinking, Fast and Slow* (London: Penguin Books, 2012).

Kajima, M., *The Emergence of Japan as a World Power 1895–1925* (Rutland, VT: Tuttle, 1978).

Kampfner, John, *Blair's Wars* (New York: Free Press, 2004).

Kaplan, Robert, *Balkan Ghosts: A Journey Through History* (London: Pan Macmillan, 1993).

Kaplan, Robert, *The Revenge of Geography: What The Map Tells Us About Coming Conflicts and the Battle Against Fate* (New York: Random House, 2012).

Kasliwal, R. R., 'The Foreign Policy of Turkey Since 1919', *Indian Journal of Political Science*, vol. 7, no. 1/2 (1945) pp. 38–97.

Kennedy, Paul, *The Rise and Fall of the Great Powers* (London: Vintage, 1989).

Kennedy, Paul, *The Rise and Fall of British Naval Mastery* (New York: Humanity Books, 2006).

Keohane, Robert, *After Hegemony* (Cambridge, MA: Harvard University Press, 1984).

Keohane, Robert (ed.), *Neorealism and its Critics* (New York: Columbia University Press, 1986).

Kettell, Steven, *The Political Economy of Exchange Rate Policy-Making: From the Gold Standard to the Euro* (London: Palgrave Macmillan, 2004).

Khong, Yuen Foong, *Analogies at War: Korea, Munich, Dien Bien Phu and the Vietnam Decisions of 1965* (Princeton, NJ: Princeton University Press, 1992).

Kindleberger, Charles, *The World in Depression 1929–1933* (London: Allen Lane, 1973).

Kinzer, Stephen, *All the Shah's Men: An American Coup and the Roots of Middle East Terror* (New York: John Wiley, 2008).

Kirkpatrick, David, 'Dilemmas in UK Defence Policy', *RUSI Defence Systems*, Vol. 15, no. 1 (2012) pp. 16–19.

Kissinger, Henry, *A World Restored: Metternich, Castlereagh and the Problems of Peace, 1812–22* (London: Weidenfeld & Nicolson, 1957).

Kissinger, Henry, *Diplomacy* (New York: Simon and Schuster, 1994).

Krishan, Y., 'Mountbatten and the Partition of India', *History*, vol. 68, no. 1 (1983), pp. 22–37.

Kyle, Keith, *Suez: Britain's End of Empire in the Middle East* (London: Weidenfeld & Nicolson, 1991).

Lakatos, Imre, 'Falsification and the Methodology of Scientific Research Programmes', in Imre Lakatos and Alan E. Musgrave (eds), *Criticism and the Growth of Knowledge* (Cambridge: Cambridge University Press, 1974), pp. 132–35.

Lane, Jan-Erik and Svante Errson, *Politics and Society in Western Europe* (London: Sage, 1987).

Lauterpacht, Hersch, *The Function of Law in the International Community* (London: Oxford University Press, 1933).

Lebow, Richard Ned, 'Miscalculation in the South Atlantic: The Origins of the Falklands War', *Journal of Strategic Studies*, vol. 6, no. 1 (1983), pp. 5–35.

Lebow, Richard Ned and Janice Gross Stein, *We All Lost the Cold War* (Princeton, NJ: Princeton University Press, 1995).

Le Carré, John, *A Delicate Truth* (London: Penguin Books, 2013).

Ledwidge, Frank, *Losing Small Wars: British Military Failure in Iraq and Afghanistan* (London: Yale University Press, 2011).

Ledwidge, Frank, *Punching Below Our Weight: How Inter-Service Rivalry Has Damaged the British Armed Forces* (Kindle E-Book: Yale University Press, 2012).

Lindberg, Leon, *Political Dynamics of European Economic Integration* (London: Oxford University Press, 1963).

Little, Richard and Mark Wickham-Jones, *New Labour's Foreign Policy: A New Moral Crusade?* (Manchester: Manchester University Press, 2000).

Longstreth, Frank, 'The City, Industry and the State', in Colin Crouch (ed.), *State and Economy in Contemporary Capitalism* (London: Croom Helm, 1979).

Louis, William Roger, *Imperialism at Bay: The United States and the Decolonisation of the British Empire, 1941–1945* (London: Oxford University Press, 1977).

Louis, William Roger, 'American Anti-Colonialism and the Dissolution of the British Empire', *International Affairs*, vol. 61, no. 3 (1985).

Louis, William Roger and Hedley Bull (eds), *The Special Relationship: Anglo-American Relations Since 1945* (Oxford: Clarendon Press, 1986).

Lowe, C. J., *The Reluctant Imperialists: British Foreign Policy, 1878–1902* (New York: Macmillan, 1969).

Luard, Evan, 'A European Foreign Policy?' *International Affairs*, vol. 62, no. 4 (1986), pp. 575–82.

Lucas, Scott, *Divided We Stand: Britain, the US and the Suez Crisis* (London: Hodder and Stoughton, 1991).

Lukes, Stephen, *Power: A Radical View* (London: Macmillan, 1975).

Lygo, Raymond, *Collision Course: Lygo Shoots Back* (Lewes, Sussex: The Book Guild 2002).

Lynn, Jonathan and Anthony Jay, *Yes, Prime Minister: The Diaries of the Rt. Hon. James Hacker, Volume II* (London: BBC Books, 1987).

Machiavelli, Niccolo, *The Prince* (translated by G. Bull) (Harmondsworth: Penguin, 1961).

Mackintosh, John, 'Britain in Europe: Historical Perspective and Contemporary Reality', *International Affairs*, vol. 45, no. 2 (1969), pp. 246–58.

Macmillan, Harold, *Riding the Storm, 1956–1959* (London: Macmillan, 1971).

Magstadt, Thomas, *An Empire If You Can Keep It: Power and Principle in American Foreign Policy* (Washington, DC: CQ Press, 2004).

Mandel, Ernest, *Late Capitalism* (London: New Left Books, 1975).

Mander, John, *Great Britain or Little England* (London: Penguin, 1963).

Mansberg, Nicholas, 'Britain, the Commonwealth and the Western Union', *International Affairs*, vol. 24, no. 4 (1948), pp. 491–504.

May, Ernest and Gregory Treverton, 'Defence Relationships: American Perspectives', in Louis and Bull (eds), *The Special Relationship: Anglo-American Relations Since 1945* (Oxford: Clarendon Press, 1986).

Mayhew, Christopher, 'British Foreign Policy Since 1945', *International Affairs*, vol. 26, no. 4 (1950), pp. 477–86.

McCourt, David, *Britain and World Power Since 1945: Constructing a Nation's Role In International Politics* (Ann Arbor, MI: University of Michigan Press, 2014).

McCourt, David, 'Role-Playing and Identity Affirmation in International Politics: Britain's Reinvasion of the Falklands, 1982', *Review of International Studies*, vol. 37, no.4 (2011), pp. 1599–1621.

McNamara, Robert, *Britain, Nasser and the Balance of Power in the Middle East, 1952–1967* (London: Routledge, 2003).

Mearsheimer, John, *The Tragedy of Great Power Politics*, Updated Edition (New York: W.W. Norton, 2014).

Medlicott, Norton, 'The Hoare-Laval Pact Reconsidered', in David Dilks (ed.), *Retreat from Power: Studies in Britain's Foreign Policy of the Twentieth Century, Volume I, 1906–1939* (London: Macmillan, 1981), pp. 118–38.

Medlicott, Norton, 'Britain and Germany: The Search for Agreement 1930–37', in Dilks (ed.), *Retreat from Power: Studies in Britain's Foreign Policy of the Twentieth Century, Volume I, 1906–1939* (London: Macmillan, 1981).

Menon, Anand, 'European Defence Policy from Lisbon to Libya', *Survival*, vol. 53, no. 3 (2011), pp. 75–90.

Middlebrook, Martin, *The Falklands War* (London: Pen and Sword, 2012).

Minns, Richard, 'A Comment on "Financial Capital and the Crisis in Britain"', *Capital and Class*, vol. 14 (1982).

Morgenthau, Hans, Kenneth Thompson and David Clinton, *Politics Among Nations*, 7th edn (New York: McGraw-Hill, 2005).

Monroe, Elisabeth, 'British Bases in the Middle East: Assets or Liabilities?', *International Affairs*, vol. 42, no. 1 (1966), pp. 25–27.

Nagl, John, *Learning to Eat Soup with a Knife: Counterinsurgency Lessons from Malaya and Vietnam* (London: University of Chicago Press, 2002).

Nardelli, Alberto and George Arnett, 'Today's Key Fact: You Are Probably Wrong About Almost Everything', *The Guardian*, 29 October 2014.

Naval Postgraduate School, *The Falklands War: Causes and Lessons* (New York: Pennyhill Press, 2014).

Northedge, F. S., 'Britain As A Second-Rank Power', *International Affairs*, vol. 46, no. 1 (1970), pp. 37–47.

Northedge, F. S., *Descent From Power: British Foreign Policy 1945–1973* (London: George Allen & Unwin, 1974).

Nye, Joseph, *Soft Power: The Means of Success in World Politics* (New York: Public Affairs, 2004).

Olson, Robert and Nurham Ince, 'Turkish Foreign Policy from 1923–1960: Kemalism and its Legacy, a Review and Critique', *Oriento Moderno*, vol. 57, No. 1 (1977), pp. 227–41.

O'Neill, Michael (ed.), *The Politics of European Integration: A Reader* (London: Routledge, 1996).

Ovendale, Ritchie, 'The Palestine Policy of the British Labour Government 1945–1946', *International Affairs*, vol. 55, no. 3 (1979), pp. 409–31.

Ovendale, Ritchie, 'Britain, the US and the Cold War in SE Asia 1949–50', *International Affairs*, vol. 58, no. 3 (1982), pp. 447–64.

Overbeek, Henk, 'Finance Capital and the Crisis in Britain', *Capital and Class*, vol. 4, no. 2 (1980), pp. 99–120.

Owen, David, 'The Effect of Prime Minister Anthony Eden's Illness on His Decision-Making During the Suez Crisis', *QJM: An International Journal of Medicine*, vol. 98, no. 6 (2005), pp. 387–402.

Page, Lewis, *Lions, Donkeys and Dinosaurs: Waste and Blundering in the Military* (London: Arrow Books, 2007).

Parry, Christopher, 'The United Kingdom's Future Carriers: What Are They Good For?', *RUSI Journal*, vol. 157, no. 6 (2012), pp. 4–9.

Payne, Kenneth, *The Psychology of Modern Conflict: Evolutionary Theory, Human Nature and a Liberal Approach to War* (Basingstoke: Palgrave Macmillan, 2015).

Paxman, Jeremy, *Empire* (London: Penguin Books, 2011).

Pearson, Jonathan, *Sir Anthony Eden and the Suez Crisis: Reluctant Gamble* (London: Palgrave Macmillan, 2002).

Pearson, Robert and Geraint Williams, *Political Thought and Public Policy in The Nineteenth Century: An Introduction* (London: Longman, 1984).

Perkins, Bradford, *The Great Rapprochement: England and the US 1895–1914* (London: Victor Gollancz, 1969).

Petersen, Michael, 'Evolutionary Political Psychology: On the Origin and Structure of Heuristics and Biases in Politics', *Advances in Political Psychology*, vol. 36, no. S1 (2015) pp. 45–78.

Pierre, Andrew, *Nuclear Politics: The British Experience with an Independent Strategic Force, 1939–70* (London: Oxford University Press, 1972).

Pohl, Benjamin, 'The Logic Underpinning EU Crisis Management Operations', *European Security*, vol. 22, no. 3 (2013), pp. 307–25.

Polk, William, *Understanding Iraq* (New York: Harper, 2005).

Porter, Bernard, *The Lion's Share: A Short History of British Imperialism*, 2nd edn (London: Longmans, 1984).

Porter, Patrick, 'Why Britain Doesn't Do Grand Strategy', *RUSI Journal*, vol. 155, no. 4 (2010), pp. 6–12.

Ravenhill, John (ed.), *Global Political Economy*, 4th edn (Oxford: Oxford University Press, 2014),

Rawnsley, Andrew, 'Where Did It All Go Wrong?', *Dispatches*, broadcast on Channel 4, 9 June 2008.

Rees, Wyn, 'The 1957 Sandys White Paper: New Priorities in British Defence Policy', vol. 12, no. 2 (1989), pp. 215–30.

Reynolds, Philip, *British Foreign Policy In The Interwar Years* (London: Longman, 1956).

Reynolds, David, 'A "Special Relationship"? America, Britain and the International Order since the Second World War', *International Affairs*, vol. 62, no. 1 (1986), pp. 1–20.

Richards, Steve, *Whatever It Takes: The Real Story of Gordon Brown and New Labour* (London: Fourth Estate, 2010).

Riddell, Peter, *The Thatcher Era and its Legacy* (Oxford: Wiley-Blackwell, 1991).

Rosamond, Ben, *Theories of European Integration* (Basingstoke: Palgrave Macmillan, 2000).

Rose, Gideon, 'Neoclassical Realism and Theories of Foreign Policy', *World Politics*, vol. 51, no. 1 (1998), pp. 144–72.

Rotberg, R. I. and Ali Mazrui (eds), *Protest and Power and Black Africa* (New York: Oxford University Press, 1970).

Rothstein, Andrew, *British Foreign Policy and Its Critics, 1830–1950* (London: Lawrence & Wishart, 1969).

Rothwell, V. H., *British War Aims and Peace Diplomacy 1914–1958* (Oxford: Clarendon Press, 1971).

Sanders, David, *Lawmaking and Co-operation in International Politics: The Idealist Case Re-examined* (London: Macmillan, 1986).

Sanders, David, *Losing An Empire, Finding a Role: British Foreign Policy Since 1945*, 1st edn (Basingstoke: Macmillan, 1990).

Sanders, David and Geoffrey Edwards, 'Consensus and Diversity in Elite Opinion: the Views of the British Foreign Policy Elite in the Early 1990s', *Political Studies*, vol. 42, no. 3 (1994), pp. 413–40.

Seldon, Anthony and Guy Lodge, *Brown at 10* (London: Biteback, 2011).

Seldon, Anthony and Peter Snowdon, *Cameron at 10* (London: Biteback, 2015).

Self, Robert, *British Foreign and Defence Policy Since 1945: Challenges and Dilemmas in a Changing World* (London: Palgrave Macmillan, 2010).

Shepherd, Alastair, 'Blair, Brown and Brussels: The European Turn in British Defence Policy', in David Brown (ed.), *The Development of British Defence Policy: Blair, Brown and Beyond* (Farnham: Ashgate, 2010).

Shonfield, Andrew, *British Economic Policy Since the War* (Harmondsworth: Penguin, 1958).

Silcock, T. H., 'Policy for Malaya, 1952', *International Affairs*, vol. 28, no. 4 (1952), pp. 445–51.

Smith, General Sir Rupert, *The Utility of Force: The Art of War in the Modern World* (New York: Knopf, 2007).

Snyder, Glenn and Paul Diesing, *Conflict Among Nations: Bargaining, Decisionmaking and System Structure in International Crises* (Princeton, NJ: Princeton University Press, 1977).

Snyder, Jack, *Myths of Empire: Domestic Politics and International Ambition* (London: Cornell University Press, 1991).

Spence, Peter, 'British Reliance on Trade with the EU Falls to an All-Time Low', *The Telegraph*, 9 June 2015.

Spinelli, Altiero, *The Eurocrats: Conflict and Crisis in the EEC* (translation C. Grove Haines) (Baltimore: Johns Hopkins Press, 1966).

Spry, Graham, 'Canada, the Emergency Force and the Commonwealth', *International Affairs*, vol. 33, no. 3 (1957), pp. 289–300.

Strange, Susan, *Sterling and British Policy* (London: Oxford University Press, 1971).

Strange, Susan, *Casino Capitalism* (London: Basil Blackwell, 1986).

Strange, Susan, *The Retreat of the State: The Diffusion of Power in the World Economy* (Cambridge: Cambridge University Press, 1996).

Strickland, Philip, 'Politics Over Strategy – Australia's Rejection of the TSR2', and 'TSR With Hindsight', *RAF Historical Journal*, Vol. 17B,

No.1 (1998) pp. 45-67. This can be accessed at http://www.raf.mod.uk/rafcms/mediafiles/EEA483B3_5056_A318_A825FD4682EDACAB.pdf.

Swanwick, H. M., *Collective Insecurity* (London: Jonathan Cape, 1937).

Swartz, Marvin, *The Politics of British Foreign Policy in the Era of Disraeli and Gladstone* (New York: St Martin's Press, 1985).

Strachan, Hew, 'The Lost Meaning of Strategy', *Survival*, vol. 47, no. 3 (2005), pp. 33–54.

Strachan, Hew, 'Capability as a Balancing Act: The UK's Dilemma', *RUSI Journal*, vol. 153, no. 3 (2008), pp. 6–10.

Strong, James, 'Why Parliament Now Decides on War: Tracing the Growth of the Parliamentary Prerogative through Syria, Libya and Iraq', *British Journal of Politics and International Relations*, vol. 17, no. 4 (2015), pp. 605–22.

Szczerbiak, Aleks and Paul Taggart, 'Comparative and Theoretical Perspectives', in Szczerbiak and Taggart (eds), *Opposing Europe? The Comparative Politics of Euroscepticism* (New York: Oxford University Press, 2008).

Talbot, I. A., 'Mountbatten and the Partition of India: A Rejoinder', *History*, vol. 69, no. 1 (1984), pp. 29–35.

Taleb, Nicholas Naseem, *The Black Swan: The Impact of the Highly Improbable*, 2nd edn (New York: Penguin Books, 2010).

Taliaferro, Jeffrey, Steven Lobell and Norrin Ripsman, 'Introduction: Neoclassical Realism, the State, and Foreign Policy', in Taliaferro, Lobell and Ripsman (eds), *Neoclassical Realism, the State and Foreign Policy* (New York: Cambridge University Press, 2009).

Tavris, Carol and Elliot Aronson, *Mistakes Were Made (But Not By Me): Why We Justify Foolish Beliefs, Bad Decisions, and Hurtful Acts* (New York: Harcourt, 2007).

Taylor, Charles Lewis and Michael C. Hudson, *World Handbook of Social and Political Indicators*, 2nd edn (New Haven: Yale University Press, 1972).

Taylor, Trevor, 'Power Politics', in Trevor Taylor (ed.), *Approaches and Theory in International Relations* (London: Longman, 1978).

The Economist, 'The Suez Crisis: An Affair to Remember', 27 July 2006.

Thompson, Grahame, 'The Relationship between the Financial and Industrial Sector in the United Kingdom Economy', *Economy and Society*, vol. 6, no. 3 (1977), pp. 235–83.

Thompson, Helen, *The British Conservative Government and the European Exchange Rate Mechanism, 1979–1994* (London: Routledge, 1996).

Thompson, J. M., *Russia, Bolshevism and the Versailles Peace* (Princeton, NJ: Princeton University Press, 1966).

Thompson, Mark, 'The Pied Piper of the Insurgency', *Time*, 2 January 2013.

Thomson, David, 'General De Gaulle and the Anglo Saxons', *International Affairs*, vol. 41, no. 1 (1965), pp. 11–21.

Thorne, Christopher, *Allies of a Kind: The United States, Britain and the War Against Japan, 1941–42* (London: Hamish Hamilton, 1978).

Thorpe, D. R., *Eden: The Life and Times of Anthony Eden, First Earl of Avon, 1897–1977* (London: Chatto & Windus, 2003).

Thucydides, *The History of the Peloponnesian War* (translated by R. Crawley) (London: Everyman's Library, 1952).

Tyler, Richard, 'Cameron Presents UK Firms with £30bn Export Challenge', *The Daily Telegraph*, 10 November 2011.

Toynbee, Arnold, 'A Turning Point in the Cold War?', *International Affairs*, vol. 26, no. 4 (1950), pp. 457–62.

Truscott, Peter, 'The Korean War in British Foreign and Domestic Policy, 1950–52' (PhD dissertation, Exeter College, Oxford, 1984).

Vasagar Jeevan, 'British Policy on Arms Sales', *The Guardian*, 15 July 2000.

Verbeek, Bertjan, 'Do Individual and Group Beliefs Matter? British Decision-Making During the 1956 Suez Crisis', *Cooperation and Conflict*, vol. 29, no. 4 (1994), pp. 307–32.

Verbeek, Bertjan, *Decision Making in Great Britain During the Suez Crisis: Small Groups and a Persistent Leader* (London: Ashgate, 2003).

Wallace, William, *The Foreign Policy Process in Britain* (London: Royal Institute of International Affairs, 1976).

Wallace, William, 'Foreign Policy and National Identity in the United Kingdom', *International Affairs*, vol. 67, no. 1 (1991), pp. 65–80.

Wallace, William, 'The Collapse of British Foreign Policy', *International Affairs*, vol. 81, no. 1 (2005), pp. 53–68.

Wallace, Helen, 'The British Presidency of the European Community's Council of Ministers: The Opportunity to Persuade', *International Affairs*, vol. 64, no. 4 (1986), pp. 583–99.

Walters, F. P., *A History of the League of Nations* (London: Oxford University Press, 1960).

Waltz, Kenneth, *Theory of International Politics* (Reading, MA: Addison-Wesley, 1979).

Waltz, Kenneth, 'International Politics Is Not Foreign Policy', *Security Studies*, vol. 6, no. 1 (1996), pp. 54–55.

Ward, Sharkey, *Sea Harrier Over The Falklands: A Maverick At War* (London: Leon Cooper, 1992).

Warner, Geoffrey, 'The Truman Doctrine and the Marshall Plan', *International Affairs*, vol. 50, no. 1 (1974), pp. 82–92.

Warner, Geoffrey, '"Collusion" and the Suez crisis of 1956', *International Affairs*, vol. 55, no. 2 (1979), pp. 226–39.

Warriner, Doreen, 'Land Reform in Egypt and its Repercussions', *International Affairs*, vol. 29, no. 1 (1953), pp. 1–10.

Watt, David, 'Introduction: The Anglo-American Relationship', in Louis and Bull (eds), *The Special Relationship: Anglo-American Relations Since 1945* (Oxford: Clarendon Press, 1986).

Webster, Sir Charles, 'Munich Reconsidered: A Survey of British Policy', *International Affairs*, vol. 37, no. 2 (1961), pp. 137–53.

Wendt, Alexander, 'The Agent-Structure Problem in International Relations Theory', *International Organization*, vol. 41, no. 3 (1987), pp. 335–70.

Wendt, Alexander, *Social Theory of International Politics* (New York: Cambridge University Press, 1999).

Wheeler, Brian and Alex Hunt, 'The UK's EU Referendum: All You Need To Know', *BBC News*, 24 June 2016. Available at http://www.bbc.com/news/uk-politics-32810887.

White, Brian, 'British Foreign Policy: Continuity and Transformation', in Ryan Beasley, Juliet Kaarbo, Jeffrey Lantis and Michael Snarr (eds), *Foreign Policy in Comparative Perspective: Domestic and International Influences on State Behavior*, 2nd edn (New York: CQ Press, 2012).

White, Rowland, *Phoenix Squadron* (London: Bantam Press, 2009).

Whyte, Anne, 'Quadripartite Rule in Berlin', *International Affairs*, vol. 23, no. 1 (1947), pp. 30–41.

Wiener, Antje and Thomas Diez, *European Integration Theory* (Oxford: Oxford University Press, 2009).

Wight, Martin, 'Brutus in Foreign Policy: The Memoirs of Sir Anthony Eden', *International Affairs*, vol. 36, no. 3 (1960), pp. 299–309.

Wight, Martin, *Power Politics*, revised edition (London: Bloomsbury, 1995).

Wilkinson, Michael and Rosa Prince, 'When Will a EU Referendum be Held?', *The Telegraph*, 28 June 2015.

Willetts, Peter, *The Non-Aligned Movement: The Origins of a Third World Alliance* (London: Francis Pinter, 1978).

Williams, Paul, *British Foreign Policy Under New Labour, 1997–2005* (Basingstoke, Hampshire: Palgrave Macmillan, 2005).

Wilson, Keith, 'British Power in the European Balance 1906–14', in David Dilks (ed.), *Retreat from Power: Studies in Britain's Foreign Policy of the Twentieth Century, Volume I, 1906–1939* (London: Macmillan, 1981).

Woodward, E. L., *British Foreign Policy in the Second World War* (5 volumes) (London: HMSO, 1970–76).

Wright, Oliver, ' "Costly Failures": Wars in Iraq and Afghanistan Cost UK Taxpayers £30bn', *The Independent*, 27 May 2014.

Wright, Quincy, *A Study of War*, vol. II (Chicago: Chicago University Press, 1942).

Wright, Walter Livingston, 'Truths about Turkey', *Foreign Affairs*, vol. 26, no. 2 (1948), pp. 349–59.

Wyatt, Caroline, 'Top General Warns Over "Hollowed-Out" Armed Forces', BBC News website, 19 December 2013.

Yergin, Daniel and Joseph Stanislaw, *The Commanding Heights: The Battle for the World Economy* (New York: Touchstone Books, 2002).

Young, Hugo, *One of Us: The Life of Margaret Thatcher* (Palgrave Macmillan, 1989).

Younger, Kenneth, 'Public Opinion and British Foreign Policy', *International Affairs*, vol. 40, no. 1 (1964), pp. 22–33.

Zakaria, Fareed, *From Wealth to Power: The Unusual Origins of America's World Role* (Princeton, NJ: Princeton University Press, 1998).

HMSO (Command) Publications

CMND 6707 *Statistical Materials Presented During the Washington Negotiations (1945).*

CMND 6743 *Statement Relating to Defence* (Feb. 1946).

CMND 7327 *Statement Relating to Defence* (Feb. 1948).

CMND 8146 *Defence Programme Statement Made by the Prime Minister in the House of Commons, January 29th 1951.*

CMND 8476 *Statement of the First Lord of the Admiralty explanatory of the Navy Estimates 1952–3* (Feb. 1952).

CMND 9075 *Statement on Defence, 1954* (Feb. 1954).

CMND 9072 *Memorandum of the Secretary of State for War relating to the Army Estimates 1954–55* (Feb. 1954).

CMND 265 *South East Asia Collective Defence Treaty,* (8 Sept. 1954).

CMND 13 *Agreement concerning the Relations between the United Kingdom and the European Coal and Steel Community* (21 Dec. 1954).

CMND 9859 *Pact of Mutual Co-operation between His Majesty the King of Iraq and the President of the Republic of Turkey* (Accessions: UK 5 April 1955; Pakistan 23 Sept. 1955; Iran 3 Nov. 1955).

CMND 9520 *Exchange of letters with the Government of the Union of South Africa on the transfer of the Simonstown Naval Base and arrangements for its future use* (30 June 1955).

CMND 9842 *Agreement between ... the United Kingdom and ... the Federal Republic of Germany for Co-operation in the Peaceful Uses of Atomic Energy* (31 July 1956).

CMND 150 *Memorandum of the Secretary of State for War Relating to the Army Estimates 1957–8* (April 1957).

CMND 1313 [Three] *Exchanges of Notes between ... the United Kingdom and ... the Federal Republic of Germany concerning Local Defence Costs of UK forces stationed in the Federal Republic ...* (7 June 1957).

CMND 124 *Defence: Outline of Future Policy* (April 1957).

CMND 458 *Agreement between ... the United Kingdom and the Government of the Italian Republic for Co-operation in the Peaceful Uses of Atomic Energy* (28 Dec. 1957).

CMND 9688 *Memorandum of the Secretary of State for War Relating to the Army Estimates 1956–57* (HMSO, Feb. 1958).

CMND 537 *Agreement between the Government of the United Kingdom ... and the government of the United States ... for co-operation on the uses of atomic energy for mutual defence purposes* (3 July 1958).

CMND 363 *Report on Defence: Britain's contribution to Peace and Security* (Feb. 1958).

CMND 1076 *Five Year Trade Agreement between the Government of the United Kingdom and the Government of the Union of Soviet Socialist Republics* (24 May 1959).

CMND 917 *Agreement between the ... United Kingdom and ... the Union of Soviet Socialist Republics on relations in the Scientific, Technological, Educational and Cultural fields, 1960-61* (1 Dec. 1959).

CMND 1080 *Exchange of Notes between the Government of the United Kingdom and the Government of the Kingdom of the Netherlands concerning the Arrangements to Facilitate Travel between the United Kingdom and the Netherlands* (1 April 1960) CMND 1157 (20 June 1960: as CMND 1080 but refers to the Federal German Republic).

CMND 1357 *Exchange of Notes between the ... United Kingdom and ... Luxembourg concerning the Acceptance of the British Visitors Passport for Travel between the UK and Luxembourg* (21 Feb. 1961); CMND 1354 (21 Feb. 1961: title as CMND 1357 but refers to Belgium); CMND 1355 (21 Feb. 1961: title as CMND 1357 but refers to the Netherlands).

CMND 2108 *Polaris. Sales Agreement between the Government of the United Kingdom ... and the Government of the United States of America* (4 June 1963).

CMND 1936 *Statement on Defence 1963* (including memoranda to accompany the Navy, Army and Air Estimates 1963–64) (Feb. 1963).

CMND 2557 *Protocol for the prolongation of the Five Year Trade Agreement between ... the United Kingdom and ... the Union of Soviet Socialist Republics* (23 April 1964).

CMND 2592 *Statement on the Defence Estimates 1965* (Feb. 1965).

CMND 2901 *Statement on the Defence Estimates 1966 Part I: The Defence Review* (Feb. 1966).

CMND 2902 *Statement on the Defence Estimates 1966 Part II: Defence Estimates 1966–67* (Feb. 1966).

CMND 3540 *Statement on the Defence Estimates 1968* (Feb. 1968).

CMND 3231 *Exchange of Notes between the Government of the United Kingdom and the Government of the United States of America concerning the availability for defence purposes of the British Indian Ocean Territory* (30 Dec. 1966).

CMND 3540 *Statement on the Defence Estimates 1968* (Feb. 1968).

CMND 3701 *Supplementary Statement on Defence Policy 1968* (July 1968).

CMND 3834 *Sterling. Exchange of Notes and Letters concerning the Guarantee by the ... United Kingdom and the Maintenance of the Minimum Sterling Proportion by certain Overseas Sterling Area Governments (the Sterling Area Agreements)* (25 Sept. 1968).

CMND 4107 *Report of the Review Committee on Overseas Representation 1968–9* (1969).

CMND 4290 *Statement on the Defence Estimates 1970* (Feb. 1970).

CMND 4705 *Long-Term Economic and Trade Agreement between the Government of the United Kingdom ... and the Government of the Polish People's Republic* (21 April 1971).

CMND 4890 *Exchange of Notes between ... the United Kingdom ... and ... Malaysia regarding Assistance for the Malaysia Armed Forces and the Arrangements for a United Kingdom Force in Malaysia* (1 Dec. 1971).

CMND 4891 *Statement on the Defence Estimates 1972* (Feb. 1972).

CMND 5016 *Long-Term Economic and Trade Agreement between the Government of the United Kingdom ... and the Government of the Hungarian People's Republic* (21 March 1972).

CMND 5074 *Long-Term Economic and Trade Agreement between the Government of the United Kingdom ... and the Government of ... Czechoslovakia* (27 June 1972).

CMND 5106 *Long-Term Economic and Trade Agreement between the Government of the United Kingdom ... and the Socialist Republic of Romania* (15 June 1972).

CMND 5179 *Treaty concerning the Accession of ... the United Kingdom ... to the European Economic Community and the European Atomic Energy Community including the Act concerning the conditions of Accession and the Adjustment to the Treaties ...* (1 Jan. 1973).

CMND 5286 *Long-Term Agreement on the Development of Economic, Industrial, Scientific and Technical Co-operation between the Government of the United Kingdom ... and the Government of the Polish People's Republic* (20 March 1973); CMND 5552 *Agreement between the Government of the United Kingdom ... and the Government of the German Democratic Republic on the Development of Economic, Industrial, Scientific and Technical Co-operation* (18 Dec. 1973).

CMND 6258 *Decisions of the Representatives of the Government of the Member States of the European Coal and Steel Community meeting in Council, opening, allocating and providing for the allocation of Tariff Quotas and opening Tariff Preferences for certain Steel Products originating in Developing Countries* (2 Dec. 1974).

CMND 5976 *Statement on the Defence Estimates 1975* (March 1975).

CMND 6413 *Exchange of Notes between ... the United Kingdom ... and ... the United States of America concerning a United States Navy Support Facility on Diego Garcia, British Indian Ocean Territory* (25 Feb. 1976).

CMND 6432 *Statement on the Defence Estimates 1976* (March 1976).

CMND 6735 *Statement on the Defence Estimates 1977* (Feb. 1977).

CMND 7099 *Statement on the Defence Estimates 1978* (Feb. 1978).

CMND 7474 *Statement on the Defence Estimates 1979* (Feb. 1979).

CMND 7826-I, *Defence in the 1980s: Statement on the Defence Estimates 1980 Vol. 1* (April 1980).

CMND 8212-I, *Statement on the Defence Estimates 1981* (April 1981).

CMND 8288 *The United Kingdom Defence Programme: The Way Forward* (1981).

CMND 8517 *The British Strategic Nuclear Force* (March 1982).

CMND 8951-I, *Statement on the Defence Estimates 1983 (Vol. 1)* (Feb. 1983).

CMND 9543 *Joint Declaration of the Government of the United Kingdom ... and the Government of the People's Republic of China on the question of Hong Kong* (19 Dec. 1984).

CMND 9763-I, *Statement on the Defence Estimates 1986* (Feb. 1987).

CMND 344-I, *Statement on the Defence Estimates 1988, Vol. 1* (Feb. 1988).

Index